the ultimate
soup
bible

the ultimate
soup
bible

Over 400 recipes for
delicious soups from
around the world with
step-by-step instructions
for every recipe

Consultant Editor:
Anne Sheasby

HH
HERMES
HOUSE

Publisher: Joanna Lorenz;
Project Editors: Felicity Forster and Molly Perham;
Designer: Nigel Partridge; Copy Editor: Molly Perham;
Production Controller: Ben Worley

Recipe contributors: Catherine Atkinson, Alex Barker, Michelle Berriedale-Johnson, Angela Boggiano, Janet Brinkworth, Carla Capalbo, Kit Chan, Jacqueline Clark, Maxine Clark, Frances Cleary, Carole Clements, Andi Clevely, Trish Davies, Roz Denny, Patrizia Diemling, Matthew Drennan, Sarah Edmonds, Joanna Farrow, Rafi Fernandez, Christine France, Sarah Gates, Shirley Gill, Rosamund Grant, Rebekah Hassan, Deh-Ta Hsiung, Shehzad Husain, Judy Jackson, Sheila Kimberley, Masaki Ko, Elisabeth Lambert Ortiz, Ruby Le Bois, Gilly Love, Lesley Mackley, Norma MacMillan, Sue Maggs, Kathy Man, Sallie Morris, Annie NIchols, Maggie Pannell, Katherine Richmond, Anne Sheasby, Jenny Stacey, Liz Trigg, Hilaire Walden, Laura Washburn, Steven Wheeler, Kate Whiteman, Elizabeth Wolf-Cohen, Jeni Wright.
Photographers: Karl Adamson, Edward Allwright, David Armstrong, Steve Baxter, James Duncan, John Freeman, Ian Garlick, Michelle Garrett, Amanda Heywood, Janine Hosegood, David Jordan, William Lingwood, Patrick McLeary, Michael MIchaels, Thomas Odulate, Juliet Piddington, Peter Reilly.

ISBN: 978-1-4351-5776-7

Manufactured in China

2 4 6 8 10 9 7 5 3 1

NOTE
Although the advice and information in this book are believed to be accurate and true at the time of going to press, neither the authors nor the copyright holder can accept any legal responsibility or liability for any errors or omissions that may have been made nor for any inaccuracies nor for any loss, harm or injury that comes about from following instructions or advice in this book.

NOTES
The nutritional analysis given for each recipe is calculated per portion (i.e. serving or item), unless otherwise stated. If the recipe gives a range, such as Serves 4–6, then the nutritional analysis will be for the smaller portion size, i.e. 6 servings. The analysis does not include optional ingredients, such as salt added to taste.
Standard spoon and cup measures are level.
Large eggs are used unless otherwise stated.
Electric oven temperatures in this book are for conventional ovens. When using a fan oven, the temperature will probably need to be reduced by about 20–40°F. Since ovens vary, you should check with your manufacturer's instruction book for guidance.

CONTENTS

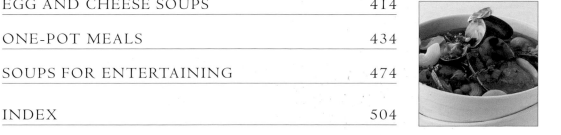

INTRODUCTION

Soups are very versatile and can be made using many different ingredients. One of the great things about soup is that you can put a selection of fresh, raw and sometimes cooked ingredients into a pan with some well-flavored stock, let the mixture bubble away for a short while, and within no time at all you have created a delicious homemade soup with very little effort.

Many soups are quick and easy to make and simply combine a few key ingredients with added flavorings, such as herbs or spices, whereas other soups —perhaps those ideal for a special occasion or a more substantial meal— may require a little more preparation.

Below: Tom Yam Gung with Tofu is a famous Thai specialty.

Some soups make ideal appetizers to a meal, and they are always a popular choice, while others are substantial enough to be meals in themselves, served with plenty of fresh crusty bread as an accompaniment. There are light and refreshing soups that are chilled, ideal for summer dining *al fresco*, and rich and creamy soups, perfect for meals shared with family and friends. Whichever kind you choose, it is well worth the effort to create fresh and flavorful soups in your own kitchen.

An essential ingredient in most soups is a good well-flavored stock, preferably homemade. Bouillon cubes, granules or powder save time, but it is hard to beat the flavor and quality of homemade stock, and they are relatively easy and inexpensive to make. Once

Above: Meatballs in Pasta Soup with Basil makes a substantial main course.

you have a good basic stock, whether it is vegetable, fish, meat or chicken stock, there is a huge range of soups that you can create in your kitchen. However, remember that your stock will only be as good as the quality of the ingredients used to make it—you cannot produce a good, tasty stock from old, limp, past-their-best vegetables! If you are really short of time, you could choose one of the chilled fresh stock products available from some supermarkets and delicatessens.

Very little specialist equipment is needed to make soups, although you will find that a food processor or blender is invaluable and will save time and effort when you want to purée soup mixtures before serving—although pressing the soup through a strainer or using a hand-held blender are perfectly good alternatives. You will probably already have in your kitchen a good-quality heavy pan, a sharp knife and chopping board, and a vegetable peeler.

The addition of an attractive garnish, perhaps a sprinkling of chopped fresh herbs, some vegetables cut in julienne strips, or a swirl of cream added at the last minute, will enhance even the simplest of soups. Soups may be served on their own or topped with a few crunchy croutons or grilled croutes.

Soups feature in every cuisine around the world—whether they are called gumbos, potages, broths, chowders or consommés. Now that once-unfamiliar ingredients are readily available in specialist food stores and many supermarkets, there is absolutely no reason why you cannot make these in your own home.

In summer, choose from cold soups such as French Vichyssoise, Chilled Avocado Soup with Cumin from Spain, or Mexican Chilled Coconut Soup. Creamy vegetable soups include Irish Parsnip Soup, Caribbean Peanut and Potato Soup, or Asparagus and Pea Soup with Parmesan Cheese. Chunky vegetable and legume soups are ideal winter warmers. You could try classic Russian Borscht with *Kvas* and Sour Cream, or Tuscan Bean Soup. Or serve a hot and spicy soup, such as North African Spiced Soup. Pasta and noodle soups range from Borlotti Bean and Pasta Soup and Avgolemono with Pasta to more exotic choices, such as Malaysian Shrimp Laksa, and Udon Noodles with Egg Broth and Ginger.

Soups made with chicken, meat, fish or shellfish are full of nourishment and make a complete meal served with

Below: Corn and Red Chile Chowder is for those who enjoy hot and spicy food.

Above: Soda bread is traditionally served with this Irish Country Soup.

slices or chunks of fresh crusty bread or bread rolls, served warm or cold. Here the choice is wide and varied—from traditional Irish Country Soup and Lobster Bisque to the more unusual and exotic Smoked Haddock Chowder, Vermouth Soup with Seared Scallops, Arugula Oil and Caviar, or Scallop and Jerusalem Artichoke Soup.

Each recipe in this book has easy-to-follow step-by-step instructions and a beautiful color photograph to show the finished dish. Few dishes give more all-round pleasure than a good homemade soup, and in this wonderful collection of recipes the world of soups is yours to explore.

VEGETABLES

Using vegetables offers the cook an infinite number of culinary possibilities, including creating a wide range of delicious and flavorful soups. The choice of vegetables is immense, and the growing demand for organic produce has led to pesticide-free vegetables becoming widely available. Vegetables are an essential component of a healthy diet and have countless nutritional benefits. They are at their most nutritious when freshly picked.

Carrots

The best carrots are not restricted to the cold winter months—summer welcomes the slender, sweet new crop, often sold with their feathery tops. Look for firm, smooth carrots—the smaller they are, the sweeter they taste. Carrots should be prepared just before use to preserve their valuable nutrients. They are delicious in Carrot and Orange Soup, as well as being an important ingredient in many other soups and in homemade stock. Raw carrots, cut into thin julienne strips, make an unusual and attractive garnish.

Beets

Beets are the key ingredient in the classic Russian Borscht. They also combine well with other flavors, for example in Beet Soup with Mascarpone Brioche, which is a light and refreshing choice, or alternatively the more substantial dish Fragrant Beet and Vegetable Soup with Spiced Lamb Kubbeh. If you are cooking beets whole, wash them carefully in order not to damage the skin or the nutrients and prevent the colour leaching out. Trim the stalks to about 1 inch above the root. Small beets are sweeter and more tender than the larger ones.

Below: Celeriac is bumpy with patchy brown, white and green skin.

Celeriac

Strictly speaking, celeriac is a root vegetable, as it is the root of certain kinds of celery. It has a similar but less pronounced flavor than celery, but when cooked it is more akin to potatoes. It is an ingredient in soups such as Cream of Celeriac and Spinach Soup.

Rutabaga

The globe-shaped rutabaga has pale orange-colored flesh with a delicate sweet flavor. Trim off the thick peel, then treat in the same way as other root vegetables. For soups, rutabaga is usually peeled and diced, and then cooked with other vegetables and stock until tender. It could be finely chopped and integrated in chunky vegetable soups, or maybe cooked with stock and other ingredients, and then pureed to create a smooth soup.

Right: Carrots give soup a sweet flavor, and add color too.

Left: Beet's deep ruby-red color adds a vibrant hue to soups. It is a classic ingredient of the Russian soup Borscht.

Above: Parsnips are best used in the winter months and make good, hearty, warming soups.

Parsnips

These winter root vegetables have a sweet, creamy flavor and are a delicious element in many soups. Parsnips are best purchased after the first frost of the year, as the cold converts their starches into sugar, enhancing their sweetness. Scrub them well before use and peel only if the skin is tough. Avoid large roots, which can be very woody.

Turnips

Turnips have many health-giving qualities, and small turnips with their green tops intact are especially nutritious. Their crisp, ivory flesh, which is enclosed in white, green and pink-tinged skin, has a pleasant, slightly peppery flavor, the intensity of which depends on their size and the time of harvesting. Turnips add a lovely flavor and a warming substance to any vegetable-based soups, such as the Russian Spinach and Root Vegetable Soup.

Jerusalem artichokes

This small, lumpy tuber has a sweet, nutty flavor. Peeling can be difficult, although scrubbing and trimming is usually sufficient. Store in the refrigerator for up to one week. Use in the same way as potatoes—they make good, creamy soups.

Potatoes

There are thousands of potato varieties, and many lend themselves to particular cooking methods. Main crop potatoes, such as Estima and Maris Piper, and sweet potatoes (preferably the orange-fleshed variety which have a better flavor than the cream-fleshed type) are ideal for using in soups. Potatoes are also good (especially when mashed or pureed) as a thickener for some soups. Discard any potatoes with green patches. Vitamins and minerals are stored in, or just beneath, the skin, so it is best to use potatoes unpeeled.

Buying and storing root vegetables

Seek out bright, firm, unwrinkled root vegetables and tubers, which do not have soft patches. When possible, choose organically grown produce, and buy in small quantities to ensure freshness. Store root vegetables in a cool, dark place.

Broccoli

This nutritious vegetable should be a regular part of everyone's diet. Two types are commonly available: purple-sprouting, which has fine, leafy stems and a delicate head, and calabrese, the more substantial green variety with a tightly budded top

Above: Trim the stalks from broccoli and divide it into florets. The stems of young broccoli can be sliced and used, too.

and thick stalk. Choose broccoli that has bright, compact florets. Yellowing florets, a limp woody stalk and a pungent smell are an indication of overmaturity. Broccoli adds flavor and texture as well as a lovely color to soups. Once cooked, it is often pureed to create an attractive green-colored soup. It is a versatile vegetable and combines well in soups with other ingredients.

Cauliflower

The cream-colored compact florets, or curds, should be encased in large, bright green leaves. There are also varieties with purple or green florets. Raw or cooked cauliflower has a mild flavor and is delicious when combined with other ingredients to make tasty soups such as Curried Cauliflower Soup or Cream of Cauliflower Soup.

Cabbage

There are several different varieties of cabbage, and one of the best to use in soups is Savoy, which has substantial, crinkly leaves with a strong flavor. Firm red and white cabbages are also good for soups, as they retain their texture well.

Left: Cauliflower can be used either raw or cooked.

Spinach

This dark green leaf provides an excellent source of cancer-fighting antioxidants. It contains about four times more beta carotene than broccoli. It is also rich in fiber, which can help to lower harmful levels of LDL cholesterol in the body, reducing the risk of heart disease and stroke. Spinach does contain iron but not in such a rich supply as was once thought. It also contains oxalic acid, which inhibits the absorption of iron and calcium in the body. However, eating spinach with a vitamin C-rich food will increase absorption. Spinach also contains vitamins C and B6, calcium, potassium, folate, thiamine and zinc. Spinach and other leafy green vegetables are ideal shredded and added to soups or cooked in them and then pureed to create flavorful, nutritious dishes with a lovely deep green color, ideal for swirling cream into just before serving.

Pumpkins

These are native to America, where they are traditionally eaten at Thanksgiving. Small pumpkins have sweeter, less fibrous flesh than the larger ones. Pumpkin can be used in smooth soups such as Pumpkin Soup with Rice. Squash, such as the butternut variety, is an alternative to pumpkin—Roasted Garlic and Butternut Squash Soup with Tomato Salsa will waken up the taste buds.

Right: Making soup is an effective way of using up an excess of zucchini in the autumn.

Below: Fresh, crisp cucumbers are excellent in chilled soups.

Above: Corn works particularly well in creamy fish-based soups.

Zucchini

The most widely available summer squash, zucchini have most flavor when they are small and young. Standard zucchini, as well as baby zucchini, may be used on their own or with other ingredients, such as mint and yogurt, to create delicious soups. They are a key ingredient in Greek Eggplant and Zucchini Soup, served with tzatziki.

Cucumbers

The Chinese say food should be enjoyed for its texture as well as for its flavor; cucumbers have a unique texture and a refreshing, cool taste. Varieties include English cucumbers, ridged cucumbers, gherkins and kirbys. Cucumbers are ideal for chilled soups such as Cucumber and Salmon Soup with Salsa, and Chilled Cucumber and Shrimp Soup.

Corn

There are several varieties of corn—the kind we eat on the cob is also known as sweetcorn. Baby corn cobs are picked when they are immature and are cooked and eaten whole. Corn and baby corn, as well as canned or frozen corn kernels, are all used in creative soup recipes such as Corn and Potato Chowder, or Corn and Red Chile Chowder.

Fennel

Florence fennel is closely related to the herb and spice of the same name. The short, fat bulbs have a similar texture to celery and are topped wtih edible feathery fronds. Fennel has a mild aniseed flavor, which is most potent when eaten raw. Cooking tempers the flavor, giving it a delicious sweetness. Fennel marries wonderfully with fish in Bourride of Red Mullet and Fennel.

Tomatoes

There are dozens of varieties to choose from, which vary in color, shape and size. The egg-shaped plum tomato is perfect for many types of cooking, including soups, as it has a rich flavor and a high proportion of flesh to seeds—but it must be used when fully ripe. Too often, store-bought tomatoes are bland and tasteless because they have been picked too young. Vine-ripened and cherry tomatoes, together with large beefsteak tomatoes, have good flavor and are also good for soups. Sun-dried tomatoes add a rich intensity to soups. Genetically engineered tomatoes are now sold in some countries; check the label. If tomatoes are cooked with their skins on, you will find that the soup may need pureeing and straining to remove skins and seeds.

Peeling and seeding tomatoes

Tomato seeds can give soups a bitter flavor. Removing them and the tomato skins will also give a smoother result, which is preferable for many soups.

1 Immerse the tomato in boiling water and leave for about 30 seconds—the base of each tomato can be slashed to make peeling easier.

2 Lift out the tomato with a slotted spoon, rinse in cold water to cool slightly, and then peel off the skin.

3 Cut the tomato in half, then scoop out the seeds with a teaspoon and remove the hard core. Dice or coarsely chop the flesh according to the recipe.

Buying and storing tomatoes

When buying tomatoes, look for deep-red fruit that has a firm, yielding flesh. Tomatoes that are grown and sold locally will generally have the best flavor. Farmers' markets are a good place to buy vegetables, or you could grow your own. To improve the flavor of a slightly hard tomato, leave it to ripen fully at room temperature. It is best to avoid refrigeration, because this stops the ripening process and adversely affects the taste and texture of the tomato.

Bell peppers

In spite of their name, bell peppers have nothing to do with the spice pepper used as a seasoning. They are actually members of the capsicum family and are called bell peppers, sweet peppers, and even bull-nose peppers. The color of the pepper tells you something about its flavor. Green peppers are the least mature of all and have a fresh "raw" flavor. Red peppers are ripened green peppers and are distinctly sweeter. Yellow/orange peppers taste more or less like red peppers, although perhaps slightly less sweet. Peppers add a lovely flavor and color to soups such as Gazpacho or Chilled Tomato and Sweet Pepper Soup.

Right: Peppers add wonderful colors to soups—red, green, yellow and orange.

Above: Pureed avocados make soups really creamy.

Chiles

Native to the Americas, this member of the capsicum family is extensively used in many cuisines, including Mexican, Indian, Thai, South American and African. There are more than 200 different varieties, and they add a fiery spiciness to soups.

Avocados

Strictly a fruit rather than a vegetable, the avocado has been known by many names—butter pear and alligator pear to name but two. There are four varieties: Hass, the purple-black small bumpy avocado, the Ettinger and Fuerte, which are pear-shaped and have smooth green skin, and the Nabal, which is rounder in shape. The black-colored Hass has golden-yellow flesh, while green avocados have pale green to yellow flesh. Avocados can be used to make tempting soups such as Avocado and Lime Soup with Green Chile Salsa.

Right: Eggplant is delicious in minestrone soups.

Eggplants

The dark-purple, glossy-skinned eggplant is the most familiar variety, although it is the small, ivory-white egg-shaped variety that has inspired its American name. There is also the bright-green pea eggplant that is used in Asian cooking, and a pale-purple Chinese eggplant. Creamy Eggplant Soup with Mozzarella and Gremolata is a delicious dish that will impress your dinner party guests.

Celery

Celery has a sharp and savory flavor, which makes it excellent for soups and stocks. The tangy, astringent flavor and crunchy texture of celery contrasts well with the other ingredients. Most supermarkets sell both green and white celery (when celery grows naturally the stalks are green; banking up earth against the shoots makes it pale and white). Look for celery with fresh-looking leaves, and avoid any that have outer stalks missing.

Onions

Every cuisine in the world includes onions in one form or another. They are an essential flavoring, offering a range of taste sensations, from the sweet and juicy red onion and powerfully pungent white onion to the light and fresh scallion. Pearl onions and shallots are the babies of the family. Shallots and leeks can be used in place of onions in many recipes, while scallions may be used as a flavoring or garnish.

Buying and storing onions

When buying, choose onions that have dry, papery skins and are heavy for their size. They will keep for 1–2 months in a cool, dark place.

Garlic

An ingredient that everyone who does any cooking at all will need, garlic is a bulb that is available in many varieties. Its papery skin can be white, pink or purple. Color makes no difference to taste, but the attraction of the large purple bulbs is that they make a beautiful display in the kitchen. As a general rule, the smaller the garlic bulb, the stronger it is likely to be. If stored in a cool, dry place and not in the refrigerator, garlic will keep for up to eight weeks.

Leeks

Like onions and garlic, leeks have a long history and are versatile, having their own distinct, subtle flavor. They are less pungent than onions, but are still therapeutically beneficial. Excellent in soups, leeks add delicious flavor and texture to many recipes. A classic combination of leeks and potatoes produces the popular soup Vichyssoise, which can be served hot or cold as a light appetizer. Commercially grown leeks are usually about 10 inches long, but you may occasionally see baby leeks, which are very mild and tender and can also be used in soups. Try winter soups such as Chicken, Leek and Celery Soup or Irish Leek and Blue Cheese Soup.

Above: Garlic is used in meat and vegetable soups.

Above: Scallions, shallots and onions add essential flavor to soups.

Above: Shiitake mushrooms are popular in Japanese soups.

Mushrooms

The most common cultivated variety of mushroom is actually one type in various stages of maturity. The white mushroom is the youngest and has a tight, white, button-like cap. It has a mild flavor. Cremini mushrooms are slightly more mature and larger in size, while the portobello mushroom is the largest variety and has dark, open gills. Flat mushrooms have the most prominent flavor. Mushrooms are a useful ingredient in many soups, and add flavor and texture, as well as color (especially cremini and portobello mushrooms). Fresh and dried wild mushrooms also add a delicious taste to some soup recipes, such as Wild Mushroom with Soft Polenta.

Several varieties of wild mushroom are now available in supermarkets, for example oyster and shiitake. Oyster mushrooms are ear-shaped fungi that grow on rotting wood. Cap, gills and stem are all the same colour, which can be greyish brown, pink or yellow. They are now widely cultivated, although they are generally thought of as wild mushrooms. Delicious in both flavor and texture, they are softer than white mushrooms

when cooked but seem more substantial, having more of a "bite" to them.

Shiitake mushrooms are Japanese fungi from the variety of tree mushrooms (called *take* in Japan, the *shii* being the hardwood tree from which they are harvested). They have a meaty, slightly acid flavor and a distinct slippery texture. Try them in Shiitake Mushroom Laksa.

Buying and storing mushrooms

Buy mushrooms that smell and look fresh. Avoid ones with damp, slimy patches and any that are discolored. Store in a paper bag in the refrigerator for up to 4 days. Wipe mushrooms with damp paper towels before use but never wash or soak them.

Arugula

Usually thought of as a salad vegetable, arugula is actually a herb with a strong peppery taste that adds flavor and color to soups such as Leek, Potato and Arugula Soup.

Sorrel

Another salad vegetable that is a herb, sorrel has a refreshing, sharp flavor. In soups it is good mixed with other herbs and green leaves, as in Sorrel, Spinach and Dill Soup. Salad leaves are best when they are very fresh, and do not keep well. Avoid leaves that are wilted or discolored. Store in the refrigerator for 3–4 days.

Cleaning leeks

Leeks need meticulous cleaning to remove any grit and earth that may hide between the layers of leaves. This method will ensure that the tiniest piece of grit will be washed away.

1 Trim off the root, them trim the top of the green part and discard. Remove any tough or damaged outer leaves.

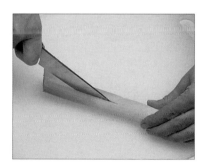

2 Slash the green part of the leek into quarters and rinse the entire leek well under cold running water, separating the layers to remove any hidden dirt or grit. Slice or leave whole, depending on the recipe.

Above: Arugula gives soups a strong, peppery flavor.

Above: Fresh sorrel mixes well with other herbs.

14

LEGUMES

Beans, lentils and peas provide the cook with a diverse range of flavors and textures, and they are a great addition to soups. They have long been a staple food in the Middle East, South America, India and the Mediterranean. Low in fat and high in complex carbohydrates, vitamins and minerals, legumes are an important source of protein for vegetarians, matching animal-based sources when eaten with cereals.

BEANS

The edible seeds from plants belonging to the legume family, pulses are packed with protein, vitamins, minerals and fiber, and are low in fat. For the cook, their ability to absorb the flavors of other foods means that beans can be used as the base for an infinite number of dishes, and many are ideal in soups.

Red kidney beans

These are dark red-brown kidney-shaped beans that keep their shape and color when cooked. They are excellent in soups as well as many other dishes. Raw kidney beans contain a substance that cannot be digested and which may cause food poisoning if the toxins are not extracted. It is therefore essential that you fast-boil red kidney beans for 15 minutes before use.

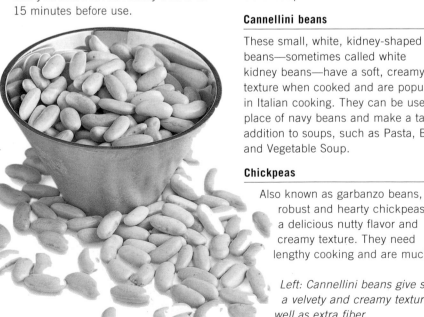

Above: Dried fava beans can be used when fresh ones are not in season.

Fava beans

Usually eaten in their fresh form, fava beans change in color from green to brown when dried, making them difficult to recognize. The outer skin can be very tough and chewy, and some people prefer to remove it after cooking. Fava beans add delicious flavor to soups—try Fava Bean Minestrone or Catalan Potato and Fava Bean Soup.

Cannellini beans

These small, white, kidney-shaped beans—sometimes called white kidney beans—have a soft, creamy texture when cooked and are popular in Italian cooking. They can be used in place of navy beans and make a tasty addition to soups, such as Pasta, Bean and Vegetable Soup.

Chickpeas

Also known as garbanzo beans, robust and hearty chickpeas have a delicious nutty flavor and creamy texture. They need lengthy cooking and are much

Left: Cannellini beans give soups a velvety and creamy texture, as well as extra fiber.

Cooking kidney beans

Most types of beans, with the exception of adzuki beans and mung beans, require soaking for 5–6 hours or overnight and then boiling rapidly for 10–15 minutes to remove any harmful toxins. This is particularly important for kidney beans, which can cause serious food poisoning if not treated in this way.

1 Put the beans in a strainer or colander and wash them well under cold running water.

2 Place the washed beans in a large bowl that allows plenty of room for expansion. Cover with cold water and leave to soak overnight or for 8–12 hours, then drain and rinse.

3 Place the beans in a large pan and cover with fresh cold water. Bring to the boil and boil rapidly for 10–15 minutes, then reduce the heat and simmer for 1–1½ hours until tender.

4 Drain and use as required.

used in Middle Eastern cuisine, including soups such as Moroccan Chickpea and Lentil Soup with Honey Buns and North African Spiced Soup.

Soybeans

These small, oval beans contain all the nutritional properties of animal products but are without the disadvantages. They are extremely dense and need to be soaked for up to 12 hours before cooking. They combine well with robust ingredients such as garlic, herbs and spices, and they make a healthy addition to soups. Soybeans are also used to make tofu, tempeh, textured vegetable protein (TVP), flour and the different versions of soy sauce. Tofu is widely used in Asian soups—try Hot and Sweet Vegetable and Tofu Soup, which uses tofu as an ingredient.

Below: Chickpeas add heartiness to soups.

Right: Soybeans vary in color from creamy-yellow through brown to black.

Buying and storing beans

Look for plump, shiny beans with unbroken skins. Beans toughen with age so, although they will keep for up to a year in a cool, dry place, it is best to buy them in small quantities from stores with a regular turnover. Avoid any that look dusty or dirty or smell musty, and store them in an airtight container in a cool, dark, dry place.

LENTILS AND PEAS

These are among our oldest foods. Lentils are hard even when fresh, so they are always sold dried. Unlike beans, they do not need soaking before being cooked.

Red lentils

Bright orange-colored red split lentils, sometimes known as Egyptian lentils, are the most familiar variety. They cook in just 20 minutes, then disintegrating into a thick puree. They are ideal for thickening soups. Try creative recipes such as Thai-style Lentil and Coconut Soup, or Spiced Lentil Soup with Parsley Cream.

Puy lentils

These tiny, dark blue-green lentils are superior in taste and texture to other varieties and are great added to soups.

Green and brown lentils

Sometimes referred to as continental lentils, these retain

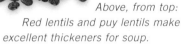

Above, from top: Red lentils and puy lentils make excellent thickeners for soup.

their disk shape when cooked. They take longer to cook than split lentils—about 40–45 minutes—and are ideal for adding to warming soups.

Peas

Dried peas come from the field pea, not the garden pea, which is eaten fresh. Unlike lentils, peas are soft when young and require drying. They are available whole or split; the latter have a sweeter flavor and cook more quickly. Like split lentils, split peas do not hold their shape when cooked, making them perfect for soups. They take about 45 minutes to cook. Dried peas require soaking overnight before use.

Buying and storing lentils and peas

Although lentils and peas can be kept for up to a year, they toughen with time. Buy from stores with a fast turnover of stock and store in airtight containers in a cool, dark place.

MEAT AND POULTRY

Packed with high-quality protein, meat is an excellent food and is used in a variety of soup recipes. Careful rearing means leaner animals and hence healthier cuts of meat, making it perfectly possible to follow current dietary advice while still enjoying meat and poultry. Nowadays we are spoilt for choice with all the types and cuts of meat available. Most butchers and many supermarkets with fresh meat counters are only too happy to advise you on the best cuts of meat to use for all your recipes, including soups.

Chicken

The stock from cooking chicken makes an ideal basis for many delicious soups. If you can, choose corn-fed, free-range or organic birds for the best flavor. Cuts used in soups include breasts, legs and thighs. Boneless thighs or breasts are a good buy.

Duck

There isn't much meat on a duck, so buy big rather than small birds, or choose duck breasts. Although leaner than it used to be, duck is still a fatty meat, so remove as much of the fat as possible before cooking. Duck goes well with oranges, and Duck Broth with Orange Spiced Dumplings is a delicious recipe. Lean duck can be used instead of chicken in some soups.

Below, from left: Corn-fed, free-range and organic chickens give the best flavor for chicken stocks.

Turkey

A turkey isn't just for Christmas—today's smaller birds are perfect for soups. Try recipes such as Chinese Chicken and Chile Soup, or Chicken, Leek and Celery Soup, using turkey in place of chicken.

Bacon

Used in soups to add flavor, bacon can be bought sliced, in lardons (thin strips or dice), or in a piece. It is available smoked or unsmoked, and in different cuts—lean or fatty. Bacon is a key ingredient in Irish Kidney and Bacon Soup, and Irish Bacon Broth.

Pancetta

Pancetta is belly of pork that is cured with salt and spices, and it is eaten either raw in very thin slices, or cut more thickly and used in cooking. It can be substituted for bacon in soup recipes. Try it in the delicious Bacon and Chickpea Soup with Tortilla Chips.

Above: Bacon and pancetta can be used interchangeably.

Beef, lamb and pork

Some soup recipes call for the addition of beef, lamb or pork. These not only bring flavor to a dish, but also make a valuable contribution in terms of nutrition, since they are a source of high-quality protein. When making soup, the best cuts of beef, lamb and pork to choose are steak, chops or tenderloin, although other cuts such as pork ribs, neck of lamb and ground beef, lamb or pork are also used, so be guided by the recipe or ask your butcher for advice. Meat bones are also used for making stocks.

Kidneys

Lamb, pork and beef kidney may all be used in soups. Beef kidney has the strongest flavor.

FISH

Fish is one of the quickest and easiest foods to cook, and makes an ideal ingredient for soups. As well as being delicious to eat, it is also very nutritious and a great source of easily digestible protein as well as other important nutrients such as B vitamins. White fish such as skinless cod, haddock and monkfish are naturally low in fat. Oily fish such as salmon, trout and mackerel are rich in omega-3 fats, which are beneficial to health, and we are actively encouraged to eat oily fish at least once a week. Oily fish are also a good source of all of the B vitamins as well as vitamins A and D.

TYPES OF FISH

We have access to a wide range of fresh sea fish, as well as river and lake fish, some caught from our local shores and others imported from further afield. Although some fish is seasonal, many varieties are available all year round from good fishmongers and supermarkets.

Both white fish, such as haddock, cod, monkfish and mullet, and oily fish, such as mackerel and salmon, are used as an ingredient in creative soup recipes. Smoked fish such as smoked haddock or smoked cod are also used to create flavorful soups.

Whichever type of fish you are using as an ingredient in your soup, it is always best to buy firm, fresh fish.

Below: Cod blends well with cream or milk to make delicious fish chowders.

Round sea fish

This is a large group of fish that includes cod, haddock, whiting and mackerel, as well as more exotic varieties such as porgy, red mullet or snapper and parrot fish. These fish have a rounded body shape with eyes at each side of the head, and swim with the dorsal fin uppermost. These fish are normally sold whole or in fillets, cutlets or steaks.

Flat sea fish

American plaice, dabs, flounder, sole and skate are common examples of flat sea fish. Flat fish swim on their sides and have both eyes on top of their head. They usually have a blind side and a darker upper surface, which is colored to camouflage them within their local habitat. Flat fish are usually sold whole or filleted.

Freshwater fish

Freshwater fish may live in freshwater rivers or lakes and include varieties such as salmon, trout and pike. They are usually sold whole or in fillets, steaks or cutlets.

Above: Trout makes a tasty alternative to the more usual clam chowder.

Smoked fish

Fish is usually smoked by one of two methods: hot smoke or cold smoke. Typical examples of smoked fish include haddock, cod, salmon, mackerel, trout and smoked herrings.

Below: Smoked haddock is sold whole, as fillets (shown here) or it can be thinly sliced.

SHELLFISH

We are fortunate to have a good selection of fresh and frozen shellfish available all year round, either shellfish caught off our local shores, or varieties that have been caught further afield and imported. Many shellfish and crustaceans have wonderfully exotic names, and almost all shellfish is considered edible, from littleneck clams to razor clams, sea snails and small scallops.

Shellfish is at its best when eaten fresh and in season. Frozen shellfish is also available and is a good substitute if fresh is not available.

SHRIMP

There are many varieties of shrimp. The smallest are tiny pink or brown shrimp. Next in size come the pink shrimp with a delicate flavor. Then there are the larger variety of shrimp, which turn bright red when they are cooked. They are highly prized for their fine, strong flavor. Best, and most expensive of all, are large succulent jumbo shrimp which have a superb flavor and texture. Similar to these is the cicala, which resembles a small, flat lobster.

Shrimp can be used in a variety of different tasty soups such as Shrimp and Egg-knot Soup, and Wonton and Shrimp Tail Soup.

Buying shrimp

Shrimp should have bright shells that feel firm to the touch; if they look limp or smell of ammonia, do not buy them.

CRUSTACEANS AND MOLLUSKS

Crustaceans range from crabs and lobsters to bright orange crayfish. Squid and cuttlefish are mollusks—their shells are located inside their bodies.

Crab

There are dozens of varieties of crab, ranging from the large common crab to tiny shore crabs that are good only for making soup. All kinds of crabmeat, both fresh and canned, can be used in creative soup recipes. Try recipes such as Crab, Coconut and Cilantro Soup, or Chinese Crab and Corn Soup.

Scallops

Scallops are available almost all year round, but are best in winter when the roes are full and firm. Always try to buy them with their delicious coral, although this is not always possible. You can buy them shelled, which saves the effort of cleaning them. But if you clean them yourself, the beard and all dark colored parts must be removed before

Below: The common or brown crab contains plenty of tasty meat.

Peeling and deveining raw shrimp

Raw shrimp are often peeled before cooking. They must have their intestinal tracts removed before cooking, a process called "deveining". It is not necessary to devein miniature shrimp.

1 Pull off the head and legs from each shrimp, then carefully peel off the body shell. Leave on the tail "fan" if you wish.

2 To remove the intestinal vein from shrimp, make a shallow incision down the center of the curved back of the shrimp using a small sharp knife, cutting all the way from the tail to the head.

3 Pick out the thin black vein that runs the length of the shrimp with the tip of the knife and discard.

Cleaning and preparing squid

Before you start, rinse the squid under cold running water.

1 Holding the body firmly in one hand, grasp the tentacles at the base with the other, and gently but firmly pull the head away from the body. As you do this the soft yellowish entrails will come away.

2 Use a sharp knife to cut off the tentacles from the head of the squid. Reserve the tentacles but discard the hard beak in the middle. Remove and reserve the ink sac, then discard the head.

3 Peel the membrane away from the body. Pull out the "quill". Wash the body under cold running water. Cut the body, flaps and tentacles to the required size.

they are cooked and eaten. Frozen scallops have little or no taste. Scallops are an ingredient in exotic soups such as Seafood Chowder, Vermouth Soup with Seared Scallops, Arugula Oil and Caviar, and Scallop and Jerusalem Artichoke Soup.

Lobsters

These are the ultimate luxury seafood. Their flesh has a delicious flavor and makes wonderful soups. Lobsters must be bought live or freshly boiled. Try the luxurious, velvety Lobster Bisque topped with heavy cream to really appreciate this superior seafood.

Squid and cuttlefish

These mollusks are indistinguishable in taste, but cuttlefish have a larger head and a wider body with stubbier tentacles. Once the bone has been removed, cuttlefish are very tender. The shell of a squid is nothing more than a long, thin, transparent quill. Both squid and cuttlefish have ten tentacles. Squid is more commonly used in soup recipes. Small squid and cuttlefish should be cooked briefly, just until they turn opaque, or they will become rubbery and tough. Larger specimens need long, slow cooking to make them tender, making them ideal for use in some soups. Try delicious Coconut and Seafood Soup.

Mussels

These shellfish have a smooth texture and sweet flavor. Both whole and shelled mussels may be used in soups, and they also make an attractive garnish, cooked and served in their open shells. Try delicious Saffron-flavored Mussel Soup.

Right: Queen scallops are smaller and cheaper than the larger king scallops, but have the same flavor.

Clams

There are many different types of clam, ranging from the tiny littleneck variety to the long, thin razor clam and the large chowder clam. All have a sweet flavor and a slightly chewy texture. Because they vary so much in size, it is best to ask at your supermarket fish counter how many clams you will need for a particular soup or be guided by the recipe. Try tempting recipes such as Clam Chowder or Chile Clam Broth.

Buying and storing shellfish

When buying fresh shellfish such as scallops, mussels, clams and oysters, look for those with tightly closed shells. They are still alive when sold fresh, and any sign of an open shell may indicate that they are far from fresh. A sharp tap on the shell may persuade the shellfish to close up, but otherwise, avoid it. When buying cooked shellfish such as crab, lobster and shrimp, make sure the shells are intact. They should feel quite heavy and have a fresh, agreeable smell.

Once purchased, keep fresh shellfish chilled, and store in the refrigerator, covered with a damp cloth, until it is ready to use. As a general rule, fresh shellfish, as well as defrosted shellfish, is best eaten on the day you purchase it, or used within 24 hours—your supermarket fish counter will be able to advise you more on the length of time recommended for storing shellfish.

EGGS AND DAIRY PRODUCE

These foods are staples in almost every kitchen in the world and have been used in cooking for thousands of years. Eggs and dairy products such as yogurt are important as thickeners in soups, as well as adding essential flavor, texture and substance.

EGGS

Both the cooking qualities of eggs and their decorative nature make them the ideal ingredient for tempting soups. They can be used to thicken soups, such as Egg and Cheese Soup and Saffron Seafood Soup, and as an attractive garnish in soups such as Spicy Tomato and Egg Drop Soup, Portuguese Garlic Soup and Shrimp and Egg-knot Soup.

CREAM

Light cream is excellent for enriching soups. Unlike heavy or whipping cream, light cream will separate if heated too fiercely. If you are planning to freeze a soup that is enriched with cream, towards the end of the cooking time, it is advisable to freeze it without adding the cream. Reheat the dish fully, then lower the heat and add the cream. Most soups in the Creamy Vegetable Soups section

Below: Eggs may be used to thicken soups or as a garnish.

contain cream, for example Cream of Red Bell Pepper Soup, Jerusalem Artichoke Soup and Simple Cream of Onion Soup.

Sour cream is a thick-textured cream that is treated with lactic acid, which gives it its typical tang. It is not the same as cream that has turned sour through age. Full-fat sour cream contains about 20 percent fat, although low- and non-fat versions are also available. Care should be taken when cooking, as it can curdle if heated to too high a temperature or too rapidly. It can be used in the same way as cream and is ideal for enriching and garnishing soups, such as Creamy Beet Soup, Roasted Root Vegetable Soup, and Sweet and Sour Cabbage, Beet and Tomato Borscht.

Crème fraîche, a rich, cultured French cream, is similar to sour cream, but is milder tasting. Its high fat

Left: Light and heavy cream can be stirred into soups or used as a garnish.

content, at around 35 percent, means that it does not curdle when cooked. It may be used to enrich soups and as a garnish. Tomato Soup with Black Olive Ciabatta Toasts, and Hungarian Cherry Soup both have a garnish of crème fraîche, which may be substituted in soups garnished with heavy cream.

MILK

Often referred to as a complete food, milk can be used in both chilled and warm soups. Used in small quantities, it is very useful for adjusting the consistency of soups. It can be used as a substitute for cream if you want a soup to taste less rich, as well as to counteract the heat of chiles in a spicy soup. Soups that contain milk rather than cream include Broccoli and Almond Soup, and Cauliflower and Walnut Cream.

YOGURT

Praised for its health-giving qualities, yogurt has earned a reputation as one of the most valuable health foods. Its consistency may be thin or thick. Strained plain and Greek-style yogurts, which are made from cow's or ewe's milk, contain about 10g of fat per 100g—just enough to prevent them from curdling during cooking. However, although these yogurts are higher in fat

Below: Mozzarella is added to soups to provide texture and absorb flavors.

Above: Stilton has a strong flavor and is a popular choice for adding to soups.

than other types of yogurt, they still contain less fat than cream and they are a healthier alternative. Cultures are added to milk to produce plain yogurt. It has a smooth, creamy texture and a fresh, slightly acidic flavor. Soy yogurt is a dairy-free yogurt that is made from soy milk and is widely available from healthfood stores and supermarkets. Soups that are made with yogurt include Spiced Mango Soup with Yogurt, and Yogurt Soup.

CHEESE

There are several cheeses that can be enjoyed in soups, the main ones being blue cheese, mozzarella and Cheddar. The type of milk, its fat content and the method used to make the cheese all help to define its individual character.

Blue cheese gives a wonderful creamy tang to soups. Stilton has a strong and robust taste that goes well with vegetables such as watercress, broccoli, leeks and zucchini—it is a key ingredient in Pear and Watercress Soup. The pears also combine well with blue cheese—another delicious example is Pear and Roquefort Soup with Caramelized Pears. If you prefer a milder flavor, try blue cheeses such as

Dolcelatte or Bleu d'Causses, which melt in the mouth just like cream. Try Creamy Zucchini and Dolcelatte Soup, which is deliciously creamy and rich.

Mozzarella, probably the most famous of Italian fresh cheeses, is a soft and springy mild white cheese and can be used in soups to add texture rather than a specific taste. The juices, oils and flavors of the other ingredients are absorbed and intensified by the mild layers of the cheese. This, and the fact that mozzarella melts to become elastic, has made it popular in soups such as Eggplant Soup with Mozzarella and Gremolata.

Cheddar cheese crumbled on top of soup creates a zingy dish quickly and elegantly. Try Cauliflower and Broccoli Soup with Cheddar Cheese Croutes.

Homemade pesto
Grated Parmesan and Pecorino cheeses are sprinkled over Italian soups to add flavor. They are also an ingredient in pesto, which makes a tasty garnish.

1 Put 3 ounces/1¹/2 cups basil, 1 ounce/2 tablespoons pine nuts, and 3 chopped garlic cloves into a mortar. Grind with a pestle until the mixture forms a chunky paste.

2 Work in 4 ounces/1¹/3 cups mixed freshly grated Parmesan and Pecorino cheese and 4 fluid ounces/¹/2 cup olive oil.

Above: Cheddar cheese can be grated and sprinkled on top of soups to add protein and flavor.

PASTA AND NOODLES

The wide range of fresh and dried pasta available to us today ensures that you have plenty of choice when it comes to selecting which pasta to cook. Pasta is a nutritious food and plays an important part in a healthy, well-balanced diet. It is low in fat and provides a good source of carbohydrate. Pasta, especially small shapes such as stellette or pastina, is ideal for use in soups and is an important ingredient in recipes such as Pasta, Bean and Vegetable Soup.

SOUP PASTA

These tiny shapes, of which there are hundreds of different varieties, are mostly made from plain durum wheat pasta, although you may find them made with egg and even flavored with carrot or spinach.

Types of soup pasta

Teeny-weeny pasta shapes are called pastina in Italian, and there are literally hundreds of different ones to choose from. In Italy they are always served in broths and clear soups, and are regarded almost as nursery food because they are so often served for children's meals.

Shapes of pastina vary enormously, and seem to get more and more fanciful as the market demands. The smallest and most plain

pasta per minestre (pasta for soups) is like tiny grains. Some look like rice and are in fact called *risi* or *risoni*, while others are more like barley and are called *orzi*. Fregola, from Sardinia, looks like couscous, and has a similar nutty texture and flavor. Semi di melone is like melon seeds, as its name suggests, while acini de pepe or peperini is named after peppercorns, which it resembles in shape and size if not in color. Coralline, grattini and occhi are three more very popular tiny pasta shapes.

The next size up are the ones that are most popular with children. These include alfabeti and alfabetini (alphabet shapes), stelline and stellette (stars), rotellini (tiny wagon wheels) and anellini, which can be tiny rings, sometimes with ridges that make them look very pretty, or larger hoops. Ditali are similar to anellini but slightly thicker, while tubettini are thicker still.

Another category of *pasta per minestre* consists of slightly larger shapes, more like miniature versions of familiar types of short pasta.

Their names end in "ine", "ette" or "etti", denoting that they are the diminutive forms. These include conchigliette (little shells), farfalline and farfallette (little bows), funghetti (little mushrooms), lumachine (little snails), quadretti and quadrettini (little squares), orecchiettini (little ears), renette (like baby penne) and tubetti (little tubes). The size of these varies: the smaller ones are for use in clear broths, while the larger ones are more often used in making thicker soups.

Buying and storing soup pasta

The quality of pasta varies tremendously —choose good-quality Italian brands made from 100 percent durum wheat, and buy fresh pasta from an Italian delicatessen rather than pre-packed fresh pasta from the supermarket.

Dried pasta will keep almost indefinitely in the pantry, but if you keep it in a storage jar, it is a good idea to use it all up before adding any from a new packet.

Fresh pasta is usually sold loose and is best cooked the same day, but can be kept in the refrigerator for a day or two. Fresh pasta from a supermarket is likely to be packed in plastic packs and bags and will keep for 3–4 days in the refrigerator. Fresh pasta freezes well and should be cooked from frozen. Convenient packs of supermarket pasta have the advantage of being easy to store in the freezer.

Left: Tiny soup pasta is available in hundreds of different shapes.

NOODLES

The fast food of the East, noodles can be made from wheat flour, rice, mung bean flour or buckwheat flour. Noodles can be used in a variety of flavorful soup recipes. Try some tasty soups such as Soba Noodles in Hot Soup with Tempura, Thai Cellophane Noodle Soup, Chiang Mai Noodle Soup, or Sapporo-style Ramen Noodles in Soup.

Wheat noodles

These are available in two types: plain and egg. Plain noodles are made from stone-ground flour and water; they can be flat or round and come in various thicknesses. Egg noodles are more common than the wheat variety, and are sold both fresh and dried. The Chinese types are available in various thicknesses. Very fine egg noodles, which resemble vermicelli, are usually sold in individual coils. More substantial wholewheat egg noodles are widely available from larger supermarkets.

Udon and ramen are types of Japanese noodles. Udon noodles are thick and can be round or flat. They are available fresh, pre-cooked or dried. Wholewheat udon noodles have a more robust flavor. Ramen egg noodles are sold in coils and in Japan are often cooked and served with an accompanying broth.

Above:
Egg noodles add flavor and texture to Chinese soups.

Rice noodles

These very fine, delicate noodles are made from rice and are opaque-white in color. Like wheat noodles, they come in various widths, from the very thin strands known as rice vermicelli, which are popular in Thailand and southern China, to the thicker rice sticks, which are used more in Vietnam and Malaysia.

Cellophane noodles

Made from mung beans, cellophane noodles are translucent and do not need to be boiled; they are simply soaked in boiling water for 10–15 minutes. They have a fantastic texture, which they retain when cooked, never becoming soggy.

Buckwheat noodles

Soba are the best-known type of buckwheat noodles. They are a much darker color than wheat noodles—almost brownish-gray. In Japan they are traditionally used in soups.

Below: Cellophane noodles do not need to be boiled.

Left: Rice noodles form the basis of many Asian soup recipes.

Buying and storing noodles

Dried noodles are readily available in supermarkets. Packets of fresh noodles are found in the chiller cabinets of Asian stores and some supermarkets. They must be stored in the refrigerator or freezer. Dried noodles will keep for many months in an airtight container in a cool, dry place.

HERBS AND SPICES

Herbs, the aromatic and fragrant plants that we use to add flavor and color to our dishes, have been cultivated all over the world for centuries. The majority of herbs are familiar as culinary herbs, but many are also good for medicinal and cosmetic purposes. In cooking, herbs are chosen mainly for their flavoring and seasoning properties as well as for adding color and texture to dishes. Herbs, both fresh and dried, add delicious flavor and aroma to a whole variety of dishes, including many hot and chilled soups.

HERBS

Herbs can make a significant difference to the flavor and aroma of a soup, and they can enliven the simplest of dishes.

Basil

This delicate aromatic herb is widely used in Italian and Thai cooking. The leaves bruise easily, so they are best used whole or torn, rather than cut with a knife.

Bay

These dark-green, glossy leaves are best left to dry for a few days before use. They have a robust, spicy flavor and are an essential ingredient in homemade stocks and for a bouquet garni.

Cilantro

Warm and spicy, cilantro looks similar to flat leaf parsley but its taste is completely different.

Dill

The mild yet distinctive, aniseed flavor of dill makes a good addition to soups, for example in Sorrel, Spinach and Dill Soup.

Kaffir lime leaves

These glossy green leaves are commonly used in Asian cuisines, lending a citrus flavor to soups. They are available fresh from Asian stores, or dried from large supermarkets.

Mint

Mint, a popular herb, has deep green leaves with an unmistakable strong and tangy scent and flavor. It is used in soup recipes such as Iced Melon Soup with Sherbet.

Oregano

This is a wild variety of marjoram with a robust flavor. It goes well with tomato-based soups.

Parsley

There are two types of parsley: flat leaf and curly. Both taste relatively similar, but the flat leaf variety is preferable in cooked dishes. Parsley is an excellent source of vitamin C, iron and calcium.

Above: Tarragon goes well with chicken and shellfish.

Above: Indian-style soups use spicy cilantro.

Tarragon

This small, perennial plant bears slim green leaves, and its distinctive taste is said to be a cross between aniseed and mint. It marries well with chicken and shellfish in soups.

Thyme

This robustly flavored aromatic herb is good in tomato-based soups, as well as soups containing lentils and beans. It is also an essential ingredient in a classic bouquet garni.

Buying and storing herbs

Fresh herbs are widely available, sold loose, in packets or growing in pots. Place stems in a jar half-filled with water and cover with a plastic bag. Sealed with an elastic band, the herbs should keep for about a week.

Right: Basil is an important herb in Italian cooking.

SPICES

Highly revered for thousands of years, spices—the seeds, fruit, pods, bark and buds of plants—add flavor, color and interest to the most unassuming of ingredients, while the evocative aroma of spices stimulates the appetite. Spices add delicious flavor to many soup recipes.

Chiles

Chiles are available fresh as well as in dried, powdered and flaked form. Dried chiles tend to be hotter than fresh, and this is certainly true of chili flakes, which contain both the seeds and the flesh. The best pure chili powders do not contain added ingredients, such as onion and garlic. All types of chile may be used in a variety of soup recipes.

Coriander

Alongside cumin, ground coriander is a key ingredient in Indian curry powders and garam masala, and in northern Europe the ivory-colored seeds are used as a pickling spice. Coriander seeds have a sweet, earthy, burnt-orange flavor that is more pronounced than the fresh leaves. The ready-ground powder rapidly loses its flavour and aroma, so it is best to buy whole seeds, which are easily ground in a mortar using a pestle, or in a coffee grinder. Before grinding, lightly dry-roast the seeds in a frying pan to enhance their flavour. Coriander adds delicious flavor and warmth to soups.

Cumin

Cumin is a familiar component of Indian, Mexican, North African and Middle Eastern cooking and is added to soups to give a delicious flavor and aroma. The seeds have a robust aroma and slightly bitter taste, which is tempered by dry-roasting. Black cumin seeds are milder and sweeter. Ground cumin can be harsh, so it is best to buy the whole seeds and grind them just before use to be sure of a fresh flavor.

Ginger

Fresh ginger root is spicy, peppery and fragrant, and adds a hot, yet refreshing, flavor to soups such as the Japanese Miso Broth with Scallions and Tofu. When buying ginger, look for firm, thin-skinned and unblemished roots and avoid withered, woody-looking roots as these are likely to be dry and fibrous.

Left: Lemon grass stalks are essential in many Asian soup recipes.

Left: Cumin adds taste and aroma.

Lemon grass

This long fibrous stalk has a fragrant citrus aroma and flavor when cut. It is familiar in Southeast Asian cooking and may be used as an ingredient in soups from this region. To use, remove the tough, woody outer layers, trim the root, then cut off the lower 2 inches and slice or pound in a mortar using a pestle. Bottled chopped lemon grass and lemon grass puree are also available.

Pepper

Undoubtedly the oldest, most widely used spice in the world, pepper is a versatile seasoning and is invaluable for soups, because it not only adds flavor of its own to a dish, but also brings out the flavor of the other ingredients.

Saffron

The world's most expensive spice is made from the dried stigmas of *Crocus salivus*. Only a tiny amount of this bright orange spice is needed to add a wonderful color and delicate flavor to fish and shellfish soups.

Salt

It is usually best to leave the seasoning of stocks and soups until the last minute, just before serving. Add salt a little bit at a time, until you have the seasoned flavor you require.

Above: Pink, black and white peppercorns bring out the flavor of your chosen soup ingredients.

Buying and storing spices

Always buy spices in small quantities from a store with a regular turnover. Store in airtight jars in a cool place.

OTHER FLAVORINGS

There are many other flavorings that are used to add depth to soups—for example, olive oil, flavored oils and vinegars, alcohol, chili sauce, pesto and soy sauce, as well as more exotic flavorings such as dashi or fish sauce. Many add that important final touch or richness to a soup, contributing an important element to the overall character. Listed below are some of the flavorings used in this book.

Oils and vinegars

Flavored oils and vinegars are brilliant for splashing into finished soups to pack an extra punch. Consider chili oil for a super-fiery flavor in a spicy soup, or basil or arugula oil to enliven a fish or Mediterranean-style soup. Infuse virgin olive oil with chiles, roasted whole garlic cloves, whole spices, woody herbs or citrus peel instead of buying flavored oil. Flavor and color oil with soft aromatic herbs such as basil. Vinegar adds bite to some soups, so look out for the many types available, including wine vinegars, balsamic vinegar, sherry vinegar and fruit-flavored vinegars, such as raspberry.

Left: Balsamic vinegar is used in Italian soups.

Alcohol

Add to soups in moderation. The golden rule is to simmer the soup for a few minutes to cook off the strong alcohol, leaving the flavor. White wine, Pernod and vermouth work very well with creamy fish soups.

Flavored creams

These provide a wonderful way to introduce contrasting flavor to a finished soup. Crème fraîche or whipped heavy cream can be transformed by adding a puree of fresh herbs, grilled bell peppers or sun-dried tomatoes. Infused saffron and pesto can also be added.

Flavored butters

Flavored butters can be spread on warm bread to accompany a soup, or added to each bowl just before serving. Flavorings range from herbs and spices to shellfish.

Coconut milk

Buy this in cans or long-life cartons, or make it yourself at home. Put 8 ounces/2²/₃ cups dry unsweetened shredded coconut into a food processor, add scant 2 cups boiling water and process for about 30 seconds. Leave to cool slightly, then transfer to a strainer lined with cheesecloth placed over a bowl and gather the ends of the cloth. Twist to extract the liquid.

Left: Raspberry vinegar adds color.

Above: Chili sauces add heat and flavor to soups.

Pesto and pistou

Pesto and pistou are closely related, the latter hailing from southern France, where it is stirred into a rich vegetable soup. Both are made by mixing crushed garlic, basil and olive oil, and pesto also contains pine nuts and Parmesan cheese. Stir into soup to add flavor and color.

Chili sauce

For those who like very hot food, chili sauce can be offered at the table, or a dash can be added to flavor soups during cooking or to individual servings of soup.

Soy sauce

Made from fermented soybeans, soy sauce is one of Asia's most important contributions to the global pantry. There are three types of Chinese soy sauce on the market: light, dark and regular. As a rule, light soy sauce is used for soups. It is the initial extraction, like the first pressing of virgin olive oil. It has the most delicate flavor and is light brown in color with a "beany" fragrance.

Left: Shoyu is a full-flavored Japanese soy sauce.

Right: Soy sauces are available in different strengths.

There are several different types of Japanese soy sauce, too. Usukuchi soy sauce is light in color and tastes less salty than the Chinese light soy. Tamari is dark and thick with a strong flavor, and is even less salty than the light type. Shoyu is a full-flavored sauce that is aged for up to two years. In between, there is the very popular Kikkoman, a brand name for the equivalent of the Chinese regular soy sauce—neither too weak nor too strong.

The Indonesian kecap manis is thick and black, with a powerful aroma but a surprisingly sweet taste.

Soy sauce is used as a flavoring in Japanese soups such as Clear Soup with Seafood Sticks, and Sapporo-style Ramen Noodles in Soup.

Fish sauce

Fish sauce is an essential seasoning for Thai and Vietnamese cooking, in the same way that soy sauce is important to the Chinese and the Japanese. In Vietnam it is often made using shrimp, but in Thailand the sauce is more often made using salted, fermented fish.

All types of fish sauce have a pungent flavor and aroma and are very salty. Thai nam pla has a slightly stronger flavor and aroma than the Vietnamese or Chinese versions. The color of fish sauce can vary considerably; lighter-colored sauces are considered to be better than darker versions. Fish sauce is used to season some soup recipes such as Coconut and Seafood Soup, and Thai Pumpkin, Shrimp and Coconut Soup.

Shrimp paste

Known in Malaysia as *blachan*, this is an essential ingredient in many Southeast Asian dishes, including soups. It is made from tiny shrimp that have been salted, dried, pounded and then left to ferment in hot humid conditions until the aroma is very pungent. The color of the paste can be anything from oyster pink to purplish brown, depending upon the type of shrimp and the precise process used. It is compressed and sold in block form or packed in tiny tubs or jars. The moment you unwrap it, the smell of rotten fish is quite overpowering, but this vanishes during cooking. Shrimp paste adds depth and pungency to a soup, for example in Balinese Vegetable Soup, a popular dish served on beans.

Miso

Many Japanese start the day with a bowl of miso soup for breakfast. Miso is one of the oldest traditional ingredients. Boiled *daizu* (soybeans) are crushed, then mixed with a culture called *koji*, which is made with wheat and rice, barley or beans. The fermented mixture is allowed to mature for up to three years. Numerous kinds and brands of miso are available in supermarkets. They are categorized into three basic grades according to strength of flavor and color: shiro-miso (white, light and made with rice), aka-miso (red, medium and made with barley), and kuro-miso (black, strong and made with soya beans). Miso is quite salty and has a strong fermented bean flavor. Try it in Miso Broth with Scallions and Tofu.

Mirin

This amber-colored, heavily sweetened sake is used only in cooking. It is one of Japan's ancient sakes and is made from *shochu* (distilled sake). There is a synthetically made, cheap mirin-like liquid available called mirin-fuhmi (mirin flavoring), as opposed to hon-mirin (real mirin). Hon-mirin has an alcohol content of 14 percent, whereas mirin-fuhmi is only 1 percent. Both are available in bottles of 1/2 pint or 1 pint from Asian stores and good supermarkets. Mirin has a syrupy texture and adds a mild sweetness to soups.

Left: Thai fish sauce adds a strong, salty flavor to soups.

EQUIPMENT AND TECHNIQUES

One advantage of making your own soups is that you won't need any specialist equipment to try a wide range of tasty recipes. You will need basic equipment such as good knives and a chopping board or two, as well as a good-quality heavy pan and utensils such as wooden spoons etc. One additional piece of equipment that is very useful in soup-making is a food processor or blender, to enable you to puree cooked soups, if you wish. However, if you don't have one of these, many of the soups that require pureeing can simply be hand-pressed to make them smooth.

Heavy pan

For making soups you should choose a good-quality heavy pan. A good pan that conducts and holds heat well allows the vegetables to cook for longer before browning, so that they can be softened without changing color. If you are health-conscious, choose a good-quality non-stick pan, and

Right: There are many different types of vegetable peeler.

Below: Using a balloon whisk.

you may be able to slightly reduce the amount of butter or oil used to sauté the vegetables.

Vegetable peelers

The quickest way to peel vegetables is to use a swivel peeler. For example, trim off the top and end of a carrot, then hold the carrot in one hand and run the peeler away from you down its length, turning the carrot as you work. Use a julienne peeler to cut vegetables such as carrots and zucchini into thin julienne strips. Use julienne strips of vegetables in recipes or as an attractive garnish for chilled or cooked hot soups.

Wooden spoon

Use a wooden spoon to stir soups. This will not damage the base of the pan (important if the pan is non-stick). However, wood absorbs flavors, so wash and dry the spoon well after use, and do not leave the spoon in the soup while it is cooking.

Below: Using a wooden mushroom or champignon.

Chopping an onion

Use a small knife to trim the root end of the onion and remove the skin with the tough layer underneath. Cut the onion in half. Place the cut side down on a chopping board and use a large sharp knife to slice down through the onion without cutting its root. Slice horizontally through the onion. Finally, cut down across all the original cuts and the onion will fall apart into fine dice.

Whisk

A balloon whisk is useful when making some soups, for quickly incorporating ingredients such as eggs and cream, which could curdle, or flour mixtures that can form lumps. Steady the pan or bowl with one hand and, holding the whisk in the other hand, make quick flicking movements.

Wooden mushroom

A wooden mushroom (or champignon), which looks like a large, flat toadstool, is useful for pressing ingredients through a fine strainer to give a smooth puree. The back of a large spoon or ladle can also be used.

Blender

A hand-held blender is brilliant, as it allows you to blend the soup directly in the pan. Controlling the speed is easy, to give the required consistency. Be careful when using a hand-held blender in a non-stick pan, and be sure not to let the blender touch the base or sides of the pan because it will cause damage to the surface.

Chopping fresh herbs

Rinse and thoroughly dry the herbs and remove the leaves from the stalks, if necessary (this is essential when chopping herbs such as rosemary, which has very tough, woody stalks. Place the herbs on a chopping board and, using a knife or other sharp tool, cut the herbs into small pieces (as finely or as coarsely as you wish), holding the tip of the blade against the chopping board and rocking the blade back and forth.

Alternatively, you can use a mezzaluna ("half-moon" in Italian). This is a curved crescent-shaped blade attached to two handles, which rocks back and forth over the herbs to chop them. It is good for chopping a lot of herbs at once.

Above: Eggplant Soup with Mozzarella and Gremolata, made smooth and creamy using a food processor or blender.

Mouli-legume

A more traditional method is to use a mouli-legume, a cooking instrument from France that is a cross between a strainer and a food mill. It sits over a bowl and has a blade to press the food through two fine strainers. The blade is turned by hand to push the soup through the strainers, leaving all the fibers and solids behind. A mouli-legume can grind food quickly into a coarse or fine texture.

Electric food processor and blender

The most common items of equipment for pureeing soups are food processors and free-standing blenders. Both types of machine are quick and efficient, but the food processor does not produce as smooth a result as a conventional blender, and for some recipes the soup must be strained afterwards. Food processors can also be used for finely chopping and slicing vegetables for salsas and garnishes.

Below: Using a mouli-legume.

Below: Using a hand-held blender.

Below: Using a food processor.

MAKING STOCKS

Fresh stocks are indispensable for creating good homemade soups. They add a depth of flavor that plain water just cannot achieve. Although many supermarkets now sell tubs of fresh stock, these may be expensive, especially if you need large quantities. Making your own is surprisingly easy and much more economical, particularly if you can use leftovers.

Homemade stocks aren't just cheaper, they are also a lot tastier, and they are much more nutritious too, precisely because they are made with fresh, natural ingredients. You can, of course, use bouillon cubes, granules or powder, but be sure to check the seasoning as these tend to be particularly high in salt.

Use the appropriate stock for the soup you are making. Onion soup, for example, is improved with a good beef stock. Be careful to use a vegetable stock, though, if you are catering for vegetarians. Recipes are given here for vegetable stock, fish stock, chicken stock, meat stock and basic stocks for Chinese and Japanese cooking.

Freezing stock

A good idea for keen and regular soup makers is to freeze portions of concentrated homemade stock in plastic freezer bags, or ice-cube trays, so you always have a supply at your disposal whenever you need some. Frozen stock can be stored in the freezer for up to 3 months (fish stock for up to 2 months). Ensure that you label each stock carefully for easy identification later.

Vegetable stock

Use this versatile stock as the basis for all vegetarian soups. It may also be used for meat, poultry or fish soups.

MAKES 10 CUPS

INGREDIENTS
2 leeks, roughly chopped
3 celery sticks, roughly chopped
1 large onion, unpeeled, roughly chopped
2 pieces fresh ginger root, chopped
1 yellow bell pepper, chopped
1 parsnip, chopped
mushroom stalks
tomato peelings
3 tablespoons light soy sauce
3 bay leaves
a bunch of parsley stalks
3 sprigs of fresh thyme
1 sprig of fresh rosemary
2 teaspoons salt
freshly ground black pepper
15 cups cold water

1 Put all the ingredients into a stockpot or large pan. Bring slowly to the boil, then lower the heat and simmer for 30 minutes, stirring from time to time.

2 Allow to cool. Strain, then discard the vegetables. The stock is ready to use.

Fish stock

Fish stock is much quicker to make than poultry or meat stock. Ask at your supermarket fish counter for heads, bones and trimmings from white fish. Lobster or crab shell pieces (taken after boiling lobster or crab and scooping out the meat) can also be used in place of fish trimmings to make a tasty fish stock, together with the other flavorings listed.

MAKES 4 CUPS

INGREDIENTS
1½ pounds heads, bones and trimmings from white fish
1 onion, sliced
2 celery sticks with leaves, chopped
1 carrot, sliced
½ lemon, sliced (optional)
1 bay leaf
a few sprigs of fresh parsley
6 black peppercorns
6 cups cold water
⅔ cup dry white wine

1 Rinse the fish heads, bones and trimmings well under cold running water. Put in a stockpot or large pan with the vegetables and lemon, if using, the herbs, peppercorns, water and wine. Bring to the boil, skimming the surface frequently, then reduce the heat and simmer for 25 minutes.

2 Strain the stock without pressing down on the ingredients in the strainer. If not using immediately, leave to cool and then refrigerate. Use within 2 days.

Chicken stock

A good homemade poultry stock is invaluable in the kitchen. If poultry giblets are available, add them (except the livers) with the wings. Once made, chicken stock can be kept in an airtight container in the refrigerator for 3–4 days, or frozen for longer storage (up to 3 months).

MAKES ABOUT 10 CUPS

INGREDIENTS
    2½–3 pounds chicken
        or turkey (wings, backs
        and necks)
    2 onions, unpeeled, quartered
    1 tablespoon olive oil
    16 cups cold water
    2 carrots, roughly chopped
    2 celery sticks, with leaves if
        possible, roughly chopped
    a small handful of
        parsley stalks
    a few sprigs of fresh thyme or
        1 teaspoon dried
    1 or 2 bay leaves
    10 black peppercorns,
        lightly crushed

1 Combine the poultry wings, backs and necks in a stockpot or large pan with the onion quarters and the oil.

2 Cook over a moderate heat, stirring occasionally, until the poultry and onions are lightly and evenly browned.

Right: Moroccan Chicken Soup with Charmoula Butter uses a good-quality homemade stock for a rich flavor.

3 Add the water and stir well to mix in the sediment on the bottom of the pan. Bring to the boil and skim off any impurities as they rise to the surface of the stock.

4 Add the chopped carrots and celery, fresh parsley, thyme, bay leaf and black peppercorns. Partly cover the stockpot and simmer the stock for 3 hours.

5 Pour the stock through a strainer into a bowl. Discard the chicken bones and the vegetables. Leave the stock to cool, then chill in the refrigerator for an hour.

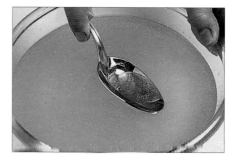

6 When cold, carefully remove the layer of fat that will have set on the surface. The stock is now ready to use in your chosen soup recipe.

Meat stock

The most delicious meat soups rely on a good homemade stock for success. A bouillon cube will do if you have no time to make your own, but fresh homemade stock will give a much better flavor and basis for soups, so it's well worth spending a little time making your own. Once it is made, meat stock can be kept in the refrigerator for up to 4 days, or frozen for up to 3 months.

MAKES ABOUT 8 CUPS

INGREDIENTS
    4 pounds beef bones, such as
        shin, leg, neck and shank, or
        veal or lamb bones, cut into
        2½ inch pieces
    2 onions, unpeeled, quartered
    2 carrots, roughly chopped
    2 celery sticks, with leaves if
        possible, roughly chopped
    2 tomatoes, coarsely chopped
    18¾ cups cold water
    a handful of parsley stalks
    few sprigs of fresh thyme or
        1 teaspoon dried
    2 bay leaves
    10 black peppercorns, lightly
        crushed

3 Transfer the bones and roasted vegetables to a stockpot or large pan. Spoon off the fat from the roasting pan. Add a little of the water to the roasting pan or casserole and bring to the boil on top of the stove, stirring well to scrape up any browned bits. Pour this liquid into the stockpot.

4 Add the remaining water to the pot. Bring just to the boil, skimming frequently to remove all the foam from the surface. Add the parsley, thyme, bay leaves and peppercorns.

5 Partly cover the stockpot and simmer the beef stock for 4–6 hours. The bones and vegetables should always be covered with enough liquid, so top up with a little boiling water from time to time if necessary.

6 Strain the stock through a colander, then skim as much fat as possible from the surface. If possible, cool the stock and then refrigerate it; the fat will rise to the top and set in a layer that can be removed easily.

Stock for Chinese cooking

This stock is an excellent basis for soup-making, and is ideal for Asian soups. Refrigerate the stock when cool—it will keep for up to 4 days. Alternatively, it can be frozen in small containers for up to 3 months and defrosted when required.

MAKES 11 CUPS

INGREDIENTS
    1½ pounds chicken portions
    1½ pounds pork spareribs
    15 cups cold water
    3–4 pieces fresh ginger root,
        unpeeled, crushed
    3–4 scallions, each tied
        into a knot
    3–4 tablespoons Chinese rice wine
        or dry sherry

Below: Braised Cabbage Soup with Beef and Horseradish Cream.

1 Preheat the oven to 450°F. Put the bones in a roasting pan or casserole dish and roast, turning occasionally, for 30 minutes, until they start to brown.

2 Add the onions, carrots, celery and tomatoes and baste with the fat in the pan. Roast for a further 20–30 minutes until the bones are well browned. Stir and baste occasionally.

1 Use a sharp knife to trim off any excess fat from the chicken and spareribs, then chop them into small pieces.

2 Place the chicken and sparerib pieces into a stockpot or large pan with the cold water. Add the crushed fresh ginger root and the scallions tied in knots.

3 Bring the stock to the boil and skim off the froth. Reduce the heat and simmer over a gentle heat, uncovered, for 2–3 hours.

4 Strain the stock, discarding the pork, chicken, ginger and scallion knots. Add the Chinese rice wine or dry sherry and return to the boil. Simmer for 2–3 minutes.

Left: A Chinese-style soup made with homemade Chinese stock.

Above: Kombu seaweed is used in Japanese stocks.

Stock for Japanese cooking

Dashi is the stock that gives the characteristically Japanese flavor to many dishes. Known as Ichiban-dashi, it is used for delicately flavored dishes, including soups. Of course instant stock is available in all Japanese supermarkets, either in granule form, in concentrate or even in a tea-bag style. Follow the instructions on the packet.

MAKES ABOUT 3½ CUPS

INGREDIENTS
¼ ounce dried kombu seaweed
¼–½ ounce dried bonito flakes

1 Wipe the kombu seaweed with a damp cloth and cut two slits in it with scissors, so that it flavors the stock effectively.

2 Soak the kombu in 3¾ cups cold water for 30–60 minutes.

3 Heat the kombu in its soaking water in a pan over a moderate heat. Just before the water boils, remove the seaweed. Add the bonito flakes and bring to the boil over a high heat, then remove the pan from the heat.

4 Leave the stock until all the bonito flakes have sunk to the bottom of the pan. Line a strainer with paper towels or cheesecloth and place it over a large mixing bowl, then gently strain the stock. Use as required or cool and refrigerate for up to 2 days.

THICKENING SOUPS

Many soups do not need any thickening ingredients added, as the pureed soup is thick enough. Vegetables such as potatoes, onions and carrots, once cooked and pureed in a soup, will often help to thicken the soup sufficiently. If your soup does need thickening, try one of the methods below.

Beurre manié

This smooth flour and butter paste is used to thicken soups at the end of the cooking time. Equal quantities of all-purpose flour and butter are kneaded together, then a small pat of the paste is added to the soup and whisked until it is fully incorporated before adding the next. The soup is brought to the boil and simmered for about 1 minute, until thickened and to avoid a raw flour flavor. A similarly useful paste can be made using flour and cream.

Cream

Heavy cream can be used to thicken a fine soup. It is added towards the end of cooking, then the soup is brought to the boil and simmered gently for a few minutes until it is slightly reduced and thickened.

Ground almonds

Ground almonds can be used as a thickener in soups, and they add extra flavor as well as texture. The delicate flavor of almonds blends particularly well with fish- and chicken-based soups. However, ground almonds

Below: Making beurre manié.

Above: Adding ground almonds.

do not thicken soup in the same way that ingredients such as flour and cornstarch do, to make a thick, smooth soup. Instead they add body, texture, flavor and richness.

Cornstarch or arrowroot

These fine flours are mixed with a little cold water (about double the volume of the dry ingredient) to make a smooth, thick, but runny paste. Stir the paste into the hot soup and simmer, stirring, until thickened. Cornstarch takes about 3 minutes to thicken completely and lose its raw flavor. Arrowroot achieves maximum thickness on boiling and tends to become slightly thinner if it is allowed to simmer for any length of time, so this is usually avoided.

Below: Mixing cornstarch with water.

Above: Adding bread crumbs.

Cornstarch gives an opaque result, but arrowroot becomes clear when it boils, so it is useful for thickening clear liquids and soups.

Bread crumbs

The more rustic approach is to use fresh white bread crumbs to thicken soup. They can be toasted in oil before being stirred into a simmering soup, or added directly to a finished dish.

Eggs

Beaten eggs, egg yolks, or a mixture of eggs and a little cream can be used to enrich and slightly thicken a smooth soup. Whisk into the hot soup, but do not allow it to boil once they are added or it will curdle.

Below: Whisking in beaten eggs.

GARNISHES

Garnishes should look attractive, be edible, complement the flavor of the soup and add that final finishing touch. Some typical ones include sprinkling the soup with chopped herbs or stirring them into it just before serving, or topping thick, rich soups with a fresh herb sprig or two for an attractive garnish. Croutons, made from either plain or flavored bread, add appeal and crunch to many soups. Below are some typical garnishes, as well as a few tips for some more unusual ones.

Swirled cream

A swirl of cream is the classic finish for many soups, such as a smooth tomato soup and Vichyssoise. This garnish gives a professional finish to your soup, although the technique is simplicity itself.

1 Transfer the cream into a jug with a good pouring lip. Pour a swirl onto the surface of each bowl of soup.

2 Draw the tip of a fine skewer quickly backward and forward through the cream to create a delicate pattern. Serve the soup immediately.

Above: Frying croutes in oil.

Herbs

Adding a handful of chopped fresh herbs to a bowl of soup just before serving can make a good soup look great. A bundle of chives makes a dainty garnish. Cut 5–6 chives to about 2½ inches long and tie them in a bundle using another length of chive.

Fried croutons

This classic garnish adds texture as well as flavor to soups. To make croutons, cut bread into small cubes and fry in a little oil. Toss the bread continuously so that the cubes are golden all over, then drain on paper towels.

Grilled croutes

Topped with grilled cheese, croutes not only look good, but taste great in all sorts of soups. To make them, toast small slices of French bread on both sides. If you like, you can rub the toast with a cut clove of garlic, then top with grated Cheddar or Parmesan, a crumbled blue cheese, such as Stilton, or a slice of goat cheese. Broil briefly until the cheese is beginning to melt.

Crisp-fried shallots

Finely sliced shallots make a quick garnish for smooth lentil and vegetable soups. Cut them crosswise into rings, then shallow fry in hot oil until crisp.

Above: Vegetable julienne make visually appealing garnishes.

Chips

Try store-bought thick-cut potato chips or tortilla chips; alternatively, make your own vegetable chips. Water-thin slices of fresh raw beet, pumpkin and parsnip can all be deep-fried in hot oil for a few moments to produce delicious and unusual chips.

Vegetable julienne

An effective way of preparing ingredients for adding a splash of color to soup is to cut them into very fine strips called julienne. Shreds of scallions or red and green chiles make great garnishes.

Below: Diced tomatoes, onions and cilantro make an attractive garnish.

CHILLED SOUPS

What could be a nicer way of starting a meal on a warm summer evening than a bowl of chilled soup, served al fresco *with a bottle of chilled white wine? In this section there are traditional favorites, such as French Vichyssoise and Spanish Gazpacho, as well as more unusual soups, such as Chilled Garlic and Almond Soup with Grapes, and Beet Soup with Mascarpone Brioche. Enjoy fresh summer herbs at their best in Melon and Basil Soup, or Sorrel, Spinach and Dill Soup.*

VICHYSSOISE

THIS CLASSIC CHILLED SUMMER SOUP WAS FIRST CREATED IN THE 1920S BY LOUIS DIAT, CHEF AT THE NEW YORK RITZ-CARLTON. HE NAMED IT AFTER VICHY, NEAR HIS HOME IN FRANCE.

3 Stir in the stock or water, 1 teaspoon salt and pepper to taste. Bring to the boil, then reduce the heat and partly cover the pan. Simmer for 15 minutes, or until the potatoes are soft.

4 Cool, then process the soup until smooth in a blender or food processor. Strain the soup into a bowl and stir in the cream. Taste and adjust the seasoning and add a little iced water if the consistency of the soup seems too thick.

5 Chill the soup for at least 4 hours or until very cold. Taste the chilled soup for seasoning and add a squeeze of lemon juice, if required. Pour the soup into bowls and sprinkle with chopped chives. Serve immediately.

SERVES 4–6

INGREDIENTS

2 ounces/¼ cup sweet butter
1 pound leeks, white parts only, thinly sliced
3 large shallots, sliced
9 ounces floury potatoes (such as Russet or Idaho), peeled and cut into chunks
4 cups light chicken stock or water
1¼ cups heavy cream
iced water (optional)
a little lemon juice (optional)
salt and ground black pepper
chopped fresh chives, to garnish

1 Melt the butter in a heavy pan and cook the leeks and shallots gently, covered, for 15–20 minutes, until soft but not browned.

2 Add the potatoes and cook, uncovered, for a few minutes.

VARIATIONS
• **Potage Bonne Femme** For this hot leek and potato soup, use 1 chopped onion instead of the shallots and 1 pound potatoes. Halve the quantity of heavy cream and reheat the pureed soup, adding a little milk if the soup seems very thick. Deep-fried shredded leek may be used to garnish the soup, instead of chopped fresh chives.
• **Chilled Leek and Sorrel or Watercress Soup** Add about 2 ounces/1 cup shredded sorrel to the soup at the end of cooking. Finish and chill as in the main recipe, then serve the soup garnished with a little pile of finely shredded sorrel. The same quantity of watercress can be used in the same way.

Energy 547kcal/2260kJ; Protein 4.6g; Carbohydrate 17.7g, of which sugars 6.8g; Fat 51.4g, of which saturates 31.7g; Cholesterol 129mg; Calcium 79mg; Fiber 3.6g; Sodium 103mg.

CUCUMBER AND SALMON SOUP WITH SALSA

CHARRED SALMON BRINGS A HINT OF HEAT TO THE REFRESHING FLAVORS OF THIS CHILLED SOUP.
GOOD-LOOKING AND BEAUTIFULLY LIGHT, IT MAKES THE PERFECT OPENER FOR AN AL FRESCO MEAL.

SERVES 4

INGREDIENTS
   3 medium cucumbers
   1¼ cups strained plain yogurt
   8 fluid ounces/1 cup vegetable
     stock, chilled
   4 fluid ounces/¼ cup crème fraîche
   1 tablespoon chopped fresh
     chervil
   1 tablespoon chopped fresh chives
   1 tablespoon chopped fresh
     Italian parsley
   1 small fresh red chile, seeded and
     very finely chopped
   a little oil, for brushing
   8 ounces salmon fillet, skinned and
     cut into eight thin slices
   salt and ground black pepper
   fresh chervil or chives, to garnish

4 Brush a griddle or frying pan with oil and heat until very hot. Add the salmon slices and sear them for 1–2 minutes, then turn over carefully and sear the other side until tender and charred.

5 Ladle the chilled soup into soup bowls. Top each portion with two slices of salmon, then pile a portion of salsa in the center. Garnish with the chervil or chives, and serve.

1 Peel two of the cucumbers and halve them lengthwise. Scoop out and discard the seeds, then roughly chop the flesh. Puree the chopped flesh in a food processor or blender.

2 Add the yogurt, stock, crème fraîche, chervil, chives and seasoning, and process until smooth. Pour the mixture into a bowl, cover and chill.

3 Peel, halve and seed the remaining cucumber. Cut the flesh into small neat dice. Mix with the chopped parsley and chilli in a bowl. Cover the salsa and chill until required.

Energy 314kcal/1299kJ; Protein 17.8g; Carbohydrate 3.9g, of which sugars 3.7g; Fat 26.1g, of which saturates 13.1g; Cholesterol 62mg; Calcium 183mg; Fiber 1.2g; Sodium 92mg.

CHILLED COCONUT SOUP

*REFRESHING, COOLING AND NOT TOO FILLING, THIS SOUP IS THE PERFECT ANTIDOTE TO HOT
WEATHER. EXCELLENT FOR SERVING AFTER AN APPETIZER, IT WILL REFRESH THE PALATE.*

SERVES 6

INGREDIENTS

5 cups milk

8 ounces/2⅔ cups dry unsweetened
  shredded coconut

14 fluid ounces/1⅔ cups
  coconut milk

14 fluid ounces/1⅔ cups
  chicken stock

7 fluid ounces/scant 1 cup
  heavy cream

½ teaspoon salt

½ teaspoon ground white pepper

1 teaspoon superfine sugar

small bunch of fresh cilantro

1 Pour the milk into a large pan. Bring
it to the boil, stir in the coconut, lower
the heat and allow to simmer for 30
minutes. Spoon the mixture into a food
processor and process until smooth.
This may take a while—up to
5 minutes—so pause frequently and
scrape down the sides of the bowl.

2 Rinse the pan to remove any coconut
that remains, pour in the processed
mixture and add the coconut milk. Stir
in the chicken stock (homemade, if
possible, which gives a better flavor
than a bouillon cube), cream, salt,
pepper and sugar. Bring to the boil,
stirring occasionally, then lower
the heat and cook for 10 minutes.

3 Reserve a few cilantro leaves to
garnish, then chop the rest finely and
stir into the soup. Pour the soup into a
large bowl, let it cool, then cover and
put into the refrigerator until chilled.
Just before serving, taste the soup and
adjust the seasoning, as chilling will
alter the taste. Serve in chilled bowls,
garnished with the cilantro leaves.

Energy 499kcal/2068kJ; Protein 9.6g; Carbohydrate 15.6g, of which sugars 15.6g; Fat 44.8g, of which saturates 33.4g; Cholesterol 58mg; Calcium 284mg; Fiber 5.1g; Sodium 341mg.

AVOCADO <u>AND</u> LIME SOUP <u>WITH A</u> GREEN CHILE SALSA

INSPIRED BY GUACAMOLE, THE POPULAR AVOCADO DIP, THIS CREAMY SOUP RELIES ON GOOD-QUALITY RIPE AVOCADOS FOR ITS FLAVOR AND COLOR.

SERVES 4

INGREDIENTS

3 ripe avocados
juice of 1½ limes
1 garlic clove, crushed
handful of ice cubes
14 fluid ounces/1⅔ cups vegetable
   stock, chilled
14 fluid ounces/1⅔ cups
   milk, chilled
⅔ cup sour cream, chilled
few drops of Tabasco sauce
salt and ground black pepper
fresh cilantro leaves,
   to garnish
extra virgin olive oil, to serve
For the salsa
4 tomatoes, peeled, seeded and
   finely diced
2 scallions, finely chopped
1 green chile, seeded and finely
   chopped
1 tablespoon chopped fresh
   cilantro leaves
juice of ½ lime

1 Prepare the salsa first. Mix all the ingredients together and season well with salt and black pepper. Leave in the refrigerator to chill until required.

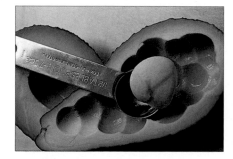

2 Halve the avocados and remove the pits. Scoop the flesh out of the avocado skins using a spoon or melon baller and place in a food processor or blender. Add the lime juice, garlic, ice cubes and ⅔ cup of the chilled vegetable stock.

3 Process the soup until smooth. Pour into a large bowl and stir in the remaining vegetable stock, chilled milk, sour cream and Tabasco sauce. Season to taste.

COOK'S TIPS
• It is easy to remove the pit from an avocado. Halve the avocado and simply tap the pit firmly with the edge of a large knife. Twist the knife gently and the pit will pop out.
• This soup may discolor if left standing for too long, but the flavor will not be spoiled. Give the soup a quick whisk just before serving.

4 Ladle the soup into bowls or glasses and spoon a little salsa on top. Add a splash of olive oil to each portion and garnish with fresh cilantro leaves. Serve immediately.

Energy 353kcal/1463kJ; Protein 7.3g; Carbohydrate 11.1g, of which sugars 9.6g; Fat 31.2g, of which saturates 10.5g; Cholesterol 28mg; Calcium 175mg; Fiber 4.8g; Sodium 73mg.

CHILLED GARLIC <u>AND</u> ALMOND SOUP <u>WITH</u> GRAPES

THIS CREAMY CHILLED SUMMER SOUP IS BASED ON AN ANCIENT MOORISH RECIPE FROM ANDALUSIA, IN SOUTHERN SPAIN. ALMONDS AND PINE NUTS ARE TYPICAL INGREDIENTS OF THIS REGION.

SERVES 6

INGREDIENTS

3 ounces/¾ cup blanched almonds
2 ounces/½ cup pine nuts
6 large garlic cloves, peeled
7 ounces good-quality day-old bread, crusts removed
3¾–4 cups still mineral water, chilled
4 fluid ounces/½ cup extra virgin olive oil, plus extra to serve
1 tablespoon sherry vinegar
2–3 tablespoons dry sherry
9 ounces grapes, peeled, halved and seeded
salt and ground white pepper
ice cubes and chopped fresh chives, to garnish

1 Roast the almonds and pine nuts together in a dry pan over a moderate heat until they are very lightly browned. Cool, then grind to a powder.

2 Blanch the garlic in boiling water for 3 minutes. Drain and rinse.

3 Soak the bread in 1¼ cup of the water for 10 minutes, then squeeze dry. Process the garlic, bread, nuts and 1 teaspoon salt in a food processor or blender until they form a paste.

4 Gradually blend in the olive oil and sherry vinegar, followed by sufficient water to make a smooth soup with a creamy consistency.

5 Stir in 2 tablespoons of the sherry. Adjust the seasoning and add more dry sherry to taste. Chill for at least 3 hours, then adjust the seasoning again and stir in a little more chilled water if the soup has thickened. Reserve a few grapes for the garnish and stir the remainder into the soup.

6 Ladle the soup into bowls (glass bowls look particularly good) and garnish with ice cubes, the reserved grapes and chopped fresh chives. Serve with additional extra virgin olive oil to drizzle over the soup to taste just before it is eaten.

COOK'S TIPS
• Toasting the nuts slightly accentuates their flavor, but you can omit this step if you prefer a paler soup.
• Blanching the garlic softens its flavor.

Energy 380kcal/1582kJ; Protein 7g; Carbohydrate 26.1g, of which sugars 8.4g; Fat 27.3g, of which saturates 3g; Cholesterol 0mg; Calcium 83mg; Fiber 2.2g; Sodium 150mg.

ROASTED PEPPER SOUP
WITH PARMESAN TOAST

THE SECRET OF THIS SOUP IS TO SERVE IT JUST COLD, NOT OVER-CHILLED, TOPPED WITH HOT PARMESAN TOAST DRIPPING WITH CHEESE AND MELTED BUTTER.

SERVES 4

INGREDIENTS

1 onion, quartered
4 garlic cloves, unpeeled
2 red bell peppers, seeded
  and quartered
2 yellow bell peppers, seeded
  and quartered
2–3 tablespoons olive oil
grated rind and juice of 1 orange
1 can (7 ounces) chopped tomatoes
2½ cups cold water
salt and ground black pepper
2 tablespoons chopped fresh chives,
  to garnish (optional)
For the hot Parmesan toast
1 medium baguette
2 ounces/¼ cup butter
6 ounces Parmesan cheese

1 Preheat the oven to 400°F. Put the onion, garlic and peppers in a roasting pan. Drizzle the oil over the vegetables and mix well, then turn the pieces of pepper skin-side up. Roast for 25–30 minutes, until slightly charred, then allow to cool slightly.

2 Squeeze the garlic flesh out of the skins into a food processor or blender. Add the roasted vegetables, orange rind and juice, tomatoes and water. Process until smooth.

COOK'S TIP
If you don't have a champignon, then use the bottom of a large ladle or the back of a wooden spoon instead.

3 Press the mixture through a strainer into a bowl using a champignon. Season well and chill for 30 minutes.

4 Make the Parmesan toasts when you are ready to serve the soup. Preheat the broiler to high. Tear the baguette in half lengthwise, then tear or cut it across to make four large pieces. Spread the pieces of bread with butter.

5 Pare most of the Parmesan into thin slices or shavings using a swivel-bladed vegetable knife or a small paring knife, then finely grate the remainder.

6 Arrange the sliced Parmesan on the toasts, then dredge with the grated cheese. Transfer the cheese-topped baguette pieces to a large baking sheet or broiler rack and toast under the broiler for a few minutes until the topping is well browned.

7 Ladle the chilled soup into large, shallow bowls and sprinkle with chopped fresh chives, if using, and plenty of freshly ground black pepper.

8 Serve the hot Parmesan toast with the chilled soup.

Energy 124kcal/516kJ; Protein 2.4g; Carbohydrate 15g, of which sugars 14.2g; Fat 6.4g, of which saturates 1g; Cholesterol 0mg; Calcium 23mg; Fiber 3.5g; Sodium 13mg.

CHILLED CUCUMBER AND SHRIMP SOUP

IF YOU'VE NEVER SERVED A CHILLED SOUP BEFORE, THIS IS THE ONE TO TRY. DELICIOUS AND LIGHT, IT'S THE PERFECT WAY TO CELEBRATE SUMMER.

2 Stir in the milk, bring almost to boiling point, then lower the heat and simmer for 5 minutes. Tip the soup into a blender or food processor and puree until very smooth. Season to taste.

3 Pour the soup into a large bowl and leave to cool. When cool, stir in the shrimp, chopped herbs and cream. Cover, transfer to the refrigerator and chill for at least 2 hours.

4 To serve, ladle the soup into four individual bowls, top each portion with a dollop of crème fraîche, if using, and place a shrimp over the edge of each dish. Sprinkle over a little extra chopped dill and tuck two or three chives under the shrimp on the edge of the bowls to garnish. Serve at once.

SERVES 4

INGREDIENTS
  1 ounce/2 tablespoons butter
  2 shallots, finely chopped
  2 garlic cloves, crushed
  1 cucumber, peeled, seeded
    and diced
  1¼ cups milk
  8 ounces cooked peeled shrimp
  1 tablespoon each finely chopped
    fresh mint, dill, chives and chervil
  1¼ cups whipping cream
  salt and ground white pepper
For the garnish
  2 tablespoons crème fraîche
    (optional)
  4 large, cooked shrimp, peeled with
    tail intact
  fresh dill and chives

1 Melt the butter in a pan and cook the shallots and garlic over a low heat until soft but not colored. Add the cucumber and cook gently, stirring frequently, until tender.

COOK'S TIP
If you prefer hot soup, reheat it gently until hot but not boiling. Do not boil, or the delicate flavor will be spoiled.

VARIATION
If you like, you can use other cooked shellfish in place of the peeled shrimp—try fresh, frozen or canned crabmeat or cooked, flaked salmon.

Energy 412kcal/1704kJ; Protein 14.2g; Carbohydrate 6g, of which sugars 6g; Fat 37g, of which saturates 23g; Cholesterol 206mg; Calcium 184mg; Fiber 0.2g; Sodium 197mg.

HUNGARIAN CHERRY SOUP

SOUPS MADE FROM SEASONAL FRUITS ARE A FAVORITE CENTRAL EUROPEAN TREAT, AND CHERRY SOUP IS ONE OF THE GLORIES OF THE HUNGARIAN TABLE. IT IS OFTEN SERVED AT THE START OF A DAIRY MEAL, SUCH AS AT THE JEWISH FESTIVAL OF SHAVUOT WHEN DAIRY FOODS ARE TRADITIONALLY FEASTED UPON, AND IS DELICIOUS SERVED WITH AN EXTRA SPOONFUL OR TWO OF SOUR CREAM.

SERVES 6

INGREDIENTS

2¼ pounds fresh, frozen or canned
  sour cherries, such as Morello or
  Montmorency, pitted
8 fluid ounces/1 cup water
6–9 ounces/about 1 cup sugar,
  to taste
1–2 cinnamon sticks, each about
  2 inches long
3 cups dry red wine
2 teaspoon almond extract,
  or to taste
8 fluid ounces/1 cup light cream
8 fluid ounces/1 cup sour cream or
  crème fraîche

1 Put the pitted cherries, water, sugar, cinnamon and wine in a large pan. Bring to the boil, reduce the heat and simmer for 20–30 minutes, until the cherries are tender. Remove from the heat and add the almond extract.

2 In a bowl, stir a few tablespoons of light cream into the sour cream or crème fraîche to thin it down, then stir in the rest until the mixture is smooth. Stir the mixture into the cherry soup, then chill until ready to serve.

Energy 518kcal/2163kJ; Protein 4.1g; Carbohydrate 51.8g, of which sugars 51.7g; Fat 24.8g, of which saturates 16.4g; Cholesterol 70mg; Calcium 107mg; Fiber 1.5g; Sodium 34mg.

CHILLED AVOCADO SOUP <u>WITH</u> CUMIN

ANDALUSIA IS HOME TO BOTH AVOCADOS AND GAZPACHO, SO IT IS NOT SURPRISING THAT THIS CHILLED AVOCADO SOUP, WHICH IS ALSO KNOWN AS GREEN GAZPACHO, WAS INVENTED THERE. IN SPAIN, THIS DELICIOUSLY MILD, CREAMY SOUP IS KNOWN AS SOPA DE AGUACATE.

SERVES 4

INGREDIENTS

 3 ripe avocados
 1 bunch scallions, white parts only,
  trimmed and roughly chopped
 2 garlic cloves, chopped
 juice of 1 lemon
 ¼ teaspoon ground cumin
 ¼ teaspoon paprika
 scant 2 cups fresh chicken
  stock, cooled and all fat
  skimmed off
 1¼ cups iced water
 salt and ground black pepper
 roughly chopped fresh Italian parsley,
  to garnish

1 Starting half a day ahead, put the flesh of one avocado in a food processor or blender. Add the scallions, garlic and lemon juice and puree until smooth. Add the second avocado and puree, then the third, with the spices and seasoning. Puree until smooth.

2 Gradually add the chicken stock. Pour the soup into a metal bowl and chill.

3 To serve, stir in the iced water, then season to taste with plenty of salt and black pepper. Garnish with chopped parsley, and serve immediately.

Energy 242kcal/1001kJ; Protein 2.8g; Carbohydrate 3g, of which sugars 1.3g; Fat 24.2g, of which saturates 5.2g; Cholesterol 0mg; Calcium 22mg; Fiber 4.6g; Sodium 9mg.

BEET SOUP WITH MASCARPONE BRIOCHE

*ALTHOUGH IT SOUNDS QUITE COMPLEX, THIS SOUP IS ACTUALLY RIDICULOUSLY EASY TO MAKE.
THE SWEET, EARTHY FLAVOR OF FRESH, COOKED BEETS IS COMBINED WITH ZESTY ORANGE
AND TART CRANBERRY JUICE.*

SERVES 4

INGREDIENTS
  12 ounces cooked beets,
    roughly chopped
  grated rind and juice of 1 orange
  2½ cups unsweetened cranberry
    juice
  scant 2 cups strained plain
    yogurt
  a little Tabasco sauce
  4 slices brioche
  4 tablespoons mascarpone
  salt and ground black pepper
  fresh mint sprigs and cooked
    cranberries, to garnish

2 Press the puree through a strainer into a clean bowl. Stir in the remaining cranberry juice and the Tabasco sauce. Season with salt and black pepper to taste. Chill the soup in the refrigerator for at least 2 hours.

3 Preheat the broiler. Using a large cookie cutter, stamp a round out of each slice of brioche.

COOK'S TIP
If the combination of cranberry and orange is a little tart, add a pinch or two of superfine sugar to the soup, according to taste.

4 Arrange the brioche rounds on a broiler rack and toast until golden. Ladle the soup into bowls and top each with brioche and mascarpone. Garnish with mint and cranberries.

1 Puree the beets with the orange rind and juice, half the cranberry juice and the yogurt in a food processor or blender until smooth.

Energy 404kcal/1695kJ; Protein 13.5g; Carbohydrate 53.5g, of which sugars 17.2g; Fat 16.6g, of which saturates 7.2g; Cholesterol 13mg; Calcium 237mg; Fiber 1.7g; Sodium 264mg.

SPICED MANGO SOUP <u>WITH</u> YOGURT

THIS DELICIOUS, LIGHT SOUP COMES FROM CHUTNEY MARY'S, AN ANGLO-INDIAN RESTAURANT IN LONDON. IT IS BEST WHEN SERVED LIGHTLY CHILLED.

SERVES 4

INGREDIENTS
  2 ripe mangoes
  1 tablespoon gram flour
  4 fluid ounces/½ cup plain yogurt
  3¾ cups cold water
  ½ teaspoon grated fresh ginger root
  2 red chiles, seeded and
    finely chopped
  2 tablespoons olive oil
  ½ teaspoon mustard seeds
  ½ teaspoon cumin seeds
  8 curry leaves
  salt and ground black pepper
  fresh mint leaves, shredded,
    to garnish
  plain yogurt, to serve

1 Peel the mangoes, remove the pits and cut the flesh into chunks. Puree in a food processor or blender until smooth.

2 Pour into a pan and stir in the flour, yogurt, water, ginger and chiles. Bring to the boil, stirring occasionally. Simmer for 4–5 minutes until thickened slightly, then set aside off the heat.

3 Heat the oil in a frying pan. Add the mustard seeds and cook for a few seconds until they begin to pop, then add the cumin seeds.

4 Add the curry leaves and then cook for 5 minutes. Stir the spice mixture into the soup, return it to the heat and cook for 10 minutes.

5 Press through a mouli-legume or a strainer, if you like, then season to taste. Leave the soup to cool completely, then chill for at least 1 hour.

6 Ladle the soup into bowls, and top each with a dollop of yogurt. Garnish with shredded mint leaves and serve.

Energy 121kcal/508kJ; Protein 2.8g; Carbohydrate 14.7g, of which sugars 12.7g; Fat 6.2g, of which saturates 1g; Cholesterol 0mg; Calcium 73mg; Fiber 2.4g; Sodium 28mg.

ICED MELON SOUP <u>WITH</u> SHERBET

USE DIFFERENT MELONS FOR THE COOL SOUP AND ICE SHERBET TO CREATE A SUBTLE CONTRAST IN FLAVOR AND COLOR. TRY A COMBINATION OF CHARENTAIS, OGEN OR CANTALOUPE.

SERVES 6–8

INGREDIENTS
    5–5¼ pounds very ripe melon
    3 tablespoons orange juice
    2 tablespoons lemon juice
    mint leaves, to garnish
For the sherbet
    1 ounce/2 tablespoons sugar
    4 fluid ounces/½ cup water
    5–5¼ pounds very ripe melon
    juice of 2 limes
    2 tablespoons chopped
      fresh mint

1 To make the melon and mint sherbet, put the sugar and water into a pan and heat gently until the sugar dissolves. Bring to the boil and simmer for 4–5 minutes, then remove from the heat and leave to cool.

2 Halve the melon. Scrape out the seeds, then scoop out the flesh. Puree in a food processor or blender with the cooled syrup and lime juice.

3 Stir in the mint and pour the melon mixture into an ice-cream maker. Churn, following the manufacturer's instructions, or until the sherbet is smooth and firm. Alternatively, pour the mixture into a suitable container and freeze until icy around the edges. Transfer to a food processor or blender and process until smooth.

4 Repeat the freezing and processing two or three times or until the mixture is smooth and holding its shape, then freeze until firm.

5 To make the chilled melon soup, prepare the melon as in step 2 and puree it in a food processor or blender. Pour the puree into a bowl and stir in the orange and lemon juice. Place the soup in the refrigerator for 30–40 minutes, but do not chill it for too long, as this will dull its flavor.

6 Ladle the soup into bowls and add a large scoop of the melon and mint sherbet to each. Garnish with mint leaves and serve at once.

Energy 117kcal/494kJ; Protein 3.1g; Carbohydrate 26g, of which sugars 26g; Fat 0.8g, of which saturates 0g; Cholesterol 0mg; Calcium 101mg; Fiber 5.3g; Sodium 39mg.

MELON AND BASIL SOUP

THIS IS A DELICIOUSLY REFRESHING CHILLED FRUIT SOUP, JUST RIGHT FOR A SUMMER LUNCH PARTY.
THE SHREDDED BASIL COMPLEMENTS THE TASTE OF THE MELON.

SERVES 4–6

INGREDIENTS

2 Charentais or cantaloupe melons
2 ounces/scant ½ cup
  superfine sugar
6 fluid ounces/¾ cup water
finely grated rind and juice
  of 1 lime
3 tablespoons shredded fresh basil,
  plus whole leaves to garnish

COOK'S TIP
Add the syrup in two stages, as the
amount of sugar needed will depend on
the sweetness of the melon.

1 Cut the melons in half across the
middle. Scrape out the seeds and
discard. Using a melon baller, scoop
out 20–24 balls and set aside to use for
the garnish.

2 Scoop out the remaining flesh and
place in a blender or food processor.

3 Place the sugar, water and lime rind
in a small pan over a low heat. Stir until
dissolved, bring to the boil and simmer
for 2–3 minutes. Remove from the heat
and leave to cool slightly. Blend half the
mixture with the melon flesh until
smooth, adding the remaining syrup
and lime juice to taste.

4 Pour the mixture into a bowl, stir in
the shredded basil and chill. Serve
garnished with whole basil leaves and
the reserved melon balls.

Energy 129kcal/550kJ; Protein 1.7g; Carbohydrate 31.7g, of which sugars 31.7g; Fat 0.3g, of which saturates 0g; Cholesterol 0mg; Calcium 50mg; Fiber 1.3g; Sodium 104mg.

WATERCRESS <u>AND</u> ORANGE SOUP

THIS IS A HEALTHY AND REFRESHING SOUP, WHICH IS GOOD SERVED CHILLED ON A SUMMER'S DAY OR HOT WHEN THERE IS A CHILL IN THE AIR.

SERVES 4

INGREDIENTS
1 large onion, chopped
1 tablespoon olive oil
2 bunches or bags of
  washed watercress
grated rind and juice of
  1 large orange
2½ cups vegetable stock
⅔ cup light cream
2 teaspoons cornstarch
salt and ground black pepper
a little heavy cream or
  plain yogurt, to garnish
4 orange wedges,
  to serve

1 Soften the onion in the oil in a large pan. Add the watercress, unchopped, to the onion. Cover and cook for 5 minutes until softened.

2 Add the orange rind and juice and the stock. Bring to the boil, cover and simmer for 10–15 minutes.

3 Process in a blender or food processor until smooth.

4 Put through a strainer if you want the soup to be even smoother.

5 Blend the cream with the cornstarch until no lumps remain, then add to the soup. Season to taste.

6 Bring the soup gently back to the boil, stirring until slightly thickened.

7 Leave to cool before chilling in the refrigerator. Serve with cream or yogurt and a wedge of orange.

Energy 144kcal/599kJ; Protein 3.6g; Carbohydrate 9.4g, of which sugars 5.6g; Fat 10.6g, of which saturates 5.1g; Cholesterol 21mg; Calcium 136mg; Fiber 1.7g; Sodium 40mg.

MIAMI CHILLED AVOCADO SOUP

AVOCADOS ARE COMBINED WITH LEMON JUICE, DRY SHERRY AND AN OPTIONAL DASH OF HOT PEPPER SAUCE, TO MAKE THIS SUBTLE CHILLED SOUP.

3 Peel the cucumber and halve it lengthwise. Scoop out and discard the seeds, then chop the flesh. Add to the avocado with the sherry and most of the scallions. Process again until smooth.

4 Combine the avocado mixture with the chicken stock. Whisk until well blended. Season with the salt and a few drops of hot pepper sauce, if you like. Cover and place in the refrigerator to chill thoroughly.

SERVES 4

INGREDIENTS
  2 large or 3 medium ripe
    avocados
  1 tablespoon fresh lemon juice
  1 small cucumber
  2 tablespoons dry sherry
  1 ounce/¼ cup coarsely chopped
    scallions, with some of the
    green stems
  16 fluid ounces/2 cups mild-
    flavored chicken stock
  1 teaspoon salt
  hot pepper sauce (optional)
  plain yogurt, to garnish

1 Halve the avocados, remove the pits and peel, and chop roughly.

2 Place the flesh in a food processor or blender. Add the lemon juice and process until very smooth.

5 To serve, fill individual bowls with the soup. Place a spoonful of yogurt in the center of each bowl and swirl with a spoon. Sprinkle the soup with the reserved chopped scallions.

Energy 155kcal/640kJ; Protein 1.8g; Carbohydrate 2.1g, of which sugars 1g; Fat 14.5g, of which saturates 3.1g; Cholesterol 0mg; Calcium 16mg; Fiber 2.8g; Sodium 7mg.

CHILLED ASPARAGUS SOUP

THIS DELICATE, PALE GREEN SOUP, GARNISHED WITH A SWIRL OF CREAM OR YOGURT, IS AS PRETTY AS IT IS DELICIOUS AND IS THE REAL TASTE OF SUMMER.

SERVES 6

INGREDIENTS

2 pounds fresh asparagus
4 tablespoons butter or olive oil
6 ounces/1½ cups sliced leeks
   or scallions
3 tablespoons flour
6¼ cups chicken stock
   or water
4 fluid ounces/½ cup light cream
   or plain yogurt
1 tablespoon chopped fresh
   tarragon or chervil
salt and ground black pepper

3 Heat the butter or oil in a pan. Add the leeks or scallions and cook over a low heat for 5–0 minutes until softened. Stir in the asparagus, cover and cook for 6–8 minutes until tender.

4 Add the flour and stir well to blend. Cook for 3–4 minutes, uncovered, stirring occasionally.

5 Add the stock or water. Bring to the boil, stirring frequently, then reduce the heat and simmer for 30 minutes. Season to taste.

6 Puree the soup in a food processor or food mill. Strain to remove any coarse fibers. Stir in the asparagus tips, most of the cream or yogurt, and the herbs. Chill well. Before serving check the seasoning. Garnish with cream or yogurt.

1 Cut the top 2½ inches off the asparagus spears and blanch in boiling water for 5–6 minutes until just tender. Drain. Cut each tip into two or three pieces and set aside.

2 Trim the ends of the stalks, removing any brown or woody parts. Chop the stalks into ½ inch pieces.

Energy 157kcal/649kJ; Protein 5.7g; Carbohydrate 4.4g, of which sugars 4.2g; Fat 13.1g, of which saturates 7.8g; Cholesterol 32mg; Calcium 72mg; Fiber 3g; Sodium 70mg.

GREEN PEA AND MINT SOUP

PERFECT PARTNERS, PEAS AND MINT REALLY CAPTURE THE FLAVORS OF SUMMER IN THIS DELICIOUS LIGHTLY CHILLED SOUP.

SERVES 4

INGREDIENTS

2 ounces/4 tablespoons butter
4 scallions, chopped
1 pound fresh or frozen peas
2½ cups vegetable stock
2 large sprigs fresh mint
2½ cups milk
a pinch of sugar (optional)
salt and freshly ground
   black pepper
small sprigs of fresh mint,
   to garnish
light cream, to serve

1 Heat the butter in a large heavy pan. Add the chopped scallions and cook gently on a low heat for 5–6 minutes until they are softened but not browned.

2 Stir the peas into the pan, add the stock and mint, and bring to the boil. Cover and simmer for about 30 minutes if you are using fresh peas (15 minutes for frozen peas), until tender. Reserve about 3 tablespoons of the peas for a garnish.

3 Pour into a food processor or blender, add the milk and puree until smooth. Season to taste, adding a pinch of sugar, if you like. Cool, then chill in the refrigerator.

4 Pour the soup into bowls. Swirl a little cream into each, then garnish with the mint and reserved peas.

Energy 258kcal/1072kJ; Protein 13.1g; Carbohydrate 20.1g, of which sugars 10g; Fat 14.6g, of which saturates 8.5g; Cholesterol 36mg; Calcium 210mg; Fiber 5.5g; Sodium 142mg.

SUMMER TOMATO SOUP

TOMATOES FLAVORED WITH FRESH SUMMER HERBS FORM THE BASIS OF THIS REFRESHING AND COLORFUL SOUP. MAKE IT WHEN THE TOMATO SEASON IS AT ITS PEAK.

SERVES 4

INGREDIENTS

1 tablespoon olive oil
1 large onion, chopped
1 carrot, chopped
2¼ pounds ripe tomatoes,
  quartered
2 garlic cloves, chopped
5 sprigs of fresh thyme, or
  ¼ teaspoon dried thyme
4 or 5 sprigs of fresh marjoram,
  or ¼ teaspoon dried marjoram
1 bay leaf
3 tablespoons crème fraîche, sour
  cream or plain yogurt, plus a little
  extra to garnish
salt and ground black pepper

1 Heat the olive oil in a large, preferably stainless-steel pan or flameproof casserole.

2 Add the onion and carrot and cook over a medium heat for 3–4 minutes until softened, stirring occasionally.

3 Add the tomatoes, garlic and herbs. Reduce the heat and simmer, covered, for 30 minutes.

4 Discard the bay leaf and press through a strainer. Stir in the crème fraîche, cream, or yogurt and season to taste. Chill in the refrigerator. Garnish with cream or yogurt.

VARIATION
Use oregano instead of marjoram, and parsley instead of thyme.

COOK'S TIP
The success of this soup depends on having ripe, full-flavored tomatoes, such as the oval plum variety.

Energy 138kcal/576kJ; Protein 3g; Carbohydrate 13.7g, of which sugars 12.4g; Fat 8.3g, of which saturates 3.7g; Cholesterol 13mg; Calcium 61mg; Fiber 4.2g; Sodium 35mg.

SORREL, SPINACH AND DILL SOUP

THE WARM FLAVOR OF HORSERADISH AND THE ANISEED FLAVOR OF DILL MELD WITH SORREL AND SPINACH TO MAKE THIS UNUSUAL RUSSIAN SOUP. AN EXCELLENT SUMMER SOUP, SERVED CHILLED.

SERVES 6

INGREDIENTS

    1 ounce/2 tablespoons butter
    8 ounces sorrel, stalks removed
    8 ounces young spinach,
      stalks removed
    1 ounce fresh horseradish,
      grated
    3 cups cider
    1 pickled cucumber,
      finely chopped
    2 tablespoons chopped fresh dill
    8 ounces cooked fish, such as
      pike, perch or salmon, skinned
      and boned
    salt and ground black pepper
    sprig of dill, to garnish

1 Melt the butter in a large pan. Add the prepared sorrel and spinach leaves together with the grated fresh horseradish.

2 Cover the pan and allow to cook gently for 3–4 minutes, or until the sorrel and spinach leaves have wilted.

3 Tip into a food processor or blender and process to a fine paste. Ladle into a tureen or bowl and stir in the cider, cucumber and dill.

4 Chop the fish into bitesize pieces. Add to the soup, then season well. Chill for at least 3 hours before serving, garnished with a sprig of dill.

Energy 156kcal/653kJ; Protein 11.4g; Carbohydrate 4.8g, of which sugars 4.7g; Fat 6.6g, of which saturates 2.8g; Cholesterol 19mg; Calcium 201mg; Fiber 1.9g; Sodium 324mg.

CHILLED TOMATO <u>AND</u> BASIL-FLOWER SOUP

THIS IS A VERY FRESH-TASTING SOUP, PACKED WITH THE COMPLEMENTARY FLAVORS OF TOMATO AND BASIL, AND TOPPED WITH PRETTY PINK AND PURPLE SWEET BASIL FLOWERS.

SERVES 4

INGREDIENTS
1 tablespoon olive oil
1 onion, finely chopped
1 garlic clove, crushed
2½ cups vegetable stock
2 pounds tomatoes, roughly chopped
20 fresh basil leaves
a few drops of balsamic vinegar
juice of ½ lemon
⅔ cup plain yogurt
sugar and salt, to taste
For the garnish
2 tablespoons plain yogurt
8 small basil leaves
2 teaspoons basil flowers, all green
   parts removed

COOK'S TIP
Basil flowers may be small but they certainly have a beautifully aromatic flavor and are surprisingly sweet. They can be used fresh in all sorts of ways by being added with basil leaves to tomato salads or pizza toppings, sprinkled on pastas, or used as flavorings in tomato juice. To remove the flowers from the stem, simply pull—they will come away easily. Purple-leaved basil has a pretty mauve flower, which is delicious too.

1 Heat the oil in a pan and add the finely chopped onion and garlic. Fry the onion and garlic in the oil for 2–3 minutes until soft and transparent, stirring occasionally.

2 Add 1¼ cups of the vegetable stock and the chopped tomatoes to the pan. Bring to the boil, then lower the heat and simmer the mixture for 15 minutes. Stir it occasionally to prevent it from sticking to the base of the pan.

3 Allow the mixture to cool slightly, then transfer it to a food processor and process until smooth. Press through a strainer placed over a bowl to remove the tomato skins and seeds.

4 Return the mixture to the food processor and add the remainder of the stock, half the basil leaves, the vinegar, lemon juice and yogurt. Season with sugar and salt to taste. Process until smooth. Pour into a bowl and chill.

5 Just before serving, finely shred the remaining basil leaves and add them to the soup. Pour the chilled soup into individual bowls. Garnish with yogurt topped with a few small basil leaves and a sprinkling of basil flowers.

Energy 89kcal/377kJ; Protein 3.7g; Carbohydrate 11g, of which sugars 10.6g; Fat 3.8g, of which saturates 0.8g; Cholesterol 1mg; Calcium 91mg; Fiber 2.5g; Sodium 52mg.

CUCUMBER <u>and</u> YOGURT SOUP <u>with</u> WALNUTS

This is a particularly refreshing cold soup, using a classic combination of cucumber and yogurt. If you prefer it smooth, blend it in a food processor before serving.

SERVES 5–6

INGREDIENTS
  1 cucumber
  4 garlic cloves
  ½ teaspoon salt
  3 ounces/¾ cup walnut pieces
  1½ ounces day-old bread, torn
    into pieces
  2 tablespoons walnut or
    sunflower oil
  14 fluid ounces/1⅔ cups
    plain yogurt
  4 fluid ounces/½ cup cold water
    or chilled still mineral water
  1–2 teaspoons lemon juice
For the garnish
  1½ ounces/scant ½ cup walnuts,
    coarsely chopped
  1½ tablespoons olive oil
  sprigs of fresh dill

1 Cut the cucumber in half and peel one half of it. Dice the cucumber flesh and set aside.

2 Using a mortar and pestle, crush together the garlic and salt well, then add the walnuts and bread.

3 When the mixture is smooth, slowly add the walnut or sunflower oil.

4 Transfer the mixture to a bowl and beat in the yogurt and cucumber. Add the cold water or mineral water and lemon juice to taste.

5 Pour the soup into chilled soup bowls. Garnish with the chopped walnuts and drizzle with the olive oil. Finally, arrange the sprigs of dill on top and serve immediately.

Energy 175kcal/728kJ; Protein 6g; Carbohydrate 9.2g, of which sugars 6g; Fat 13.1g, of which saturates 1.5g; Cholesterol 1mg; Calcium 152mg; Fiber 0.7g; Sodium 92mg.

BABY CHERRY TOMATO SOUP
WITH ARUGULA PESTO

FOR THEIR SIZE, BABY TOMATOES ARE A POWERHOUSE OF SWEETNESS AND FLAVOR. HERE THEY ARE COMPLEMENTED BEAUTIFULLY BY A RICH PASTE OF PEPPERY ARUGULA.

SERVES 4

INGREDIENTS

    8 ounces baby cherry
      tomatoes, halved
    8 ounces baby plum
      tomatoes, halved
    8 ounces vine-ripened
      tomatoes, halved
    2 shallots, roughly chopped
    1½ tablespoons sun-dried
      tomato paste
    2½ cups vegetable stock
    salt and ground black pepper
    ice cubes, to serve
For the pesto
    ½ ounce arugula leaves
    5 tablespoons olive oil
    ½ ounce/2 tablespoons pine nuts
    1 garlic clove
    1 ounce/⅓ cup freshly grated
      Parmesan cheese

1 Puree all the tomatoes and the shallots in a food processor or blender. Add the sun-dried tomato paste and process until smooth. Press the combined paste through a strainer into a pan.

2 Add the vegetable stock, bring to the boil and simmer gently for 4–5 minutes. Season well with salt and black pepper. Leave to cool, then chill in the refrigerator for at least 4 hours.

3 To make the pesto, puree the arugula, oil, pine nuts and garlic using a mortar and pestle. Alternatively, use a food processor.

4 Stir the Parmesan cheese into the pesto mix, grinding it well.

5 Ladle the soup into bowls and add a few ice cubes to each. Spoon some of the arugula pesto into the center of each portion and serve.

VARIATION
The pesto can be made with other soft-leaved herbs in place of arugula. Try fresh basil, cilantro or mint, or use a mixture of herb leaves, if you like. Parsley and mint are a good flavor combination and make delicious pesto.

Energy 197kcal/819kJ; Protein 4.9g; Carbohydrate 7.9g, of which sugars 7.6g; Fat 16.5g, of which saturates 3.3g; Cholesterol 6mg; Calcium 101mg; Fiber 2.4g; Sodium 105mg.

CHILLED TOMATO AND SWEET PEPPER SOUP

A RECIPE INSPIRED BY THE SPANISH GAZPACHO, WHERE RAW INGREDIENTS ARE COMBINED TO MAKE A CHILLED SOUP. IN THIS RECIPE THE INGREDIENTS ARE COOKED FIRST AND THEN CHILLED.

SERVES 4

INGREDIENTS

2 red bell peppers, halved
3 tablespoons olive oil
1 onion, finely chopped
2 garlic cloves, crushed
1½ pounds ripe, well-flavored
  tomatoes
⅔ cup red wine
2½ cups vegetable stock
salt and ground black pepper
chopped fresh chives, to garnish
For the croutons
2 slices day-old white bread,
  crusts removed
4 tablespoons olive oil

COOK'S TIP
Any juice that accumulates in the pan after broiling the peppers, or in the bowl, should be stirred into the soup. It will add a delectable flavor.

1 Cut each pepper half into quarters and seed. Place skin-side up on a broiler rack and cook until the skins have charred. Transfer to a bowl and cover with a plate.

2 Heat the oil in a large pan. Add the onion and garlic, and cook until soft. Meanwhile, remove the skin from the peppers and roughly chop them. Cut the tomatoes into chunks.

3 Add the peppers and tomatoes to the pan, then cover and cook gently for 10 minutes. Add the red wine and cook for a further 5 minutes, then add the stock and salt and pepper, and simmer for 20 minutes.

4 To make the croutons, cut the bread into cubes. Heat the oil in a small frying pan, add the bread and fry until golden. Drain on paper towels, cool, then store in an airtight box.

5 Process the soup in a blender or food processor until smooth. Pour into a clean glass or ceramic bowl and leave to cool thoroughly before chilling for at least 3 hours. When the soup is cold, season to taste.

6 Serve the soup in bowls, topped with the croutons and garnished with chopped chives.

Energy 292kcal/1216kJ; Protein 3.4g; Carbohydrate 18.8g, of which sugars 11.8g; Fat 20.4g, of which saturates 3g; Cholesterol 0mg; Calcium 40mg; Fiber 3.5g; Sodium 92mg.

CHILLED ALMOND SOUP

UNLESS YOU ARE PREPARED TO SPEND TIME POUNDING ALL THE INGREDIENTS BY HAND, A FOOD PROCESSOR IS ESSENTIAL FOR THIS SPANISH SOUP.

SERVES 6

INGREDIENTS
    4 ounces fresh white bread
    3 cups cold water
    4 ounces/1 cup blanched almonds
    2 garlic cloves, sliced
    5 tablespoons olive oil
    1½ tablespoons sherry vinegar
    salt and ground black pepper
For the garnish
    toasted sliced almonds
    seedless green and black grapes,
        halved and skinned

1 Break the bread into a bowl and pour ⅔ cup of the water on top. Leave for 5 minutes.

2 Put the almonds and garlic in a blender or food processor and process until finely ground. Blend the soaked bread into the mixture.

3 Gradually add the oil until the mixture forms a smooth paste. Add the sherry vinegar and remaining water and process until smooth.

4 Transfer to a bowl and season to taste. Chill for 2–3 hours. Garnish with toasted almonds and grapes.

Energy 366kcal/1523kJ; Protein 6.8g; Carbohydrate 24.2g, of which sugars 8.2g; Fat 26.7g, of which saturates 2.9g; Cholesterol 0mg; Calcium 74mg; Fiber 1.9g; Sodium 177mg.

LIGHT AND REFRESHING SOUPS

As an appetizer before the main meal, a light and refreshing

soup is a good choice. Tomatoes, peas, carrots, asparagus, and

mushrooms, teamed with fresh herbs such as basil, tarragon and

cilantro, make appetizing soups that are full of flavor.

For an international flavor, try Balinese Vegetable Soup,

or Light and Fragrant Broth with Stuffed Cabbage Leaves,

which in Vietnam is often served at New Year celebrations.

ITALIAN PEA AND BASIL SOUP

THE PUNGENT FLAVOR OF BASIL LIFTS THIS APPETIZING ITALIAN SOUP, WHILE THE ONION AND GARLIC GIVE DEPTH. SERVE IT WITH GOOD CRUSTY BREAD TO ENJOY IT AT ITS BEST.

2 Add the peas and stock to the pan and bring to the boil. Reduce the heat, add the basil and seasoning, then simmer for 10 minutes.

3 Spoon the soup into a food processor or blender (you may have to do this in batches) and process until the soup is smooth.

4 Return the soup to the rinsed pan and reheat gently until piping hot. Ladle into warm bowls, sprinkle with shaved Parmesan and garnish with basil.

VARIATION
You can also use mint or a mixture of parsley, mint and chives in place of the basil, if you like.

SERVES 4

INGREDIENTS
   5 tablespoons olive oil
   2 large onions, chopped
   1 celery stick, chopped
   1 carrot, chopped
   1 garlic clove, finely chopped
   14 ounces/3½ cups frozen
     baby peas
   3¾ cups vegetable stock
   1 ounce/1 cup fresh basil leaves,
     roughly torn, plus extra to garnish
   salt and ground black pepper
   shaved Parmesan cheese,
     to serve

1 Heat the oil in a large pan and add the onions, celery, carrot and garlic. Cover the pan and cook over a low heat for 45 minutes, or until the vegetables are soft, stirring occasionally to prevent the vegetables from sticking.

Energy 261kcal/1078kJ; Protein 8.8g; Carbohydrate 22.9g, of which sugars 10.9g; Fat 15.7g, of which saturates 2.3g; Cholesterol 0mg; Calcium 73mg; Fiber 7.3g; Sodium 16mg.

FRESH TOMATO SOUP

THE COMBINATION OF INTENSELY FLAVORED SUN-RIPENED AND FRESH TOMATOES NEEDS LITTLE EMBELLISHMENT IN THIS TASTY ITALIAN SOUP. CHOOSE THE RIPEST-LOOKING TOMATOES.

SERVES 6

INGREDIENTS
3–3½ pounds ripe tomatoes
14 fluid ounces/1⅔ cups chicken or vegetable stock
3 tablespoons sun-dried tomato paste
2–3 tablespoons balsamic vinegar
2–3 teaspoons sugar
a small handful of fresh basil leaves, plus extra to garnish
salt and ground black pepper
toasted cheese croutes and crème fraîche, to serve

COOK'S TIP
Use a sharp knife to cut a cross in the base of each tomato before plunging it into the boiling water. The skin will then peel back easily from the crosses.

1 Plunge the tomatoes into boiling water for 30 seconds, then refresh in cold water. Peel off the skins and quarter the tomatoes. Put them in a large pan and pour over the chicken or vegetable stock. Bring just to the boil, reduce the heat, cover and simmer gently for 10 minutes until the tomatoes are pulpy.

2 Stir in the tomato paste, vinegar, sugar and basil. Season with salt and pepper, then cook gently, stirring, for 2 minutes. Process the soup in a blender or food processor, then return to a clean pan and reheat gently. Serve in bowls, topped with one or two toasted cheese croutes and a spoonful of crème fraîche, garnished with basil leaves.

Energy 52kcal/225kJ; Protein 1.9g; Carbohydrate 10.4g, of which sugars 10.4g; Fat 0.7g, of which saturates 0.2g; Cholesterol 0mg; Calcium 19mg; Fiber 2.4g; Sodium 38mg.

CARROT AND ORANGE SOUP

THIS TRADITIONAL BRIGHT AND SUMMERY SOUP IS ALWAYS POPULAR FOR ITS WONDERFULLY CREAMY CONSISTENCY AND VIBRANTLY FRESH CITRUS FLAVOR. USE A GOOD, HOMEMADE CHICKEN OR VEGETABLE STOCK IF YOU CAN, FOR THE BEST RESULTS.

SERVES 4

INGREDIENTS
2 ounces/¼ cup butter
3 leeks, sliced
1 pound carrots, sliced
5 cups chicken or vegetable
  stock
rind and juice of 2 oranges
½ teaspoon freshly grated
  nutmeg
⅔ cup strained plain yogurt
salt and ground black pepper
fresh sprigs of cilantro,
  to garnish

1 Melt the butter in a large pan. Add the leeks and carrots and stir well, coating the vegetables with the butter. Cover and cook for about 10 minutes, until the vegetables are beginning to soften but not color.

2 Pour in the stock and the orange rind and juice. Add the nutmeg and season to taste with salt and pepper. Bring to the boil, lower the heat, cover and simmer for about 40 minutes, or until the vegetables are tender.

3 Leave to cool slightly, then puree the soup in a food processor or blender until smooth.

4 Return the soup to the pan and add 2 tablespoons of the yogurt, then taste the soup and adjust the seasoning, if necessary. Reheat gently.

5 Ladle the soup into warm individual bowls and put a swirl of yogurt in the center of each. Sprinkle the fresh sprigs of cilantro over each bowl to garnish, and serve immediately.

Energy 206kcal/856kJ; Protein 5g; Carbohydrate 15.8g, of which sugars 14.2g; Fat 14.4g, of which saturates 8.3g; Cholesterol 27mg; Calcium 111mg; Fiber 5.8g; Sodium 131mg.

LIGHT AND FRAGRANT BROTH WITH STUFFED CABBAGE LEAVES

THE ORIGINS OF THIS VIETNAMESE SOUP, CANH BAP CUON, *COULD BE ATTRIBUTED TO THE FRENCH DISH,* CHOU FARCI, *OR TO THE CHINESE TRADITION OF COOKING DUMPLINGS IN A CLEAR BROTH.*

SERVES 4

INGREDIENTS

10 Chinese cabbage or savoy cabbage leaves, halved, main ribs removed

4 scallions, green tops left whole, white part chopped

5 or 6 dried wood ears, soaked in hot water for 15 minutes

4 ounces ground pork

4 ounces shrimp, shelled, deveined and finely chopped

1 Thai chile, seeded and chopped

2 tablespoons *nuoc mam*

1 tablespoon soy sauce

1½ inches fresh ginger root, peeled and very finely sliced

chopped fresh cilantro, to garnish

For the stock

1 meaty chicken carcass

2 onions, peeled and quartered

4 garlic cloves, crushed

1½ inches fresh ginger root, chopped

2 tablespoons *nuoc mam*

2 tablespoons soy sauce

6 black peppercorns

a few sprigs of fresh thyme

sea salt

1 To make the stock, put the chicken carcass into a deep pan. Add the other stock ingredients and cover with water. Bring to the boil, skim off any foam, then reduce the heat and simmer gently with the lid on for 1½–2 hours. Remove the lid and simmer for a further 30 minutes to reduce the stock. Skim off any fat, then strain the stock and measure out 6¼ cups.

2 Blanch the cabbage leaves in boiling water for 2 minutes. Remove with tongs or a slotted spoon and refresh under cold water. Add the green tops of the scallions to the boiling water and blanch for 1 minute, then drain and refresh under cold water. Tear each piece into five thin strips and set aside.

3 Squeeze the wood ear dry, then trim and finely chop and mix with the pork, shrimp, scallion whites, chile, *nuoc mam* and soy sauce. Lay a cabbage leaf flat and put a teaspoon of the filling ½ inch from the bottom edge. Fold the edge over the filling, then fold in the sides. Roll all the way to the top of the leaf to form a tight bundle. Tie a piece of blanched scallion green around the bundle. Repeat with the remaining leaves and filling.

4 Bring the stock to the boil in a wok or deep pan. Stir in the finely sliced ginger, then reduce the heat and drop in the cabbage bundles. Bubble very gently over a medium heat for about 20 minutes to ensure that the filling is thoroughly cooked.

5 Ladle into bowls and sprinkle with fresh cilantro leaves.

Energy 87kcal/362kJ; Protein 11.8g; Carbohydrate 3.1g, of which sugars 3g; Fat 3.2g, of which saturates 1.1g; Cholesterol 75mg; Calcium 54mg; Fiber 1.2g; Sodium 527mg.

BALINESE VEGETABLE SOUP

*THE BALINESE BASE THIS POPULAR SOUP ON BEANS, BUT ANY SEASONAL VEGETABLES CAN BE ADDED
OR SUBSTITUTED. THE RECIPE ALSO INCLUDES SHRIMP PASTE, WHICH IS KNOWN LOCALLY AS TERASI.*

2 Finely grind the chopped garlic, macadamia nuts or almonds, shrimp paste and the coriander seeds to a paste using a pestle and mortar or in a food processor.

3 Heat the oil in a wok, and fry the onion until transparent. Remove with a slotted spoon. Add the nut paste to the wok and fry it for 2 minutes without allowing it to brown.

4 Pour in the reserved vegetable water. Spoon off 3–4 tablespoons of the cream from the top of the coconut milk and set it aside. Add the remaining coconut milk to the wok, bring to the boil and add the bay leaves. Cook, uncovered, for 15–20 minutes.

5 Just before serving, reserve a few beans, fried onions and bean sprouts to garnish and stir the rest into the soup. Add the lemon wedges, reserved coconut cream, lemon juice and seasoning; stir well. Pour into individual soup bowls and serve, garnished with the reserved beans, onion and bean sprouts.

SERVES 8

INGREDIENTS

8 ounces green beans
5 cups lightly salted water
1 garlic clove, roughly chopped
2 macadamia nuts or 4 almonds,
  finely chopped
1/2-inch cube shrimp paste
2–3 teaspoons coriander seeds,
  dry fried
2 tablespoons vegetable oil
1 onion, finely sliced
1 can (14 fluid ounces)
  coconut milk
2 bay leaves
8 ounces/4 cups bean sprouts
8 thin lemon wedges
2 tablespoons lemon juice
salt and ground black pepper

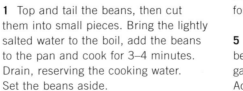

1 Top and tail the beans, then cut them into small pieces. Bring the lightly salted water to the boil, add the beans to the pan and cook for 3–4 minutes. Drain, reserving the cooking water. Set the beans aside.

COOK'S TIP
Dry-fry the coriander seeds for about 2 minutes until the aroma is released.

Energy 54kcal/224kJ; Protein 2.1g; Carbohydrate 5.2g, of which sugars 4.2g; Fat 2.8g, of which saturates 0.4g; Cholesterol 0mg; Calcium 38mg; Fiber 1.3g; Sodium 57mg.

PEA SOUP WITH GARLIC

THIS DELICIOUS SOUP HAS A WONDERFULLY SWEET TASTE AND SMOOTH TEXTURE, AND IS GREAT SERVED WITH CRUSTY BREAD AND GARNISHED WITH MINT.

SERVES 4

INGREDIENTS

1 ounce/2 tablespoons butter
1 garlic clove, crushed
2 pounds/8 cups frozen peas
2 5 cups chicken stock
salt and ground black pepper

1 Heat the butter in a large pan and add the garlic. Fry gently for 2–3 minutes, until softened, then add the peas. Cook for 1–2 minutes more, then pour in the stock.

COOK'S TIP
If you keep a bag of frozen peas in the freezer, you can rustle up this soup at very short notice.

2 Bring the soup to the boil, then reduce the heat to a simmer. Cover and cook for 5–6 minutes, until the peas are tender. Leave to cool slightly, then transfer the mixture to a food processor and process until smooth (you may have to do this in two batches).

3 Return the soup to the pan and heat through gently. Season with salt and pepper to taste.

Energy 233kcal/965kJ; Protein 15.6g; Carbohydrate 25.5g, of which sugars 5.2g; Fat 8.5g, of which saturates 3.9g; Cholesterol 13mg; Calcium 49mg; Fiber 10.6g; Sodium 40mg.

SUMMER HERB SOUP <u>WITH</u> CHARGRILLED RADICCHIO

THE SWEETNESS OF SHALLOTS AND LEEKS IN THIS SOUP IS BALANCED BEAUTIFULLY BY THE SLIGHTLY ACIDIC SORREL WITH ITS HINT OF LEMON, AND A BOUQUET OF SUMMER HERBS.

SERVES 4–6

INGREDIENTS
    2 tablespoons dry white wine
    2 shallots, finely chopped
    1 garlic clove, crushed
    2 leeks, sliced
    1 large potato, about 8 ounces,
      roughly chopped
    2 zucchini, chopped
    2½ cups water
    4 ounces sorrel, torn
    large handful of fresh chervil
    large handful of fresh Italian parsley
    large handful of fresh mint
    1 butterhead lettuce, separated
      into leaves
    2½ cups vegetable stock
    1 small head of radicchio
    1 teaspoon peanut oil
    salt and ground black pepper

1 Put the wine, shallots and garlic into a heavy-based pan and bring to the boil. Cook for 2–3 minutes, until softened.

2 Add the leeks, potato and zucchini with enough of the water to come about halfway up the vegetables. Lay a wetted piece of waxed paper over the vegetables and put a lid on the pan, then cook for 10–15 minutes, until soft.

3 Remove the paper and add the fresh herbs and lettuce. Cook for 1–2 minutes, or until wilted.

4 Pour in the remaining water and the vegetable stock and simmer for 10–12 minutes. Cool the soup slightly, then process it in a food processor or blender until smooth. Return the soup to the rinsed-out pan and season well.

5 Cut the radicchio into thin wedges that hold together, then brush the cut sides with the oil. Heat a ridged griddle or frying pan until very hot and add the radicchio wedges.

6 Cook the radicchio for 1 minute on each side until slightly charred. Reheat the soup over a low heat, then ladle it into warmed shallow bowls. Serve a wedge of charred radicchio on top.

Energy 102kcal/428kJ; Protein 5g; Carbohydrate 15.1g, of which sugars 5.7g; Fat 2.2g, of which saturates 0.4g; Cholesterol 0mg; Calcium 135mg; Fiber 4.9g; Sodium 57mg.

TOMATO, CIABATTA <u>AND</u> BASIL OIL SOUP

THROUGHOUT EUROPE, BREAD IS A POPULAR INGREDIENT FOR THICKENING SOUP, AND THIS RECIPE SHOWS HOW WONDERFULLY QUICK AND EASY THIS METHOD CAN BE.

SERVES 4

INGREDIENTS

    3 tablespoons olive oil
    1 red onion, chopped
    6 garlic cloves, chopped
    1¼ cups white wine
    ⅔ cup water
    12 plum tomatoes, quartered
    2 cans (28 ounces) plum tomatoes
    ½ teaspoon sugar
    ½ ciabatta loaf
    salt and ground black pepper
    basil leaves, to garnish
For the basil oil
    4 ounces basil leaves
    4 fluid ounces/½ cup olive oil

1 For the basil oil, process the basil and oil in a food processor or blender to make a paste. Line a bowl with cheesecloth and scrape the paste into it. Gather up the muslin and squeeze firmly to extract all the oil. Set aside.

2 Heat the oil in a large pan and cook the onion and garlic for 4–5 minutes until softened.

3 Add the wine, water, fresh and canned tomatoes. Bring to the boil, reduce the heat and cover the pan, then simmer for 3–4 minutes. Add the sugar and season well with salt and black pepper.

4 Break the bread into bitesize pieces and stir into the soup.

5 Ladle the soup into bowls. Garnish with basil and drizzle the basil oil over each portion.

Energy 332kcal/1396kJ; Protein 7.8g; Carbohydrate 35.4g, of which sugars 16.3g; Fat 13.4g, of which saturates 2g; Cholesterol 0mg; Calcium 98mg; Fiber 5g; Sodium 306mg.

ROASTED PEPPER SOUP

GRILLING INTENSIFIES THE FLAVOR OF SWEET RED AND YELLOW BELL PEPPERS AND HELPS THIS DELICIOUS SOUP TO KEEP ITS STUNNING COLOR.

SERVES 4

INGREDIENTS
  3 red bell peppers
  1 yellow bell pepper
  1 medium onion, chopped
  1 garlic clove, crushed
  3 cups vegetable stock
  1 tablespoon all-purpose flour
  salt and ground black pepper
  diced red and yellow bell pepper,
    to garnish

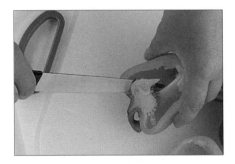

1 Preheat the broiler to hot. Cut the peppers in half, remove their stalks, cores and white pith, and scrape out the seeds.

2 Line a broiler pan with foil and arrange the halved peppers, skin-side up, in a single layer on the foil. Broil for 8–10 minutes, until the skins have blackened and blistered.

VARIATION
If you prefer, garnish the soup before serving with a swirl of plain yogurt or crème fraîche instead of the diced peppers.

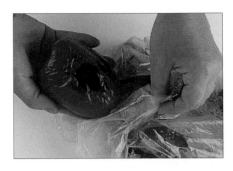

3 Transfer the peppers to a plastic bag and leave until cool, then peel away their skins and discard. Roughly chop the pepper flesh.

4 Put the onion, garlic clove and ⅔ cup of the stock in a large pan. Boil for about 5 minutes until the stock has reduced in volume. Reduce the heat and stir until softened and just beginning to color.

5 Sprinkle the flour over the onion, then gradually add the remaining stock, stirring to prevent lumps from forming.

6 Add the chopped, roasted peppers and bring to the boil. Cover and simmer for a further 5 minutes.

7 Leave to cool slightly, then puree in a food processor or blender until smooth. Season to taste with salt and ground black pepper.

8 Return to the pan and reheat until the soup is piping hot.

9 Ladle into four soup bowls and garnish each with a sprinkling of diced peppers before serving.

COOK'S TIP
Stir any juice that accumulates in the pan after broiling the peppers into the soup for extra flavor.

Energy 87kcal/364kJ; Protein 2.7g; Carbohydrate 18.1g, of which sugars 13.5g; Fat 0.9g, of which saturates 0.2g; Cholesterol 0mg; Calcium 32mg; Fiber 3.6g; Sodium 9mg.

BEET AND APRICOT SWIRL

THIS SOUP IS MOST ATTRACTIVE IF YOU SWIRL TOGETHER THE TWO DIFFERENTLY COLORED MIXTURES, BUT IF YOU PREFER THEY CAN BE MIXED TOGETHER TO SAVE TIME.

SERVES 4

INGREDIENTS
   4 large cooked beets,
     roughly chopped
   1 small onion, roughly chopped
   2½ cups chicken stock
   7 ounces/1 cup ready-to-eat
     dried apricots
   8 fluid ounces/1 cup orange juice
   salt and ground black pepper

1 Place the beets and half the onion in a pan with the stock. Bring to the boil, reduce the heat, cover and simmer for 10 minutes. Puree until smooth in a food processor or blender.

2 Place the rest of the onion in a pan with the apricots and orange juice, cover and simmer gently for about 15 minutes, until tender. Puree in a food processor or blender to the same consistency as the beet mixture.

3 Return the two mixtures to the pans and reheat. Season to taste with salt and pepper. To serve, swirl the two mixtures together in individual soup bowls for a marbled effect. Serve while still hot.

Energy 143kcal/609kJ; Protein 4.2g; Carbohydrate 32.5g, of which sugars 31.6g; Fat 0.5g, of which saturates 0g; Cholesterol 0mg; Calcium 67mg; Fiber 5.3g; Sodium 80mg.

TAMARIND SOUP WITH VEGETABLES

Known in Indonesia as Sayur Asam, this is a colorful and refreshing soup from Jakarta, with more than a hint of sharpness.

SERVES 4 AS AN APPETIZER OR 8 AS PART OF A BUFFET

INGREDIENTS

5 shallots or 1 medium red onion, sliced

3 garlic cloves, peeled and crushed

1-inch galangal, peeled and sliced

1 or 2 fresh red chiles, seeded and sliced

1 ounce/¼ cup raw peanuts

½-inch cube shrimp paste, prepared

5 cups well-flavored stock

2–3 ounces/½–¾ cup salted peanuts, lightly crushed

1–2 tablespoons soft dark brown sugar

1 teaspoon tamarind pulp, soaked in 5 tablespoons warm water for 15 minutes

salt

For the vegetables

1 chayote, thinly peeled, seeds removed, flesh finely sliced

4 ounces green beans, trimmed and finely sliced

2 ounces corn kernels (optional)

a handful of green leaves, such as watercress, arugula or Chinese cabbage, washed and finely shredded

1 fresh green chile, sliced, to garnish

1 Put the shallots or onion, garlic, galangal, chiles, raw peanuts and shrimp paste in a food processor or pestle and mortar and grind to a paste.

3 Strain the tamarind pulp, discarding the seeds, and reserve the juice.

2 Pour in some of the stock to moisten and then pour this mixture into a pan or wok, adding the rest of the stock. Cook for 15 minutes with the crushed salted peanuts and sugar.

4 About 5 minutes before serving, add the chayote slices, beans and corn, if using, to the soup and cook fairly rapidly. At the last minute, add the green leaves and salt to taste. Add the tamarind juice and adjust the seasoning. Serve immediately, garnished with slices of green chile.

Energy 80kcal/334kJ; Protein 3.8g; Carbohydrate 6.2g, of which sugars 4.9g; Fat 4.6g, of which saturates 0.9g; Cholesterol 0mg; Calcium 46mg; Fiber 1.7g; Sodium 19mg.

CHICKEN RICE SOUP <u>WITH</u> LEMONGRASS

SHNOR CHROOK IS CAMBODIA'S ANSWER TO THE CHICKEN NOODLE SOUP OF THE WEST. LIGHT AND REFRESHING, IT IS A PERFECT DISH FOR A HOT DAY, AS WELL AS A GREAT PICK-ME-UP WHEN YOU ARE FEELING LOW OR TIRED. THE FRESH, CITRUS AROMA OF LEMONGRASS AND LIME, COMBINED WITH THE WARMTH OF THE CHILES, IS INVIGORATING AND AWAKENS THE SENSES.

SERVES 4

INGREDIENTS
For the stock
　1 small chicken or 2 meaty
　　chicken legs
　1 onion, quartered
　2 garlic cloves, crushed
　1 ounce fresh ginger root, sliced
　2 lemongrass stalks
　2 dried red chiles
　2 tablespoons *nuoc mam*
For the soup
　2 lemongrass stalks, trimmed and
　　cut into 3 pieces
　1 tablespoon Thai fish sauce
　3½ ounces/½ cup short grain
　　rice, rinsed
　sea salt and ground black pepper
　a small bunch of cilantro leaves,
　　finely chopped, and 1 green or red
　　chile, to garnish
　1 lime, quartered, to serve

1 Put the chicken into a deep pan and add all the other stock ingredients.

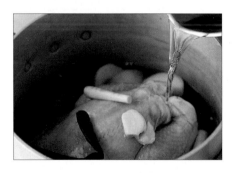

2 Bring the water to the boil for a few minutes, then reduce the heat and simmer gently with the lid on for about 2 hours, until the chicken is tender.

3 Skim off any fat from the stock, strain and reserve. Remove the skin from the chicken and shred the meat. Set aside while you make the soup.

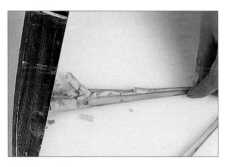

4 Bruise the lemongrass stalks with the blunt edge of a chopping knife.

5 Pour the stock back into the deep pan and bring to the boil. Reduce the heat and stir in the bruised lemongrass stalks and the fish sauce.

6 Stir in the rice and simmer, uncovered, for about 40 minutes. Add the shredded chicken and season to taste with salt and black pepper.

7 Slice the chile in half, remove the seeds and cut the flesh into very thin strips. It is a good idea to wear gloves when handling chiles.

8 Ladle the soup into individual bowls, garnish with cilantro and the thin strips of chile and serve with lime wedges to squeeze over.

Energy 124kcal/519kJ; Protein 10.9g; Carbohydrate 18.1g, of which sugars 0g; Fat 0.7g, of which saturates 0.1g; Cholesterol 26mg; Calcium 8mg; Fiber 0g; Sodium 226mg.

HOT AND SPICY SOUPS

Make your taste buds tingle with these hot and spicy soups from all around the world. In the recipes in this section, chiles, ginger, cayenne pepper and garlic add punch to vegetables, legumes, meat and shellfish. Choose from exotic dishes such as the richly flavored Thai-style Lentil and Coconut Soup, traditional North African Spiced Soup, Goan Potato Soup with Spiced Pea Samosas, or Mexican Beef Chili with Monterey Jack Nachos.

CURRIED PARSNIP SOUP WITH CROUTONS

THE MILD SWEETNESS OF PARSNIPS AND MANGO CHUTNEY IS GIVEN AN EXCITING LIFT WITH A BLEND OF SPICES IN THIS SIMPLE SOUP GARNISHED WITH NAAN CROUTONS.

SERVES 4

INGREDIENTS

2 tablespoons olive oil
1 onion, chopped
1 garlic clove, crushed
1 small green chile, seeded and
    finely chopped
1 tablespoon grated fresh
    ginger root
5 large parsnips, diced
1 teaspoon cumin seeds
1 teaspoon ground coriander
½ teaspoon ground turmeric
2 tablespoons mango chutney
5 cups water
juice of 1 lime
salt and ground black pepper
4 tablespoons plain yogurt and
    mango chutney, to serve
chopped fresh cilantro,
    to garnish (optional)

For the sesame naan croutons
    45ml/3 tablespoons olive oil
    1 large naan
    1 tablespoon sesame seeds

1 Heat the oil in a large pan and add the onion, garlic, chile and ginger. Cook for 4–5 minutes, until the onion has softened. Add the parsnips and cook for 2–3 minutes. Sprinkle in the cumin seeds, coriander and turmeric and cook for 1 minute, stirring constantly.

2 Add the chutney and the water. Season well and bring to the boil. Reduce the heat and simmer for 15 minutes, until the parsnips are soft.

3 Cool the soup slightly, then process it in a food processor or blender until smooth, and return it to the pan. Stir in the lime juice.

4 For the naan croutons, cut the naan into small dice. Heat the oil in a large frying pan and cook until golden all over. Remove from the heat and drain off any excess oil. Add the sesame seeds and return to the heat for 30 seconds, until the seeds are golden.

5 Ladle the soup into bowls. Add a little yogurt and top with mango chutney and the naan croutons.

Energy 189kcal/792kJ; Protein 4g; Carbohydrate 26.6g, of which sugars 15.5g; Fat 8.2g, of which saturates 1.2g; Cholesterol 0mg; Calcium 101mg; Fiber 7.5g; Sodium 110mg.

SPICED LENTIL SOUP WITH PARSLEY CREAM

CRISPY SHALLOTS AND A PARSLEY CREAM TOP THIS RICH SOUP, WHICH IS INSPIRED BY THE DHALS OF INDIAN COOKING. CHUNKS OF SMOKED BACON ADD TEXTURE.

SERVES 6

INGREDIENTS

  1 teaspoon cumin seeds
  ½ teaspoon coriander seeds
  1 teaspoon ground turmeric
  2 tablespoons olive oil
  1 onion, chopped
  2 garlic cloves, chopped
  1 smoked bacon hock
  5 cups vegetable stock
  10 ounces/1¼ cups red lentils
  1 can (14 ounces) chopped
    tomatoes
  1 tablespoon vegetable oil
  3 shallots, thinly sliced
For the parsley cream
  3 tablespoons chopped
    fresh parsley
  ⅔ cup strained plain yogurt
  salt and ground black pepper

1 Heat a frying pan and add the cumin and coriander seeds. Roast them over a high heat for a few seconds, shaking the pan until they smell aromatic. Transfer the seeds to a mortar and crush using a pestle. Mix in the turmeric. Set aside.

2 Heat the oil in a large pan. Add the onion and garlic and cook for 4–5 minutes, until softened.

3 Add the spice mixture and cook for 2 minutes, stirring continuously.

COOK'S TIP
Tip lentils into a strainer or colander and pick them over to remove any pieces of grit before rinsing.

4 Place the bacon in the pan and pour in the stock. Bring to the boil, cover and simmer gently for 30 minutes.

5 Add the red lentils and cook for 20 minutes or until the lentils and bacon hock are tender. Stir in the tomatoes and cook for a further 5 minutes.

6 Remove the bacon from the pan and set it aside until cool enough to handle. Leave the soup to cool slightly, then process in a food processor or blender until almost smooth. Return the soup to the rinsed-out pan. Cut the meat from the hock, discarding skin and fat, then stir it into the soup and reheat.

7 Heat the oil in a frying pan and fry the shallots for 10 minutes until crisp and golden. Remove using a slotted spoon and drain on paper towels.

8 To make the parsley cream, stir the chopped parsley into the yogurt and season well. Ladle the soup into bowls and add a dollop of the parsley cream to each. Pile some crisp shallots onto each portion and serve at once.

Energy 235kcal/991kJ; Protein 13g; Carbohydrate 28.4g, of which sugars 3.7g; Fat 8.8g, of which saturates 2.2g; Cholesterol 0mg; Calcium 66mg; Fiber 2.9g; Sodium 40mg.

TOMATO SOUP <u>WITH</u> RED PEPPER CREAM

THIS DAZZLING SOUP CAN BE MADE AS FIERY OR AS MILD AS YOU LIKE BY INCREASING OR REDUCING THE NUMBER OF CHILES.

4 Transfer the pepper for the pepper cream to a bowl as soon as it is cooked. Cover with plastic wrap and leave to cool. Peel away the skin and puree the flesh in a food processor or blender with half the crème fraîche. Pour into a bowl and stir in the remaining crème fraîche. Season and add a dash of Tabasco sauce. Chill in the refrigerator until required.

5 Process the roasted vegetables in batches, adding a ladleful of stock to each batch to make a smooth, thick paste. Depending on how juicy the tomatoes are, you may not need all the vegetable stock.

6 Press the paste through a strainer into a pan and stir in more stock if you want to thin the soup. Heat gently and season well. Ladle the soup into bowls and spoon red pepper cream into the center of each bowl. Pile wild arugula leaves on top to garnish.

SERVES 4

INGREDIENTS
  3–3½ pounds plum tomatoes, halved
  5 red chiles, seeded
  1 red bell pepper, halved
    and seeded
  2 red onions, roughly chopped
  6 garlic cloves, crushed
  2 tablespoons sun-dried tomato paste
  3 tablespoons olive oil
  14 fluid ounces/1⅔ cups
    vegetable stock
  salt and ground black pepper
  wild arugula, to garnish
For the pepper cream
  1 red bell pepper, halved
    and seeded
  2 teaspoons olive oil
  4 fluid ounces/½ cup crème fraîche
  a few drops of Tabasco sauce

1 Preheat the oven to 400°F. Place the tomatoes, chiles, red pepper, onions, garlic and tomato paste in a roasting pan. Toss all the vegetables, drizzle with the oil and toss again, then roast for 40 minutes, until tender and when the pepper skin is slightly charred.

2 Meanwhile make the pepper cream. Lay the red pepper halves skin-side up on a baking tray and brush with the olive oil.

3 Roast with the mixed vegetables for about 30–40 minutes, until blistered.

COOK'S TIP
The pepper cream may be a bit runny when first processed, but it firms up when chilled.

Energy 319kcal/1330kJ; Protein 5.3g; Carbohydrate 23.5g, of which sugars 22g; Fat 23.4g, of which saturates 10g; Cholesterol 34mg; Calcium 67mg; Fiber 6.2g; Sodium 72mg.

NORTH AFRICAN SPICED SOUP

CLASSICALLY KNOWN AS HARIRA, THIS SOUP IS OFTEN SERVED IN THE EVENING DURING RAMADAN, THE MUSLIM RELIGIOUS FESTIVAL WHEN FOLLOWERS FAST DURING THE DAYTIME FOR A MONTH.

SERVES 6

INGREDIENTS
1 large onion, chopped
5 cups stock
1 teaspoon ground cinnamon
1 teaspoon turmeric
1 tablespoon grated ginger
pinch of cayenne pepper
2 carrots, diced
2 celery sticks, diced
1 can (14 ounces) chopped tomatoes
1 pound floury potatoes, diced
5 strands saffron
1 can (14 ounces) chickpeas, drained
2 tablespoons chopped
  fresh cilantro
1 tablespoon lemon juice
salt and ground black pepper
fried wedges of lemon, to serve

1 Place the chopped onion in a large pot with 1¼ cups of the vegetable stock. Bring the mixture to the boil and simmer gently for about 10 minutes.

2 Meanwhile, mix together the cinnamon, turmeric, ginger, cayenne pepper and 2 tablespoons of stock to form a paste. Stir into the onion mixture with the carrots, celery and remaining stock.

3 Bring the mixture to a boil, reduce the heat, then cover and gently simmer for 5 minutes.

4 Add the tomatoes and potatoes and simmer gently, covered, for 20 minutes. Add the saffron, chickpeas, cilantro and lemon juice. Season to taste and when piping hot serve with fried wedges of lemon.

Energy 158kcal/668kJ; Protein 7.2g; Carbohydrate 28.4g, of which sugars 7g; Fat 2.5g, of which saturates 0.4g; Cholesterol 0mg; Calcium 64mg; Fiber 5.4g; Sodium 173mg.

CURRIED CAULIFLOWER SOUP

THIS SPICY, CREAMY SOUP IS PERFECT FOR LUNCH ON A COLD WINTER'S DAY SERVED WITH CRUSTY BREAD AND GARNISHED WITH FRESH CILANTRO.

SERVES 4

INGREDIENTS
    3 cups milk
    1 large cauliflower
    1 tablespoon garam masala
    salt and ground black pepper

1 Pour the milk into a large pan and place over a medium heat. Cut the cauliflower into florets and add to the milk with the garam masala and season with salt and pepper.

2 Bring the milk to the boil, then reduce the heat, partially cover the pan with a lid and simmer for about 20 minutes, or until the cauliflower is tender.

3 Let the mixture cool for a few minutes, then transfer to a food processor and process until smooth (you may have to do this in two separate batches).

4 Return the puree to the pan and heat through gently without boiling, checking and adjusting the seasoning to taste. Serve immediately.

Energy 143kcal/601kJ; Protein 12g; Carbohydrate 13.9g, of which sugars 12.6g; Fat 4.8g, of which saturates 2.3g; Cholesterol 11mg; Calcium 271mg; Fiber 3.2g; Sodium 104mg.

CORN AND RED CHILE CHOWDER

CORN AND CHILES MAKE GOOD BEDFELLOWS, AND HERE THE COOL COMBINATION OF CREAMED CORN AND MILK IS THE PERFECT FOIL FOR THE RAGING HEAT OF THE CHILES.

SERVES 6

INGREDIENTS

2 tomatoes, skinned
1 onion, roughly chopped
1 can (13 ounces) creamed corn
2 red bell peppers, halved
  and seeded
1 tablespoon olive oil, plus extra
  for brushing
3 red chiles, seeded and sliced
2 garlic cloves, chopped
1 teaspoon ground cumin
1 teaspoon ground coriander
2½ cups milk
12 fluid ounces/1½ cups
  chicken stock
3 cobs of corn, kernels removed
1 pound potatoes, finely diced
4 tablespoons heavy cream
4 tablespoons chopped
  fresh parsley
salt and ground black pepper

1 Process the tomatoes and onion in a food processor or blender to a smooth paste. Add the creamed corn and process again, then set aside. Preheat the broiler to high.

2 Put the peppers, skin-sides up, on a broiler rack and brush with oil. Broil for 8–10 minutes, until the skins blacken and blister. Transfer to a bowl and cover with plastic wrap, then leave to cool. Peel and dice the peppers, then set them aside.

3 Heat the oil in a large pan and add the chiles and garlic. Cook, stirring, for 2–3 minutes, until softened.

4 Add the ground cumin and coriander, and cook for a further 1 minute. Stir in the corn paste and cook for about 8 minutes, stirring occasionally.

5 Pour in the milk and stock, then stir in the corn kernels, potatoes, red pepper and seasoning to taste. Cook for 15–20 minutes, until the corn and potatoes are tender.

6 Pour into deep bowls and add the cream, then sprinkle over the chopped parsley and serve at once.

Energy 343kcal/1448kJ; Protein 9.4g; Carbohydrate 55.4g, of which sugars 23.2g; Fat 10.9g, of which saturates 5.1g; Cholesterol 20mg; Calcium 147mg; Fiber 4g; Sodium 383mg.

FRAGRANT BEET AND VEGETABLE SOUP WITH SPICED LAMB KUBBEH

THE JEWISH COMMUNITY FROM COCHIN IN INDIA IS SCATTERED NOW BUT IS STILL FAMOUS FOR ITS CUISINE. THIS TANGY SOUP IS SERVED WITH DUMPLINGS MADE OF BRIGHT YELLOW PASTA WRAPPED AROUND A SPICY LAMB FILLING, AND A DOLLOP OF FRAGRANT GREEN HERB PASTE.

SERVES 6–8

INGREDIENTS
    1 tablespoon vegetable oil
    ½ onion, finely chopped
    6 garlic cloves
    1 carrot, diced
    1 zucchini, diced
    ½ celery stick, diced (optional)
    4–5 cardamom pods
    ½ teaspoon curry powder
    4 vacuum-packed beets (cooked
        not pickled), finely diced and
        juice reserved
    4 cups vegetable stock
    1 can (14 ounces) chopped tomatoes
    3–4 tablespoons chopped fresh
        cilantro leaves
    2 bay leaves
    1 tablespoon sugar
    salt and ground black pepper
    1–2 tablespoons white wine vinegar,
        to serve
For the kubbeh
    2 large pinches of saffron threads
    1 tablespoon hot water
    1 tablespoon vegetable oil
    1 large onion, chopped
    9 ounces lean ground lamb
    1 teaspoon vinegar
    ½ bunch fresh mint, chopped
    4 ounces/1 cup all-purpose flour
    2–3 pinches of salt
    ½–1 teaspoon ground turmeric
    3–4 tablespoons cold water
For the ginger and cilantro paste
    4 garlic cloves, chopped
    1–1½ tablespoons chopped
        fresh ginger root
    ½–4 fresh mild chiles
    ½ large bunch fresh cilantro
    2 tablespoons white wine vinegar
    1 tablespoon extra virgin olive oil
    salt

COOK'S TIP
Serve any leftover paste with meatballs
or spread on sandwiches.

1 For the paste, process the garlic, ginger and chiles in a food processor. Add the cilantro, vinegar, oil and salt and process to a paste. Set aside.

2 To make the kubbeh filling, place the saffron and hot water in a small bowl and leave to steep. Meanwhile, heat the oil in a pan and fry the onion until softened. Put the onion and saffron water in a food processor and blend. Add the lamb, season and blend. Add the vinegar and mint, then chill.

3 To make the kubbeh dough, put the flour, salt and ground turmeric in a food processor, then gradually add the water, processing until it forms a sticky dough. Knead on a floured surface for 5 minutes, wrap in a plastic bag and leave to stand for 30 minutes.

4 Divide the dough into 10–15 pieces. Roll each into a ball, then, using a pasta machine, roll into very thin rounds.

5 Lay the rounds on a well-floured surface. Place a spoonful of filling in the middle of each. Dampen the edges of the dough, then bring them together and seal. Set aside on a floured surface.

6 To make the soup, heat the oil in a pan, add the onion and fry for about 10 minutes, or until softened but not browned. Add half the garlic, the carrot, zucchini, celery (if using), cardamom pods and curry powder, and cook for 2–3 minutes.

7 Add three of the diced beets, the stock, tomatoes, cilantro, bay leaves and sugar to the pan. Bring to the boil, then reduce the heat and simmer for about 20 minutes.

8 Add the remaining beets, beet juice and garlic to the soup. Season with salt and pepper to taste and set aside until ready to serve.

9 To serve, reheat the soup and poach the dumplings in a large pan of salted boiling water for about 4 minutes. Using a slotted spoon, remove the dumplings from the water as they are cooked and place on a plate to keep warm.

10 Ladle the soup into bowls, adding a dash of vinegar to each bowl, then add two or three dumplings and a small spoonful of the ginger and cilantro paste to each. Serve immediately.

Energy 210kcal/881kJ; Protein 11.6g; Carbohydrate 22.1g, of which sugars 6.8g; Fat 9g, of which saturates 2.7g; Cholesterol 32mg; Calcium 55mg; Fiber 2.5g; Sodium 74mg.

GOAN POTATO SOUP <u>WITH</u> SPICED PEA SAMOSAS

IN GOA THIS SOUP WOULD BE SERVED AS A COMPLETE MEAL. BOTH SOUP AND SAMOSAS ARE SIMPLE TO PREPARE, AND MAKE A SUBSTANTIAL VEGETARIAN LUNCH.

SERVES 4

INGREDIENTS
    4 tablespoons sunflower oil
    2 teaspoons black mustard seeds
    1 large onion, chopped
    1 red chile, seeded and chopped
    ½ teaspoon ground turmeric
    ¼ teaspoon cayenne pepper
    2 pounds potatoes, cut into
        ½-inch cubes
    4 fresh curry leaves
    3 cups water
    8 ounces spinach leaves, torn if large
    14 fluid ounces/1⅔ cups
        coconut milk
    handful of fresh cilantro leaves
    salt and ground black pepper
For the samosa dough
    10 ounces/2½ cups all-purpose flour
    ¼ teaspoon salt
    2 tablespoons sunflower oil
    ⅔ cup warm water
For the samosa filling
    4 tablespoons sunflower oil
    1 small onion, finely chopped
    6 ounces/1½ cups frozen peas,
        thawed
    1 tablespoon grated fresh ginger root
    1 green chile, seeded and
        finely chopped
    3 tablespoons water
    12 ounces cooked potatoes,
        finely diced
    1½ teaspoons ground coriander
    1 teaspoon garam masala
    1½ teaspoons ground cumin
    ¼ teaspoon cayenne pepper
    2 teaspoons lemon juice
    2 tablespoons chopped fresh
        cilantro
    vegetable oil, for deep frying

1 Make the samosa dough. Mix the flour and salt in a bowl and make a well in the middle. Add the oil and water and mix in the flour to make a soft dough. Knead briefly on a lightly floured surface. Wrap in plastic wrap and chill for 30 minutes.

2 To make the filling, heat the oil in a frying pan and add the onion. Cook for 6–7 minutes until golden. Add the peas, ginger, chile and water. Cover and simmer for 5–6 minutes, until the peas are cooked. Add the potatoes, spices and lemon juice. Cook over a low heat for 2–3 minutes. Stir in the cilantro and season well. Leave to cool.

3 Divide the dough into eight. On a floured surface, roll out one piece into a 7-inch round. Keep the remaining dough covered. Cut the round in half and place 2 tablespoons of the filling on each half toward one corner.

4 Dampen the edges and fold the dough over the filling. Pinch the edges together to form triangles. Repeat with the remaining dough and filling.

5 Heat the oil for deep frying to 375°F, or until a cube of bread rises and sizzles in 30 seconds. Fry the samosas for 4–5 minutes, turning once. Drain on paper towels.

6 To make the soup, heat the oil in a large pan. Add the mustard seeds, cover and cook until they begin to pop. Add the onion and chile and cook for 5–6 minutes, until softened. Stir in the turmeric, cayenne, potatoes, curry leaves and water. Cover and cook over a low heat for 15 minutes, stirring occasionally, until the potatoes are soft.

7 Add the spinach and cook for 5 minutes. Stir in the coconut milk and cook for a further 5 minutes. Season and add the cilantro leaves before ladling the soup into bowls. Serve with the vegetable samosas.

Energy 836kcal/3503kJ; Protein 16.7g; Carbohydrate 112g, of which sugars 8.6g; Fat 38.7g, of which saturates 4.9g; Cholesterol 0mg; Calcium 227mg; Fiber 8.9g; Sodium 117mg.

MEXICAN BEEF CHILI WITH MONTEREY JACK NACHOS

STEAMING BOWLS OF BEEF CHILI SOUP, PACKED WITH BEANS, ARE DELICIOUS TOPPED WITH CRUSHED TORTILLAS AND CHEESE. POP THE BOWLS UNDER THE BROILER TO MELT THE CHEESE, IF YOU WISH.

SERVES 4

INGREDIENTS

- 3 tablespoons olive oil
- 12 ounces rump steak, cut into small pieces
- 2 onions, chopped
- 2 garlic cloves, crushed
- 2 green chiles, seeded and finely chopped
- 2 tablespoons mild chili powder
- 1 teaspoon ground cumin
- 2 bay leaves
- 2 tablespoons tomato paste
- 3¾ cups beef stock
- 2 cans (28 ounces) mixed beans, drained and rinsed
- 3 tablespoons chopped fresh cilantro leaves
- salt and ground black pepper

For the topping
- bag of plain tortilla chips, lightly crushed
- 8 ounces/2 cups Monterey Jack cheese, grated

1 Heat the oil in a large pan over a high heat and cook the meat all over until golden. Use a slotted spoon to remove it from the pan.

2 Reduce the heat and add the onions, garlic and chiles, then cook for 4–5 minutes, until softened.

VARIATION
Use Cheddar cheese instead of Monterey Jack if you prefer.

3 Add the chili powder and ground cumin, and cook for a further 2 minutes. Return the meat to the pan, then stir in the bay leaves, tomato paste and beef stock. Bring to the boil.

4 Reduce the heat, cover the pan and simmer for about 45 minutes, or until the meat is tender.

5 Put a quarter of the beans into a bowl and mash with a potato masher. Stir these into the soup to thicken it slightly. Add the remaining beans and simmer for about 5 minutes. Season and stir in the chopped cilantro. Ladle the soup into warmed bowls and spoon tortilla chips on top. Pile grated cheese over the tortilla chips and serve.

Energy 749kcal/3135kJ; Protein 50g; Carbohydrate 54.1g, of which sugars 10.3g; Fat 37.2g, of which saturates 16.1g; Cholesterol 106mg; Calcium 609mg; Fiber 14.5g; Sodium 1473mg.

SPICY TOMATO AND CILANTRO SOUP

HEART-WARMING TOMATO SOUP IS ALWAYS A FAVORITE. DELICIOUSLY SPICY, IT IS ALSO THE PERFECT SOUP TO PREPARE FOR A COLD WINTER'S DAY.

SERVES 4

INGREDIENTS

1½ pounds tomatoes
2 tablespoons vegetable oil
1 bay leaf
4 scallions, chopped
1 teaspoon salt
½ teaspoon crushed garlic
1 teaspoon crushed black
  peppercorns
2 tablespoons chopped fresh cilantro
3 cups water
1 tablespoon cornstarch
2 tablespoons light cream,
  to serve

2 In a medium pan, heat the oil and fry the chopped tomatoes, bay leaf and chopped scallions for a few minutes until soft and translucent, but not browned.

5 Remove the soup from the heat and press through a strainer over a bowl. Discard the strained vegetables.

1 To peel the tomatoes, plunge them into very hot water, then lift them out more or less right away using a slotted spoon. The skin should now peel off quickly and easily. Once this is done, chop the tomatoes roughly.

3 Gradually add the salt, garlic, peppercorns and fresh cilantro to the tomato mixture, finally adding the water.

4 Bring to the boil, lower the heat and simmer for 15–20 minutes. Meanwhile, dissolve the cornstarch in a little cold water, and set aside.

6 Return to the pan, add the cornstarch mixture and simmer over a gentle heat, stirring continuously, for about 3 minutes until thickened.

7 Pour into individual warmed soup bowls and serve piping hot, with a swirl of cream.

VARIATION
Instead of cream, add a dollop of plain yogurt or crème fraîche to the individual servings.

COOK'S TIP
The best tomatoes to use for this soup are ripe Italian plum tomatoes. If the only fresh tomatoes available are rather pale and under-ripe, add 1 tablespoon tomato paste to the pan with the chopped tomatoes. This will enhance the color and flavor of the soup.

Energy 63kcal/267kJ; Protein 2g; Carbohydrate 9.5g, of which sugars 6g; Fat 2.2g, of which saturates 1.1g; Cholesterol 4mg; Calcium 48mg; Fiber 2.5g; Sodium 24mg.

SPICY CARROT SOUP <u>WITH</u> GARLIC CROUTONS

CARROT SOUP IS GIVEN A HINT OF SPICE WITH CORIANDER, CUMIN AND CHILI POWDER. THE FINAL TOUCH COMES WITH A GARNISH OF GARLIC CROUTONS.

<u>SERVES 6</u>

INGREDIENTS
    1 tablespoon olive oil
    1 large onion, chopped
    1½ pounds/3¾ cups carrots, sliced
    1 teaspoon each ground coriander,
      ground cumin and hot chili powder
    3¾ cups vegetable stock
    salt and ground black pepper
    fresh cilantro, to garnish
For the garlic croutons
    a little olive oil
    2 garlic cloves, crushed
    4 slices bread, crusts removed, cut
      into ½-inch cubes

1 To make the soup, heat the oil in a large pan, add the onion and carrots and cook gently for 5 minutes, stirring occasionally. Add the ground spices and cook gently for 1 minute, continuing to stir.

2 Stir in the stock, bring to the boil, then cover and cook gently for about 45 minutes until the carrots are tender.

3 Meanwhile, make the garlic croutons. Heat the oil in a frying pan, add the garlic and cook for 30 seconds. Add the bread cubes, turn them over in the oil and fry until crisp and golden brown all over, turning frequently. Drain on paper towels and keep warm.

4 Puree the soup in a blender or food processor. Return it to the rinsed-out pan, season and reheat gently. Serve hot, sprinkled with garlic croutons and garnished with cilantro sprigs.

Energy 124kcal/517kJ; Protein 2.5g; Carbohydrate 19.7g, of which sugars 10.6g; Fat 4.4g, of which saturates 0.6g; Cholesterol 0mg; Calcium 55mg; Fiber 3.4g; Sodium 116mg.

ROASTED GARLIC AND BUTTERNUT SQUASH SOUP WITH TOMATO SALSA

THIS IS A WONDERFUL, RICHLY FLAVORED DISH. A SPOONFUL OF THE HOT AND SPICY TOMATO SALSA GIVES BITE TO THE SWEET-TASTING SQUASH AND GARLIC SOUP.

SERVES 4–5

INGREDIENTS

    2 garlic bulbs, outer skin removed
    5 tablespoons olive oil
    a few fresh thyme sprigs
    1 large butternut squash, halved
      and seeded
    2 onions, chopped
    1 teaspoon ground coriander
    5 cups vegetable or
      chicken stock
    2–3 tablespoons chopped fresh
      oregano or marjoram
    salt and ground black pepper
For the salsa
    4 large ripe tomatoes, halved
      and seeded
    1 red bell pepper, halved
      and seeded
    1 large fresh red chile, halved
      and seeded
    2–3 tablespoons extra virgin
      olive oil
    1 tablespoon balsamic vinegar
    pinch of superfine sugar

1 Preheat the oven to 425°F. Place the garlic bulbs on a piece of foil and pour over half the olive oil. Add the thyme sprigs, then fold the foil around the garlic bulbs to enclose them completely. Place the foil parcel on a baking sheet with the butternut squash and brush the squash with 1 tablespoon of the remaining olive oil. Add the tomatoes, red pepper and fresh chile for the salsa.

2 Roast the vegetables for 25 minutes, then remove the tomatoes, pepper and chilli. Reduce the temperature to 375°F and cook the squash and garlic for 20–25 minutes more, or until the squash is tender.

3 Heat the remaining oil in a large, heavy pan and cook the onions and ground coriander gently for about 10 minutes, or until softened.

4 Skin the pepper and chile and process in a food processor or blender with the tomatoes and 2 tablespoons olive oil. Stir in the vinegar and seasoning to taste, adding a pinch of superfine sugar. Add the remaining oil if you think the salsa needs it.

5 Squeeze the roasted garlic out of its papery skin into the onions and scoop the squash out of its skin, adding it to the pan. Add the stock, 1 teaspoon salt and plenty of black pepper. Bring to the boil and simmer for 10 minutes.

6 Stir in half the oregano or marjoram and cool the soup slightly, then process it in a blender or food processor. Alternatively, press the soup through a fine strainer.

7 Reheat the soup without allowing it to boil, then taste for seasoning before ladling it into warmed bowls. Top each with a spoonful of salsa and sprinkle over the remaining chopped oregano or marjoram. Serve immediately.

Energy 303kcal/1256kJ; Protein 4.2g; Carbohydrate 20.7g, of which sugars 16.6g; Fat 23.2g, of which saturates 3.5g; Cholesterol 0mg; Calcium 107mg; Fiber 5.7g; Sodium 15mg.

CURRIED CELERY SOUP

AN UNUSUAL BUT STIMULATING COMBINATION OF FLAVORS, THIS WARMING SOUP IS AN EXCELLENT WAY TO TRANSFORM CELERY. SERVE WITH WARM WHOLE-WHEAT BREAD ROLLS.

SERVES 4–6

INGREDIENTS

2 teaspoons olive oil
1 onion, chopped
1 leek, sliced
1½ pounds celery, chopped
1 tablespoon medium or hot
  curry powder
8 ounces unpeeled potatoes,
  washed and diced
3¾ cups vegetable stock
bouquet garni
2 tablespoons chopped fresh
  mixed herbs
salt
celery seeds and leaves,
  to garnish

1 Heat the oil in a large pan. Add the onion, leek and celery, cover and cook gently for about 10 minutes, stirring occasionally.

2 Add the curry powder and cook gently for 2 minutes, stirring from time to time to prevent it sticking to the pan.

3 Add the potatoes, stock and bouquet garni, cover and bring to the boil. Simmer for about 20 minutes, until the vegetables are tender but not too soft.

4 Remove and discard the bouquet garni and set the soup aside to cool slightly before it is processed.

COOK'S TIP
For a change, use celeriac and sweet potatoes for this soup in place of celery and standard potatoes.

5 Transfer the soup to a blender or food processor and process in batches until smooth.

6 Add the mixed herbs, season to taste with salt and process briefly again. Return to the pan and reheat gently until piping hot.

7 Ladle into bowls and garnish each one with a sprinkling of celery seeds and a few celery leaves before serving.

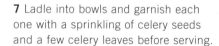

Energy 50kcal/212kJ; Protein 1.8g; Carbohydrate 8.7g, of which sugars 2.7g; Fat 1.2g, of which saturates 0.2g; Cholesterol 0mg; Calcium 58mg; Fiber 2.4g; Sodium 73mg.

YOGURT SOUP

MAKE THIS TRADITIONAL INDIAN SOUP AS HOT AS YOU LIKE BY ADDING MORE OR LESS SPICE. SOME COMMUNITIES IN INDIA ADD SUGAR.

SERVES 4–6

INGREDIENTS

scant 2 cups plain yogurt,
 beaten
1 ounce/¼ cup gram flour
½ teaspoon chili powder
½ teaspoon turmeric
2 or 3 fresh green chiles, chopped
4 tablespoons vegetable oil
1 whole dried red chile
1 teaspoon cumin seeds
3 or 4 curry leaves
3 garlic cloves, crushed
2-inch piece fresh ginger root,
 peeled and crushed
2 tablespoons chopped fresh cilantro
salt

1 Mix together the yogurt, flour, chili powder, turmeric and salt and strain into a pan.

2 Add the green chiles and cook gently for about 10 minutes, stirring occasionally. Be careful not to let the soup boil over.

3 Heat the oil in a frying pan and fry the remaining spices with the garlic and ginger until the dried chile turns black. Stir in 1 tablespoon of the cilantro.

4 Add the spices to the soup, cover and rest for 5 minutes. Reheat. Serve hot, garnished with the remaining cilantro.

Energy 125kcal/520kJ; Protein 4.5g; Carbohydrate 9.1g, of which sugars 5.9g; Fat 8.2g, of which saturates 1.2g; Cholesterol 1mg; Calcium 165mg; Fiber 0.6g; Sodium 65mg.

SPICY CHICKEN AND MUSHROOM SOUP

THIS CREAMY CHICKEN SOUP MAKES A HEARTY MEAL. SERVE IT PIPING HOT WITH FRESH GARLIC BREAD AND GARNISHED WITH CHOPPED CILANTRO.

SERVES 4

INGREDIENTS

3 ounces/6 tablespoons
  sweet butter
½ teaspoon crushed garlic
1 teaspoon garam masala
1 teaspoon crushed black
  peppercorns
1 teaspoon salt
¼ teaspoon freshly grated nutmeg
8 ounces chicken, skinned
  and boned
1 medium leek, sliced
3 ounces/generous 1 cup
  mushrooms, sliced
2 ounces/⅓ cup corn kernels
1¼ cups water
8 fluid ounces/1 cup light cream
2 tablespoons chopped
  fresh cilantro
1 teaspoon crushed dried red chili,
  to garnish (optional)

1 Melt the butter in a medium pan. Lower the heat slightly and add the garlic and garam masala. Lower the heat even further and add the black peppercorns, salt and nutmeg.

2 Cut the chicken pieces into very fine strips and add to the pan with the leek, mushrooms and corn. Cook for 5–7 minutes until the chicken is cooked through, stirring constantly.

COOK'S TIP
Any type of mushrooms may be used for this soup, for example portobello or white.

3 Remove the pan from the heat and allow to cool slightly.

4 Transfer three-quarters of the mixture into a food processor or blender. Add the water and process for about 1 minute.

5 Pour the paste back into the pan and bring to the boil over a medium heat. Lower the heat and stir in the cream.

6 Add the fresh cilantro. Taste and adjust the seasoning. Serve garnished with crushed red chili, if you like.

Energy 335kcal/1388kJ; Protein 17.1g; Carbohydrate 3.1g, of which sugars 2.7g; Fat 28.3g, of which saturates 17.6g; Cholesterol 114mg; Calcium 75mg; Fiber 1.4g; Sodium 310mg.

LIGHTLY SPICED TOMATO SOUP

SIMPLE AND QUICK TO MAKE, THIS TOMATO SOUP WILL SOON BECOME ONE OF YOUR FIRM FAVORITES.
SERVE SPRINKLED WITH PLENTY OF COARSELY GROUND BLACK PEPPER IF YOU LIKE IT REALLY SPICY.

SERVES 4

INGREDIENTS

1 tablespoon corn or peanut oil
1 onion, finely chopped
2 pounds tomatoes, peeled, seeded and chopped
16 fluid ounces/2 cups chicken stock
2 sprigs of fresh cilantro
salt
coarsely ground black pepper

1 Heat the oil in a large pan and fry the onion for about 5 minutes until it is soft and transparent but not brown.

2 Add the chopped tomatoes, chicken stock and cilantro to the pan. Bring to the boil, then lower the heat, cover the pan and simmer gently for 15 minutes or until the tomatoes are soft.

3 Remove and discard the cilantro. Press the soup through a strainer and return it to the clean pan. Season and heat through. Serve sprinkled with coarsely ground pepper.

Energy 71kcal/299kJ; Protein 2g; Carbohydrate 8.4g, of which sugars 8g; Fat 3.6g, of which saturates 0.6g; Cholesterol 0mg; Calcium 35mg; Fiber 2.8g; Sodium 23mg.

MUSHROOM, CELERY AND GARLIC SOUP

A ROBUST SOUP IN WHICH THE DOMINANT FLAVOR OF MUSHROOMS IS ENHANCED WITH GARLIC, WHILE CELERY INTRODUCES A CONTRASTING NOTE.

SERVES 4

INGREDIENTS

    12 ounces/4½ cups chopped
        mushrooms
    4 celery sticks, chopped
    3 garlic cloves
    3 tablespoons dry sherry or
        white wine
    3 cups chicken stock
    2 tablespoons Worcestershire sauce
    1 teaspoon freshly grated nutmeg
    salt and ground black pepper
    celery leaves, to garnish

1 Place the mushrooms, celery and garlic in a pan and stir in the sherry or wine. Cover and cook over a low heat for 30–40 minutes until the vegetables are tender.

COOK'S TIP
Any type of mushrooms may be used for this soup, for example portobello or white.

2 Add half the stock and puree in a food processor or blender until smooth. Return to the pan and add the remaining stock, the Worcestershire sauce and nutmeg.

3 Bring to the boil and season to taste with salt and pepper.

4 Ladle into warmed soup bowls and serve hot, garnished with celery leaves.

Energy 26kcal/109kJ; Protein 1.9g; Carbohydrate 1.9g, of which sugars 1.6g; Fat 0.5g, of which saturates 0.1g; Cholesterol 0mg; Calcium 33mg; Fiber 1.3g; Sodium 113mg.

HOT-AND-SOUR SHRIMP SOUP <u>WITH</u> LEMONGRASS

THIS CLASSIC SEAFOOD SOUP, KNOWN AS TOM YAM GOONG, IS PROBABLY THE MOST POPULAR AND BEST-KNOWN SOUP FROM THAILAND.

SERVES 4–6

INGREDIENTS
- 1 pound jumbo shrimp
- 4 cups chicken stock or water
- 3 lemongrass stalks
- 10 kaffir lime leaves, torn in half
- 1 can (8 ounces) straw mushrooms, drained
- 3 tablespoons Thai fish sauce
- 2 fluid ounces/¼ cup lime juice
- 2 tablespoons chopped scallion
- 1 tablespoon fresh cilantro leaves
- 4 fresh red chiles, seeded and chopped
- 2 scallions, finely chopped, to garnish

1 Shell and devein the shrimp and set aside. Rinse the shrimp shells, place in a large pan with the stock or water and bring to the boil.

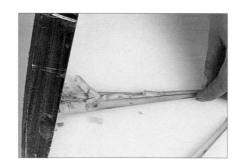

2 Bruise the lemongrass stalks with the blunt edge of a chopping knife and add them to the stock, together with half the lime leaves. Simmer gently for 5–6 minutes until the stalks change color.

3 Strain the stock, return to the pan and reheat. Add the mushrooms and shrimp, then cook until the shrimp turn pink.

4 Stir in the fish sauce, lime juice, scallon, cilantro, red chiles and the rest of the lime leaves. Taste and adjust the seasoning. The soup should be sour, salty, spicy and hot. Garnish with finely chopped scallions.

Energy 63kcal/268kJ; Protein 14g; Carbohydrate 0.4g, of which sugars 0.3g; Fat 0.7g, of which saturates 0.1g; Cholesterol 146mg; Calcium 64mg; Fiber 0.5g; Sodium 145mg.

PORK AND PICKLED MUSTARD GREENS SOUP

THIS HIGHLY FLAVORED SOUP MAKES AN INTERESTING START TO A MEAL. ADD MORE SLICED FRESH CHILES TO GARNISH IF YOU REALLY WANT TO PACK A PUNCH.

SERVES 4–6

INGREDIENTS

    8 ounces pickled mustard leaves,
      soaked
    2 ounces cellophane noodles, soaked
    1 tablespoon vegetable oil
    4 garlic cloves, finely sliced
    4 cups chicken stock
    1 pound pork ribs, cut into
      large chunks
    2 tablespoons Thai fish sauce
    a pinch of sugar
    ground black pepper
    2 fresh chiles, seeded and finely
      sliced, to garnish

1 Cut the pickled mustard leaves into bitesize pieces. Taste to check the seasoning. If they are too salty, soak them for a little longer.

2 Drain the cellophane noodles, discarding the soaking water, and cut them into pieces about 2 inches long.

COOK'S TIP
The color of Thai fish sauce can vary. Lighter sauces are considered to be better than darker vesions.

3 Heat the oil in a small frying pan, add the garlic and stir-fry until golden. Transfer to a bowl and set aside.

4 Pour the stock into a pan, bring to the boil, then add the pork ribs and simmer gently for 10–15 minutes.

5 Add the pickled mustard leaves and cellophane noodles. Bring back to the boil. Season to taste with Thai fish sauce, sugar and ground black pepper.

6 Garnish with the fried garlic and the red chiles and serve hot.

Energy 218kcal/910kJ; Protein 24.5g; Carbohydrate 7.8g, of which sugars 0.9g; Fat 9.7g, of which saturates 3g; Cholesterol 74mg; Calcium 90mg; Fiber 0.8g; Sodium 454mg.

SPICED PARSNIP SOUP

THIS PALE, CREAMY-TEXTURED SOUP IS GIVEN A SPECIAL TOUCH WITH AN AROMATIC, SPICED GARLIC AND CORIANDER GARNISH.

SERVES 4–6

INGREDIENTS

1½ ounces/3 tablespoons butter
1 onion, chopped
1½ pounds parsnips, diced
1 teaspoon ground coriander
½ teaspoon ground cumin
½ teaspoon ground turmeric
¼ teaspoon chilli powder
5 cups stock
⅔ cup light cream
1 tablespoon sunflower oil
1 garlic clove, cut into julienne strips
2 teaspoons yellow mustard seeds
salt and ground black pepper

1 Melt the butter in a large pan, add the chopped onion and parsnips and fry gently for about 3 minutes.

2 Stir in the spices and cook for 1 minute more.

3 Add the stock, season and bring to the boil. Reduce the heat, cover and simmer for 45 minutes, or until tender.

4 Cool slightly, then puree in a blender or food processor until smooth.

5 Return the soup to the pan, add the cream and heat through gently.

6 Heat the oil in a small pan, add the julienne strips of garlic and the yellow mustard seeds and fry quickly until the garlic is beginning to brown and the mustard seeds start to pop and splutter.

7 Ladle the soup into warmed soup bowls and pour a little of the spice mixture over each one. Serve hot.

Energy 191kcal/795kJ; Protein 3.1g; Carbohydrate 15.6g, of which sugars 7.6g; Fat 13.4g, of which saturates 7g; Cholesterol 28mg; Calcium 72mg; Fiber 5.4g; Sodium 59mg.

LEEK, PARSNIP <u>AND</u> GINGER SOUP

A FLAVORSOME WINTER WARMER, WITH THE ADDED SPICINESS OF FRESH GINGER. GARNISH WITH A SWIRL OF MASCARPONE AND A SPRINKLING OF PAPRIKA.

SERVES 4–6

INGREDIENTS

 2 tablespoons olive oil
 8 ounces/2 cups leeks, washed
  and sliced
 1 ounce fresh ginger root, peeled
  and finely chopped
 1½ pounds/5 cups parsnips,
  roughly chopped
 1¼ cups dry white wine
 5 cups vegetable stock
  or water
 salt and ground black pepper
 mascarpone and paprika,
  to garnish

1 Heat the oil in a large pan and add the leeks and ginger. Cook gently, stirring, for 2–3 minutes until the leeks start to soften.

2 Add the parsnips and cook for a further 7–8 minutes until they are beginning to soften.

VARIATION
Heavy cream, crème fraîche or plain yogurt may be used to garnish in place of mascarpone.

3 Pour in the wine and stock or water and bring to the boil. Reduce the heat and simmer for 20–30 minutes or until the parsnips are tender.

4 Puree in a blender or food processor until smooth. Season to taste. Reheat and garnish with a swirl of mascarpone and a light dusting of paprika.

Energy 146kcal/613kJ; Protein 2.7g; Carbohydrate 15.5g, of which sugars 7.5g; Fat 5.1g, of which saturates 0.8g; Cholesterol 0mg; Calcium 60mg; Fiber 6g; Sodium 14mg.

SPICY BEAN SOUP

A FILLING SOUP MADE WITH TWO KINDS OF BEANS FLAVORED WITH CUMIN. SERVE IT GARNISHED WITH A SWIRL OF SOUR CREAM AND CHOPPED FRESH CILANTRO.

SERVES 6–8

INGREDIENTS

6 ounces/1 cup dried black beans,
   soaked overnight and drained
6 ounces/1 cup dried kidney beans,
   soaked overnight and drained
2 bay leaves
6 tablespoons coarse salt
2 tablespoons olive or vegetable oil
3 carrots, chopped
1 onion, chopped
1 celery stick
1 garlic clove, crushed
1 teaspoon ground cumin
¼–½ teaspoon cayenne pepper
½ teaspoon dried oregano
2 fluid ounces/¼ cup red wine
5 cups beef stock
8 fluid ounces/1 cup water
salt and ground black pepper
For the garnish
   sour cream
   chopped fresh cilantro

1 Put the black beans and kidney beans in two separate pans with cold water to cover and a bay leaf in each. Boil rapidly for 10 minutes, then cover and simmer for 20 minutes.

2 Add 3 tablespoons coarse salt to each pan and continue simmering for a further 30 minutes until the beans are tender. Drain.

COOK'S TIP
Beans toughen with age, so, although they will keep for up to a year in a cool, dry place, it is best to buy small quantities from a store with a regular turnover.

3 Heat the oil in a large heavy pan or flameproof casserole. Add the carrots, onion, celery and garlic and cook over a low heat for 8–10 minutes, stirring, until softened.

4 Stir in the cumin, cayenne, oregano and salt to taste.

5 Add the wine, stock and water and stir to mix all the ingredients together. Remove the bay leaves from the cooked beans and add the beans to the casserole.

6 Bring to the boil, reduce the heat, then cover and simmer for about 20 minutes, stirring occasionally to prevent sticking to the base of the pan.

7 Transfer half the soup (including most of the solids) to a food processor or blender. Process until smooth. Return to the pan and stir to combine well.

8 Reheat the soup and adjust the seasoning. Serve hot, garnished with sour cream and chopped cilantro.

Energy 161kcal/681kJ; Protein 9.9g; Carbohydrate 23g, of which sugars 3g; Fat 3.5g, of which saturates 0.6g; Cholesterol 0mg; Calcium 47mg; Fiber 5.6g; Sodium 506mg.

CURRIED CARROT AND APPLE SOUP

THE COMBINATION OF CARROT, CURRY AND APPLE IS A HIGHLY SUCCESSFUL ONE. CURLS OF FRESH CARROT MAKE AN ATTRACTIVE GARNISH.

SERVES 4

INGREDIENTS

2 teaspoons sunflower oil
1 tablespoon mild Korma
  curry powder
1¼ pounds carrots, chopped
1 large onion, chopped
1 cooking apple, chopped
3 cups chicken stock
salt and ground black pepper
plain yogurt and carrot curls,
  to garnish

1 Heat the oil in a large, heavy pan and very gently fry the curry powder for 2–3 minutes.

2 Add the chopped carrots and onion and the cooking apple, stir well until coated with the curry powder, then cover the pan. Cook over a low heat for about 15 minutes, shaking the pan occasionally to prevent sticking to the base of the pan, until softened.

3 Spoon the vegetable mixture into a food processor or blender, then add half the stock and process until smooth.

4 Return to the pan and pour in the remaining stock. Bring the soup to the boil and adjust the seasoning before serving in bowls, garnished with a swirl of yogurt and a few curls of raw carrot.

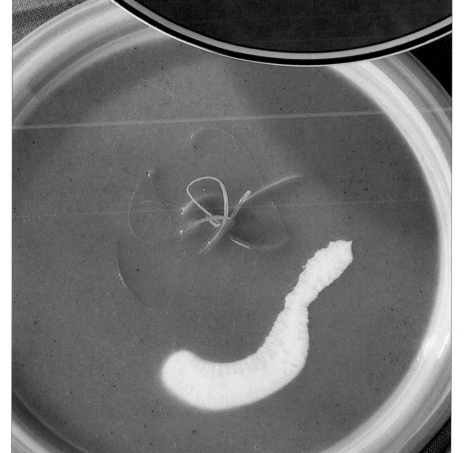

Energy 90kcal/376kJ; Protein 1.7g; Carbohydrate 17.3g, of which sugars 15g; Fat 2.1g, of which saturates 0.3g; Cholesterol 0mg; Calcium 51mg; Fiber 4.3g; Sodium 34mg.

SPICY PEANUT SOUP

A THICK AND WARMING VEGETABLE SOUP, EXCITINGLY FLAVORED WITH CHILI AND PEANUTS. ADD A
SPRINKLING OF ROUGHLY CHOPPED PEANUTS AS A CRUNCHY GARNISH.

SERVES 6

INGREDIENTS

2 tablespoons oil
1 large onion, finely chopped
2 garlic cloves, crushed
1 teaspoon mild chili powder
2 red bell peppers, seeded and
    finely chopped
8 ounces carrots, finely chopped
8 ounces potatoes, finely chopped
3 celery sticks, sliced
3¾ cups vegetable stock
6 tablespoons crunchy peanut butter
4 ounces/⅔ cup corn
salt and ground black pepper
roughly chopped unsalted roasted
    peanuts, to garnish

1 Heat the oil in a large pan and
cook the onion and garlic for about
3 minutes. Add the chili powder and
cook for a further 1 minute.

2 Add the red peppers, carrots, potatoes
and celery. Stir well, then cook for a
further 4 minutes, stirring occasionally.

3 Add the vegetable stock, followed by
the peanut butter and corn. Stir until
thoroughly combined.

4 Season well. Bring to the boil, cover
and simmer for about 20 minutes until
all the vegetables are tender. Serve
garnished with chopped peanuts.

Energy 211kcal/880kJ; Protein 6.3g; Carbohydrate 20.5g, of which sugars 12g; Fat 12.1g, of which saturates 2.5g; Cholesterol 0mg; Calcium 46mg; Fiber 4.4g; Sodium 298mg.

SOUTH INDIAN PEPPER WATER

THIS IS A HIGHLY SOOTHING BROTH FOR COLD WINTER EVENINGS. SERVE WITH THE WHOLE SPICES OR STRAIN AND REHEAT IF YOU WISH. THE LEMON JUICE CAN BE ADJUSTED TO TASTE.

SERVES 2–4

INGREDIENTS

2 tablespoons vegetable oil
½ teaspoon ground black pepper
1 teaspoon cumin seeds
½ teaspoon mustard seeds
¼ teaspoon asafetida powder
2 whole dried red chiles
4–6 curry leaves
½ teaspoon ground turmeric
2 garlic cloves, crushed
1¼ cups tomato juice
juice of 2 lemons
4 fluid ounces/½ cup water
salt
fresh cilantro leaves, chopped,
  to garnish

1 In a large frying pan, heat the vegetable oil and fry the spices and garlic until the chiles are nearly black and the garlic is a golden brown.

COOK'S TIP
Asafetida can smell unpleasant but this disappears when added to your cooking.

2 Lower the heat and add the tomato juice, lemon juice, water and salt to taste. Bring to the boil, then simmer for 10 minutes.

3 Ladle the soup into warmed bowls, garnish with chopped cilantro and serve piping hot.

Energy 63kcal/262kJ; Protein 0.7g; Carbohydrate 2.6g, of which sugars 2.3g; Fat 5.6g, of which saturates 0.7g; Cholesterol 0mg; Calcium 16mg; Fiber 0.8g; Sodium 178mg.

SPICED RED LENTIL SOUP
WITH COCONUT MILK

A SUBTLE BLEND OF SPICES TAKES THIS WARMING SOUP TO NEW HEIGHTS. SERVE IT WITH CRUSTY BREAD FOR A FILLING AND SATISFYING LUNCH.

SERVES 6

INGREDIENTS

2 onions, finely chopped
2 garlic cloves, crushed
4 tomatoes, roughly chopped
½ teaspoon ground turmeric
1 teaspoon ground cumin
6 cardamom pods
½ cinnamon stick
8 ounces/1 cup red lentils, rinsed
  and drained
3¾ cups water
1 can (14 ounces) coconut milk
1 tablespoon lime juice
salt and ground black pepper
cumin seeds, to garnish

COOK'S TIP
Unlike other legumes, lentils do not need soaking before being cooked.

1 Put the onions, garlic, tomatoes, turmeric, cumin, cardamom pods, cinnamon, lentils and water into a large pan. Bring to the boil, lower the heat, cover and simmer gently for 20 minutes or until the lentils are soft.

2 Remove the cardamom pods and cinnamon stick, then puree the mixture in a blender or food processor.

3 Press the soup through a strainer, then return to the clean pan.

4 Reserve a little of the coconut milk for the garnish and add the remainder to the pan with the lime juice. Stir well and season with salt and pepper. Reheat the soup gently without boiling. Swirl in the reserved coconut milk, garnish with cumin seeds and serve piping hot.

Energy 163kcal/694kJ; Protein 10.2g; Carbohydrate 30.4g, of which sugars 9g; Fat 1g, of which saturates 0.3g; Cholesterol 0mg; Calcium 56mg; Fiber 3.2g; Sodium 94mg.

SPICY ROASTED PUMPKIN SOUP
WITH PUMPKIN CHIPS

THE PUMPKIN IS ROASTED WHOLE, THEN SPLIT OPEN AND SCOOPED OUT TO MAKE THIS DELICIOUS SOUP; TOPPED WITH CRISP STRIPS OF FRIED PUMPKIN, IT IS A REAL TREAT.

SERVES 6–8

INGREDIENTS
3–3½ pounds pumpkin
6 tablespoons olive oil
2 onions, chopped
3 garlic cloves, chopped
3-inch piece fresh ginger
   root, grated
1 teaspoon ground coriander
½ teaspoon ground turmeric
pinch of cayenne pepper
4 cups vegetable stock
salt and ground black pepper
1 tablespoon sesame seeds
   and fresh cilantro leaves,
   to garnish
For the pumpkin chips
   wedge of fresh pumpkin, seeded
   4 fluid ounces/½ cup extra virgin
   olive oil

1 Preheat the oven to 400°F. Prick the pumpkin around the top several times with a fork. Brush the pumpkin with plenty of the oil and bake for 45 minutes or until tender. Leave until cool enough to handle.

2 Take care when cutting the pumpkin, as there may still be a lot of hot steam inside. When cool enough to handle, scoop out and discard the seeds. Scoop out and chop the flesh.

3 Heat 4 tablespoons of the remaining oil (you may not have to use all of it) in a large pan and add the onions, garlic and ginger, then cook gently for 4–5 minutes. Add the coriander, turmeric and cayenne, and cook for 2 minutes. Stir in the pumpkin flesh and stock. Bring to the boil, reduce the heat and simmer for 20 minutes.

COOK'S TIP
If only large pumpkins are available, cut off two or three large wedges weighing 3–3½ pounds in total. Brush with oil and roast for 20–30 minutes until tender.

4 Cool the soup slightly, then puree it in a food processor or blender until smooth. Return the soup to the rinsed pan and season well.

5 Meanwhile, prepare the pumpkin chips. Using a swivel-blade potato peeler, pare off long thin strips.

6 Heat the oil in a small pan and fry the strips in batches for 2–3 minutes, until crisp. Drain on paper towels.

7 Reheat the soup and ladle it into bowls. Top with the pumpkin chips and garnish each portion with sesame seeds and cilantro leaves.

Energy 271kcal/1119kJ; Protein 3.1g; Carbohydrate 11.1g, of which sugars 8.2g; Fat 24.1g, of which saturates 3.6g; Cholesterol 0mg; Calcium 110mg; Fiber 3.8g; Sodium 3mg.

CASTILIAN GARLIC SOUP

THIS RICH, DARK GARLIC SOUP COMES FROM LA MANCHA IN CENTRAL SPAIN, AND IS SIMILAR TO PORTUGUESE GARLIC SOUP. THE REGION IS FAMOUS FOR ITS SUMMER SUNSHINE, AND THE LOCAL SOUP HAS A STRONG TASTE TO MATCH THE CLIMATE.

SERVES 4

INGREDIENTS
    2 tablespoons olive oil
    4 large garlic cloves, peeled
    4 slices stale rustic bread
    4 tablespoons paprika
    4 cups beef stock
    ¼ teaspoon ground cumin
    4 farm-fresh eggs
    salt and ground black pepper
    chopped fresh parsley, to garnish

VARIATION
If you prefer, you can simply whisk the eggs into the hot soup.

1 Preheat the oven to 450°F. Heat the olive oil in a large pan. Add the whole peeled garlic cloves and cook until they are golden, then remove and set aside. Fry the slices of bread in the oil until golden, then set these aside.

2 Add 1 tablespoon of the paprika to the pan, and fry for a few seconds. Stir in the beef stock, cumin and remaining paprika, then add the reserved garlic, crushing the cloves with the back of a wooden spoon. Season to taste, then cook for about 5 minutes.

3 Break up the slices of fried bread into bitesize pieces and stir them into the soup. Ladle the soup into four ovenproof bowls. Carefully break an egg into each bowl of soup and place in the oven for about 3 minutes, until the eggs are set. Sprinkle the soup with chopped fresh parsley and serve immediately.

Energy 202kcal/843kJ; Protein 9.3g; Carbohydrate 15.3g, of which sugars 1.5g; Fat 12.2g, of which saturates 2.4g; Cholesterol 190mg; Calcium 69mg; Fiber 0.6g; Sodium 202mg.

THAI-STYLE LENTIL AND COCONUT SOUP

HOT, SPICY AND RICHLY FLAVORED, THIS SUBSTANTIAL SOUP IS ALMOST A MEAL IN ITSELF. IF YOU ARE REALLY HUNGRY, SERVE WITH CHUNKS OF WARM NAAN BREAD OR THICK SLICES OF TOAST.

SERVES 4

INGREDIENTS

2 tablespoons sunflower oil
2 red onions, finely chopped
1 Thai chile, seeded and finely sliced
2 garlic cloves, chopped
1-inch piece fresh lemongrass,
  outer layers removed and inside
  finely sliced
7 ounces/scant 1 cup red
  lentils, rinsed
1 teaspoon ground coriander
1 teaspoon paprika
14 fluid ounces/1⅔ cups
  coconut milk
juice of 1 lime
3 scallions, chopped
¾ ounce/scant 1 cup fresh cilantro,
  finely chopped
salt and freshly ground black pepper

1 Heat the oil in a large pan and add the onions, chile, garlic and lemon grass. Cook for 5 minutes or until the onions have softened but not browned, stirring occasionally.

COOK'S TIP
When using canned coconut milk, shake it before opening. This ensures that the layers of milk are well combined.

2 Add the lentils and spices. Pour in the coconut milk and 3¾ cups water, and stir. Bring to the boil, reduce the heat and simmer for 40–45 minutes, until the lentils are soft.

3 Pour in the lime juice and add the scallions and cilantro, reserving a little of each for the garnish. Season, ladle into bowls and garnish.

Energy 245kcal/1034kJ; Protein 12.9g; Carbohydrate 35.8g, of which sugars 8.1g; Fat 6.6g, of which saturates 1g; Cholesterol 0mg; Calcium 75mg; Fiber 3.2g; Sodium 131mg.

CREAMY
VEGETABLE SOUPS

A bowl of smooth and creamy vegetable soup served with some crusty bread makes an excellent light lunch at any time of year. Choose whichever vegetables are fresh and in season—tomatoes and herbs in the summer, pumpkins and squash for the autumn, leeks and root vegetables during the winter months. In this section you will find Simple Cream of Onion Soup and Parsnip Soup from Ireland alongside exotic dishes such as Creamy Heart of Palm Soup and Jerusalem Artichoke Soup.

CREAMY HEART OF PALM SOUP

THIS DELICATE SOUP HAS A LUXURIOUS, CREAMY, ALMOST VELVETY TEXTURE. THE SUBTLE YET DISTINCTIVE FLAVOR OF THE PALM HEARTS IS LIKE NO OTHER, ALTHOUGH IT IS MILDLY REMINISCENT OF ARTICHOKES AND ASPARAGUS. SERVE WITH FRESH BREAD FOR A SATISFYING LUNCH.

SERVES 4

INGREDIENTS

1 ounce/2 tablespoons butter
2 teaspoons olive oil
1 onion, finely chopped
1 large leek, finely sliced
1 tablespoon all-purpose flour
4 cups well-flavored chicken stock
12 ounces potatoes, peeled
  and cubed
2 cans (28 ounces) hearts of palm,
  drained and sliced
8 fluid ounces/1 cup heavy cream
salt and ground black pepper
cayenne pepper and chopped fresh
  chives, to garnish

1 Heat the butter and oil in a large pan over a low heat. Add the onion and leek and stir well until coated in butter. Cover and cook for 5 minutes until softened and translucent.

2 Sprinkle over the flour. Cook, stirring, for 1 minute.

3 Pour in the stock and add the potatoes. Bring to the boil, then lower the heat and simmer for 10 minutes. Stir in the hearts of palm and the cream, and simmer gently for 10 minutes.

4 Process in a blender or food processor until smooth. Return the soup to the pan and heat gently, adding a little water if necessary. The consistency should be thick but not too heavy. Season with salt and ground black pepper.

5 Ladle the soup into heated bowls and garnish each with a pinch of cayenne pepper and a scattering of fresh chives. Serve immediately.

VARIATION
For a richer, buttery flavor, add the flesh of a ripe avocado when blending.

Energy 486kcal/2016kJ; Protein 4.9g; Carbohydrate 25.9g, of which sugars 3g; Fat 41.1g, of which saturates 24.4g; Cholesterol 99mg; Calcium 127mg; Fiber 3.7g; Sodium 97mg.

PARSNIP SOUP

THIS LIGHTLY SPICED SOUP HAS BECOME VERY POPULAR IN IRELAND IN RECENT YEARS, AND MANY VARIATIONS ABOUND, INCLUDING THIS TRADITIONAL IRISH COMBINATION WHERE PARSNIP AND APPLE ARE USED IN EQUAL PROPORTIONS.

SERVES 6

INGREDIENTS
2 pounds parsnips
2 ounces/¼ cup butter
1 onion, chopped
2 garlic cloves, crushed
2 teaspoons ground cumin
1 teaspoon ground coriander
about 5 cups hot chicken stock
⅔ cup light cream
salt and ground black pepper
chopped fresh chives or parsley
 and/or croutons, to garnish

COOK'S TIP
Parsnips taste best after the first frost, as the cold converts their starches into sugar, enhancing their sweetness.

1 Peel and thinly slice the parsnips. Heat the butter in a large heavy pan and add the peeled parsnips and chopped onion with the crushed garlic. Cook until softened but not colored, stirring occasionally. Add the ground cumin and ground coriander to the vegetable mixture and cook, stirring, for 1–2 minutes, and then gradually blend in the hot chicken stock and mix well.

2 Cover and simmer for about 20 minutes, or until the parsnip is soft. Puree the soup, adjust the texture with extra stock or water if it seems too thick, and check the seasoning. Add the cream and reheat without boiling.

3 Serve immediately, sprinkled with chopped chives or parsley and/or croutons, to garnish.

Energy 215kcal/899kJ; Protein 3.9g; Carbohydrate 21.3g, of which sugars 10.6g; Fat 13.3g, of which saturates 7.7g; Cholesterol 32mg; Calcium 92mg; Fiber 7.3g; Sodium 74mg.

CREAM OF MUSHROOM SOUP WITH GOAT CHEESE CROSTINI

CLASSIC CREAM OF MUSHROOM SOUP IS STILL A FIRM FAVORITE, ESPECIALLY WITH THE ADDITION OF LUXURIOUSLY CRISP AND GARLICKY CROUTES.

SERVES 6

INGREDIENTS

1 ounce/2 tablespoons butter
1 onion, peeled and chopped
1 garlic clove, peeled and
   chopped
1 pound/6 cups white or cremini
   mushrooms, roughly chopped
1 tablespoon all-purpose flour
3 tablespoons dry sherry
3¾ cups vegetable stock
⅔ cup heavy cream
salt and ground black pepper
fresh chervil sprigs,
   to garnish

For the crostini
1 tablespoon olive oil, plus extra
   for brushing
1 shallot, chopped
4 ounces/1½ cups white mushrooms,
   finely chopped
1 tablespoon chopped
   fresh parsley
6 cremini mushrooms
6 slices baguette
1 small garlic clove
4 ounces/1 cup soft goat cheese

1 Melt the butter in a pan and cook the onion and garlic for 5 minutes. Stir in the mushrooms, cover and cook for 10 minutes, stirring occasionally.

2 Stir in the flour and cook for 1 minute. Stir in the sherry and stock and bring to the boil, then simmer for 15 minutes. Cool slightly, then puree the soup in a food processor or blender until smooth.

3 Meanwhile, prepare the crostini. Heat the oil in a small pan. Add the shallot and mushrooms, and cook for 8–10 minutes, until softened. Drain well and transfer to a food processor. Add the parsley and process until finely chopped.

4 Preheat the broiler. Brush the cremini mushrooms with oil and cook for 5–6 minutes.

5 Toast the slices of baguette, rub with the garlic and put a spoonful of cheese on each. Top the broiled mushrooms with the mushroom mixture and place on the crostini.

6 Return the soup to the pan and stir in the cream. Season, then reheat gently. Ladle the soup into six bowls. Float a crostini in the center of each and garnish with chervil.

Energy 313kcal/1305kJ; Protein 6.2g; Carbohydrate 26.8g, of which sugars 2.5g; Fat 20g, of which saturates 11g; Cholesterol 43mg; Calcium 75mg; Fiber 2.2g; Sodium 283mg.

ASPARAGUS AND PEA SOUP WITH PARMESAN CHEESE

THIS BRIGHT AND TASTY SOUP USES EVERY INCH OF THE ASPARAGUS, INCLUDING THE WOODY ENDS, WHICH ARE USED FOR MAKING THE STOCK.

SERVES 6

INGREDIENTS

    12 ounces asparagus
    2 leeks
    1 bay leaf
    1 carrot, roughly chopped
    1 celery stick, chopped
    few stalks of fresh parsley
    7½ cups cold water
    1 ounce/2 tablespoons butter
    5 ounces fresh garden peas
    1 tablespoon chopped
       fresh parsley
    4 fluid ounces/½ cup
       heavy cream
    grated rind of ½ lemon
    salt and ground black pepper
    shavings of Parmesan cheese,
       to serve

1 Cut the woody ends from the asparagus, then set the spears aside. Roughly chop the woody ends and place them in a large pan. Cut off and chop the green parts of the leeks and add to the asparagus stalks with the bay leaf, carrot, celery, parsley stalks and the cold water. Bring to the boil and simmer for 30 minutes. Strain the stock and discard the vegetables.

2 Cut the tips off the asparagus and set aside, then cut the stems into short pieces. Chop the remainder of the leeks.

3 Melt the butter in a large pan and add the leeks. Cook for 3–4 minutes until softened, then add the asparagus stems, peas and chopped parsley. Pour in 5 cups of the asparagus stock. Bring to the boil, reduce the heat and cook for 6–8 minutes, until all the vegetables are tender. Season well with salt and pepper.

4 Cool the soup slightly, then puree it in a food processor or blender until smooth. Press the puree through a very fine strainer into the rinsed pan. Stir in the cream and lemon rind.

5 Bring a small pan of water to the boil and cook the asparagus tips for about 2–3 minutes until just tender. Drain and refresh under cold water. Reheat the soup, but do not allow it to boil.

6 Ladle the soup into six warmed bowls and garnish with the asparagus tips. Serve immediately, with shavings of Parmesan cheese and plenty of ground black pepper.

VARIATION

For a lighter soup, you could replace the cream with lowfat milk, but the finished dish will not taste as rich.

Energy 221kcal/912kJ; Protein 8.1g; Carbohydrate 7.1g, of which sugars 4.3g; Fat 18g, of which saturates 10.8g; Cholesterol 45mg; Calcium 151mg; Fiber 3.8g; Sodium 129mg.

SIMPLE CREAM OF ONION SOUP

THIS WONDERFULLY SOOTHING SOUP HAS A DEEP, BUTTERY FLAVOR THAT IS COMPLEMENTED BY CRISP CROUTONS OR CHOPPED CHIVES, SPRINKLED OVER JUST BEFORE SERVING.

SERVES 4

INGREDIENTS
    4 ounces/½ cup sweet butter
    2¼ pounds yellow onions, sliced
    1 fresh bay leaf
    7 tablespoons dry white vermouth
    4 cups good chicken or vegetable
      stock
    ⅔ cup heavy cream
    a little lemon juice (optional)
    salt and ground black pepper
    croutons or chopped fresh chives,
      to garnish

COOK'S TIP
Adding the second batch of onions gives texture and a buttery flavor to this soup. Make sure they do not brown.

1 Melt 3 ounces/6 tablespoons of the butter in a large heavy pan. Set about 7 ounces of the onions aside and add the rest to the pan with the bay leaf. Stir to coat in the butter, then cover and cook very gently for about 30 minutes. The onions should be very soft and tender, but not browned.

2 Add the vermouth, increase the heat and boil rapidly until the liquid has evaporated. Add the stock, 1 teaspoon salt and pepper to taste. Bring to the boil, lower the heat and simmer for 5 minutes, then remove from the heat.

3 Leave to cool, then discard the bay leaf and process the soup in a blender or food processor. Return the soup to the rinsed pan.

4 Meanwhile, melt the remaining butter in another pan and cook the remaining onions slowly, covered, until soft but not browned. Uncover and continue to cook gently until golden yellow.

5 Add the cream to the soup and reheat it gently until hot, but do not allow it to boil. Taste and adjust the seasoning, adding a little lemon juice if liked. Add the buttery onions and stir for 1–2 minutes, then ladle the soup into bowls. Sprinkle with croutons or chopped chives and serve.

CREAM OF CAULIFLOWER SOUP

THIS SOUP IS LIGHT IN FLAVOR YET SATISFYING ENOUGH FOR A LUNCHTIME SNACK.
YOU CAN TRY GREEN CAULIFLOWER FOR A COLORFUL CHANGE.

SERVES 6

INGREDIENTS
    2 tablespoons olive oil
    2 large onions, finely diced
    1 garlic clove, crushed
    3 large floury potatoes,
      finely diced
    3 celery sticks, finely diced
    7½ cups stock
    2 carrots, finely diced
    1 medium cauliflower, chopped
    1 tablespoon chopped fresh dill
    1 tablespoon lemon juice
    1 teaspoon mustard powder
    ¼ teaspoon caraway seeds
    1¼ cups light cream
    salt and ground black pepper
    shredded scallions

3 Add the cauliflower, fresh dill, lemon juice, mustard powder and caraway seeds to the pan and simmer gently for 20 minutes, until the vegetables are just tender.

4 Process the soup in a blender or food processor until smooth, return to the pan and stir in the cream. Season to taste and serve garnished with shredded scallions.

1 Heat the oil in a large pan, add the onions and garlic and fry them for a few minutes until they soften. Add the potatoes, celery and stock and simmer for 10 minutes.

2 Add the carrots and simmer for a further 10 minutes.

Energy 258kcal/1075kJ; Protein 6.9g; Carbohydrate 26.9g, of which sugars 9.8g; Fat 14.4g, of which saturates 6.9g; Cholesterol 28mg; Calcium 95mg; Fiber 3.8g; Sodium 46mg.

CAULIFLOWER AND WALNUT CREAM

EVEN THOUGH THERE'S NO CREAM ADDED TO THIS SOUP, THE CAULIFLOWER GIVES IT A DELICIOUS, RICH, CREAMY TEXTURE, FOR PLEASURE WITHOUT THE CALORIES.

SERVES 4

INGREDIENTS

1 medium cauliflower
1 medium onion, roughly chopped
scant 2 cups chicken or vegetable
  stock
scant 2 cups skimmed milk
3 tablespoons walnut pieces
salt and ground black pepper
paprika and chopped walnuts,
  to garnish

VARIATION

If you prefer, you can make this soup using broccoli instead of cauliflower.

1 Trim the cauliflower of outer leaves and break into small florets. Place the cauliflower, onion and stock in a pan.

2 Bring to the boil, cover and simmer for about 15 minutes until soft. Add the milk and walnut pieces, then puree in a blender or food processor until smooth.

3 Season the soup to taste with salt and black pepper, then reheat and bring to the boil.

4 Serve sprinkled with a dusting of paprika and chopped walnuts.

Energy 175kcal/727kJ; Protein 10g; Carbohydrate 14.3g, of which sugars 12g; Fat 9.1g, of which saturates 1g; Cholesterol 4mg; Calcium 188mg; Fiber 3.3g; Sodium 62mg.

BROCCOLI <u>AND</u> ALMOND SOUP

THE CREAMINESS OF THE TOASTED ALMONDS COMBINES PERFECTLY WITH THE SLIGHTLY BITTER TASTE OF THE BROCCOLI IN THIS APPETIZING SOUP.

SERVES 4–6

INGREDIENTS

    2 ounces/½ cup ground almonds
    1½ pounds broccoli
    3¾ cups vegetable stock
     or water
    1¼ cups skimmed milk
  salt and ground black pepper

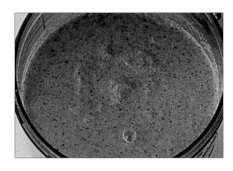

3 Place the remaining toasted almonds, broccoli, stock or water and milk in a blender and blend until smooth.

4 Season to taste with salt and pepper. Reheat and serve sprinkled with the reserved toasted almonds.

1 Preheat the oven to 350°F. Spread the ground almonds evenly on a baking sheet and toast in the oven for about 10 minutes until golden. Reserve one quarter of the almonds and set aside to garnish the finished dish.

2 Cut the broccoli into small florets and steam for about 6–7 minutes until just tender.

COOK'S TIP
Make sure that you choose broccoli that has bright, compact florets. Yellowing florets, a limp woody stalk and a pungent smell are an indication of over-maturity and loss of flavor.

Energy 104kcal/435kJ; Protein 8.4g; Carbohydrate 4.8g, of which sugars 4.2g; Fat 5.8g, of which saturates 0.7g; Cholesterol 2mg; Calcium 144mg; Fiber 3.6g; Sodium 32mg.

Jerusalem Artichoke Soup

TOPPED WITH SAFFRON CREAM, THIS DELICIOUS SOUP IS WONDERFUL ON A CHILLY DAY.
THE SAFFRON GIVES IT AN ATTRACTIVE COLOR.

SERVES 4

INGREDIENTS
    2 ounces/4 tablespoons butter
    1 onion, peeled and
      chopped
    1 pound Jerusalem artichokes,
      peeled and cut into chunks
    3¾ cups chicken stock
    ⅔ cup milk
    ⅔ cup heavy cream
    a good pinch of saffron powder
    salt and ground black pepper
    chopped fresh chives,
      to garnish

1 Melt the butter in a large, heavy pan and cook the onion for 5–8 minutes until soft but not browned, stirring from time to time.

2 Add the Jerusalem artichokes to the pan and stir until coated in the butter. Cover and cook gently for 10–15 minutes, being careful not to allow the artichokes to brown. Pour in the chicken stock and milk, then cover and simmer for 15 minutes. Cool slightly, then process in a blender or food processor until smooth.

3 Strain the soup back into the pan. Add half the cream, season to taste and reheat gently. Lightly whip the remaining cream and the saffron powder. Ladle the soup into warmed soup bowls and put a spoonful of saffron cream in the center of each. Sprinkle the chopped chives over the top and serve at once.

Energy 310kcal/1277kJ; Protein 2.7g; Carbohydrate 4.7g, of which sugars 4.3g; Fat 31.3g, of which saturates 19.4g; Cholesterol 80mg; Calcium 116mg; Fiber 1.5g; Sodium 168mg.

FRESH PEA SOUP ST. GERMAIN

THIS SOUP TAKES ITS NAME FROM A SUBURB OF PARIS WHERE PEAS WERE CULTIVATED IN MARKET GARDENS. SERVE IT IN EARLY SUMMER, WHEN FRESH PEAS ARE AT THEIR BEST.

SERVES 2–3

INGREDIENTS

a small pat of butter
2 or 3 shallots, finely chopped
14 ounces/3 cups shelled fresh
  peas (from about 3 pounds
  garden peas)
17 fluid ounces/2¼ cups water
3–4 tablespoons whipping cream
  (optional)
salt and ground black pepper
croutons, to garnish

1 Melt the butter in a heavy pan or flameproof casserole. Add the shallots and cook for about 3 minutes, stirring them occasionally.

2 Add the peas and water and season with salt and a little pepper. Cover and simmer for about 12 minutes for young peas and up to 18 minutes for large or older peas, stirring occasionally.

COOK'S TIP
If fresh peas are not available, use frozen peas, but thaw and rinse them before use.

3 When the peas are tender, ladle them into a food processor or blender with a little of the cooking liquid and process until smooth.

4 Strain the soup into the pan or casserole, stir in the cream, if using, and heat through without boiling. Add the seasoning and serve hot, garnished with croutons.

Energy 143kcal/591kJ; Protein 9.5g; Carbohydrate 16.7g, of which sugars 4.2g; Fat 4.8g, of which saturates 2.1g; Cholesterol 7mg; Calcium 34mg; Fiber 6.5g; Sodium 22mg.

CREAM OF RED PEPPER SOUP

GRILLING PEPPERS GIVES THEM A SWEET, SMOKY FLAVOR, WHICH IS DELICIOUS IN SALADS OR, AS HERE, IN A VELVETY SOUP WITH A SECRET FLAVORING OF ROSEMARY TO ADD AROMATIC DEPTH.

SERVES 4

INGREDIENTS
  4 bell peppers
  1 ounce/2 tablespoons butter
  1 onion, finely chopped
  1 sprig of fresh rosemary
  5 cups chicken or light vegetable
    stock
  3 tablespoons tomato paste
  4 fluid ounces/½ cup heavy cream
  paprika
  salt and ground black pepper

1 Preheat the broiler. Line the broiler pan with foil. Put the peppers in the pan under the broiler and turn them regularly until the skins have blackened all around.

2 Put the peppers into plastic bags, sealing them tightly, and leave them for 20 minutes.

3 Peel off the blackened skins. Avoid rinsing them under the tap, as this removes some of the natural oil and flavor.

4 Halve the peppers, removing the seeds, stalks and pith, then roughly chop the flesh.

5 Melt the butter in a deep pan. Add the onion and rosemary and cook gently over a low heat for about 5 minutes. Remove the rosemary and discard.

6 Add the peppers and stock to the onion, bring to the boil and simmer for 15 minutes. Stir in the tomato paste, then process or strain the soup to a smooth paste.

7 Stir in half the cream and season with paprika, salt, if necessary, and pepper.

8 Serve the soup hot or chilled, with the remaining cream swirled delicately on top. Speckle the cream very lightly with a pinch of paprika.

Energy 265kcal/1097kJ; Protein 3g; Carbohydrate 14.5g, of which sugars 13.7g; Fat 22g, of which saturates 13.5g; Cholesterol 54mg; Calcium 38mg; Fiber 3.3g; Sodium 79mg.

CREAMY TOMATO SOUP

TOMATO SOUP IS AN OLD FAVORITE. THIS VERSION IS MADE SPECIAL BY THE ADDITION OF FRESH HERBS AND CREAM.

SERVES 4

INGREDIENTS

1 ounce/2 tablespoons butter
  or margarine
1 onion, chopped
2 pounds tomatoes, peeled
  and quartered
2 carrots, chopped
scant 2 cups chicken stock
2 tablespoons chopped fresh parsley
½ teaspoon fresh thyme leaves,
  plus extra to garnish
5 tablespoons whipping cream
  (optional)
salt and ground black pepper

COOK'S TIP
Meaty and flavorful, ripe Italian plum tomatoes are the best choice for making this soup.

1 Melt the butter or margarine in a large pan. Add the onion and cook for 5 minutes until softened.

2 Stir in the tomatoes, chopped carrots, chicken stock, parsley and thyme. Bring to the boil. Reduce the heat to low, cover the pan, and simmer gently for 15–20 minutes until the vegetables are tender.

3 Puree the soup in a vegetable mill until it is smooth. Return the pureed soup to the pan.

4 Stir in the cream, if using, and reheat gently. Season the soup to taste with salt and freshly ground black pepper. Ladle into warmed soup bowls and serve piping hot, garnished with fresh thyme leaves.

Energy 107kcal/447kJ; Protein 2.3g; Carbohydrate 11.4g, of which sugars 10.9g; Fat 6.1g, of which saturates 3.5g; Cholesterol 13mg; Calcium 50mg; Fiber 3.9g; Sodium 71mg.

CREAM OF SCALLION SOUP

THE ONIONY FLAVOR OF THIS SOUP IS SURPRISINGLY DELICATE, AND RELIES ON THE USE OF A GOOD-QUALITY STOCK. IT IS EQUALLY DELICIOUS SERVED HOT OR COLD.

3 Add the potatoes and the stock. Bring to the boil, then cover again and simmer over moderately low heat for about 30 minutes. Cool slightly.

4 Puree the soup in a blender or food processor.

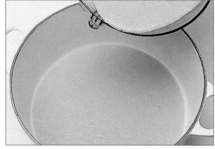

5 If serving the soup hot, pour it back into the pan. Add the cream and season with salt and pepper. Reheat gently, stirring occasionally. Add the lemon juice.

SERVES 4–6

INGREDIENTS

1 ounce/2 tablespoons butter
1 small onion, chopped
5 ounces/1¾ cups scallions, chopped
8 ounces potatoes, peeled
  and chopped
2½ cups vegetable stock
12 fluid ounces/1½ cups
  light cream
2 tablespoons lemon juice
salt and ground white pepper
chopped scallion greens or
  fresh chives, to garnish

1 Melt the butter in a large pan and add all the onions. Stir to coat with the melted butter.

2 Cover and cook over very low heat for about 10 minutes or until softened.

6 If serving the soup cold, pour it into a bowl. Stir in the cream and lemon juice and season with salt and pepper. Cover the bowl and chill for at least 1 hour. Sprinkle with the chopped scallion greens or chives before serving.

Energy 179kcal/744kJ; Protein 3.2g; Carbohydrate 8.9g, of which sugars 3.1g; Fat 14.8g, of which saturates 9.3g; Cholesterol 41mg; Calcium 67mg; Fiber 0.9g; Sodium 48mg.

CREAM OF MUSHROOM SOUP

A GOOD MUSHROOM SOUP MAKES THE MOST OF THE SUBTLE AND SOMETIMES RATHER ELUSIVE FLAVOR OF MUSHROOMS. WHITE MUSHROOMS ARE USED HERE FOR THEIR PALE COLOR.

SERVES 4

INGREDIENTS
10 ounces white mushrooms
1 tablespoon sunflower oil
1½ ounces/3 tablespoons butter
1 small onion, peeled and finely chopped
1 tablespoon all-purpose flour
scant 2 cups vegetable stock
scant 2 cups milk
a pinch of dried basil
2–3 tablespoons light cream (optional)
salt and ground black pepper
fresh basil leaves, to garnish

1 Separate the mushroom caps from the stalks. Finely slice the caps and finely chop the stalks.

2 Heat the oil and half the butter in a heavy pan. Add the onion, mushroom stalks and about three-quarters of the mushroom caps. Fry for about 1–2 minutes, stirring frequently, then cover and sweat over gentle heat for 6–7 minutes, stirring from time to time.

3 Stir in the flour and cook for about 1 minute. Gradually add the stock and milk, to make a smooth, thin sauce. Add the dried basil, and season to taste. Bring to the boil and simmer, partly covered, for 15 minutes.

VARIATION
Cremini or portobello mushrooms may be used instead of white mushrooms. They give a fuller flavor but turn the soup brown.

4 Pour into a food processor or blender and process until smooth.

5 Melt the rest of the butter in a frying pan and fry the remaining mushroom caps gently for 3–4 minutes until they are just tender.

6 Pour the soup into a clean pan and stir in the fried mushrooms. Heat until very hot and adjust the seasoning. Add the cream, if using.

7 Sprinkle with fresh basil leaves and serve hot.

Energy 178kcal/742kJ; Protein 5.7g; Carbohydrate 9.7g, of which sugars 6.4g; Fat 13.3g, of which saturates 6.8g; Cholesterol 28mg; Calcium 150mg; Fiber 1.1g; Sodium 113mg.

CREAMY CORN SOUP

THIS MEXICAN-STYLE SOUP IS SIMPLE TO PREPARE YET FULL OF FLAVOR. IT IS SOMETIMES MADE WITH SOUR CREAM AND CREAM CHEESE.

SERVES 4

INGREDIENTS
    2 tablespoons corn oil
    1 onion, finely chopped
    1 red bell pepper, seeded
      and chopped, plus ½, seeded and
      finely diced, to garnish
    1 pound/2⅔ cups corn kernels,
      thawed if frozen
    3 cups chicken stock
    8 fluid ounches/1 cup light cream
    salt and ground black pepper

VARIATION
Poblano chiles may be added to this soup, but these are rather difficult to locate outside Mexico.

1 Heat the oil in a frying pan and sauté the onion and red pepper for about 5 minutes, until soft. Add the corn and sauté for 2 minutes.

2 Carefully transfer the contents of the pan to a food processor or blender. Process until smooth, scraping down the sides of the blender and adding a little of the stock, if necessary.

3 Transfer the mixture to a pan and stir in the stock. Season to taste with salt and pepper, bring to a simmer and cook for 5 minutes.

4 Gently stir in the cream. Serve the soup hot or chilled, sprinkled with the diced red pepper. If serving hot, reheat gently after adding the cream, but do not allow the soup to boil.

Energy 327kcal/1367kJ; Protein 6g; Carbohydrate 35.3g, of which sugars 15.7g; Fat 19g, of which saturates 8.7g; Cholesterol 34mg; Calcium 68mg; Fiber 2.5g; Sodium 324mg.

CREAM ₒF AVOCADO SOUP

AVOCADOS MAKE WONDERFUL SOUP—PRETTY, DELICIOUS AND REFRESHING. THIS SOUP TASTES JUST AS GOOD SERVED CHILLED AS IT DOES HOT.

SERVES 4

INGREDIENTS
2 large ripe avocados
4 cups chicken stock
8 fluid ounces/1 cup light cream
salt and ground white pepper
1 tablespoon finely chopped fresh
   cilantro, to garnish (optional)

COOK'S TIP
It is important to choose really ripe avocadoes for this soup. To test whether an avocado is ripe, gently press the stalk end with your thumb and forefinger to see if it is soft.

1 Cut the avocados in half, remove the pits and mash the flesh.

2 Put the flesh into a strainer and press it through with a wooden spoon into a warm soup bowl.

3 Heat the chicken stock with the cream in a pan.

4 When the mixture is hot, but not boiling, whisk it into the pureed avocado in the bowl.

5 Season to taste with salt and pepper. Serve immediately, sprinkled with chopped fresh cilantro, if you like.

Energy 263kcal/1087kJ; Protein 3.5g; Carbohydrate 2.8g, of which sugars 1.8g; Fat 26.4g, of which saturates 10.7g; Cholesterol 34mg; Calcium 64mg; Fiber 2.6g; Sodium 23mg.

BUTTERNUT SQUASH BISQUE

THIS IS A FRAGRANT, CREAMY AND DELICATELY FLAVORED SOUP WITH A WONDERFUL COLOR.
SUBSTITUTE VEGETABLE STOCK IF YOU ARE CATERING FOR VEGETARIANS.

SERVES 4

INGREDIENTS
  1 ounce/2 tablespoons butter
    or margarine
  2 small onions, finely chopped
  1 pound butternut squash, peeled,
    seeded and cubed
  5 cups chicken stock
  8 ounces potatoes, cubed
  1 teaspoon paprika
  4 fluid ounces/½ cup whipping cream
    (optional)
  1½ tablespoons chopped fresh
    chives, plus a few whole chives
    to garnish
salt and ground black pepper

1 Melt the butter or margarine in a large pan. Add the onions and cook for about 5 minutes until soft.

2 Add the squash, stock, potatoes and paprika. Bring to the boil. Reduce the heat to low, cover the pan and simmer for about 35 minutes until all the vegetables are soft.

3 Pour the soup into a food processor or blender and process until smooth. Return the soup to the pan.

4 Stir in the cream, if using. Season with salt and pepper and reheat gently. Stir in the chopped chives just before serving. Garnish each serving with a few whole chives.

Energy 106kcal/443kJ; Protein 2g; Carbohydrate 12.8g, of which sugars 3.5g; Fat 5.6g, of which saturates 3.4g; Cholesterol 13mg; Calcium 41mg; Fiber 1.9g; Sodium 45mg.

PEAR <u>AND</u> WATERCRESS SOUP

THIS UNUSUAL SOUP COMBINES SWEET PEARS WITH SLIGHTLY SHARP WATERCRESS. A MORE TRADITIONAL PARTNER, STILTON CHEESE, APPEARS IN THE FORM OF CRISP CROUTONS.

SERVES 6

INGREDIENTS
   1 bunch of watercress
   4 medium pears, sliced
   3¾ cups chicken stock, preferably
      homemade
   4 fluid ounces/½ cup heavy cream
   juice of 1 lime
   salt and ground black pepper
For the Stilton croutons
   1 ounce/2 tablespoons butter
   1 tablespoon olive oil
   7 ounces/3 cups cubed stale bread
   4 ounces/1 cup Stilton cheese,
      chopped

1 Place two-thirds of the watercress leaves and all the stalks in a pan with the pears, stock and a little seasoning. Simmer for about 15–20 minutes.

2 Reserving some of the watercress leaves for the garnish, add the rest to the soup and immediately blend in a food processor until smooth.

3 Put the mixture into a bowl and stir in the cream and the lime juice to mix the flavors thoroughly. Season again with salt and pepper to taste.

4 Pour the soup back into the pan and reheat, stirring gently, until warmed through but not boiling.

5 To make the Stilton croutons, melt the butter and oil and fry the cubes of bread until golden brown. Drain on paper towels. Sprinkle the cheese on top and heat under a hot broiler until bubbling.

6 Pour the soup into warmed bowls. Divide the Stilton croutons and reserved watercress among the bowls and serve piping hot.

Energy 351kcal/1463kJ; Protein 9g; Carbohydrate 27g, of which sugars 11.4g; Fat 23.6g, of which saturates 13.6g; Cholesterol 55mg; Calcium 177mg; Fiber 3.2g; Sodium 373mg.

CREAMY BEET SOUP

A SIMPLY STUNNING COLOR, THIS DELICIOUSLY CREAMY BEET SOUP IS THE PERFECT DISH TO SERVE WHEN YOU WANT TO OFFER SOMETHING A LITTLE DIFFERENT.

SERVES 6

INGREDIENTS
  1 onion, peeled and chopped
  1 pound raw beets, peeled
   and chopped
  2 celery sticks, chopped
  ½ red bell pepper, seeded
   and chopped
  4 ounces mushrooms, chopped
  1 large cooking apple, chopped
  1 ounce/2 tablespoons butter
  2 tablespoons sunflower oil
  9 cups stock or water
  1 teaspoon cumin seeds
  a pinch of dried thyme
  1 large bay leaf
  fresh lemon juice, to taste
  salt and ground black pepper
For the garnish
  ⅔ cup sour cream
  a few sprigs of fresh dill

1 Place the chopped vegetables and apple in a large pan with the butter, oil and 3 tablespoons of the stock or water. Cover and cook gently for about 15 minutes, shaking the pan occasionally.

2 Stir in the cumin seeds and cook for 1 minute, then add the remaining stock or water, the thyme, bay leaf and lemon juice and seasoning to taste.

3 Bring the mixture to the boil, then cover the pan and turn down the heat to a gentle simmer. Cook for about 30 minutes.

4 Strain the vegetables and reserve the liquid. Process the vegetables in a food processor or blender until they are smooth and creamy.

COOK'S TIP
The flavor of this marvelous soup matures and improves if it is made the day before it is needed.

5 Return the vegetables to the pan, add the reserved stock and reheat. Check the seasoning.

6 Divide between individual serving bowls. Garnish each with swirls of sour cream and top with a few sprigs of fresh dill.

Energy 162kcal/674kJ; Protein 2.9g; Carbohydrate 10.5g, of which sugars 9.7g; Fat 12.4g, of which saturates 5.8g; Cholesterol 24mg; Calcium 50mg; Fiber 2.5g; Sodium 94mg.

CREAM OF CELERIAC AND SPINACH SOUP

CELERIAC HAS A WONDERFUL FLAVOR THAT IS REMINISCENT OF CELERY, BUT ALSO ADDS A SLIGHTLY NUTTY TASTE. HERE IT IS COMBINED WITH SPINACH TO MAKE A DELICIOUS SOUP.

SERVES 6

INGREDIENTS
4 cups water
8 fluid ounces/1 cup dry white wine
1 leek, thickly sliced
1¼ pounds celeriac, diced
7 ounces fresh spinach leaves
freshly grated nutmeg
salt and ground black pepper
1 ounce/¼ cup pine nuts, to garnish

COOK'S TIP
If the soup is too thick, thin it with a little water or low-fat milk when pureeing.

1 Mix the water and wine in a jug. Place the leek, celeriac and spinach in a deep pan and pour the liquid over the top. Bring to the boil, lower the heat and simmer for 10–15 minutes until the vegetables are soft.

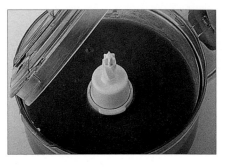

2 Pour the celeriac mixture into a blender or food processor and puree until smooth, in batches if necessary. Return to the clean pan and season to taste with salt, ground black pepper and nutmeg. Reheat gently.

3 Heat a non-stick frying pan (do not add any oil) and add the pine nuts. Roast until golden brown, stirring occasionally so that they do not stick. Sprinkle them over the soup and serve.

Energy 77kcal/319kJ; Protein 2.4g; Carbohydrate 2.6g, of which sugars 2.3g; Fat 3.4g, of which saturates 0.3g; Cholesterol 0mg; Calcium 102mg; Fiber 2.3g; Sodium 99mg.

APPLE SOUP

A DELICIOUS SOUP THAT MAKES THE MOST OF FRESHLY PICKED APPLES. SERVE IT WITH LEMON WEDGES TO ENHANCE THE FLAVOR, AND SOME FRESH CRUSTY BREAD.

SERVES 6

INGREDIENTS

    3 tablespoons oil
    1 kohlrabi, diced
    3 carrots, diced
    2 celery sticks, diced
    1 green bell pepper, diced
    2 tomatoes, diced
    9 cups chicken stock
    6 large green apples
    3 tablespoons all-purpose flour
    ⅔ cup heavy cream
    1 tablespoon sugar
    2–3 tablespoons lemon juice
    salt and ground black pepper
    lemon wedges, to serve

1 Heat the oil in a large pan. Add the kohlrabi, carrots, celery, green pepper and tomatoes and fry for 5–6 minutes until just softened.

2 Pour in the chicken stock, bring to the boil, then reduce the heat and simmer for about 45 minutes.

3 Meanwhile, peel and core the apples, then chop into small cubes. Add to the pan and simmer for 15 minutes.

4 Mix together the flour and cream and stir into the soup. Bring to the boil. Add the sugar, lemon juice and seasoning. Serve with lemon wedges.

Energy 278kcal/1159kJ; Protein 2.4g; Carbohydrate 24.8g, of which sugars 18.8g; Fat 19.5g, of which saturates 9.2g; Cholesterol 34mg; Calcium 63mg; Fiber 4.6g; Sodium 54mg.

CHUNKY VEGETABLE SOUPS

In this section you will find a collection of traditional soups using colorful Mediterranean vegetables, such as Greek Eggplant and Zucchini Soup, Summer Minestrone, and Provençal Vegetable Soup. In winter root vegetables come into their own—now is the time to try Russian Spinach and Root Vegetable Soup with Dill, Winter Vegetable Soup, or Leek and Thyme Soup. And winter meets summer in Roast Vegetable Medley with Sun-dried Tomato Bread.

GREEK EGGPLANT AND ZUCCHINI SOUP

A FUSION OF FLAVORS FROM THE SUNNY GREEK ISLANDS CREATES THIS FABULOUS SOUP, WHICH IS SERVED WITH TZATZIKI, THE POPULAR COMBINATION OF CUCUMBER AND CREAMY YOGURT.

SERVES 4

INGREDIENTS

    2 large eggplants, roughly diced
    4 large zucchini, roughly diced
    1 onion, roughly chopped
    4 garlic cloves, roughly chopped
    3 tablespoons olive oil
    5 cups vegetable stock
    1 tablespoon chopped
      fresh oregano
    salt and ground black pepper
    mint sprigs, to garnish
For the tzatziki
    1 cucumber
    2 teaspoons salt
    2 garlic cloves, crushed
    1 teaspoon white wine vinegar
    8 ounces/1 cup strained
      plain yogurt
    small bunch of fresh mint
      leaves, chopped

1 Preheat the oven to 400ºF. Place the eggplants and zucchini in a roasting pan. Add the onion and garlic, and drizzle over the olive oil. Roast for 35 minutes, turning once, until tender and slightly charred.

2 Place half the roasted vegetables in a food processor or blender. Add the stock and process until almost smooth. Pour into a large pan and add the remaining vegetables. Bring to the boil, season and stir in the chopped oregano.

3 For the tzatziki, peel, seed and dice the cucumber. Place the flesh in a colander and sprinkle with salt. Leave for 30 minutes. Mix the garlic with the vinegar and stir into the yogurt. Pat the cucumber dry on paper towels and fold it into the yogurt. Season to taste and stir in the mint. Chill until required.

4 Ladle the soup into bowls and garnish with mint sprigs. Hand round the bowl of tzatziki so that your guests can add a dollop or two to their soup.

Energy 188kcal/778kJ; Protein 6.9g; Carbohydrate 8.5g, of which sugars 7.3g; Fat 14.9g, of which saturates 4.3g; Cholesterol 0mg; Calcium 134mg; Fiber 3.6g; Sodium 1027mg.

CORN AND SWEET POTATO SOUP

THE COMBINATION OF CORN AND SWEET POTATO GIVES THIS SOUP A REAL DEPTH OF FLAVOR AS WELL AS MAKING IT LOOK VERY COLORFUL.

SERVES 6

INGREDIENTS
   1 tablespoon olive oil
   1 onion, finely chopped
   2 garlic cloves, crushed
   1 small red chile, seeded
     and finely chopped
   7½ cups vegetable stock
   2 teaspoons ground cumin
   1 medium sweet potato,
     diced
   ½ red bell pepper, seeded and
     finely chopped
   1 pound corn kernels
   salt and ground black pepper
   lime wedges, to serve

COOK'S TIP
Wear rubber gloves to protect your hands when seeding and chopping fresh chiles.

1 Heat the oil and fry the onion for 5 minutes until softened. Add the garlic and chile and fry for a further 2 minutes.

2 In the same pan, add 1¼ cups of the vegetable stock. Bring to the boil and simmer for 10 minutes.

3 Mix the cumin with a little stock to form a paste and then stir into the soup. Add the diced sweet potato, stir and simmer for 10 minutes. Season and stir again.

4 Add the pepper, corn and remaining stock and simmer for 10 minutes. Process half of the soup until smooth and then stir into the chunky soup. Season and serve with lime wedges for squeezing over.

Energy 188kcal/778kJ; Protein 6.9g; Carbohydrate 8.5g, of which sugars 7.3g; Fat 14.9g, of which saturates 4.3g; Cholesterol 0mg; Calcium 134mg; Fiber 3.6g; Sodium 1027mg.

SUMMER VEGETABLE SOUP

THIS BRIGHTLY COLORED, FRESH-TASTING TOMATO SOUP MAKES THE MOST OF SUMMER VEGETABLES IN SEASON. ADD LOTS OF RED AND YELLOW BELL PEPPERS TO MAKE A SWEETER VERSION.

SERVES 4

INGREDIENTS

1 pound ripe plum tomatoes
8 ounces ripe yellow tomatoes
3 tablespoons olive oil
1 large onion, finely chopped
1 tablespoon sun-dried
  tomato paste
8 ounces zucchini, trimmed
  and chopped
8 ounces yellow zucchini, trimmed
  and chopped
3 waxy new potatoes, diced
2 garlic cloves, crushed
about 5 cups chicken stock or water
4 tablespoons shredded fresh basil
2 ounces/⅔ cup freshly grated
  Parmesan cheese
sea salt and freshly ground
  black pepper

1 Plunge all the tomatoes in boiling water for 30 seconds, refresh in cold water, then peel and chop finely. Heat the oil in a large pan, add the onion and cook gently for about 5 minutes, stirring constantly, until softened. Stir in the sun-dried tomato paste, chopped tomatoes, zucchini, diced potatoes and garlic. Mix well and cook gently for 10 minutes, shaking the pan often.

2 Pour in the stock or water. Bring to the boil, lower the heat, half cover the pan and simmer gently for 15 minutes or until the vegetables are just tender. Add more stock or water if necessary.

3 Remove the pan from the heat and stir in the basil and half the cheese. Taste for seasoning. Serve hot, sprinkled with the remaining cheese.

Energy 243kcal/1012kJ; Protein 10.3g; Carbohydrate 20.9g, of which sugars 12g; Fat 13.7g, of which saturates 4.1g; Cholesterol 13mg; Calcium 215mg; Fiber 4.3g; Sodium 169mg.

CORN AND POTATO CHOWDER

THIS CREAMY YET CHUNKY SOUP IS RICH WITH THE SWEET TASTE OF CORN. IT'S EXCELLENT SERVED WITH THICK CRUSTY BREAD AND TOPPED WITH SOME MELTED CHEDDAR CHEESE.

SERVES 4

INGREDIENTS

1 onion, chopped
1 garlic clove, crushed
1 medium baking potato, chopped
2 celery sticks, sliced
1 small green bell pepper, seeded, halved and sliced
2 tablespoons sunflower oil
1 ounce/2 tablespoons butter
2½ cups stock or water
1¼ cups milk
1 can (7 ounces) flageolet beans
1 can (11 ounces) corn kernels
good pinch dried sage
salt and ground black pepper
Cheddar cheese, grated, to serve

1 Put the onion, garlic, potato, celery and green pepper into a large heavy-based pan with the oil and butter.

2 Heat the ingredients until sizzling then reduce the heat to low. Cover and cook gently for about 10 minutes, shaking the pan occasionally to prevent the ingredients from sticking.

3 Pour in the stock or water, season with salt and pepper to taste and bring to the boil. Reduce the heat, cover again and simmer gently for about 15 minutes until the vegetables are tender.

4 Add the milk, beans and corn—including their liquids—and the sage. Simmer, uncovered, for 5 minutes. Check the seasoning and serve hot, sprinkled with grated cheese.

Energy 251kcal/1052kJ; Protein 9.7g; Carbohydrate 25.9g, of which sugars 9.3g; Fat 12.9g, of which saturates 4.9g; Cholesterol 18mg; Calcium 128mg; Fiber 5.5g; Sodium 1154mg.

ROAST VEGETABLE MEDLEY WITH SUN-DRIED TOMATO BREAD

WINTER MEETS SUMMER IN THIS SOUP RECIPE FOR CHUNKY ROASTED ROOTS. SERVE IT WITH BREAD BAKED WITH A HINT OF ADDED SUMMER FLAVOR IN THE FORM OF SUN-DRIED TOMATOES.

SERVES 4

INGREDIENTS
    4 parsnips, quartered lengthwise
    2 red onions, cut into thin wedges
    4 carrots, thickly sliced
    2 leeks, thickly sliced
    1 small rutabaga, cut into
      bitesize pieces
    4 potatoes, cut into chunks
    4 tablespoons olive oil
    few sprigs of fresh thyme
    1 garlic bulb, broken into
      cloves, unpeeled
    4 cups vegetable stock
    salt and ground black pepper
    fresh thyme sprigs, to garnish
For the sun-dried tomato bread
    1 ciabatta loaf (about 10 ounces)
    3 ounces/6 tablespoons
      butter, softened
    1 garlic clove, crushed
    4 sun-dried tomatoes, finely chopped
    2 tablespoons chopped fresh parsley

1 Preheat the oven to 400ºF. Cut the thick ends of the parsnip quarters into four, then place them in a large roasting pan. Add the onions, carrots, leeks, rutabaga and potatoes, and spread them in an even layer.

2 Drizzle the olive oil over the vegetables. Add the thyme sprigs and the unpeeled garlic cloves. Toss well to coat with oil and roast for about 45 minutes, until all the vegetables are tender and slightly charred.

3 Meanwhile, to make the sun-dried tomato bread, cut diagonal slits along the loaf, taking care not to cut right through it. Mix the butter with the garlic, sun-dried tomatoes and parsley. Spread the mixture into each slit, then press the bread back together. Wrap the loaf in foil and bake for 15 minutes, opening the foil for the last 5 minutes.

4 Discard the thyme from the roasted vegetables. Squeeze the garlic cloves from their skins over the vegetables.

5 Process about half the vegetables with the stock in a food processor or blender until almost smooth. Pour into a pan and add the remaining vegetables. Bring to the boil and season well with salt and black pepper.

6 Ladle the soup into bowls and garnish with fresh thyme leaves. Serve the hot bread with the soup.

Energy 511kcal/2146kJ; Protein 13.9g; Carbohydrate 72.6g, of which sugars 18.9g; Fat 20.4g, of which saturates 10.6g; Cholesterol 40mg; Calcium 218mg; Fiber 12.1g; Sodium 521mg.

SWEET AND SOUR CABBAGE, BEET AND TOMATO BORSCHT

THERE ARE MANY VARIATIONS OF THIS CLASSIC JEWISH SOUP, WHICH MAY BE SERVED HOT OR COLD. THIS VERSION INCLUDES PLENTIFUL AMOUNTS OF CABBAGE, TOMATOES AND POTATOES.

SERVES 6

INGREDIENTS
1 onion, chopped
1 carrot, chopped
4–6 raw or vacuum-packed (cooked, not pickled) beets, 3–4 diced and 1–2 coarsely grated
1 can (14 ounces) tomatoes
4–6 new potatoes, cut into bitesize pieces
1 small white cabbage, thinly sliced
4 cups vegetable stock
3 tablespoons sugar
2–3 tablespoons white wine, cider vinegar or citric acid
3 tablespoons chopped fresh dill, plus extra to garnish
salt and ground black pepper
sour cream, to garnish
buttered rye bread, to serve

1 Put the onion, carrot, diced beets, tomatoes, potatoes, cabbage and stock in a large pan. Bring to the boil, reduce the heat and simmer for 30 minutes, or until the potatoes are tender.

VARIATION
To make meat borscht, place 2¼ pounds chopped beef in a large pan. Pour over water to cover and crumble in 1 beef bouillon cube. Bring to the boil, then reduce the heat and simmer until tender. Skim any fat from the surface, then add the vegetables and proceed as above. For Kashrut, omit the sour cream and serve with unbuttered rye bread.

2 Add the grated beets, sugar and wine, vinegar or citric acid to the soup and cook for 10 minutes. Taste for a good sweet-sour balance and add more sugar and/or vinegar if necessary. Season.

3 Stir the chopped dill into the soup and ladle into warmed bowls immediately. Garnish each bowl with a generous spoonful of sour cream and more dill and serve with buttered rye bread.

Energy 111kcal/470kJ; Protein 3.2g; Carbohydrate 24.6g, of which sugars 17.8g; Fat 0.6g, of which saturates 0.1g; Cholesterol 0mg; Calcium 65mg; Fiber 3.8g; Sodium 52mg.

LEEK <u>AND</u> THYME SOUP

THIS IS A FILLING, HEART-WARMING SOUP, WHICH CAN BE LIQUIDIZED TO A SMOOTH PUREE OR SERVED AS IT IS HERE, IN ITS ORIGINAL PEASANT STYLE.

SERVES 4

INGREDIENTS

   2 pounds leeks
   1 pound potatoes
   4 ounces/½ cup butter
   1 large sprig fresh thyme, plus extra
     to garnish (optional)
   1¼ cups milk
   salt and ground black pepper
   4 tablespoons heavy cream,
     to serve

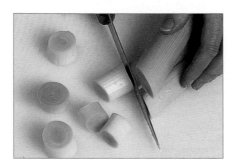

1 Trim the leeks. If you are using big winter leeks, strip away all the coarse outer leaves, then cut the leeks into thick slices. Wash thoroughly under cold running water.

2 Cut the potatoes into rough dice, about 1 inch, and dry thoroughly on paper towels.

3 Melt the butter in a large pan and add the leeks and 1 sprig of thyme. Cover and cook for 4–5 minutes until softened. Add the potato pieces and just enough cold water to cover the vegetables. Re-cover and cook over a low heat for 30 minutes.

4 Pour in the milk and season with salt and pepper. Cover and simmer for a further 30 minutes. You will find that some of the potato breaks up, leaving you with a semi-pureed and rather lumpy soup.

5 Remove the sprig of thyme (the leaves will have fallen into the soup) and serve, adding 1 tablespoon cream and a garnish of thyme to each bowl.

COOK'S TIP
Leeks need meticulous cleaning to remove any grit and earth between the layers of leaves. Slice the green part of the leek and separate the leaves before washing under cold running water.

Energy 377kcal/1570kJ; Protein 8.2g; Carbohydrate 28.3g, of which sugars 10.1g; Fat 26.4g, of which saturates 16.1g; Cholesterol 66mg; Calcium 156mg; Fiber 6.1g; Sodium 223mg.

WINTER VEGETABLE SOUP

NO FEWER THAN EIGHT VARIETIES OF VEGETABLE ARE PACKED INTO THIS HEARTY AND NUTRITIOUS SOUP. SERVE IT FOR LUNCH ON A COLD WINTER'S DAY, WITH PLENTY OF CRUSTY BREAD.

SERVES 8

INGREDIENTS

1 medium savoy cabbage, quartered and cored
2 tablespoons corn oil
4 carrots, finely sliced
2 celery stalks, finely sliced
2 parsnips, diced
6¼ cups chicken stock
3 medium potatoes, diced
2 zucchini, sliced
1 red bell pepper, seeded and diced
4 ounces/2 cups cauliflower florets
2 tomatoes, seeded and diced
½ teaspoon fresh thyme leaves or ¼ teaspoon dried thyme
2 tablespoons chopped fresh parsley
salt and ground black pepper

1 Using a sharp knife, slice the cabbage quarters into thin strips across the leaves.

2 Heat the oil in a large pan. Add the cabbage, carrots, celery and parsnips and cook for 10–15 minutes over medium heat, stirring frequently to prevent the vegetables from sticking.

3 Stir the stock into the vegetables and bring to the boil, skimming off any foam that rises to the surface.

4 Add the potatoes, zucchini, pepper, cauliflower and tomatoes, with the herbs, and salt and pepper to taste.

5 Bring back to the boil. Reduce the heat to low, cover the pan and simmer for 15–20 minutes until the vegetables are tender. Serve hot.

VARIATION
Other vegetables can be used for this soup in place of the ones listed. White winter cabbage, sweet potato, leeks, rutabaga and turnip would all be good choices.

Energy 105kcal/441kJ; Protein 3.4g; Carbohydrate 15.4g, of which sugars 8.2g; Fat 3.7g, of which saturates 0.6g; Cholesterol 0mg; Calcium 56mg; Fiber 3.9g; Sodium 23mg.

VEGETABLE AND HERB CHOWDER

A MEDLEY OF FRESH VEGETABLES AND HERBS COMBINES TO MAKE A DELICIOUS LUNCHTIME SOUP TO SERVE WITH SOME CRUSTY BREAD.

SERVES 4

INGREDIENTS

   1 ounce/2 tablespoons butter
   1 onion, finely chopped
   1 leek, finely sliced
   1 celery stick, diced
   1 yellow or green bell pepper, seeded
     and diced
   2 tablespoons chopped fresh parsley
   1 tablespoon all-purpose flour
   5 cups vegetable stock
   12 ounces potatoes, diced
   a few sprigs of fresh thyme or
     ½ teaspoon dried thyme
   1 bay leaf
   4 ounces/1 cup young green beans,
     diagonally sliced
   4 fluid ounces/½ cup milk
   salt and ground black pepper

1 Melt the butter in a heavy pan or flameproof casserole and add the onion, leek, celery, yellow or green pepper and parsley. Cover and cook gently over low heat until the vegetables are soft.

2 Add the flour and stir until well blended. Gradually stir in the stock. Bring the mixture to the boil, stirring frequently.

3 Add the potatoes, thyme and bay leaf. Simmer, uncovered, for 10 minutes.

4 Add the beans and simmer for a further 10–15 minutes until all the vegetables are tender.

5 Stir in the milk. Season with salt and pepper. Heat through. Before serving, discard the thyme stalks and bay leaf.

Energy 172kcal/723kJ; Protein 4.9g; Carbohydrate 24.9g, of which sugars 8g; Fat 6.6g, of which saturates 3.8g; Cholesterol 15mg; Calcium 80mg; Fiber 3.7g; Sodium 68mg.

VEGETABLE SOUP <u>WITH</u> COCONUT

THE COCONUT COMPLEMENTS THE VEGETABLES IN THIS FINE SOUP, AND THE VARIOUS GROUND SPICES PROVIDE ADDITIONAL FLAVOR.

SERVES 4

INGREDIENTS

   1 ounce/2 tablespoons butter
     or margarine
   ½ red onion, finely chopped
   6 ounces each turnip, sweet potato
     and pumpkin, roughly diced
   1 teaspoon dried marjoram
   ½ teaspoon ground ginger
   ¼ teaspoon ground cinnamon
   1 tablespoon chopped scallion
   4 cups well-flavored vegetable
     stock
   2 tablespoons sliced almonds
   1 fresh chile, seeded and chopped
   1 teaspoon sugar
   1 ounce creamed coconut or
     1½ tablespoons coconut cream
salt and ground black pepper
cilantro, to garnish

1 Melt the butter or margarine in a large, non-stick pan. Fry the onion for 4–5 minutes.

2 Add the diced vegetables and fry for 3–4 minutes. Add the marjoram, ginger, cinnamon, scallion and fry over a low heat for about 10 minutes, stirring.

3 Add the vegetable stock, flaked almonds, chile and sugar and stir well to mix. Cover and simmer gently for 10–15 minutes until the vegetables are just tender.

4 Add the creamed coconut or coconut cream to the soup and stir to mix thoroughly. Spoon into warmed bowls, sprinkle with chopped cilantro and serve immediately.

Energy 227kcal/953kJ; Protein 3.5g; Carbohydrate 27.4g, of which sugars 8.3g; Fat 12.3g, of which saturates 5.9g; Cholesterol 13mg; Calcium 54mg; Fiber 3.7g; Sodium 88mg.

FAVA BEAN <u>AND</u> RICE SOUP

THIS THICK SOUP MAKES THE MOST OF FRESH FAVA BEANS WHILE THEY ARE IN SEASON. IT WORKS WELL WITH FROZEN BEANS FOR THE REST OF THE YEAR.

SERVES 4

INGREDIENTS

   2¼ pounds fava beans in their pods
   6 tablespoons olive oil
   1 medium onion, finely chopped
   2 medium tomatoes, peeled and
     finely chopped
   8 ounces/1 cup arborio or other
     non-parboiled rice
   1 ounce/2 tablespoons butter
   4 cups boiling water
   salt and ground black pepper
   grated Parmesan cheese, to serve
     (optional)

COOK'S TIP
If fresh fava beans are not in season, use 14 ounces frozen shelled broad beans, thawed, instead.

1 Bring a large pan of water to the boil and blanch the beans for 3–4 minutes. Drain and rinse under cold water. Peel off the skins.

2 Heat the oil in a large pan. Add the onion and cook over low to moderate heat until it softens. Stir in the beans and cook for about 5 minutes, stirring to coat them with the oil.

3 Season with salt and pepper. Add the tomatoes and cook for 5 minutes more, stirring. Add the rice and cook for a further 1–2 minutes, stirring constantly.

4 Add the butter and stir until it melts. Pour in the water, a little at a time. Adjust the seasoning to taste. Continue cooking until the rice is tender. Serve with grated Parmesan, if you like.

Energy 507kcal/2111kJ; Protein 14.4g; Carbohydrate 61.3g, of which sugars 3.1g; Fat 22.7g, of which saturates 5.8g; Cholesterol 13mg; Calcium 87mg; Fiber 8.5g; Sodium 50mg.

ITALIAN VEGETABLE SOUP

THE SUCCESS OF THIS CLEAR SOUP DEPENDS ON THE QUALITY OF THE STOCK, SO USE HOMEMADE VEGETABLE STOCK RATHER THAN STOCK OR BOUILLON CUBES.

SERVES 4

INGREDIENTS
  1 small carrot
  1 baby leek
  1 celery stick
  2 ounces green cabbage
  3¾ cups vegetable stock
  1 bay leaf
  4 ounces/1 cup cooked
    cannellini beans
  1 ounce/¼ cup soup pasta, such
    as tiny shells, bows, stars
    or elbows
salt and ground black pepper
chopped fresh chives, to garnish

1 Cut the carrot, leek and celery into 2-inch long julienne strips. Finely shred the cabbage.

2 Put the stock and bay leaf into a large pan and bring to the boil. Add the carrot, leek and celery, cover and simmer for 6 minutes, until the vegetables are softened, but not tender.

VARIATION
Cooked small cannellini beans can be used to vary this recipe.

3 Add the cabbage, beans and pasta, then simmer, uncovered, for a further 4–5 minutes, or until the vegetables are tender and the pasta is *al dente*.

4 Remove the bay leaf and season to taste. Ladle the soup into four warmed soup bowls and garnish with chopped chives. Serve immediately.

Energy 55kcal/234kJ; Protein 3.1g; Carbohydrate 10.1g, of which sugars 3g; Fat 0.5g, of which saturates 0.1g; Cholesterol 0mg; Calcium 28mg; Fiber 2.7g; Sodium 133mg.

FRESH TOMATO <u>AND</u> BEAN SOUP

THIS IS A RICH, CHUNKY TOMATO SOUP, WITH BEANS AND CILANTRO. SERVE WITH OLIVE CIABATTA
FOR A SATISFYING SUMMER LUNCH DISH.

SERVES 4

INGREDIENTS
 2 pounds ripe plum tomatoes
 2 tablespoons olive oil
 10 ounces onions, peeled and
  roughly chopped
 2 garlic cloves, peeled andcrushed
 3¾ cups vegetable stock
 2 tablespoons sun-dried
  tomato paste
 2 teaspoons paprika
 1 tablespoon cornstarch
 1 can (15 ounces) cannellini beans,
  rinsed and drained
 2 tablespoons chopped
  fresh cilantro
salt and ground black pepper
olive ciabatta, to serve

1 First, peel the tomatoes. Using a
sharp knife, make a small cross in each
one and place in a bowl. Pour over
boiling water to cover and leave to stand
for 30–60 seconds.

2 Drain the tomatoes and cover with
cold water. When they are cool enough
to handle, drain again. Using a sharp
knife, peel off the skins. Quarter them
and then cut each piece in half again.

3 Heat the oil in a large pan and cook
the chopped onions and garlic for about
3 minutes or until they are just
beginning to soften.

4 Add the tomatoes to the onions and
stir in the stock, sun-dried tomato
paste and paprika. Season with a little
salt and pepper.

5 Bring to the boil and simmer gently
for about 10 minutes until the tomatoes
are softened.

6 In a small bowl, mix the cornstarch to
a smooth paste with 2 tablespoons cold
water. Stir the beans into the soup
with the cornstarch paste. Cook for a
further 5 minutes.

7 Taste and adjust the seasoning if
necessary. Stir in the chopped cilantro
just before serving with chunks of
olive ciabatta.

Energy 216kcal/911kJ; Protein 9.3g; Carbohydrate 31g, of which sugars 13.3g; Fat 7g, of which saturates 1.1g; Cholesterol 0mg; Calcium 70mg; Fiber 8.8g; Sodium 492mg.

PROVENÇAL VEGETABLE SOUP

THIS SATISFYING CHUNKY VEGETABLE SOUP CAPTURES ALL THE FLAVORS OF SUMMER IN PROVENCE. THE BASIL AND GARLIC PUREE, PISTOU, GIVES IT EXTRA COLOR AND A WONDERFUL AROMA—SO DON'T LEAVE IT OUT.

SERVES 6–8

INGREDIENTS

10 ounces/1½ cups shelled
  fresh fava beans or 6 ounces/
  ¾ cup dried navy beans,
  soaked overnight
½ teaspoon dried *herbes de Provence*
2 garlic cloves, finely chopped
1 tablespoon olive oil
1 onion, finely chopped
1 large leek, finely sliced
1 celery stick, finely sliced
2 carrots, finely diced
2 small potatoes, finely diced
4 ounces green beans
5 cups water
2 small zucchini, finely chopped
3 medium tomatoes, peeled, seeded
  and finely chopped
4 ounces/1 cup shelled garden peas
a handful of spinach leaves, cut into
  thin ribbons
salt and ground black pepper
sprigs of fresh basil, to garnish

For the *pistou*

1 or 2 garlic cloves, finely chopped
½ ounce/½ cup (packed)
  basil leaves
4 tablespoons grated Parmesan
  cheese
4 tablespoons extra virgin olive oil

1 To make the *pistou*, put the garlic, basil and Parmesan cheese in a food processor and process until smooth, scraping down the sides once. With the machine running, slowly add the olive oil through the feed tube.

2 To make the soup, if using dried navy beans, drain them, place in a pan and cover with water. Boil vigorously for 10 minutes and drain.

3 Place the par-boiled beans, or fresh fava beans if using, in a pan with the *herbes de Provence* and one of the garlic cloves. Add water to cover by 1 inch. Bring to the boil, reduce the heat and simmer over medium-low heat until tender, about 10 minutes for fresh beans or 1 hour for dried beans. Set aside in the cooking liquid.

4 Heat the oil in a large pan or flameproof casserole. Add the onion and leek and cook for 5 minutes, stirring occasionally, until they are beginning to soften.

COOK'S TIPS
• Both the *pistou* and the soup can be made 1 or 2 days in advance and chilled. To serve, reheat gently, stirring occasionally to prevent sticking.
• Alternatively, you can pound the garlic, basil and cheese for the pistou with a mortar and pestle. Then stir in the oil.

5 Add the celery, carrots and the remaining garlic clove and cook, covered, for 10 minutes, stirring occasionally.

6 Add the potatoes, green beans and water, then season lightly with salt and pepper. Bring to the boil, skimming any foam that rises to the surface, then reduce the heat, cover and simmer gently for 10 minutes.

7 Add the zucchini, tomatoes and peas, together with the reserved beans and their cooking liquid, and simmer for about 25–30 minutes until all the vegetables are tender. Add the spinach and simmer for 5 minutes.

8 Season the soup and swirl a spoonful of *pistou* into each bowl. Garnish with fresh basil and serve.

Energy 168kcal/700kJ; Protein 8.2g; Carbohydrate 11.7g, of which sugars 4.4g; Fat 10.2g, of which saturates 2.7g; Cholesterol 8mg; Calcium 136mg; Fiber 4.7g; Sodium 95mg.

MIXED MUSHROOM SOLYANKA
WITH PICKLED CUCUMBER

THE TART FLAVORS OF PICKLED CUCUMBER, CAPERS AND LEMON ADD EXTRA BITE TO THIS TRADITIONAL RUSSIAN SOUP. THIS IS THE PERFECT DISH TO SERVE WHEN YOU WANT TO OFFER SOMETHING A LITTLE DIFFERENT.

2 Add the remaining vegetable stock with the sliced mushrooms, bring to the boil, cover and simmer gently for about 30 minutes.

3 In a small bowl, blend the tomato paste with 2 tablespoons of stock.

4 Add the tomato paste to the pan with the pickled cucumber, bay leaf, capers, salt and peppercorns. Cook gently for a further 10 minutes.

5 Ladle the soup into warmed bowls and sprinkle lemon rind curls, a few olives and a sprig of Italian parsley over each bowl before serving.

SERVES 4

INGREDIENTS

2 onions, chopped
5 cups vegetable stock
1 pound/6 cups mushrooms, sliced
4 teaspoons tomato paste
1 pickled cucumber, chopped
1 bay leaf
1 tablespoon capers in brine, drained
pinch of salt
6 peppercorns, crushed
lemon rind curls, green olives and
  sprigs of Italian parsley, to garnish

1 Put the onions in a large pan with 2 fluid ounces/¼ cup of the stock. Cook, stirring occasionally, until all the liquid has evaporated.

COOK'S TIP

Using a mixture of mushrooms gives this soup its character. Try using varieties such as cremini, portobello and white mushrooms.

RUSSIAN SPINACH AND ROOT VEGETABLE SOUP WITH DILL

THIS IS A TYPICAL RUSSIAN SOUP, TRADITIONALLY PREPARED WHEN THE FIRST VEGETABLES OF SPRINGTIME APPEAR. EARTHY ROOT VEGETABLES, COOKED WITH FRESH SPINACH LEAVES, ARE ENLIVENED WITH A TART, FRESH TOPPING OF DILL, LEMON AND SOUR CREAM.

SERVES 4–6

INGREDIENTS

1 small turnip, cut into chunks
2 carrots, sliced or diced
1 small parsnip, cut into large dice
1 potato, peeled and diced
1 onion, chopped or cut into chunks
1 garlic clove, finely chopped
¼ celeriac bulb, diced
4 cups vegetable or chicken stock
7 ounces spinach, washed and
 roughly chopped
1 small bunch fresh dill, chopped
salt and ground black pepper
For the garnish
2 hard-boiled eggs, sliced
1 lemon, cut into slices
8 fluid ounces/1 cup sour cream
2 tablespoons fresh parsley and dill

1 Put the turnip, carrots, parsnip, potato, onion, garlic, celeriac and stock into a large pan. Bring to the boil, then simmer for 25–30 minutes, or until the vegetables are very tender.

COOK'S TIP
For the best results, use a really good-quality vegetable stock.

2 Add the spinach to the pan and cook for a further 5 minutes, or until the spinach is tender but still green and leafy. Season with salt and pepper.

3 Stir the dill into the soup, then ladle into bowls and serve garnished with egg, lemon, sour cream and a sprinkling of parsley and dill.

Energy 229kcal/952kJ; Protein 7.8g; Carbohydrate 14.3g, of which sugars 9.2g; Fat 16.2g, of which saturates 8.7g; Cholesterol 133mg; Calcium 197mg; Fiber 4.1g; Sodium 148mg.

PISTOU

SERVE THIS DELICIOUS TRADITIONAL VEGETABLE SOUP, FROM NICE IN THE SOUTH OF FRANCE, WITH A SPOONFUL OF SUN-DRIED TOMATO PESTO STIRRED INTO EACH BOWL, AND HAND ROUND A BOWL OF FRESH PARMESAN CHEESE. ANY TYPE OF SMALL PASTA SHAPES MAY BE USED, SUCH AS TINY SHELLS, BOWS, STARS OR ELBOWS.

SERVES 4

INGREDIENTS
1 zucchini, diced
1 small potato, diced
1 shallot, chopped
1 carrot, diced
1 can (8 ounces) chopped tomatoes
5 cups vegetable stock
2 ounces green beans, cut into
  ½ inch lengths
2 ounces/½ cup frozen baby peas
2 ounces/½ cup small pasta shapes
4–6 tablespoons pesto
1 tablespoon sun-dried
  tomato paste
salt and ground black pepper
grated Parmesan cheese,
  to serve

1 Place the zucchini, potato, shallot, carrot and tomatoes in a large pan. Add the vegetable stock and season with salt and pepper. Bring to the boil, then cover and simmer for 20 minutes.

2 Add the green beans, baby peas, and pasta shapes. Cook for a further 10 minutes, until the pasta is tender.

3 Taste the soup and adjust the seasoning as necessary. Ladle the soup into individual bowls. Mix together the pesto and sun-dried tomato paste, and stir a spoonful into each serving.

4 Serve, handing round a bowl of grated Parmesan cheese for sprinkling into each bowl.

Energy 156kcal/651kJ; Protein 4.1g; Carbohydrate 21.3g, of which sugars 6.1g; Fat 6.3g, of which saturates 1g; Cholesterol 0mg; Calcium 36mg; Fiber 2.9g; Sodium 16mg.

GRANDFATHER'S SOUP

THIS TRADITIONAL EASTERN EUROPEAN SOUP DERIVES ITS NAME FROM THE FACT THAT IT IS EASILY DIGESTED AND THEREFORE THOUGHT TO BE SUITABLE FOR THE ELDERLY. TO GET THE CORRECT TEXTURE FOR THE DISH, USE OLD POTATOES OF A FLOURY TEXTURE, SUCH AS THE IDAHO OR LONG WHITE VARIETIES.

SERVES 4

INGREDIENTS
  1 large onion, finely sliced
  1 ounce/2 tablespoons butter
  12 ounces potatoes, peeled
    and diced
  3¾ cups beef stock
  1 bay leaf
  salt and ground black pepper
For the drop noodles
  3 ounces/⅔ cup self-rising flour
  pinch of salt
  ½ ounce/1 tablespoon butter
  1 tablespoon chopped fresh parsley,
    plus a little extra to garnish
  1 egg, beaten
  chunks of bread, to serve

1 In a wide heavy pan, cook the onion gently in the butter for 10 minutes, or until it begins to soften and go golden brown.

2 Add the diced potatoes and cook for 2-3 minutes, then pour in the stock. Add the bay leaf, salt and pepper. Bring to the boil, then reduce the heat, cover and simmer for about 10 minutes.

3 To make the noodles, sift the flour and salt into a bowl and rub in the butter. Stir in the parsley, then add the egg and mix to a soft dough.

4 Drop half-teaspoonfuls of the dough into the simmering soup. Cover and simmer gently for a further 10 minutes. Ladle into warmed soup bowls, sprinkle over a little parsley, and serve.

Energy 239kcal/1001kJ; Protein 5.5g; Carbohydrate 33.3g, of which sugars 5g; Fat 10.2g, of which saturates 5.7g; Cholesterol 69mg; Calcium 96mg; Fiber 2.3g; Sodium 157mg.

WINTER WARMING SOUPS

A hot soup is the ideal dish for a cold winter day. The soups in this section are hearty and nourishing, made with ingredients such as potatoes, root vegetables, leeks and pumpkins. Bread and oatmeal are used to add body and texture— for example in Broccoli and Bread Soup, Tomato and Bread Soup, Yellow Broth, and Leek and Oatmeal Soup. Garlic is thought to help ward off winter colds, so why not try it in Garlic Soup or Potato and Roasted Garlic Broth.

POTATO <u>AND</u> ROASTED GARLIC BROTH

ROASTED GARLIC TAKES ON A SUBTLE, SWEET FLAVOR IN THIS DELICIOUS VEGETARIAN SOUP. SERVE IT PIPING HOT WITH MELTED CHEDDAR OR GRUYÈRE CHEESE ON FRENCH BREAD, AS A WINTER WARMER.

SERVES 4

INGREDIENTS
  2 small or 1 large whole head of
    garlic (about 20 cloves)
  4 medium potatoes
    (about 1¼ pounds in total), diced
  7½ cups good-quality hot vegetable
    stock
  salt and ground black pepper
  chopped Italian parsley, to garnish

COOK'S TIP
Choose floury potatoes such as the Idaho
or long white varieties to give the soup a
delicious velvety texture.

VARIATION
Use chicken or beef stock for a slightly
different flavor, if you like.

1 Preheat the oven to 375°F. Place
the unpeeled garlic bulbs or bulb in
a small roasting pan and bake in the
oven for 30 minutes until soft in
the center.

2 Meanwhile, par-boil the potatoes in a
large pan of lightly salted boiling water
for 10 minutes.

3 Simmer the stock in another pan for
5 minutes. Drain the potatoes and add
them to the stock.

4 Squeeze the garlic pulp into the soup,
reserving a few whole cloves, stir and
season to taste. Simmer for 15 minutes
and serve topped with the whole garlic
cloves and parsley.

Energy 115kcal/488kJ; Protein 4.3g; Carbohydrate 24.3g, of which sugars 2.1g; Fat 0.7g, of which saturates 0.2g; Cholesterol 0mg; Calcium 14mg; Fiber 2.3g; Sodium 219mg.

GREEN PEA SOUP WITH SPINACH

THIS LOVELY GREEN SOUP WAS INVENTED BY THE WIFE OF A 17TH-CENTURY BRITISH MEMBER OF PARLIAMENT, AND IT HAS STOOD THE TEST OF TIME.

SERVES 6

INGREDIENTS

1 pound/generous 3 cups podded
   fresh or frozen peas
1 leek, finely sliced
2 garlic cloves, crushed
2 rindless lean back bacon
   strips, diced
5 cups ham or chicken stock
2 tablespoons olive oil
2 ounces fresh spinach, shredded
1½ ounces/⅓ cup white cabbage,
   finely shredded
½ small lettuce, finely shredded
1 celery stick, finely chopped
a large handful of parsley, coarsely
   chopped
4 teaspoons chopped fresh mint
a pinch of ground mace
salt and ground black pepper

3 About 5 minutes before the pea mixture is ready, heat the oil in a deep frying pan. Add the spinach, cabbage, lettuce, celery and herbs. Cover and sweat the mixture until soft.

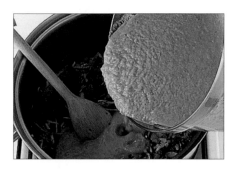

4 Add the processed pea mixture to the vegetables and herbs, and heat through.

5 Season with mace, and salt and pepper, and serve hot.

1 Put the peas, leek, garlic and bacon in a large pan. Add the stock, bring to the boil, then lower the heat and simmer for 20 minutes.

2 Transfer to a blender or food processor and process until smooth.

Energy 127kcal/527kJ; Protein 7.7g; Carbohydrate 10.1g, of which sugars 2.8g; Fat 6.5g, of which saturates 1.3g; Cholesterol 4mg; Calcium 58mg; Fiber 4.6g; Sodium 146mg.

MUSHROOM SOUP

USING A MIXTURE OF MUSHROOMS GIVES THIS SOUP CHARACTER. THIS MAKES A FLAVORSOME LIGHT MEAL SERVED WITH FRESH CRUSTY BREAD.

SERVES 4–6 AS A LIGHT MEAL
OR 6–8 AS A SOUP COURSE

INGREDIENTS
  ¾ ounce/1½ tablespoons butter
  1 tablespoon oil
  1 onion, roughly chopped
  4 potatoes, about 9–12 ounces,
    roughly chopped
  12 ounces mixed mushrooms,
    such as cremini, portobello,
    and white, cleaned and
    roughly chopped
  1 or 2 garlic cloves, crushed
  ⅔ cup white wine or hard cider
  5 cups good chicken stock
  bunch of fresh parsley, chopped
  salt and ground black pepper
  whipped or sour cream,
    to garnish

1 Heat the butter and oil in a large pan over medium heat. Add the chopped onion, turning it in the butter until well coated. Stir in the potatoes. Cover and sweat over a low heat for 5–10 minutes until softened but not browned.

2 Add the mushrooms, garlic and white wine or cider and stock. Season, bring to the boil and cook for 15 minutes, until all the ingredients are tender.

3 Put the mixture through a food mill, using the coarse blade, or blend. Return the soup to the rinsed pan, and add three-quarters of the parsley. Bring back to the boil, season, and garnish with cream and the remaining parsley.

GARLIC SOUP

THIS INTERESTING AND SURPRISINGLY SUBTLY FLAVORED IRISH SOUP MAKES GOOD USE OF AN ANCIENT INGREDIENT THAT IS NOT ONLY DELICIOUS BUT IS ALSO BELIEVED TO HAVE HEALTH-GIVING PROPERTIES. IT CERTAINLY BRINGS A GREAT SENSE OF WELL-BEING AND IS A REAL TREAT FOR GARLIC-LOVERS. SERVE IT WITH SOME CRUSTY BREAD AS A REAL WINTER WARMER.

SERVES 8

INGREDIENTS
  12 large garlic cloves, peeled
  1 tablespoon olive oil
  1 tablespoon melted butter
  1 small onion, finely chopped
  ½ ounce/2 tablespoons
    all-purpose flour
  1 tablespoon white wine vinegar
  4 cups good chicken stock
  2 egg yolks, lightly beaten
  bread croutons, fried in butter,
    to serve

VARIATION
Broiled croutes make a nice change in place of the croutons. Toast small slices of baguette, top with grated Cheddar and broil until the cheese melts.

1 Crush the garlic. Put the oil and butter into a pan, add the garlic and onion, and cook them gently for 20 minutes, until soft but not brown.

2 Add the flour and stir with a wooden spoon to make a roux. Cook for a few minutes, then stir in the wine vinegar, stock and 4 cups water. Simmer for about 30 minutes.

3 When ready to serve the soup, whisk in the lightly beaten egg yolks. Put the croutons into eight soup bowls and pour over the hot soup.

COOK'S TIP
When adding egg yolks to thicken a soup, reheat the soup gently but do not bring it back to the boil, otherwise the egg will curdle.

Top: Energy 155kcal/648kJ; Protein 3.2g; Carbohydrate 13.6g, of which sugars 3.4g; Fat 7.6g, of which saturates 3.2g; Cholesterol 11mg; Calcium 23mg; Fiber 2.1g; Sodium 44mg.
Bottom: Energy 55kcal/229kJ; Protein 1.6g; Carbohydrate 3.6g, of which sugars 0.6g; Fat 4g, of which saturates 1.3g; Cholesterol 53mg; Calcium 13mg; Fiber 0.4g; Sodium 11mg.

ROASTED ROOT VEGETABLE SOUP

ROASTING THE VEGETABLES GIVES THIS WINTER SOUP A WONDERFUL DEPTH OF FLAVOR. YOU CAN USE OTHER VEGETABLES, IF YOU WISH, OR ADAPT THE QUANTITIES DEPENDING ON WHAT'S IN SEASON.

SERVES 6

INGREDIENTS
2 fluid ounces/¼ cup olive oil
1 small butternut squash, peeled, seeded and cubed
2 carrots, cut into thick rounds
1 large parsnip, cubed
1 small rutabaga, cubed
2 leeks, thickly sliced
1 onion, quartered
3 bay leaves
4 thyme sprigs, plus extra to garnish
3 rosemary sprigs
5 cups vegetable stock
salt and freshly ground black pepper
sour cream, to serve

1 Preheat the oven to 400°F.

2 Pour the olive oil into a large bowl. Add the prepared vegetables and toss thoroughly with a spoon until they are all coated in the oil.

3 Spread out the vegetables in a single layer on one large or two small baking sheets. Tuck the bay leaves and the thyme and rosemary sprigs among the vegetables.

4 Roast the vegetables for about 50 minutes until tender, turning them occasionally to make sure they brown evenly. Remove from the oven, discard the herbs and transfer the vegetables to a large pan.

5 Pour the stock into the pan and bring to the boil. Reduce the heat, season to taste, then simmer for 10 minutes. Transfer the soup to a food processor or blender (or use a hand blender) and process for a few minutes until thick and smooth.

6 Return the soup to the pan to heat through. Season and serve with a swirl of sour cream. Garnish each serving with a sprig of thyme.

COOK'S TIP
Dried herbs can be used in place of fresh: sprinkle ½ teaspoon of each type over the vegetables in step 2 above.

Energy 65kcal/272kJ; Protein 2.5g; Carbohydrate 11.3g, of which sugars 8.8g; Fat 1.3g, of which saturates 0.3g; Cholesterol 0mg; Calcium 93mg; Fiber 4.4g; Sodium 13mg.

LEEK, POTATO AND ARUGULA SOUP

ARUGULA ADDS ITS DISTINCTIVE, PEPPERY TASTE TO THIS WONDERFULLY SATISFYING SOUP.
SERVE IT HOT, GARNISHED WITH A GENEROUS SPRINKLING OF TASTY CIABATTA CROUTONS.

SERVES 4–6

INGREDIENTS

2 ounces/4 tablespoons butter
1 onion, peeled and chopped
3 leeks, chopped
2 medium floury potatoes, cut into
  ½-inch dice
3¾ cups light chicken stock
or water
2 large handfuls arugula
⅔ cup heavy cream
salt and ground black pepper
garlic-flavored ciabatta croutons,
  to serve

1 Melt the butter in a large heavy-based pan, then add the onion, leeks and potatoes and stir until the vegetables are coated in butter. Heat the ingredients until sizzling then reduce the heat to low.

2 Cover and sweat the vegetables for 15 minutes. Pour in the stock or water and bring to the boil then reduce the heat, cover again and simmer for 20 minutes until the vegetables are tender.

3 Press the soup through a strainer or pass through a food mill and return to the rinsed pan. (When pureeing the soup, don't use a blender or food processor, as these will give it a gluey texture.) Chop the arugula, add it to the pan and cook the soup gently, uncovered, for 5 minutes.

4 Stir in the cream, then season to taste and reheat gently. Ladle the soup into warmed soup bowls and serve with a scattering of garlic-flavored ciabatta croutons in each.

Energy 393kcal/1631kJ; Protein 5.2g; Carbohydrate 23.6g, of which sugars 7.1g; Fat 31.5g, of which saturates 19.3g; Cholesterol 78mg; Calcium 87mg; Fiber 4.5g; Sodium 116mg.

CABBAGE AND POTATO SOUP WITH CARAWAY

EARTHY FLOURY POTATOES ARE ESSENTIAL TO THE SUCCESS OF THIS SOUP, SO CHOOSE YOUR VARIETY CAREFULLY. CARAWAY SEEDS COME FROM A PLANT IN THE PARSLEY FAMILY. THEY ARE AROMATIC AND NUTTY, WITH A DELICATE ANISE FLAVOR, ADDING A SUBTLE ACCENT TO THIS SATISFYING DISH.

SERVES 4

INGREDIENTS

2 tablespoons olive oil
2 small onions, sliced
6 garlic cloves, halved
12 ounces/3 cups shredded
  green cabbage
4 potatoes, unpeeled
1 teaspoon caraway seeds
1 teaspoon sea salt
5 cups water

COOK'S TIP

Use floury potatoes to achieve the correct texture for this soup. Russet or Idaho are excellent choices.

1 Pour the olive oil into a large pan and cook the onion for 3–4 minutes, until soft. Add the garlic and the cabbage and cook over a low heat for a further 10 minutes, stirring occasionally to prevent the cabbage from sticking to the base of the pan.

2 Add the potatoes, caraway seeds, sea salt and water. Bring to the boil then simmer until the vegetables are cooked.

3 Remove from the heat and allow to cool slightly before serving, strained or mashed.

Energy 144kcal/601kJ; Protein 3.1g; Carbohydrate 20.4g, of which sugars 8.1g; Fat 6g, of which saturates 0.9g; Cholesterol 0mg; Calcium 60mg; Fiber 3.3g; Sodium 507mg.

PEANUT <u>AND</u> POTATO SOUP

PEANUT SOUP IS A FIRM FAVORITE THROUGHOUT CENTRAL AND SOUTH AMERICA, AND IS PARTICULARLY POPULAR IN BOLIVIA AND ECUADOR. AS IN MANY LATIN AMERICAN RECIPES, THE PEANUTS ARE USED AS A THICKENING AGENT, WITH UNEXPECTEDLY DELICIOUS RESULTS.

SERVES 6

INGREDIENTS

4 tablespoons peanut oil
1 onion, finely chopped
2 garlic cloves, crushed
1 red bell pepper, seeded
  and chopped
9 ounces potatoes, peeled and diced
2 fresh red chiles, seeded
  and chopped
7 ounces canned chopped tomatoes
5 ounces/1¼ cups unsalted peanuts
6¼ cups beef stock
salt and ground black pepper
2 tablespoons chopped fresh cilantro,
  to garnish

1 Heat the oil in a large heavy pan over a low heat. Stir in the onion and cook for 5 minutes, until it begins to soften. Add the garlic, pepper, potatoes, chiles and tomatoes. Stir well to coat the vegetables evenly in the oil, cover and cook for 5 minutes, until softened.

2 Meanwhile, toast the peanuts by gently cooking them in a large dry frying pan over a medium heat. Keep a close eye on them, moving the peanuts around the pan until they are evenly golden. Take care not to burn them.

COOK'S TIP
Replace the unsalted peanuts with peanut butter if you like. Use equal quantities of chunky and smooth peanut butter for the ideal texture.

3 Set 2 tablespoons of the peanuts aside, to use as garnish. Transfer the remaining peanuts to a food processor and process until finely ground. Add the vegetables and process again until smooth.

4 Return the mixture to the pan and stir in the beef stock. Bring to the boil, then lower the heat and simmer for 10 minutes.

5 Pour the soup into heated bowls. Garnish with a generous sprinkling of cilantro and the remaining peanuts.

Energy 260kcal/1079kJ; Protein 8g; Carbohydrate 14.7g, of which sugars 6.2g; Fat 19.2g, of which saturates 3.6g; Cholesterol 0mg; Calcium 30mg; Fiber 3g; Sodium 20mg.

Tomato Soup with Black Olive Ciabatta Toasts

Tomato soup is everybody's favorite, particularly when made with fresh sun-ripened tomatoes. This delicious soup is wonderfully warming and has an earthy richness.

SERVES 6

INGREDIENTS

1 pound very ripe fresh tomatoes
2 tablespoons olive oil
1 onion, chopped
1 garlic clove, crushed
2 tablespoons sherry vinegar
2 tablespoons tomato paste
1 tablespoon cornstarch or
  potato flour
1¼ cups bottled strained tomatoes
1 bay leaf
3¾ cups vegetable or chicken
  stock
7 fluid ounces/scant 1 cup
  crème fraîche
salt and ground black pepper
basil leaves, to garnish
For the black olive ciabatta toasts
1 plain or black olive ciabatta
1 small red bell pepper
3 whole garlic cloves, skins on
8 ounces black olives (preferably
  a wrinkly Greek variety)
2–3 tablespoons salted capers or
  capers in vinegar
12 drained canned anchovy fillets
  or 1 small can tuna in oil, drained
about ⅔ cup good-quality extra virgin
  olive oil
fresh lemon juice and ground black
  pepper, to taste
3 tablespoons chopped fresh basil

1 Make the ciabatta toasts first. Preheat the oven to 400°F. Split the ciabatta in half and cut each half into nine fingers to give 18 in total. Arrange on a baking sheet and bake for 10–15 minutes until golden and crisp.

2 Place the whole pepper and garlic cloves under a hot broiler and cook for 15 minutes, turning, until charred all over. If you prefer, you can bake them in the oven for about 25 minutes. Once charred, put the garlic and pepper in a plastic bag, seal and leave to cool for about 10 minutes.

3 When the pepper is cool, peel off the skin (do not wash) and remove the stalk and seeds. Peel the skin off the garlic. Pit the olives. Rinse the capers under running water to remove the salt or vinegar. Place the prepared ingredients in a food processor with the anchovies or tuna and process until roughly chopped.

4 With the machine running, slowly add the olive oil until you have a fairly smooth dark paste. Alternatively, just stir in the olive oil for a chunkier result. Season to taste with lemon juice and pepper. Stir in the basil.

5 Spread the paste on the finger toasts, or, if not using immediately, transfer to a jar, cover with a layer of olive oil and keep in the refrigerator for up to three weeks.

6 For the soup, cut the tomatoes in half and remove the seeds and pulp using a lemon squeezer. Press the pulp through a strainer and reserve the liquid.

7 Heat the oil in a pan and add the onion, garlic, sherry vinegar, tomato paste and the tomato halves. Stir, then cover the pan and cook over a low heat for 1 hour, stirring occasionally. When done, process the soup in a blender or food processor until smooth, then pass through a sieve to remove any pieces of skin. Return to the pan.

8 Mix the cornstarch or potato flour with the reserved tomato pulp, then stir into the hot soup with the bottled strained tomatoes, bay leaf and stock. Simmer for 30 minutes. Stir in the crème fraîche and garnish with the basil leaves. Serve piping hot, with the ciabatta toasts.

Energy 532kcal/2211kJ; Protein 11.9g; Carbohydrate 29.3g, of which sugars 7.6g; Fat 41.7g, of which saturates 13.2g; Cholesterol 50mg; Calcium 120mg; Fiber 3.5g; Sodium 1352mg.

RUSSIAN BORSCHT <u>WITH</u> *KVAS* <u>AND</u> SOUR CREAM

BEET IS THE MAIN INGREDIENT OF BORSCHT, AND ITS FLAVOR AND COLOR DOMINATE THIS WELL-KNOWN SOUP. IT IS A CLASSIC OF BOTH RUSSIA AND POLAND.

SERVES 4–6

INGREDIENTS

2 pounds uncooked beets, peeled
2 carrots, peeled
2 celery sticks
1½ ounces/3 tablespoons butter
2 onions, sliced
2 garlic cloves, peeled and
    crushed
4 tomatoes, peeled, seeded
    and chopped
1 bay leaf
1 large parsley sprig
2 cloves
4 whole peppercorns
5 cups beef or chicken stock
⅔ cup beet *kvas* (see Cook's Tip)
    or the liquid from pickled beets
salt and ground black pepper
sour cream, garnished with chopped
    fresh chives or sprigs of dill,
    to serve

1 Cut the beets, carrots and celery into thick strips. Melt the butter in a pan and cook the onions over a low heat for 5 minutes, stirring occasionally.

2 Add the beets, carrots and celery and cook for a further 5 minutes.

COOK'S TIP
Beet *kvas* adds an intense color and a slight tartness. If unavailable, peel and grate 1 beet, add ⅔ cup stock and 2 teaspoons lemon juice. Bring to the boil, cover and leave for 30 minutes. Strain before using.

3 Add the crushed garlic and chopped tomatoes to the pan and cook, stirring, for 2 more minutes.

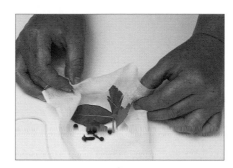

4 Place the bay leaf, parsley, cloves and peppercorns in a piece of cheesecloth and tie with string.

5 Add the cheesecloth bag to the pan with the stock. Bring to the boil, reduce the heat, cover and simmer for 1¼ hours, until the vegetables are tender. Discard the bag. Stir in the *kvas* and season. Ladle into bowls and serve with sour cream. Garnish with chives or dill.

Energy 125kcal/532kJ; Protein 5.3g; Carbohydrate 26.2g, of which sugars 23.5g; Fat 0.7g, of which saturates 0.1g; Cholesterol 0mg; Calcium 71mg; Fiber 6.6g; Sodium 166mg.

BROCCOLI AND BREAD SOUP

BROCCOLI GROWS ABUNDANTLY AROUND ROME AND IS SERVED IN THIS SOUP WITH GARLIC TOASTS, SPRINKLED WITH PARMESAN CHEESE.

SERVES 6

INGREDIENTS
1½ pounds broccoli spears
7½ cups chicken or vegetable stock
1 tablespoon lemon juice
salt and ground black pepper
To serve
6 slices white bread
1 large garlic clove, cut in half
grated Parmesan cheese (optional)

COOK'S TIP
Choose broccoli that has bright, compact florets. Yellowing florets, a limp woody stalk and a pungent smell are an indication of overmaturing, and the flavor will not be so good.

1 Using a small, sharp knife, peel the broccoli stems, starting from the base and pulling gently up toward the florets. (The peel should come off easily.) Chop the broccoli into small chunks.

2 Bring the stock to the boil in a large pan. Add the broccoli and simmer for about 10 minutes until soft.

3 Puree about half of the soup and mix into the rest of the soup. Season with salt, pepper and lemon juice.

4 Reheat the soup. Toast the bread, rub with garlic and cut into quarters. Place 3 or 4 pieces of toast in the bottom of each soup plate. Ladle on the soup. Serve immediately, with Parmesan if you like.

TOMATO AND BREAD SOUP

THIS COLORFUL FLORENTINE RECIPE WAS CREATED TO USE UP STALE BREAD. IT CAN BE MADE WITH VERY RIPE FRESH TOMATOES OR CANNED PLUM TOMATOES.

SERVES 4

INGREDIENTS
6 tablespoons olive oil
small piece dried chili, crumbled
(optional)
6 ounces/1½ cups stale bread,
cut into 1-inch cubes
1 medium onion, finely chopped
2 garlic cloves, finely chopped
1½ pounds ripe tomatoes, peeled
and chopped, or 2 cans
(28 ounces) peeled plum
tomatoes, chopped
3 tablespoons chopped fresh basil
6¼ cups light meat stock or water,
or a combination
salt and ground black pepper
extra virgin olive oil, to serve
(optional)

1 Heat 4 tablespoons of the oil in a large pan. Add the chili, if using, and stir for 1–2 minutes.

2 Add the bread cubes and cook until golden, then remove to a plate and drain on paper towels.

3 Add the remaining oil, the onion and garlic to the pan and cook until the onion softens.

4 Stir in the tomatoes, basil and the reserved bread cubes. Season with salt. Cook over a moderate heat, stirring occasionally, for about 15 minutes.

5 Meanwhile, heat the stock or water to simmering point. Add it to the tomato mixture and stir well. Bring to the boil. Lower the heat slightly and simmer gently for 20 minutes.

6 Remove the soup from the heat. Use a fork to mash together the tomatoes and bread. Season with pepper, and more salt if necessary. Allow to stand for 10 minutes.

7 Just before serving, swirl in a little extra virgin olive oil, if you like.

Top: Energy 101kcal/426kJ; Protein 7.2g; Carbohydrate 15.3g, of which sugars 2.4g; Fat 1.5g, of which saturates 0.2g; Cholesterol 0mg; Calcium 93mg; Fiber 3.3g; Sodium 149mg.
Bottom: Energy 289kcal/1210kJ; Protein 5.4g; Carbohydrate 28.3g, of which sugars 7.5g; Fat 18g, of which saturates 2.5g; Cholesterol 0mg; Calcium 86mg; Fiber 3.1g; Sodium 247mg.

MUSHROOM <u>AND</u> HERB POTAGE

DO NOT WORRY IF THIS SOUP IS NOT COMPLETELY SMOOTH—IT IS ESPECIALLY NICE WHEN IT HAS A SLIGHTLY NUTTY, TEXTURED CONSISTENCY. THE SHERRY INTENSIFIES THE FLAVOR OF THE STOCK AND ADDS A LITTLE PUNCH.

SERVES 4

INGREDIENTS

2 ounces smoked fatty bacon
1 onion, chopped
1 tablespoon sunflower oil
12 ounces portobello mushrooms
   or a mixture of wild and
   brown mushrooms
2½ cups good meat stock
2 tablespoons sweet sherry
2 tablespoons chopped fresh mixed
   herbs, such as sage, rosemary,
   thyme and marjoram, or
   2 teaspoons mixed dried herbs
salt and ground black pepper
a few sprigs of fresh sage or
   marjoram, to garnish
4 tablespoons strained plain yogurt
   or crème fraîche

1 Roughly chop the bacon and place in a large pan. Cook gently until all the fat comes out.

COOK'S TIP
For the best flavor, use homemade meat stock for this soup (see page 32). Once it is made, the stock will keep in the refrigerator for up to 4 days, or in the freezer for up to 3 months.

2 Add the onion and soften, adding oil if necessary. Wipe the mushrooms clean, roughly chop and add to the pan. Cover and sweat until they have completely softened and their liquid has run out.

3 Add the stock, sherry, herbs and seasoning, cover and simmer for 10–12 minutes. Process the soup in a food processor or blender until smooth, but don't worry if you still have a slightly textured result.

4 Check the seasoning and heat through. Serve with a dollop of yogurt or crème fraîche and a sprig of fresh sage or marjoram in each bowl.

Energy 111kcal/460kJ; Protein 4.7g; Carbohydrate 2g, of which sugars 1.4g; Fat 8.7g, of which saturates 2.4g; Cholesterol 8mg; Calcium 33mg; Fiber 1.2g; Sodium 174mg.

LEEK AND POTATO SOUP

*THIS IS A HEARTY SCOTTISH STAPLE, SUITABLE FOR EVERYTHING FROM A WARMING LUNCH TO A HOT
DRINK FROM A FLASK ON A COLD AFTERNOON. THE CHOPPED VEGETABLES PRODUCE A CHUNKY SOUP.
IF YOU PREFER A SMOOTH TEXTURE, PRESS THE MIXTURE THROUGH A STRAINER.*

SERVES 4

INGREDIENTS
2 ounces/¼ cup butter
2 leeks, washed thoroughly
    and chopped
1 small onion, peeled and
    finely chopped
12 ounces potatoes, peeled
    and chopped
3¾ cups chicken or
    vegetable stock
salt and ground black pepper

1 Heat 1 ounce/2 tablespoons of the butter
in a large pan over a medium heat. Add
the leeks and onion and cook gently, for
about 7 minutes, until they are softened.

2 Add the potatoes to the pan and cook
for about 2–3 minutes, then add the
stock and bring to the boil. Cover and
simmer for 30–35 minutes, until the
potatoes are tender.

COOK'S TIP
This soup tastes better if you make your
own chicken or vegetable stock (see
pages 30–1).

3 Season to taste and remove the pan
from the heat. Chop up and stir in the
remaining butter. Serve hot, with fresh
crusty bread.

Energy 179kcal/747kJ; Protein 3.2g; Carbohydrate 17.9g, of which sugars 4g; Fat 11g, of which saturates 6.7g; Cholesterol 27mg; Calcium 32mg; Fiber 3g; Sodium 88mg.

YELLOW BROTH

THIS IS ONE OF MANY VERSIONS OF THIS FAMOUS NORTHERN IRISH SOUP, WHICH IS BOTH THICKENED WITH, AND GIVEN ITS FLAVOR BY, OATMEAL. IT'S THE PERFECT SOUP TO SERVE ON A REALLY COLD WINTER'S DAY, GARNISHED WITH CHOPPED FRESH PARSLEY.

SERVES 4

INGREDIENTS

    1 ounce/2 tablespoons butter
    1 onion, finely chopped
    1 celery stick, finely chopped
    1 carrot, finely chopped
    1 ounce/¼ cup all-purpose flour
    3¾ cups chicken stock
    1 ounce/¼ cup medium oatmeal
    4 ounces spinach, chopped
    2 tablespoons cream
    salt and ground black pepper
    chopped fresh parsley, to garnish
      (optional)

1 Melt the butter in a large pan. Add the onion, celery and carrot and stir to coat with the melted butter. Cook for about 2 minutes until the onion is beginning to soften.

2 Stir in the flour and cook gently for a further 1 minute, stirring constantly. Pour in the chicken stock, bring to the boil and cover. Reduce the heat and simmer for 30 minutes until the vegetables are tender.

3 Stir in the oatmeal and chopped spinach and cook for a further 15 minutes, stirring from time to time.

4 Stir in the cream and season well. Serve hot, garnished with chopped fresh parsley.

Energy 127kcal/530kJ; Protein 2.8g; Carbohydrate 12.8g, of which sugars 3g; Fat 7.5g, of which saturates 4.2g; Cholesterol 17mg; Calcium 81mg; Fiber 2g; Sodium 92mg.

LEEK <u>AND</u> OATMEAL SOUP

THIS TRADITIONAL IRISH SOUP IS KNOWN AS BROTCHÁN FOLTCHEP OR BROTCHÁN ROY, AND COMBINES LEEKS, OATMEAL AND MILK—THREE INGREDIENTS THAT HAVE BEEN STAPLE FOODS IN IRELAND FOR CENTURIES. SERVE WITH FRESHLY BAKED BREAD AND BUTTER.

SERVES 4–6

INGREDIENTS

   about 5 cups chicken stock and
     milk, mixed
   2 tablespoons medium pinhead
     oatmeal
   1 ounce/2 tablespoons butter
   6 large leeks, sliced into ¾-inch
     pieces and washed
   pinch of ground mace
   2 tablespoons chopped fresh parsley
   sea salt and ground black pepper
   light cream and chopped fresh
     parsley or chives, to garnish
     (optional)

1 Bring the stock and milk mixture to the boil over medium heat and sprinkle in the oatmeal. Stir well to prevent lumps forming, and then simmer gently.

2 Melt the butter in a separate pan and cook the leeks over a gentle heat until softened slightly, then add them to the stock. Simmer for 15–20 minutes, until the oatmeal is cooked.

VARIATION

Make nettle and oatmeal soup in the spring, when the nettle tops are young and tender. Strip 10 ounces leaves from the stems, chop and add to the leeks.

3 Season with salt, pepper and mace, stir in the parsley and serve in warmed bowls. Decorate with a swirl of cream and some chopped fresh parsley or chives, if you like.

Energy 121kcal/505kJ; Protein 4.2g; Carbohydrate 11.3g, of which sugars 4.5g; Fat 6.8g, of which saturates 3.5g; Cholesterol 13mg; Calcium 53mg; Fiber 4.9g; Sodium 44mg.

IRISH POTATO SOUP

THIS MOST IRISH OF ALL SOUPS IS NOT ONLY EXCELLENT AS IT IS, BUT VERSATILE TOO, AS IT CAN BE USED AS A BASE FOR NUMEROUS OTHER SOUPS. USE A FLOURY POTATO, SUCH AS RUSSET.

SERVES 6–8

INGREDIENTS

2 ounces/¼ cup butter
2 large onions, peeled and
    finely chopped
1½ pounds potatoes, diced
about 7½ cups hot chicken
    stock
a little milk, if necessary
sea salt and ground black pepper
chopped fresh chives, to garnish

1 Melt the butter in a large heavy pan and add the onions, turning them in the butter until well coated. Cover and leave to sweat over a very low heat for about 10 mintues.

2 Add the potatoes to the pan, and mix well with the butter and onions. Season with salt and pepper, cover and cook without coloring over a gentle heat for about 10 minutes. Add the stock, bring to the boil and simmer for 25 minutes, or until the vegetables are tender.

3 Remove from the heat and allow to cool slightly. Puree the soup in batches in a blender or food processor.

4 Reheat the soup over a low heat and adjust the seasoning. If the soup seems too thick, add a little extra stock or milk to achieve the right consistency.

5 Serve the soup very hot, sprinkled with chopped chives.

COOK'S TIP
The best potatoes to use in soups are the floury ones, because they cook more quickly and disintegrate easily. Choose varieties such as Russet, Idaho, and long white.

Energy 167kcal/699kJ; Protein 2.9g; Carbohydrate 23.5g, of which sugars 5.3g; Fat 7.5g, of which saturates 4.5g; Cholesterol 18mg; Calcium 26mg; Fiber 2.1g; Sodium 201mg.

NETTLE SOUP

A COUNTRY-STYLE SOUP THAT IS A TASTY VARIATION OF THE CLASSIC IRISH POTATO SOUP. USE WILD NETTLES IF YOU CAN FIND THEM, OR A WASHED HEAD OF BUTTERHEAD LETTUCE IF YOU PREFER.

SERVES 4

INGREDIENTS

4 ounces/½ cup butter
1 pound onions, sliced
1 pound potatoes, cut into chunks
3 cups chicken stock
1 ounce nettle leaves, removed from the stalks
a small bunch of chives, chopped
salt and ground black pepper
heavy cream, to serve

COOK'S TIP
Wear rubber gloves when handling the nettle leaves to avoid being stung. The leaves lose their sting when cooked.

1 Melt the butter in a large pan and add the sliced onions. Cover and cook for about 5 minutes until just softened.

2 Add the potatoes to the pan with the chicken stock. Cover and cook for 25 minutes, until soft.

3 Wash the nettle leaves and add to the pan. Cook for 5 minutes.

4 Puree the soup in a blender or food processor. Return it to the pan, season and stir in the chives. Serve with a swirl of cream and a sprinkle of pepper.

Energy 338kcal/1404kJ; Protein 3.9g; Carbohydrate 27.6g, of which sugars 8.3g; Fat 24.4g, of which saturates 15.1g; Cholesterol 61mg; Calcium 71mg; Fiber 3.3g; Sodium 202mg.

SWEET POTATO AND RED PEPPER SOUP

As colorful as it is good to eat, this soup is a sure winner. Serve it with some fresh rustic bread for a warming winter treat.

SERVES 6

INGREDIENTS
    2 red bell peppers (about 8 ounces)
      seeded and cubed
    1¼ pounds sweet potatoes, cubed
    1 onion, roughly chopped
    2 large garlic cloves, roughly chopped
    1¼ cups dry white wine
    5 cups vegetable stock
    Tabasco sauce, to taste
    salt and ground black pepper
    fresh rustic bread, to serve

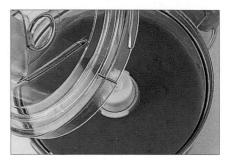

1 Dice a small quantity of red pepper for the garnish and set aside. Put the rest into a pan with the sweet potato, onion, garlic, wine and vegetable stock. Bring to the boil, lower the heat and simmer for 30 minutes or until all the vegetables are quite soft.

2 Transfer the mixture to a blender or food processor and process until smooth. Season to taste with salt, pepper and a generous dash of Tabasco. Cool slightly. Garnish with the reserved diced red pepper and serve warm or at room temperature.

Energy 124kcal/526kJ; Protein 1.6g; Carbohydrate 21.8g, of which sugars 8.6g; Fat 0.5g, of which saturates 0.1g; Cholesterol 0mg; Calcium 29mg; Fiber 2.9g; Sodium 38mg.

Sweet Potato and Parsnip Soup

The sweetness of the two root vegetables comes through strongly in this delicious soup. Roasted vegetable strips add an unusual garnish.

SERVES 6

INGREDIENTS

1 tablespoon sunflower oil
1 large leek, sliced
2 celery sticks, chopped
1 pound sweet potatoes, diced
8 ounces/1½ cups parsnips, diced
3¾ cups vegetable stock
salt and ground black pepper
For the garnish
1 tablespoon chopped fresh parsley
roasted strips of sweet potatoes
  and parsnips

1 Heat the oil in a large pan and add the leek, celery, sweet potatoes and parsnips. Cook gently for about 5 minutes, stirring to prevent them browning or sticking to the pan.

2 Stir in the vegetable stock and bring to the boil, then cover and simmer gently for about 25 minutes, or until the vegetables are tender, stirring occasionally. Season to taste. Remove the pan from the heat and allow the soup to cool slightly.

COOK'S TIP
Cut some narrow strips of sweet potato and parsnip, drizzle with olive oil and roast in a hot oven for 10–15 minutes.

3 Puree the soup in a blender or food processor until smooth, then return the soup to the pan and reheat gently.

4 To serve, sprinkle over the chopped parsley and roasted strips of sweet potatoes and parsnips.

Energy 113kcal/479kJ; Protein 2.1g; Carbohydrate 21.6g, of which sugars 7.2g; Fat 2.6g, of which saturates 0.4g; Cholesterol 0mg; Calcium 45mg; Fiber 4.3g; Sodium 40mg.

LEGUME SOUPS

Soups made with legumes—peas, beans, and lentils—are very nutritious as they contain protein, fiber, minerals and B vitamins, and are low in fat. The recipes in this section are particularly suitable for vegetarians, if made with vegetarian stock. For a quick and easy lunch, try a simple Potage of Lentils, or Catalan Potato and Fava Bean Soup. On special occasions, impress your guests with cinnamon-scented Moroccan Chickpea and Lentil Soup with Honey Buns.

CATALAN POTATO AND FAVA BEAN SOUP

FAVA BEANS ARE ALSO KNOWN AS BROAD BEANS. WHILE THEY ARE IN SEASON, FRESH BEANS ARE IDEAL, BUT TINNED OR FROZEN WILL MAKE A PERFECTLY GOOD SUBSTITUTE.

SERVES 6

INGREDIENTS

   2 tablespoons olive oil
   2 onions, chopped
   3 large floury potatoes, diced
   1 pound fresh fava beans
   7½ cups vegetable stock
   1 bunch cilantro, finely chopped
   ⅔ cup light cream
   salt and ground black pepper
   fresh cilantro, to garnish

COOK'S TIP
Fava beans sometimes have a tough outer skin, particularly if they are large. To remove this, first cook the beans briefly, peel off the skin, and add the tender center part to the soup.

1 Heat the oil in a large pan and fry the onions, stirring occasionally, for about 5 minutes until softened but not brown.

2 Add the potatoes, beans (reserving a few for garnishing) and stock to the mixture in the pan and bring to the boil, then simmer for 5 minutes.

3 Stir in the cilantro and simmer for a further 10 minutes.

4 Process the mixture in a blender or food processor (you may have to do this in batches) then return the soup to the pan.

5 Stir in the cream (reserving a little for garnishing). Season to taste with salt and pepper, and bring to a simmer.

6 Serve garnished with more cilantro leaves, beans and cream.

Energy 187kcal/784kJ; Protein 8.1g; Carbohydrate 19.2g, of which sugars 3.5g; Fat 9.2g, of which saturates 3.7g; Cholesterol 14mg; Calcium 89mg; Fiber 6.1g; Sodium 22mg.

FAVA BEAN MINESTRONE

THE CLASSIC, WINTRY MINESTRONE SOUP TAKES ON A SUMMER-FRESH IMAGE IN THIS LIGHT RECIPE.
ANY SMALL PASTA SHAPES CAN BE USED INSTEAD OF THE SPAGHETTINI IF YOU PREFER.

SERVES 6

INGREDIENTS

2 tablespoons olive oil
2 onions, peeled and
  finely chopped
2 garlic cloves, peeled and
  finely chopped
2 carrots, very finely chopped
1 celery stick, very finely chopped
5⅔ cups boiling water
1 pound shelled fresh fava beans
8 ounces snow peas, cut into
  fine strips
3 tomatoes, peeled and chopped
1 teaspoon tomato paste
2 ounces spaghettini, broken into
  1½-inch lengths
8 ounces baby spinach
2 tablespoons chopped
  fresh parsley
handful of fresh basil leaves
salt and ground black pepper
basil sprigs, to garnish
freshly grated Parmesan cheese,
  to serve

1 Heat the oil in a pan and add the chopped onions and garlic. Cook over a low heat for 4–5 minutes, until softened but not browned.

2 Add the carrots and celery, and cook for 2–3 minutes. Add the boiling water and simmer for 15 minutes, until the vegetables are tender.

3 Cook the fava beans in boiling salted water for 4–5 minutes. Remove with a slotted spoon, refresh under cold water and set aside.

4 Bring the pan of water back to the boil, add the snow peas and cook for 1 minute until just tender. Drain, then refresh under cold water and set aside.

5 Add the tomatoes and the tomato puree to the soup. Cook for 1 minute. Puree two or three large ladlefuls of the soup and a quarter of the fava beans in a food processor or blender until smooth. Set aside.

6 Add the spaghettini to the remaining soup and cook for 6–8 minutes, until tender. Stir in the puree and spinach and cook for 2–3 minutes. Add the rest of the fava beans, the snow peas and parsley, and season well.

7 When you are ready to serve the soup, stir in the basil leaves, ladle the soup into deep cups or bowls and garnish with sprigs of basil. Serve a little grated Parmesan with the soup.

Energy 162kcal/682kJ; Protein 9.9g; Carbohydrate 20.8g, of which sugars 6.5g; Fat 4.9g, of which saturates 0.7g; Cholesterol 0mg; Calcium 137mg; Fiber 7.9g; Sodium 72mg.

POTAGE OF LENTILS

THIS TRADITIONAL JEWISH SOUP IS SOMETIMES KNOWN AS ESAU'S SOUP. RED LENTILS AND VEGETABLES ARE COOKED AND PUREED, THEN SHARPENED WITH LOTS OF LEMON JUICE.

SERVES 4

INGREDIENTS

3 tablespoons olive oil
1 onion, chopped
2 celery sticks, chopped
1 or 2 carrots, sliced
8 garlic cloves, chopped
1 potato, peeled and diced
9 ounces/generous 1 cup red lentils,
  picked over and rinsed
4 cups vegetable stock
2 bay leaves
1 or 2 lemons, halved
½ teaspoon ground cumin, or
  to taste
cayenne pepper or Tabasco sauce,
  to taste
salt and ground black pepper
lemon slices and chopped fresh
  Italian parsley, to serve

1 Heat the oil in a large pan. Add the onion and cook for about 5 minutes, or until softened. Stir in the celery, carrots, half the garlic and all the potato. Cook for a few minutes until beginning to soften.

2 Add the lentils and stock to the pan and bring to the boil. Reduce the heat, cover and simmer for about 30 minutes, until the potato and lentils are tender.

3 Add the bay leaves, remaining garlic and half the lemons to the pan and cook the soup for a further 10 minutes. Remove the bay leaves. Squeeze the juice from the remaining lemons, then stir into the soup, to taste.

4 Pour the soup into a food processor or blender and process until smooth. (You may need to do this in batches.) Tip the soup back into the pan, stir in the cumin, cayenne pepper or Tabasco sauce, and season with salt and pepper.

5 Ladle the soup into bowls and top each portion with lemon slices and a sprinkling of chopped fresh Italian parsley.

VARIATION
On a hot day, serve this soup cold, with even more lemon juice.

Energy 330kcal/1391kJ; Protein 16.3g; Carbohydrate 48.1g, of which sugars 4.7g; Fat 9.4g, of which saturates 1.4g; Cholesterol 0mg; Calcium 50mg; Fiber 4.5g; Sodium 44mg.

BEAN <u>AND</u> PISTOU SOUP

THIS HEARTY VEGETARIAN SOUP IS A TYPICAL PROVENÇAL-STYLE SOUP, RICHLY FLAVORED WITH A HOMEMADE GARLIC AND FRESH BASIL PISTOU SAUCE.

SERVES 4–6

INGREDIENTS

    5 ounces/scant 1 cup dried navy
      beans, soaked overnight
    5 ounces/scant 1 cup dried
      small cannellini beans,
      soaked overnight
    1 onion, chopped
    5 cups hot vegetable stock
    2 carrots, roughly chopped
    8 ounces savoy cabbage,
      shredded
    1 large potato, about 8 ounces,
      roughly chopped
    8 ounces green beans, chopped
    salt and ground black pepper
    basil leaves, to garnish
For the pistou
    4 garlic cloves
    8 large sprigs basil leaves
    6 tablespoons olive oil
    4 tablespoons freshly grated
      Parmesan cheese

1 Soak a bean pot in cold water for 20 minutes, then drain. Drain the soaked navy and small cannellini beans and place in the bean pot. Add the chopped onion and pour over sufficient cold water to come 2 inches above the beans. Cover and place the pot in an unheated oven. Set the oven to 400°F and cook for about 1½ hours, or until the beans are tender.

2 Drain the beans and onions. Place half the beans and onions in a food processor or blender and process to a paste. Return the beans and paste to the bean pot. Add the vegetable stock.

3 Add the chopped carrots, shredded cabbage, chopped potato and green beans to the bean pot. Season with salt and pepper, cover and return the pot to the oven. Reduce the oven temperature to 350°F and cook for 1 hour, or until all the vegetables are cooked right through.

4 Meanwhile place the garlic and basil in a mortar and pound with a pestle, then gradually beat in the oil. Stir in the grated Parmesan. Stir half the pistou into the soup and then ladle into warmed soup bowls. Top each bowl of soup with a spoonful of the remaining pistou and serve garnished with basil.

Energy 286kcal/1214kJ; Protein 19.8g; Carbohydrate 50.9g, of which sugars 11.1g; Fat 1.8g, of which saturates 0.3g; Cholesterol 0mg; Calcium 142mg; Fiber 16.1g; Sodium 36mg.

LIMA BEAN, SUN-DRIED TOMATO AND PESTO SOUP

THIS SOUP IS SO QUICK AND EASY TO MAKE, AND USING PLENTY OF PESTO AND SUN-DRIED TOMATO PASTE GIVES IT A RICH, MINESTRONE-LIKE FLAVOR.

SERVES 4

INGREDIENTS

3¾ cups chicken or vegetable stock
2 cans (28 ounces) lima beans
4 tablespoons sun-dried
  tomato paste
5 tablespoons pesto

COOK'S TIP
Use a good-quality homemade or bought fresh stock for the best results. Vegetarians should use vegetable stock.

VARIATION
As an alternative to lima beans, use navy or cannellini beans.

1 Drain and rinse the lima beans. Put the drained beans in a large pan with the stock and bring just to the boil.

2 Reduce the heat and stir in the tomato puree and pesto. Cover, bring back to simmering point and cook gently for 5 minutes.

3 Transfer six ladlefuls of the soup to a blender or food processor, scooping up plenty of the beans. Process until smooth, then return to the pan.

4 Heat gently, stirring frequently, for 5 minutes, then season if necessary. Ladle into four warmed soup bowls.

Energy 264kcal/1109kJ; Protein 14.8g; Carbohydrate 27.4g, of which sugars 3.6g; Fat 11.3g, of which saturates 2.7g; Cholesterol 6mg; Calcium 109mg; Fiber 9.5g; Sodium 932mg.

AMERICAN RED BEAN SOUP
WITH GUACAMOLE SALSA

THIS SOUP IS IN TEX-MEX STYLE, AND IT IS SERVED WITH A COOLING AVOCADO AND LIME SALSA. IF YOU RELISH CHILES, ADD A LITTLE MORE CAYENNE FOR A TRULY FIERY EXPERIENCE.

SERVES 6

INGREDIENTS
  2 tablespoons olive oil
  2 onions, chopped
  2 garlic cloves, chopped
  2 teaspoons ground cumin
  ¼ teaspoon cayenne pepper
  1 tablespoon paprika
  1 tablespoon tomato paste
  ½ teaspoon dried oregano
  1 can (14 ounces) chopped tomatoes
  2 cans (28 ounces) red kidney beans,
   drained and rinsed
  3¾ cups water
  salt and ground black pepper
  Tabasco sauce, to serve
For the guacamole salsa
  2 avocados
  1 small red onion, finely chopped
  1 green chile, seeded and chopped
  1 tablespoon chopped
   fresh cilantro
  juice of 1 lime

1 Heat the oil in a pan and add the onions and garlic. Cook for 4–5 minutes, until softened. Add the cumin, cayenne and paprika, and cook for 1 minute.

2 Stir in the tomato paste and cook for a few seconds, then stir in the oregano. Add the chopped tomatoes, kidney beans and water. Bring to the boil and simmer for 15–20 minutes.

3 Cool the soup slightly, then puree it in a food processor or blender until smooth. Return to the pan and season.

4 To make the guacamole salsa, halve, pit and peel the avocados, then dice them finely. Place in a small bowl and gently, but thoroughly, mix with the finely chopped red onion and chile, and the cilantro and lime juice.

5 Reheat the soup and ladle into bowls. Spoon a little guacamole salsa into the middle of each and serve, offering Tabasco sauce separately.

Energy 244kcal/1023kJ; Protein 10.5g; Carbohydrate 27.5g, of which sugars 7.4g; Fat 11g, of which saturates 2g; Cholesterol 0mg; Calcium 108mg; Fiber 10g; Sodium 535mg.

BLACK-EYED PEA
AND TOMATO BROTH

THIS DELICIOUS BLACK-EYED PEA SOUP—KNOWN AS LUBIYA IN ISRAEL—IS FLAVORED WITH TANGY LEMON AND SPECKLED WITH CHOPPED FRESH CILANTRO. IT IS IDEAL FOR SERVING AT PARTIES. SIMPLY MULTIPLY THE QUANTITIES AS REQUIRED.

SERVES 4

INGREDIENTS

6 ounces/1 cup black-eyed peas
1 tablespoon olive oil
2 onions, chopped
4 garlic cloves, chopped
1 medium-hot or 2–3 mild fresh
  chiles, chopped
1 teaspoon ground cumin
1 teaspoon ground turmeric
9 ounces fresh or canned
  tomatoes, diced
2½ cups chicken, beef or
  vegetable stock
1 ounce fresh cilantro leaves,
  roughly chopped
juice of ½ lemon
pitta bread, to serve

1 Put the beans in a pan, cover with cold water, bring to the boil and cook for 5 minutes. Remove from the heat, cover and leave to stand for 2 hours. Drain the beans, return to the pan, cover with fresh cold water, then simmer for 35–40 minutes, or until the beans are tender. Drain and set aside.

2 Heat the oil in a pan, add the onions, garlic and chile and cook for 5 minutes, or until the onion is soft. Stir in the cumin, turmeric, tomatoes, stock, half the cilantro and the beans and simmer for 20–30 minutes. Stir in the lemon juice and remaining cilantro and serve at once with pitta bread.

Energy 168kcal/712kJ; Protein 10.7g; Carbohydrate 25g, of which sugars 2.3g; Fat 3.6g, of which saturates 0.6g; Cholesterol 0mg; Calcium 52mg; Fiber 4.1g; Sodium 10mg.

MOROCCAN CHICKPEA AND LENTIL SOUP WITH HONEY BUNS

THIS THICK PULSE AND VEGETABLE SOUP IS SAID TO ORIGINATE FROM A SEMOLINA GRUEL THAT THE BERBERS ATE DURING THE COLD WINTERS IN THE ATLAS MOUNTAINS. TODAY, IT IS SERVED IN RESTAURANTS AND CAFÉS AS A HEARTY SNACK WITH HONEY-SWEETENED SPICED BREAD OR BUNS.

SERVES 8

INGREDIENTS
  2–3 tablespoons olive oil
  2 onions, halved and sliced
  ½ teaspoon ground ginger
  ½ teaspoon ground turmeric
  1 teaspoon ground cinnamon
  pinch of saffron threads
  2 cans (28 ounces) chopped
    tomatoes
  1–2 teaspoons superfine sugar
  6 ounces/¾ cup brown or green
    lentils, picked over and rinsed
  about 7½ cups meat or vegetable
    stock, or water
  7 ounces/1 generous cup dried
    chickpeas, soaked overnight,
    drained and boiled until tender
  7 ounces/1 generous cup dried fava
    beans, soaked overnight, drained
    and boiled until tender
  small bunch of fresh cilantro,
    chopped
  small bunch of Italian parsley,
    chopped
  salt and ground black pepper
For the buns
  ½ teaspoon dried yeast
  11 ounces/1¼ cups unbleached
    white bread flour
  1–2 tablespoons clear honey
  1 teaspoon fennel seeds
  8 fluid ounces/1 cup milk
  1 egg yolk, stirred with
    a little milk
  salt

1 Make the buns. Dissolve the yeast in about 1 tablespoon lukewarm water. Sift the flour and a pinch of salt into a bowl. Make a well in the center and add the dissolved yeast, honey and fennel seeds. Gradually pour in the milk, using your hands to work it into the flour along with the honey and yeast, until the mixture forms a dough—if the dough becomes too sticky to handle, add more flour.

2 Turn the dough out onto a floured surface and knead well for about 10 minutes, until it is smooth and elastic. Flour the surface under the dough and cover it with a damp cloth, then leave the dough to rise until it has doubled in size.

3 Preheat the oven to 450°F. Grease two baking sheets. Divide the dough into 12 balls. On a floured surface, flatten the balls of dough with the palm of your hand, then place them on a baking sheet. Brush the tops of the buns with egg yolk and bake for about 15 minutes until they are risen slightly and sound hollow when tapped underneath. Transfer to a wire rack to cool.

4 To make the soup, heat the olive oil in a stockpot or large pan. Add the onions and stir for about 15 minutes, or until they are soft.

5 Add the ginger, turmeric, cinnamon, saffron, tomatoes and sugar. Stir in the lentils and pour in the stock or water. Bring to the boil, then reduce the heat, cover and simmer for about 25 minutes, or until the lentils are tender.

6 Stir in the cooked chickpeas and beans, bring back to the boil, then cover and simmer for a further 10–15 minutes. Stir in the fresh herbs and season the soup to taste. Serve piping hot, with the honey buns.

Energy 368kcal/1558kJ; Protein 18.3g; Carbohydrate 64.9g, of which sugars 9.7g; Fat 5.7g, of which saturates 1g; Cholesterol 2mg; Calcium 172mg; Fiber 7.5g; Sodium 74mg.

TUSCAN CANNELLINI BEAN SOUP
WITH CAVOLO NERO

CAVOLO NERO IS A VERY DARK GREEN CABBAGE WITH A NUTTY FLAVOR FROM TUSCANY AND SOUTHERN ITALY. IT IS IDEAL FOR THIS TRADITIONAL RECIPE.

SERVES 4

INGREDIENTS
    2 cans (28 ounces) chopped
      tomatoes with herbs
    9 ounces cavolo nero leaves, or savoy
      cabbage
    1 can (14 ounces) cannellini beans,
      drained and rinsed
    4 tablespoons extra virgin olive oil
    salt and ground black pepper

1 Pour the tomatoes into a large pan and add a can of cold water. Season with salt and pepper and bring to the boil, then reduce the heat to a simmer.

2 Roughly shred the cabbage leaves and add them to the pan. Partially cover the pan and simmer gently for about 15 minutes, or until the cabbage is tender.

3 Add the cannellini beans to the pan and warm through for a few minutes. Check and adjust the seasoning, then ladle the soup into bowls, drizzle each one with a little olive oil and serve.

Energy 227kcal/950kJ; Protein 8.2g; Carbohydrate 22.3g, of which sugars 10.4g; Fat 12.2g, of which saturates 1.9g; Cholesterol 0mg; Calcium 60mg; Fiber 7.9g; Sodium 443mg.

OLD COUNTRY MUSHROOM, BEAN AND BARLEY SOUP

THIS HEARTY JEWISH SOUP IS PERFECT ON A FREEZING COLD DAY. SERVE IN WARMED BOWLS, WITH PLENTY OF RYE OR PUMPERNICKEL BREAD.

SERVES 6–8

INGREDIENTS

2–3 tablespoons small navy beans, soaked overnight
3–4 tablespoons green split peas
3–4 tablespoons yellow split peas
6–7 tablespoons pearl barley
1 onion, chopped
2 carrots, sliced
3 celery sticks, diced or sliced
½ baking potato, peeled and cut into chunks
¼ ounce or 3 tablespoons mixed flavorful dried mushrooms
5 garlic cloves, sliced
8 cups water
2 vegetable bouillon cubes
salt and ground black pepper
2–3 tablespoons chopped fresh parsley, to garnish

1 In a large pan, put the beans, green and yellow split peas, pearl barley, onion, carrots, celery, potato, mushrooms, garlic and water.

2 Bring the mixture to the boil, then reduce the heat, cover and simmer gently for about 1½ hours, or until the beans are tender.

3 Crumble the bouillon cubes into the soup and taste for seasoning. Ladle into warmed bowls, garnish with parsley and serve with rye or pumpernickel bread.

COOK'S TIP
Do not add the bouillon cubes until the end of cooking, as the salt will stop the beans from becoming tender.

Energy 171kcal/726kJ; Protein 7.7g; Carbohydrate 35.4g, of which sugars 3.7g; Fat 0.8g, of which saturates 0.1g; Cholesterol 0mg; Calcium 37mg; Fiber 3.3g; Sodium 27mg.

RUSSIAN PEA AND BARLEY SOUP

THIS THICK AND WARMING SOUP, GROCHOWKA, MAKES A SUBSTANTIAL APPETIZER, OR IT MAY BE SERVED AS A MEAL IN ITS OWN RIGHT, EATEN WITH HOT CRUSTY BREAD.

3 Dry-fry the bacon cubes in a frying pan for 5 minutes, or until well browned and crispy. Remove from the pan with a slotted spoon, leaving the fat behind, and set aside.

4 Add the butter to the frying pan, add the onion and garlic and cook gently for 5 minutes. Add the celeriac and cook for a further 5 minutes, or until the onion is just starting to color.

5 Add the softened vegetables and bacon to the pan of stock, peas and barley. Season lightly with salt and pepper, then cover and simmer for 20 minutes, or until the soup is thick. Stir in the marjoram, add extra black pepper to taste and serve with bread.

SERVES 6

INGREDIENTS

8 ounces/1¼ cups yellow split peas, rinsed in cold water
1 ounce/¼ cup pearl barley, rinsed in cold water
7½ cups vegetable or ham stock
2 ounces smoked fatty bacon, cubed
1 ounce/2 tablespoons butter
1 onion, finely chopped
2 garlic cloves, crushed
8 ounces celeriac, cubed
1 tablespoon roughly chopped fresh marjoram
salt and ground black pepper
bread, to serve

1 Put the peas and barley in a bowl, cover with plenty of water and leave to soak overnight.

2 The next day, drain and rinse the peas and barley. Put them in a large pan, pour in the stock and bring to the boil. Turn down the heat and simmer gently for 40 minutes.

Energy 189kcal/799kJ; Protein 11g; Carbohydrate 25.8g, of which sugars 1.8g; Fat 5.5g, of which saturates 2.8g; Cholesterol 13mg; Calcium 39mg; Fiber 2.4g; Sodium 190mg.

LENTIL ᴬᴺᴰ BACON SOUP

THIS IS A WONDERFULLY HEARTY GERMAN SOUP. A LIGHTER VERSION CAN BE MADE BY OMITTING THE FRANKFURTERS, IF YOU PREFER.

SERVES 6

INGREDIENTS

    8 ounces/1 cup brown lentils
    1 tablespoon sunflower oil
    1 onion, finely chopped
    1 leek, finely chopped
    1 carrot, finely diced
    2 celery sticks, chopped
    4-ounce piece lean bacon
    2 bay leaves
    6¼ cups water
    2 tablespoons chopped fresh parsley,
      plus extra to garnish
    8 ounces frankfurters, sliced
    salt and ground black pepper

1 Rinse the lentils thoroughly under cold running water, then drain.

2 Heat the oil in a large pan and gently fry the onion for 5 minutes until soft. Add the leek, carrot, celery, bacon and bay leaves.

3 Add the lentils. Pour in the water, then slowly bring to the boil. Skim the surface, then simmer, half-covered, for about 45–50 minutes, or until the lentils are soft.

4 Remove the piece of bacon from the soup and cut into small cubes. Trim off any fat.

5 Return the bacon to the soup with the parsley and sliced frankfurters, and season well with salt and freshly ground black pepper. Simmer for 2–3 minutes, then remove the bay leaves.

6 Transfer to individual soup bowls and serve garnished with chopped parsley.

COOK'S TIP
Unlike most legumes, brown lentils do not need to be soaked before cooking.

Energy 260kcal/1091kJ; Protein 14.8g; Carbohydrate 24.6g, of which sugars 3.8g; Fat 12.1g, of which saturates 3.8g; Cholesterol 29mg; Calcium 41mg; Fiber 3.2g; Sodium 370mg.

WHITE BEAN SOUP

*USE EITHER NAVY BEANS OR LIMA BEANS FOR THIS VELVETY SOUP. DRIED BEANS NEED TO BE SOAKED
IN COLD WATER OVERNIGHT BEFORE THEY ARE COOKED.*

SERVES 4

INGREDIENTS
6 ounces/¾ cup dried white beans,
  soaked in cold water overnight
2–3 tablespoons oil
2 large onions, chopped
4 celery sticks, chopped
1 parsnip, chopped
4 cups chicken stock
salt and ground black pepper
chopped fresh cilantro and paprika,
  to garnish

1 Drain the beans and boil rapidly in
fresh water for 10 minutes. Drain, cover
with fresh water and simmer for 1–2
hours until soft. Reserve the liquid and
discard any bean skins on the surface.

2 Heat the oil in a heavy pan and
sauté the onions, celery and parsnip
for 3 minutes.

3 Add the cooked beans and stock and
continue cooking until the vegetables
are tender.

4 Allow the soup to cool slightly and,
using a food processor or hand
blender, puree the soup until it is
velvety smooth.

5 Reheat the soup gently, gradually
adding some of the bean liquid or a
little water if it is too thick. Season to
taste with salt and pepper.

6 To serve, transfer the soup into wide
bowls. Garnish with fresh cilantro and a
sprinkling of paprika. Serve hot.

VARIATIONS
• You can, if you prefer, use 1 can
(14 ounces) cannellini or lima beans
instead of dried beans. Drain and rinse
them before adding to the dish.
• Garnish the soup with chopped parsley
instead of cilantro, and sprinkle with a
little cayenne pepper.

Energy 220kcal/926kJ; Protein 11.5g; Carbohydrate 30.6g, of which sugars 8.4g; Fat 6.7g, of which saturates 0.9g; Cholesterol 0mg; Calcium 91mg; Fiber 9.8g; Sodium 32mg.

BLACK AND WHITE BEAN SOUP

ALTHOUGH THIS SOUP TAKES A WHILE TO PREPARE, THE RESULTS ARE SO STUNNING THAT IT IS WELL WORTH THE EFFORT.

SERVES 8

INGREDIENTS

12 ounces/2 cups dried black beans, soaked overnight and drained
10½ cups water
6 garlic cloves, crushed
12 ounces/2 cups dried white beans, soaked overnight and drained
6 tablespoons balsamic vinegar
4 jalapeño peppers, seeded and chopped
6 scallions, finely chopped
juice of 1 lime
2 fluid ounces/¼ cup olive oil
½ ounce/¼ cup chopped fresh cilantro, plus extra to garnish
salt and ground black pepper

1 Drain and rinse the black beans under cold running water. Place in a large pan with half the water and garlic. Bring to the boil. Reduce the heat to low, cover the pan, and simmer for about 1½ hours until the beans are soft.

2 Meanwhile, drain and rinse the white beans and put in another pan with the remaining water and garlic. Bring to the boil, cover the pan and simmer for about 1 hour until soft.

3 Puree the cooked white beans in a food processor or blender. Stir in the vinegar, jalapeños, and half of the scallions. Return to the pan and reheat gently.

4 Puree the cooked black beans in the food processor or blender. Return them to the pan and stir in the lime juice, olive oil, cilantro and remaining scallions. Reheat gently.

5 Season both soups with salt and freshly ground black pepper. To serve, place a ladleful of each pureed soup in each soup bowl, side by side. Swirl the two soups together with a toothpick or skewer. Garnish with fresh cilantro and serve hot.

Energy 281kcal/1189kJ; Protein 19.7g; Carbohydrate 40.2g, of which sugars 3.7g; Fat 5.7g, of which saturates 0.8g; Cholesterol 0mg; Calcium 92mg; Fiber 14.2g; Sodium 17mg.

SPLIT PEA AND PUMPKIN SOUP

THIS IS A TASTY VEGETARIAN VERSION OF A TRADITIONAL PEA SOUP. THE SPLIT PEAS MUST BE SOAKED IN COLD WATER OVERNIGHT.

2 In a separate pan, melt the butter and sauté the onion until it is soft but not browned.

3 Add the pumpkin, tomatoes, tarragon, cilantro, cumin and chili powder, and crumble in the bouillon cube. Bring to the boil over high heat.

4 Stir the vegetable mixture into the cooked split peas and their liquid. Simmer over a gentle heat for about 20 minutes or until the vegetables are tender. If the soup is too thick, add about another ⅔ cup water and reheat gently.

5 Ladle into warm bowls and serve hot, garnished with sprigs of cilantro.

SERVES 4

INGREDIENTS

   8 ounces/1 cup split peas
   5 cups water
   1 ounce/2 tablespoons butter
   1 onion, finely chopped
   8 ounces pumpkin, chopped
   3 tomatoes, peeled and chopped
   1 teaspoon dried tarragon, crushed
   1 tablespoon chopped fresh cilantro
   ½ teaspoon ground cumin
   chili powder, to taste
   1 vegetable bouillon cube
   sprigs of fresh cilantro,
     to garnish

1 Soak the split peas overnight in enough water to cover them completely, then drain. Place them in a large pan, add the water and boil for about 30 minutes until tender.

Energy 251kcal/1061kJ; Protein 14.5g; Carbohydrate 36.5g, of which sugars 5.5g; Fat 6.2g, of which saturates 3.5g; Cholesterol 13mg; Calcium 55mg; Fiber 4.3g; Sodium 65mg.

CAULIFLOWER, CANNELLINI AND FENNEL SOUP

THE SWEET, ANISE-LIQUORICE FLAVOR OF THE FENNEL SEEDS GIVES A DELICIOUS EDGE TO THIS HEARTY VEGETARIAN SOUP.

SERVES 4–6

INGREDIENTS

1 tablespoon olive oil
1 garlic clove, crushed
1 onion, chopped
2 teaspoons fennel seeds
1 cauliflower, cut into small florets
2 cans (28 ounces) small cannellini
   beans, drained and rinsed
5 cups vegetable stock
   or water
salt and ground black pepper
chopped fresh parsley, to garnish
toasted slices of French bread,
   to serve

3 Bring the mixture to the boil. Reduce the heat and simmer for about 10 minutes or until the cauliflower is tender. Pour the soup into a blender or food processor and blend until smooth.

4 Stir in the remaining beans and season to taste. Reheat and pour into bowls. Sprinkle with chopped parsley and serve with toasted slices of French bread.

1 Heat the olive oil. Add the garlic, onion and fennel seeds and cook gently for 5 minutes or until softened.

2 Add the cauliflower florets, half the beans and the vegetable stock or water.

COOK'S TIP
When purchasing a cauliflower, look for one with cream-colored, compact, firm florets, or curds, encased in large, bright green leaves.

Energy 170kcal/719kJ; Protein 11.1g; Carbohydrate 26g, of which sugars 6.6g; Fat 3.1g, of which saturates 0.5g; Cholesterol 0mg; Calcium 108mg; Fiber 9.3g; Sodium 525mg.

EASTERN EUROPEAN CHICKPEA SOUP

CHICKPEAS FORM PART OF THE STAPLE DIET IN THE BALKANS, WHERE THIS SOUP ORIGINATES. IT IS ECONOMICAL TO MAKE, AND IS A HEARTY AND SATISFYING DISH.

SERVES 4–6

INGREDIENTS

1¼ pounds/5 cups chickpeas, soaked overnight
9 cups vegetable stock
3 large waxy potatoes, cut into bitesize chunks
2 fluid ounces/¼ cup olive oil
8 ounces spinach leaves
salt and ground black pepper
spicy sausage, cooked (optional)

1 Drain the chickpeas and rinse under cold water. Place in a large pan with the vegetable stock. Bring to the boil, then reduce the heat and cook gently for about 1 hour.

2 Add the potatoes, olive oil, and salt and pepper to taste. Cook for 20 minutes until the potatoes are tender.

COOK'S TIP
Dried chickpeas toughen with age so, although they will keep for up to a year in a cool dry place, it is best to buy them in small quantities.

3 Add the spinach and sliced, cooked sausage (if using) 5 minutes before the end of cooking. Serve the soup in individual warmed soup bowls.

Energy 399kcal/1685kJ; Protein 20.6g; Carbohydrate 58.1g, of which sugars 4.1g; Fat 11g, of which saturates 1.4g; Cholesterol 0mg; Calcium 209mg; Fiber 10.8g; Sodium 101mg.

CHICKPEA AND SPINACH SOUP WITH GARLIC

THIS DELICIOUS, THICK AND CREAMY SOUP IS RICHLY FLAVORED AND PERFECT FOR VEGETARIANS.
SERVED WITH SOME FRESH CRUSTY BREAD, IT MAKES A COMPLETE MEAL.

SERVES 4

INGREDIENTS

2 tablespoons olive oil
4 garlic cloves, crushed
1 onion, roughly chopped
2 teaspoons ground cumin
2 teaspoons ground coriander
5 cups vegetable stock
12 ounces potatoes,
 finely chopped
1 can (15 ounces) chickpeas,
 drained
1 tablespoon cornstarch
⅔ cup heavy cream
2 tablespoons light tahini
7 ounces spinach, shredded
cayenne pepper
salt and ground black pepper

1 Heat the oil in a large pan and cook the garlic and onion for about 5 minutes or until the onion is softened and golden brown.

2 Stir in the ground cumin and coriander and cook for 1 minute. Add the stock and potatoes. Bring to the boil and simmer for 10 minutes.

3 Add the chickpeas and simmer for a further 5 minutes or until the potatoes are just tender.

4 Blend together the cornstarch, cream, tahini and plenty of seasoning. Stir into the soup a little at a time. Add the shredded spinach.

5 Bring to the boil, stirring, and simmer for a further 2 minutes. Adjust the seasoning with salt, pepper and cayenne pepper to taste.

6 Spoon into four warmed bowls and serve sprinkled with a little extra cayenne pepper.

COOK'S TIPS
• Tahini is a paste made with sesame seeds and is available from many health food stores.
• You can use dried chickpeas instead of canned ones if you prefer, but remember that they must be soaked overnight.
• For a lighter soup, use low-fat milk instead of cream, but the result will not be so rich and creamy.

Energy 496kcal/2066kJ; Protein 12.7g; Carbohydrate 37.3g, of which sugars 3.8g; Fat 33.9g, of which saturates 14.4g; Cholesterol 51mg; Calcium 210mg; Fiber 7.1g; Sodium 326mg.

CHICKPEA AND PARSLEY SOUP

PARSLEY AND A HINT OF LEMON BRING FRESHNESS TO CHICKPEAS. USE VEGETABLE STOCK INSTEAD OF CHICKEN STOCK FOR THIS SOUP IF YOU ARE CATERING FOR VEGETARIANS.

2 Place the onion and parsley in a food processor or blender and process until finely chopped.

3 Heat the olive and sunflower oils in a large pan or flameproof casserole and fry the onion mixture for about 4 minutes over a low heat until the onion is slightly softened.

4 Add the chickpeas, cook gently for 1–2 minutes then add the stock. Season well. Bring the soup to the boil, then cover and simmer for 20 minutes.

5 Allow the soup to cool a little and then mash the chickpeas using a fork until the soup is thick but still quite chunky.

6 Reheat the soup and add the lemon juice. Serve garnished with lemon wedges and rind.

SERVES 6

INGREDIENTS

8 ounces/1⅓ cups chickpeas, soaked overnight
1 small onion
1 bunch of fresh parsley (about 1½ ounces)
2 tablespoons olive and sunflower oils, mixed
5 cups chicken stock
juice of ½ lemon
salt and ground black pepper
lemon wedges and finely pared strips of rind, to garnish

1 Drain the chickpeas and rinse under cold running water. Place in a large pan covered with fresh water, bring to the boil and cook for 1–1½ hours until tender. Drain and peel.

VARIATIONS

• This soup is equally good made with cilantro instead of parsley.
• If you do not have time to soak dried chickpeas overnight, use canned ones instead—drain before adding to the soup.

Energy 159kcal/668kJ; Protein 8.3g; Carbohydrate 19.6g, of which sugars 1.7g; Fat 5.8g, of which saturates 0.6g; Cholesterol 0mg; Calcium 76mg; Fiber 4.5g; Sodium 17mg.

GREEN LENTIL SOUP

LENTIL SOUP IS AN EASTERN MEDITERRANEAN CLASSIC, VARYING IN ITS SPICINESS ACCORDING TO THE REGION IT COMES FROM.

SERVES 4–6

INGREDIENTS

8 ounces/1 cup green lentils
5 tablespoons extra virgin
    olive oil
3 onions, finely chopped
2 garlic cloves, finely sliced
2 teaspoons cumin seeds, crushed
¼ teaspoon ground turmeric
2½ cups vegetable stock
2½ cups water
salt and ground black pepper
2 tablespoons roughly chopped fresh
    cilantro, to garnish
warm crusty bread, to serve

1 Put the lentils in a pan and cover with cold water. Boil for 10 minutes. Drain.

2 Heat 2 tablespoons of the oil and fry two-thirds of the onions with the garlic, cumin and turmeric for 3 minutes.

3 Add the lentils, stock and water. Bring to the boil, reduce the heat, cover and simmer for 30 minutes until the lentils are soft.

4 Heat the remaining oil and fry the rest of the onion until golden brown, stirring frequently.

5 Use a potato masher to lightly mash the lentils and make the soup pulpy in texture. Reheat gently and season with salt and freshly ground pepper to taste.

6 Pour the soup into warmed bowls. Stir the fresh cilantro into the fried onion and sprinkle over the soup as a garnish. Serve hot with warm crusty bread.

COOK'S TIP
Red or Puy lentils make an equally good substitute for green lentils. The lentils do not need to be soaked before cooking.

Energy 220kcal/921kJ; Protein 9.5g; Carbohydrate 25.1g, of which sugars 3.7g; Fat 9.8g, of which saturates 1.4g; Cholesterol 0mg; Calcium 32mg; Fiber 2.5g; Sodium 15mg.

GARLICKY LENTIL SOUP

HIGH IN FIBER, LENTILS MAKE A PARTICULARLY TASTY SOUP. UNLIKE MANY PULSES, THEY DO NOT NEED TO BE SOAKED BEFORE BEING COOKED.

SERVES 6

INGREDIENTS

8 ounces/1 cup red lentils, rinsed
  and drained
2 onions, finely chopped
2 large garlic cloves, finely chopped
1 carrot, finely chopped
2 tablespoons olive oil
2 bay leaves
a generous pinch of dried marjoram
  or oregano
6¼ cups vegetable stock
2 tablespoons red wine vinegar
salt and ground black pepper
celery leaves, to garnish
crusty bread rolls, to serve

1 Put all the ingredients except for the vinegar, seasoning and garnish in a large, heavy pan. Bring to the boil over a medium heat, then lower the heat and simmer for 1½ hours, stirring the soup occasionally to prevent the lentils from sticking to the bottom.

2 Remove the bay leaves and add the red wine vinegar, with salt and pepper to taste. If the soup is too thick, thin it with a little extra vegetable stock or water. Serve the soup in heated bowls, garnished with celery leaves. Serve with warmed crusty rolls.

Energy 176kcal/742kJ; Protein 9.6g; Carbohydrate 26.4g, of which sugars 4.9g; Fat 4.3g, of which saturates 0.6g; Cholesterol 0mg; Calcium 36mg; Fiber 2.9g; Sodium 19mg.

LENTIL SOUP <u>WITH</u> ROSEMARY

A CLASSIC RUSTIC ITALIAN SOUP FLAVORED WITH ROSEMARY, THIS IS DELICIOUS SERVED WITH WARMED GARLIC BREAD.

SERVES 4

INGREDIENTS

8 ounces/1 cup dried green or
  brown lentils
3 tablespoons extra virgin
  olive oil
3 rindless fatty bacon strips,
  cut into small dice
1 onion, finely chopped
2 celery sticks, finely chopped
2 carrots, finely chopped
2 sprigs fresh rosemary,
  finely chopped
2 bay leaves
1 can (14 ounces) plum tomatoes
7½ cups vegetable stock
salt and ground black pepper
fresh bay leaves and sprigs of fresh
  rosemary, to garnish

1 Place the lentils in a bowl and cover with cold water. Leave to soak for at least 2 hours. Rinse and drain well.

2 Heat the oil in a large pan. Add the bacon and cook for about 3 minutes, then stir in the onion and cook for 5 minutes until softened.

3 Stir in the celery, carrots, rosemary, bay leaves and lentils. Toss over the heat for 1 minute until coated in the oil.

COOK'S TIP
Look out for the small green lentils in Italian groceries or delicatessens. If you buy your lentils loose, remember to put them in a strainer or colander and pick them over, removing any pieces of grit, before rinsing them.

4 Stir in the tomatoes and stock, and bring to the boil. Lower the heat, half-cover the pan and simmer gently for about 1 hour until the lentils are perfectly tender.

5 Remove the bay leaves, add salt and freshly ground black pepper to taste and serve with a garnish of fresh bay leaves and sprigs of rosemary.

Energy 334kcal/1403kJ; Protein 18.2g; Carbohydrate 38.1g, of which sugars 7.3g; Fat 13.1g, of which saturates 2.8g; Cholesterol 12mg; Calcium 53mg; Fiber 4.7g; Sodium 392mg.

Split Pea and Ham Soup

The main ingredient for this dish is bacon hock, which is the narrow piece of bone cut from a leg of ham. You could use a pork rib instead, if you prefer.

SERVES 4

INGREDIENTS

1 pound/2½ cups green split peas
4 rindless bacon strips
1 onion, roughly chopped
2 carrots, sliced
1 celery stick, sliced
10½ cups cold water
1 sprig of fresh thyme
2 bay leaves
1 large potato, roughly diced
1 bacon hock
ground black pepper

4 Drain the split peas and add to the pan with the thyme, bay leaves, potato and bacon hock. Bring to the boil, reduce the heat, cover and cook gently for 1 hour.

5 Remove the thyme, bay leaves and hock. Process the soup in a blender or food processor until smooth. Return to a clean pan. Cut the meat from the hock, add to the soup and heat through gently. Season with plenty of freshly ground black pepper. Ladle into warm soup bowls and serve.

1 Put the split peas into a bowl, cover with cold water and leave to soak overnight.

2 Cut the bacon into small pieces. In a large pan, dry-fry the bacon for 4–5 minutes or until crisp. Remove from the pan with a slotted spoon.

3 Add the chopped onion, carrots and celery to the fat in the pan and cook for 3–4 minutes until the onion is softened but not brown. Return the bacon to the pan with the water.

Energy 466kcal/1974kJ; Protein 32.2g; Carbohydrate 75.6g, of which sugars 6.2g; Fat 5.9g, of which saturates 1.9g; Cholesterol 13mg; Calcium 75mg; Fiber 7g; Sodium 443mg.

TUSCAN BEAN SOUP

THIS ITALIAN SOUP IS KNOWN AS RIBOLLITA. IT IS SIMILAR TO MINESTRONE, BUT MADE WITH BEANS INSTEAD OF PASTA, AND IS TRADITIONALLY LADLED OVER A RICH GREEN VEGETABLE, SUCH AS SPINACH.

SERVES 6

INGREDIENTS
3 tablespoons olive oil
2 onions, chopped
2 carrots, sliced
4 garlic cloves, crushed
2 celery sticks, thinly sliced
1 fennel bulb, trimmed
    and chopped
2 large zucchini, thinly sliced
1 can (14 ounces) chopped tomatoes
2 tablespoons homemade or
    bought pesto
3¾ cups vegetable stock
1 can (14 ounces) navy or borlotti
    beans, drained
salt and ground black pepper
For the base
1 tablespoon extra virgin olive oil,
    plus extra for drizzling
1 pound fresh young spinach
ground black pepper

1 Heat the oil in a large pan. Add the chopped onions, carrots, crushed garlic, celery and fennel and fry gently for about 10 minutes. Add the zucchini and fry for a further 2 minutes.

2 Stir in the chopped tomatoes, pesto, stock and beans and bring to the boil. Lower the heat, cover and simmer gently for 25–30 minutes, until the vegetables are completely tender. Season with salt and black pepper to taste.

3 Heat the oil in a frying pan and fry the spinach for 2 minutes, or until wilted. Spoon the spinach into heated soup bowls, then ladle the soup over the spinach. Just before serving, drizzle with olive oil and sprinkle with ground black pepper.

VARIATION
Use other dark greens, such as Chard or cabbage, instead of the spinach. Simply shred and cook until tender, then ladle the soup over the top.

Energy 197kcal/822kJ; Protein 6.8g; Carbohydrate 20.8g, of which sugars 10.3g; Fat 10.2g, of which saturates 1.5g; Cholesterol 0mg; Calcium 93mg; Fiber 7.7g; Sodium 287mg.

PASTA SOUPS

In Italy hearty pasta soups are often served with bread for a light supper. There are hundreds of little pasta shapes, called pastina, to choose from—which means an endless variety of dishes is possible. Most of the soups in this section are rustic Italian classics such as Borlotti Bean and Pasta Soup, and Meatballs in Pasta Soup with Basil. For something more unusual, try Tomato Soup with Israeli Couscous—a toasted round pasta much larger than regular couscous.

LENTIL AND PASTA SOUP

THIS RUSTIC VEGETARIAN SOUP MAKES A FILLING LUNCH OR SUPPER AND GOES WELL WITH WHOLE-WHEAT OR CRUSTY ITALIAN BREAD.

SERVES 4–6

INGREDIENTS

6 ounces/¾ cup brown lentils
3 garlic cloves
4 cups water
3 tablespoons olive oil
1 ounce/2 tablespoons butter
1 onion, finely chopped
2 celery sticks, finely chopped
2 tablespoons sun-dried tomato paste
7½ cups vegetable stock
a few fresh marjoram leaves, plus
extra to garnish
a few fresh basil leaves
leaves from a sprig of fresh thyme
2 ounces/½ cup small pasta shapes,
such as tubetti
salt and ground black pepper

1 Put the lentils in a large pan. Smash one of the garlic cloves (there's no need to peel it first) and add it to the lentils. Pour in the water and bring to the boil. Lower the heat to a gentle simmer and cook for about 20 minutes, stirring occasionally, until the lentils are just tender.

2 Drain the lentils, then remove the cooked garlic clove and set it aside.

3 Rinse the lentils under cold water, then leave them to drain again. Heat 2 tablespoons of the oil with half the butter in a large pan. Add the onion and celery and cook over low heat, stirring frequently to prevent sticking, for 5–7 minutes until softened.

4 Crush the remaining garlic and peel and mash the reserved cooked garlic clove. Add to the vegetables with the remaining oil, the tomato paste and lentils. Stir to mix.

5 Add the stock, herbs and salt and pepper to taste. Bring to the boil, stirring, and simmer for 30 minutes.

6 Add the pasta and bring to the boil, stirring. Simmer, stirring frequently, for 7–8 minutes or according to the instructions on the packet, until the pasta is *al dente*.

7 Add the remaining butter and adjust the seasoning.

8 Ladle into warmed bowls and garnish with marjoram leaves. Serve hot.

COOK'S TIPS
• Use green lentils instead of brown, if you like, but the orange or red ones are not so good for this soup because they tend to become mushy.
• Put lentils in a strainer or colander and pick them over to remove any pieces of grit before rinsing.

Energy 206kcal/865kJ; Protein 8.1g; Carbohydrate 23.5g, of which sugars 1.7g; Fat 9.5g, of which saturates 3g; Cholesterol 9mg; Calcium 24mg; Fiber 1.9g; Sodium 42mg.

BORLOTTI BEAN AND PASTA SOUP

A COMPLETE MEAL IN A BOWL, THIS IS A VERSION OF A CLASSIC ITALIAN SOUP. TRADITIONALLY, THE PERSON WHO FINDS THE BAY LEAF IS HONORED WITH A KISS FROM THE COOK.

SERVES 4

INGREDIENTS

1 onion, chopped
1 celery stick, chopped
2 carrots, chopped
5 tablespoons olive oil
1 bay leaf
1 glass white wine (optional)
4 cups vegetable stock
1 can (14 ounces) chopped tomatoes
1¼ cups bottled strained tomatoes
6 ounces/1½ cups dried pasta shapes,
  such as farfalle or conchiglie
1 can (14 ounces) borlotti
  beans, drained
salt and ground black pepper
9 ounces spinach, washed
  and drained
2 ounces/⅔ cup freshly grated
  Parmesan cheese, to serve

VARIATION

Other pulses, such as cannellini beans, navy beans or chickpeas, are equally good in this soup.

1 Place the chopped onion, celery and carrots in a large pan with the olive oil. Cook over a medium heat for 5 minutes or until the vegetables soften, stirring occasionally.

2 Add the bay leaf, wine, vegetable stock, the chopped and the strained tomatoes, and bring to the boil. Lower the heat and simmer for 10 minutes until the vegetables are just tender.

3 Add the pasta and beans, and bring the soup back to the boil, then simmer for 8 minutes until the pasta is *al dente*. Stir frequently to prevent the pasta from sticking.

4 Season to taste with salt and pepper. Remove any thick stalks from the spinach and add it to the mixture. Cook for a further 2 minutes. Serve in heated soup bowls sprinkled with the freshly grated Parmesan.

VARIATIONS

• This soup is also delicious with chunks of cooked spicy sausage or pieces of crispy cooked pancetta or bacon—simply add to the soup at the end of Step 3 and stir in, ensuring that the meat is piping hot before serving.

• For vegetarians, you could use fried chunks of smoked or marinated tofu as an alternative to meat.

Energy 488kcal/2049kJ; Protein 20.5g; Carbohydrate 59.8g, of which sugars 14.1g; Fat 20.1g, of which saturates 4.9g; Cholesterol 13mg; Calcium 366mg; Fiber 11.1g; Sodium 808mg.

BROCCOLI, ANCHOVY <u>AND</u> PASTA SOUP

THIS SOUP IS FROM APULIA IN THE SOUTH OF ITALY, WHERE ANCHOVIES AND BROCCOLI ARE USED TOGETHER IN MANY DELICIOUS DISHES.

SERVES 4

INGREDIENTS

2 tablespoons olive oil
1 small onion, finely chopped
1 garlic clove, finely chopped
¼–⅓ fresh red chile, seeded and
   finely chopped
2 canned anchovy fillets, drained
7 fluid ounces/scant 1 cup bottled
   strained tomatoes
3 tablespoons dry white wine
5 cups vegetable stock
11 ounces/2 cups broccoli florets
7 ounces/1¾ cups orecchiette
salt and ground black pepper
grated Pecorino cheese, to serve

COOK'S TIP
Wear rubber gloves to protect your hands
when seeding and chopping the chile.

1 Heat the oil in a large pan. Add the
onion, garlic, chile and anchovies and
cook over a low heat, stirring all the
time, for 5–6 minutes.

2 Add the tomatoes and white wine,
with salt and ground black pepper to
taste. Bring to the boil, cover the pan,
then cook over a low heat, stirring
occasionally to prevent sticking, for
12–15 minutes.

3 Pour in the stock. Bring to the boil,
then add the broccoli and simmer for
about 5 minutes. Add the pasta and
bring back to the boil, stirring. Simmer
for 7–8 minutes or according to the
instructions on the packet, stirring
frequently, until the pasta is *al dente*.

4 Taste and adjust the seasoning. Serve
hot, in individual warmed bowls. Hand
round the Pecorino cheese separately.

Energy 268kcal/1131kJ; Protein 10.3g; Carbohydrate 41.2g, of which sugars 5.2g; Fat 7.3g, of which saturates 1.1g; Cholesterol 1mg; Calcium 69mg; Fiber 3.9g; Sodium 182mg.

PASTA, BEAN <u>AND</u> VEGETABLE SOUP

THIS IS A CALABRIAN SPECIALTY KNOWN AS MILLECOSEDDE. THE NAME COMES FROM THE ITALIAN WORD MILLECOSE, MEANING "A THOUSAND THINGS." LITERALLY ANYTHING EDIBLE CAN GO IN THIS SOUP.

SERVES 4–6

INGREDIENTS

3 ounces/scant ½ cup brown lentils
½ ounce dried mushrooms
4 tablespoons olive oil
1 carrot, diced
1 celery stick, diced
1 onion, finely chopped
1 garlic clove, finely chopped
a little chopped fresh Italian parsley
a good pinch of crushed red chiles (optional)
6¼ cups vegetable stock
5 ounces/scant 1 cup each canned red kidney beans, cannellini beans and chickpeas, rinsed and drained
4 ounces/1 cup dried small pasta shapes, such as rigatoni, penne or penne rigate
salt and ground black pepper
freshly grated Pecorino cheese, to serve
chopped Italian parsley, to garnish

1 Put the lentils in a medium pan, add 16 fluid ounces/2 cups water and bring to the boil over a high heat. Lower the heat to a gentle simmer and cook, stirring occasionally, for 15–20 minutes or until the lentils are just tender. Meanwhile, soak the dried mushrooms in 6 fluid ounces/¾ cup warm water for 15–20 minutes.

2 Put the lentils in a strainer to drain, then rinse under the cold tap. Drain the soaked mushrooms and reserve the soaking liquid. Finely chop the mushrooms and set aside.

3 Heat the oil in a large pan and add the carrot, celery, onion, garlic, parsley and chiles, if using. Cook over a low heat, stirring constantly, for 5–7 minutes, until the vegetables are soft.

4 Add the stock, then the mushrooms and their soaking liquid. Bring to the boil, then add the beans, chickpeas and lentils. Season to taste. Cover, and simmer gently for 20 minutes.

5 Add the pasta and bring back to the boil, stirring. Simmer for 7–8 minutes, until the pasta is *al dente*. Season, then serve hot in soup bowls, with grated Pecorino and chopped parsley.

COOK'S TIP
You can freeze the soup at the end of Step 4. Thaw and bring to the boil, add the pasta and simmer until tender.

Energy 668kcal/2831kJ; Protein 41.4g; Carbohydrate 100.8g, of which sugars 7.5g; Fat 14g, of which saturates 2g; Cholesterol 0mg; Calcium 178mg; Fiber 26.1g; Sodium 44mg.

TOMATO SOUP WITH ISRAELI COUSCOUS

NEWLY POPULAR ISRAELI COUSCOUS IS A TOASTED, ROUND PASTA WHICH IS MUCH LARGER THAN REGULAR COUSCOUS. IT MAKES A WONDERFUL ADDITION TO THIS WARM AND COMFORTING SOUP. IF YOU LIKE YOUR SOUP REALLY GARLICKY, ADD AN EXTRA CLOVE OF CHOPPED GARLIC BEFORE SERVING.

SERVES 4–6

INGREDIENTS

2 tablespoons olive oil
1 onion, chopped
1 or 2 carrots, diced
1 can (14 ounces) chopped tomatoes
6 garlic cloves, roughly chopped
6¼ cups vegetable or chicken stock
7–9 ounces/1–1½ cups
  Israeli couscous
2 or 3 mint sprigs, chopped, or
  several pinches of dried mint
¼ teaspoon ground cumin
¼ bunch fresh ciiantro, or
  about 5 sprigs, chopped
cayenne pepper, to taste
salt and ground black pepper

1 Heat the oil in a large pan, add the onion and carrots and cook gently for about 10 minutes until softened. Add the tomatoes, half the garlic, stock, couscous, mint, ground cumin, cilantro, and cayenne pepper, salt and pepper to taste.

2 Bring the soup to the boil, add the remaining chopped garlic, then reduce the heat slightly and simmer gently for 7–10 minutes, stirring occasionally, or until the couscous is just tender. Serve piping hot, ladled into individual serving bowls.

Energy 191kcal/797kJ; Protein 4.2g; Carbohydrate 31.3g, of which sugars 5g; Fat 6.2g, of which saturates 0.8g; Cholesterol 0mg; Calcium 30mg; Fiber 1.4g; Sodium 44mg.

MEATBALLS IN PASTA SOUP WITH BASIL

THESE HOMEMADE MEATBALLS ARE DELICIOUS—SCENTED WITH ORANGE AND GARLIC, THEY ARE SERVED IN A RUSTIC PASTA SOUP, WHICH IS THICKENED WITH PUREED CANNELLINI BEANS. THE DISH IS A FILLING AND SATISFYING ITALIAN CLASSIC.

SERVES 4

INGREDIENTS
 1 can (14 ounces) cannellini beans,
   drained and rinsed
 4 cups vegetable stock
 3 tablespoons olive oil
 1 onion, finely chopped
 2 garlic cloves, chopped
 1 small red chile, seeded
   and chopped
 2 celery sticks, finely chopped
 1 carrot, finely chopped
 1 tablespoon tomato paste
 11 ounces small pasta shapes
 large handful of fresh basil, torn
 salt and ground black pepper
 basil leaves, to garnish
 freshly grated Parmesan cheese,
   to serve
For the meatballs
 1 thick slice white bread,
   crusts removed
 4 tablespoons milk
 12 ounces lean ground beef
   or veal
 2 tablespoons chopped fresh parsley
 grated rind of 1 orange
 2 garlic cloves, crushed
 1 egg, beaten
 2 tablespoons olive oil

1 First prepare the meatballs. Break the bread into small pieces and place them in a bowl. Add the milk and leave to soak for about 10 minutes. Add the minced beef or veal, parsley, orange rind and garlic, and season well. Mix well with your hands.

2 When the bread is thoroughly incorporated with the meat, add enough beaten egg to bind the mixture. Shape small spoonfuls of the mixture into balls about the size of a large olive.

COOK'S TIP
Choose hollow pasta shapes for this soup, which will scoop up the soup as you eat. Look for small and medium-size shapes that are made especially for soup.

3 Heat the oil in a frying pan and fry the meatballs in batches for 6–8 minutes until browned all over. Use tongs or a draining spoon to remove them from the pan, and set them aside.

4 Puree the cannellini beans with a little of the stock in a food processor or blender until smooth. Set aside.

5 Heat the olive oil in a large pan. Add the chopped onion and garlic, chile, celery and carrot, and cook for 4–5 minutes. Cover and cook gently for a further 5 minutes.

6 Stir in the tomato puree, the bean puree and the remaining vegetable stock. Bring the soup to the boil and cook for about 10 minutes.

7 Stir in the pasta shapes and simmer for 8–10 minutes, until the pasta is tender, but not soft. Add the meatballs and basil and cook for a further 5 minutes. Season the soup well before ladling it into warmed bowls. Garnish each bowl of soup with a basil leaf, and serve freshly grated Parmesan cheese with the soup.

Energy 718kcal/3014kJ; Protein 35g; Carbohydrate 80.9g, of which sugars 10g; Fat 30.5g, of which saturates 8.5g; Cholesterol 53mg; Calcium 152mg; Fiber 9.7g; Sodium 529mg.

AVGOLEMONO WITH PASTA

*THIS IS THE MOST POPULAR OF GREEK SOUPS. THE NAME MEANS EGG AND LEMON, THE TWO
MOST IMPORTANT INGREDIENTS, WHICH PRODUCE A LIGHT, NOURISHING SOUP. ORZO IS A GREEK
RICE-SHAPED PASTA, BUT YOU CAN USE ANY SMALL SOUP PASTA.*

SERVES 4–6

INGREDIENTS
  7½ cups chicken stock
  4 ounces/½ cup orzo pasta
  3 eggs
  juice of 1 large lemon
  salt and ground black pepper
  lemon slices, to garnish

COOK'S TIP
This egg and lemon combination is also
widely used in Greece as a sauce for
pasta or with meatballs.

1 Pour the stock into a large pan, and
bring it to a rolling boil. Add the pasta
and cook for 5 minutes.

2 Beat the eggs until frothy, then
add the lemon juice and 1 tablespoon
of cold water. Slowly stir in a ladleful of
the hot chicken stock, then add one or
two more.

3 Return this mixture to the pan,
remove from the heat and stir well.
(Do not let the soup boil once the
eggs have been added, or it will curdle.)

4 Season the soup to taste with salt
and freshly ground black pepper and
serve immediately, garnished with a
few lemon slices.

Energy 154kcal/648kJ; Protein 8.1g; Carbohydrate 21.3g, of which sugars 1g; Fat 4.7g, of which saturates 1.2g; Cholesterol 143mg; Calcium 29mg; Fiber 0.8g; Sodium 53mg.

OLD-FASHIONED CHICKEN NOODLE SOUP

THIS IS A REALLY TRADITIONAL CHICKEN NOODLE SOUP—CLEAR, GOLDEN AND WARMING, AND FILLED WITH LIGHTLY COOKED PASTA. IT IS GUARANTEED TO MAKE YOU FEEL BETTER WHENEVER YOU HAVE A COLD. THE SECRET LIES IN BEGINNING WITH A GOOD-QUALITY STOCK.

SERVES 4–6

INGREDIENTS

4½ pounds stewing chicken with
  the giblets (except the liver)
1 large onion, peeled
  and halved
2 large carrots, halved lengthwise
6 celery sticks, roughly chopped
1 bay leaf
6 ounces vermicelli pasta
3 tablespoons chopped fresh parsley
  or whole parsley leaves
salt and ground black pepper

1 Put the chicken into a large pan with all the vegetables and the bay leaf. Cover with 10 cups cold water. Bring slowly to the boil, carefully skimming off any scum that rises to the top. Add 1 teaspoon salt and some ground black pepper.

2 Turn down the heat and simmer the soup slowly for at least 2 hours, or until the fowl is tender. When simmering, the surface of the liquid should just tremble. If it is allowed to boil, the soup will become cloudy.

3 When tender, remove the bird from the broth and strip the flesh off the carcass. (Use the meat in sandwiches or a risotto.) Return the bones to the soup and simmer for another hour.

VARIATION
For a change you can use the same weight of guinea fowl and chicken wings and thighs, mixed.

4 Strain the soup into a bowl, cool, then chill overnight. The next day the soup should have set to a solid jelly and will be covered with a thin layer of solidified chicken fat. Carefully remove the fat.

5 To serve the soup, reheat in a large pan. Add the vermicelli and chopped parsley, and simmer for 6–8 minutes until the pasta is cooked. Taste and season well. Serve piping hot.

Energy 176kcal/748kJ; Protein 6.3g; Carbohydrate 37.5g, of which sugars 5.7g; Fat 1.2g, of which saturates 0.1g; Cholesterol 0mg; Calcium 66mg; Fiber 3.4g; Sodium 39mg.

FARMHOUSE SOUP

ROOT VEGETABLES FORM THE BASE OF THIS CHUNKY, MINESTRONE-STYLE, MAIN-MEAL SOUP. SERVE IT WITH CRUSTY BREAD FOR A FILLING AND SATISFYING LUNCH DISH.

SERVES 4

INGREDIENTS

2 tablespoons olive oil
1 onion, roughly chopped
3 carrots, cut into large chunks
6–7 ounces turnips, chopped
6 ounces rutabaga, chopped
1 can (14 ounces) chopped tomatoes
1 tablespoon tomato paste
1 teaspoon dried mixed herbs
1 teaspoon dried oregano
2 ounces/½ cup dried peppers, finely sliced (optional)
6¼ cups vegetable stock or water
2 ounces/½ cup small macaroni or conchiglie
1 can (14 ounces) red kidney beans, rinsed and drained
2 tablespoons chopped Italian parsley
salt and ground black pepper
grated Parmesan cheese, to serve

1 Heat the oil in a large pan, add the onion and cook over a low heat for about 5 minutes until softened.

2 Add the fresh vegetables, canned tomatoes, tomato paste, dried herbs and dried peppers, if using. Stir in salt and pepper to taste.

3 Pour in the stock or water and bring to the boil. Stir well, cover, lower the heat and simmer for 30 minutes, stirring occasionally.

COOK'S TIPS

• Packets of dried Italian peppers are sold in many supermarkets and in delicatessens. They are piquant and firm with a "meaty" bite to them, which makes them ideal for adding substance to vegetarian soups.
• You can vary the vegetables according to what you have at hand.

4 Add the pasta and bring to the boil, stirring. Lower the heat and simmer, uncovered, for about 5 minutes or according to the instructions on the packet, until the pasta is just *al dente*.

5 Stir in the beans. Heat through for 2–3 minutes, then remove from the heat and stir in the parsley. Taste and adjust the seasoning. Serve hot in warmed soup bowls and hand round the grated Parmesan separately.

Energy 262kcal/1101kJ; Protein 10.4g; Carbohydrate 41.5g, of which sugars 17.6g; Fat 7.1g, of which saturates 1.1g; Cholesterol 0mg; Calcium 148mg; Fiber 11.5g; Sodium 432mg.

PASTA SOUP WITH CHICKEN LIVERS

THIS SOUP CAN BE SERVED AS A FIRST OR MAIN COURSE. YOU WILL FIND THAT THE FRIED CHICKEN LIVERS ARE REALLY DELICIOUS, EVEN IF YOU DO NOT NORMALLY LIKE THEM.

SERVES 4–6

INGREDIENTS

4 ounces/½ cup chicken livers, thawed if frozen
1 tablespoon olive oil
a pat of butter
4 garlic cloves, crushed
3 sprigs each fresh parsley, marjoram and sage, chopped
1 sprig fresh thyme, chopped
5 or 6 fresh basil leaves, chopped
1–2 tablespoons dry white wine
2 cans (22 ounces) condensed chicken consommé
8 ounces/2 cups frozen peas
2 ounces/½ cup small pasta shapes, such as farfalle
2 or 3 scallions, sliced
salt and ground black pepper

1 Cut the chicken livers into pieces with scissors. Heat the oil and butter in a frying pan, add the garlic, herbs, and seasoning, and fry for a few minutes. Add the livers, increase the heat to high and stir-fry until they change color and become dry. Add the wine, cook until it evaporates, then remove from the heat.

2 Empty both cans of chicken consommé into a large pan and add water to the condensed soup as directed on the labels. Add an extra can of water, then stir in a little salt and pepper to taste and bring to the boil.

3 Add the frozen peas to the pan and simmer for about 5 minutes, then add the small pasta shapes and bring the soup back to the boil, stirring. Allow to simmer, stirring frequently to prevent sticking, for about 5 minutes or according to the instructions on the packet, until the pasta is *al dente*.

4 Add the fried chicken livers and spring onions and heat through for 2–3 minutes. Taste and adjust the seasoning. Serve hot, in warmed bowls.

Energy 105kcal/440kJ; Protein 7.7g; Carbohydrate 11.1g, of which sugars 1.5g; Fat 3.5g, of which saturates 0.5g; Cholesterol 73mg; Calcium 33mg; Fiber 2.5g; Sodium 426mg.

CHICKEN STELLETTE SOUP

SIMPLE AND QUICK TO PREPARE, PROVIDED YOU HAVE SOME GOOD STOCK AT HAND, THIS LIGHT, CLEAR SOUP IS EASY ON THE PALATE AND THE EYE.

SERVES 4–6

INGREDIENTS
    3¾ cups chicken stock
    1 bay leaf
    4 scallions, sliced
    8 ounces white mushrooms, sliced
    4 ounces cooked chicken breast
    2 ounces small soup pasta (stellette)
    150ml/⅔ cup dry white wine
    1 tablespoon chopped parsley
    salt and ground black pepper

COOK'S TIP
This soup tastes best if you make your own chicken stock rather than using a bouillon cube.

1 Put the stock and bay leaf into a large pan and bring to the boil. Add the sliced scallions and mushrooms.

2 Remove the skin from the chicken and discard. Slice the chicken, add to the soup and season to taste with salt and pepper. Heat for 2–3 minutes.

3 Add the pasta to the soup, cover and leave to simmer for 7–8 minutes until the pasta is *al dente*.

4 Just before serving, add the wine and chopped parsley and heat through for 2–3 minutes. Pour into individual warmed soup bowls and serve hot.

Energy 72kcal/303kJ; Protein 6.4g; Carbohydrate 6.7g, of which sugars 0.7g; Fat 0.6g, of which saturates 0.1g; Cholesterol 13mg; Calcium 10mg; Fiber 0.8g; Sodium 15mg.

ZUCCHINI SOUP WITH PASTA

THIS IS A PRETTY, FRESH-TASTING SOUP, WHICH IS ALWAYS A WELCOME DISH IN HOT WEATHER. ADD A DECORATIVE SWIRL OF SOUR CREAM TO FINISH.

SERVES 4–6

INGREDIENTS

4 tablespoons olive or
  sunflower oil
2 onions, finely chopped
6¼ cups chicken stock
2 pounds zucchini
4 ounces small soup pasta
  (stellette)
a little lemon juice
2 tablespoons chopped fresh chervil
salt and ground black pepper
sour cream, to serve

1 Heat the oil in a large pan and add the onions. Cover and cook gently for about 20 minutes, stirring occasionally, until soft but not colored.

2 Add the stock to the pan and bring the mixture to the boil.

VARIATION
You can use cucumber instead of zucchini, if you prefer, and other soup pasta such as tiny shells.

3 Meanwhile, grate the zucchini and stir into the boiling stock with the pasta. Reduce the heat, cover the pan and simmer for 15 minutes until the pasta is tender, or *al dente*.

4 Season to taste with lemon juice, salt and pepper. Stir in the chopped fresh chervil. Pour into bowls and add a swirl of sour cream before serving.

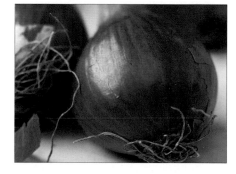

Energy 183kcal/765kJ; Protein 5.9g; Carbohydrate 22.2g, of which sugars 7g; Fat 8.4g, of which saturates 1.2g; Cholesterol 0mg; Calcium 64mg; Fiber 3g; Sodium 5mg.

BEET SOUP WITH RAVIOLI

BEET AND PASTA MAKE AN UNUSUAL COMBINATION, BUT THIS SOUP IS NO LESS GOOD FOR THAT.
SERVE IT WITH SOME CRUSTY BREAD.

SERVES 4–5

INGREDIENTS

1 quantity of basic pasta dough
  (see page 251)
1 egg white, beaten, for brushing
flour, for dusting
1 small onion or shallot, chopped
2 garlic cloves, crushed
1 teaspoon fennel seeds
2½ cups chicken or vegetable stock
8 ounces cooked beets
2 tablespoons fresh orange juice
fresh fennel or dill leaves, to garnish
For the filling
4 ounces mushrooms, finely chopped
1 shallot or small onion, chopped
1 or 2 garlic cloves, crushed
1 teaspoon chopped fresh thyme
1 tablespoon chopped fresh parsley
6 tablespoons fresh white bread
  crumbs
salt and ground black pepper
a large pinch of grated nutmeg

1 Process all the filling ingredients in a food processor or blender.

2 Roll the pasta into thin sheets. Lay one piece over a ravioli tray and put 1 teaspoon of the filling into each depression. Brush around the edges of each ravioli with egg white. Cover with another sheet of pasta and press the edges together well to seal. Transfer to a floured dish towel and leave to rest for one hour before cooking.

3 Cut into individual ravioli. Cook in boiling, salted water for 2 minutes (in batches to stop them sticking together). Remove and drop into a bowl of cold water for 5 seconds before placing on a tray. (You can make these a day in advance and store in the refrigerator.)

4 Put the onion, garlic and fennel seeds into a pan with ⅔ cup of the stock. Bring to the boil, cover and simmer for 5 minutes until tender.

5 Peel and finely dice the beets, reserving 4 tablespoons for the garnish. Add the rest of it to the soup with the remaining stock, and bring to the boil.

6 Add the orange juice and cooked ravioli and simmer for 2 minutes.

7 Serve in shallow soup bowls, garnished with the reserved diced beets and fresh fennel or dill leaves.

Energy 260kcal/1101kJ; Protein 9.8g; Carbohydrate 51g, of which sugars 6.1g; Fat 3.3g, of which saturates 0.7g; Cholesterol 76mg; Calcium 108mg; Fiber 3.1g; Sodium 198mg.

CHUNKY PASTA SOUP

SERVE THIS HEARTY, MAIN-MEAL SOUP WITH TASTY, PESTO-TOPPED FRENCH BREAD CROUTONS. ANY KIND OF PASTA SHAPE CAN BE USED—SHELLS, SPIRALS OR TUBES.

SERVES 4

INGREDIENTS

4 ounces/½ cup dried beans—a mixture of red kidney and navy beans—soaked overnight
5 cups water
1 tablespoon oil
1 onion, peeled and roughly chopped
2 celery sticks, finely sliced
2 or 3 garlic cloves, crushed
2 leeks, finely sliced
1 vegetable bouillon cube
1 can or jar (14 ounces) pimientos
3–4 tablespoons tomato paste
4 ounces pasta shapes
4 slices French bread
1 tablespoon pesto sauce
4 ounces/1 cup baby corn cobs, halved
2 ounces each broccoli and cauliflower florets
a few drops of Tabasco sauce
salt and ground black pepper

1 Drain the beans and place in a large pan with the water. Bring to the boil and simmer for about 1 hour, or until nearly tender.

2 When the beans are almost ready, heat the oil in a large pan and fry the vegetables for 2 minutes. Add the stock cube and the beans with about 2½ cups of their liquid. Cover and simmer for 10 minutes.

COOK'S TIP
Make your own stock (see page 30) instead of using a bouillon cube.

3 Meanwhile, puree the pimientos with a little of their liquid and add to the pan. Stir in the tomato paste and pasta and cook for 15 minutes.

4 Preheat the oven to 400°F.

5 Meanwhile, make the pesto croutons. Spread the French bread with the pesto sauce and bake in the preheated oven for 10 minutes or until crisp.

6 When the pasta is just cooked, add the corn, broccoli and cauliflower florets, Tabasco sauce and seasoning to taste. Heat through for 2–3 minutes.

7 Ladle into warmed soup bowls and serve immediately with the croutons.

Energy 387kcal/1641kJ; Protein 20.1g; Carbohydrate 70.3g, of which sugars 14.9g; Fat 4.7g, of which saturates 1.2g; Cholesterol 3mg; Calcium 185mg; Fiber 12.5g; Sodium 654mg.

TINY PASTA IN BROTH

IN ITALY THIS SOUP IS OFTEN SERVED WITH BREAD FOR A LIGHT SUPPER. HAND ROUND A BOWL OF GRATED PARMESAN CHEESE FOR SPRINKLING ON TOP.

SERVES 4

INGREDIENTS

5 cups beef stock
3 ounces/¾ cup small soup pasta, such as stellette
2 pieces bottled roasted red bell pepper (about 2 ounces)
salt and ground black pepper
grated Parmesan cheese, to serve

1 Bring the beef stock to the boil in a large pan. Add salt and pepper to taste, then drop in the soup pasta. Stir well and bring the stock back to the boil.

2 Lower the heat to a simmer and cook for 7–8 minutes, or according to the packet instructions, until the pasta is *al dente*. Stir often during cooking to prevent the pasta shapes from sticking together.

3 Drain the pieces of bottled roasted pepper and dice them finely. Place them in the bottom of four warmed soup plates, and set them aside.

4 Taste the soup and adjust the seasoning. Ladle into the soup plates and serve immediately, with grated Parmesan handed round separately.

LITTLE STUFFED HATS IN BROTH

THIS SOUP IS SERVED IN NORTHERN ITALY ON SANTO STEFANO (ST. STEPHEN'S DAY) AND ON NEW YEAR'S DAY. IT MAKES A WELCOME CHANGE FROM ALL THE SPECIAL CELEBRATION FOOD AT THIS TIME OF YEAR. IT IS TRADITIONALLY MADE WITH THE CHRISTMAS CAPON CARCASS, BUT CHICKEN STOCK WORKS EQUALLY WELL.

SERVES 4

INGREDIENTS

5 cups chicken stock
3½–4 ounces/1 cup fresh or dried cappelletti
2 tablespoons dry white wine (optional)
about 1 tablespoon finely chopped fresh Italian parsley (optional)
salt and ground black pepper
about 2 tablespoons grated Parmesan cheese, to serve

1 Pour the chicken stock into a large pan and bring to the boil. Add a little salt and pepper to taste, then drop in the pasta. Stir well to separate the pasta and bring back to the boil.

2 Lower the heat to a simmer and cook according to the instructions on the packet, until the pasta is *al dente*. Stir frequently during cooking to ensure the pasta cooks evenly.

3 Swirl in the wine and parsley, if using, then taste and adjust the seasoning.

4 Ladle into four warmed soup plates, then sprinkle with grated Parmesan. Serve immediately.

COOK'S TIP
Cappelletti is just another name for tortellini, which come from Romagna. You can either buy them ready-made or make your own.

Top: *Energy 68kcal/290kJ; Protein 2.6g; Carbohydrate 14.7g, of which sugars 1.4g; Fat 0.5g, of which saturates 0.1g; Cholesterol 0mg; Calcium 6mg; Fiber 0.8g; Sodium 183mg.*
Bottom: *Energy 77kcal/328kJ; Protein 2.9g; Carbohydrate 16.7g, of which sugars 0.8g; Fat 0.5g, of which saturates 0.1g; Cholesterol 0mg; Calcium 6mg; Fiber 0.7g; Sodium 183mg.*

ROASTED TOMATO AND PASTA SOUP

WHEN THE ONLY TOMATOES YOU CAN BUY ARE NOT PARTICULARLY FLAVORSOME, MAKE THIS SOUP. THE ROASTING COMPENSATES FOR LACK OF FLAVOR, AND THE SOUP HAS A LOVELY SMOKY TASTE.

SERVES 4

INGREDIENTS

1 pound ripe Italian plum tomatoes, halved lengthwise
1 large red bell pepper, quartered lengthwise and seeded
1 large red onion, quartered lengthwise
2 garlic cloves, unpeeled
1 tablespoon olive oil
5 cups vegetable stock or water
a good pinch of sugar
3½ ounces/scant 1 cup small pasta shapes, such as tubetti or small macaroni
salt and ground black pepper
fresh basil leaves, to garnish

1 Preheat the oven to 375°F. Spread out the tomatoes, red pepper, onion and garlic in a roasting pan and drizzle with the olive oil.

2 Roast for 30–40 minutes until the vegetables are soft and charred, turning them halfway through cooking.

3 Transfer the vegetables to a food processor, add about 8 fluid ounces/ 1 cup of the stock or water, and process until pureed. Scrape into a strainer placed over a large pan and press the puree through into the pan.

4 Add the remaining stock or water, the sugar and salt and pepper to taste. Bring to the boil.

5 Add the pasta and simmer for 7–8 minutes (or according to the instructions on the packet), stirring frequently, until *al dente*. Taste and adjust the seasoning with salt and freshly ground black pepper. Serve hot in warmed bowls, garnished with the fresh basil leaves.

COOK'S TIP
You can roast the vegetables in advance, allow them to cool, then leave them in a covered bowl in the refrigerator overnight before pureeing.

Energy 128kcal/543kJ; Protein 4.5g; Carbohydrate 26.9g, of which sugars 9.7g; Fat 1g, of which saturates 0.2g; Cholesterol 0mg; Calcium 30mg; Fiber 3.2g; Sodium 14mg.

PASTA AND CHICKPEA SOUP

THIS IS A SIMPLE, FILLING, COUNTRY-STYLE SOUP. THE SHAPE OF THE PASTA AND THE BEANS COMPLEMENT ONE ANOTHER BEAUTIFULLY.

SERVES 4–6

INGREDIENTS

4 tablespoons olive oil
1 onion, finely chopped
2 carrots, finely chopped
2 celery sticks, finely chopped
1 can (14 ounces) chickpeas, rinsed and drained
1 can (7 ounces) cannellini beans, rinsed and drained
⅔ cup bottled strained tomatoes
4 fluid ounces/½ cup water
2½ pints/6¼ cups vegetable or chicken stock
1 sprig fresh rosemary, plus a few leaves to garnish
7 ounces/scant 2 cups dried conchiglie
salt and ground black pepper
shavings of Parmesan cheese, to serve

1 Heat the oil in a large pan, add the vegetables and cook over a low heat, stirring frequently, for 5–7 minutes.

2 Add the chickpeas and cannellini beans, stir well to mix, then cook for 5 minutes. Stir in the tomatoes and water. Cook, stirring, for 2–3 minutes.

3 Add 16 fluid ounces/2 cups of the stock, the rosemary sprig, and salt and freshly ground black pepper to taste. Bring to the boil, cover, then simmer gently, stirring occasionally, for 1 hour.

COOK'S TIP
If you use dried chickpeas, soak them overnight and boil until tender.

4 Pour in the remaining stock, add the pasta and bring to the boil. Lower the heat and simmer for 7–8 minutes (or according to the instructions on the packet), until the pasta is *al dente*. Remove the rosemary sprig. Serve the soup sprinkled with rosemary leaves and Parmesan shavings.

VARIATION
You can use other pasta shapes, but conchiglie are ideal because they scoop up the chickpeas and beans.

Energy 317kcal/1336kJ; Protein 12g; Carbohydrate 45.6g, of which sugars 5.4g; Fat 11g, of which saturates 1.4g; Cholesterol 0mg; Calcium 71mg; Fiber 6.2g; Sodium 290mg.

PASTA SQUARES AND PEAS IN BROTH

THIS THICK SOUP IS FROM LAZIO, WHERE IT IS TRADITIONALLY MADE WITH FRESH HOMEMADE PASTA
AND PEAS. IN THIS MODERN VERSION, READY-MADE PASTA IS USED WITH FROZEN PEAS TO SAVE TIME.

SERVES 4–6

INGREDIENTS

1 ounce/2 tablespoons butter
2 ounces/⅓ cup pancetta or
  rindless smoked fatty bacon,
  roughly chopped
1 small onion, finely chopped
1 celery stick, finely chopped
14 ounces/3½ cups frozen peas
1 teaspoon tomato paste
1–2 teaspoon finely chopped fresh
  Italian parsley
4 cups chicken stock
11 ounces fresh lasagne sheets
about 2 ounces/⅓ cup prosciutto,
  cut into cubes
salt and ground black pepper
grated Parmesan cheese, to serve

1 Melt the butter in a large pan and add the pancetta or bacon, onion and celery. Cook over a low heat for 5 minutes.

2 Add the peas and cook for 3 minutes. Stir in the tomato paste, parsley, stock and seasoning. Bring to the boil, cover and simmer gently for 10 minutes.

3 Cut the lasagne sheets into ¾-inch squares. Taste the soup and adjust the seasoning. Drop in the pasta, stir and bring to the boil. Simmer for 2–3 minutes or until the pasta is *al dente*, then stir in the prosciutto. Serve hot in warmed bowls, with grated Parmesan handed round separately.

Energy 240kcal/1013kJ; Protein 9.2g; Carbohydrate 38.4g, of which sugars 2.7g; Fat 6.6g, of which saturates 3.1g; Cholesterol 19mg; Calcium 20mg; Fiber 1.7g; Sodium 241mg.

CONSOMMÉ WITH AGNOLOTTI

SHRIMP, CRAB AND CHICKEN JOSTLE FOR THE UPPER HAND IN THIS RICH AND SATISFYING CONSOMMÉ.
GARNISH WITH COOKED SHRIMP AND FRESH CILANTRO LEAVES.

SERVES 4–6

INGREDIENTS
  3 ounces cooked peeled shrimp
  3 ounces canned crab meat,
    drained
  1 teaspoon finely grated fresh
    ginger root
  1 tablespoon fresh white
    bread crumbs
  1 teaspoon light soy sauce
  1 scallion, finely chopped
  1 garlic clove, peeled and
    crushed
  1 egg white, beaten
  1 can (14 ounces) chicken or
    fish consommé
  2 tablespoons sherry or vermouth
  salt and ground black pepper
For the pasta
  7 ounces/1¾ cups all-purpose
    flour
  2 eggs
  2 teaspoons cold water
For the garnish
  2 ounces cooked peeled shrimp
  fresh cilantro leaves

1 For the pasta, sift the flour and a
pinch of salt onto a work surface and
make a well in the center with your
hand. Put the eggs and water into the
well. Using a fork, beat the eggs gently
together, then draw in the flour from the
sides to make a thick paste.

2 When the mixture becomes too stiff to
use a fork, use your hands to mix to a
firm dough. Knead the dough for about
5 minutes until smooth. Wrap in plastic
wrap to prevent it drying out and leave
to rest for 20–30 minutes.

3 Meanwhile, put the shrimp, crab
meat, ginger, bread crumbs, soy sauce,
scallion, garlic and seasoning into a
food processor or blender and process
until smooth.

4 Roll the rested pasta into thin sheets.
Stamp out 32 x 2-inch rounds using a
fluted cookie cutter.

5 Place 1 teaspoon of the filling in the
centre of half the pasta rounds. Brush
the edges of each round with egg white
and sandwich with a second round on
top. Pinch the edges together to prevent
the filling from seeping out.

6 Cook the pasta in a large pan of boiling,
salted water for 5 minutes (in batches
to prevent it from sticking together).
Remove and drop into a bowl of cold
water for 5 seconds before placing on a
tray. (You can make these pasta shapes
a day in advance. Cover with plastic
wrap and store in the refrigerator.)

7 Heat the consommé in a pan with the
sherry or vermouth. Add the cooked
pasta shapes to the soup and simmer
for 1–2 minutes.

8 Serve the pasta in soup bowls covered
with hot consommé. Garnish with
peeled shrimp and cilantro leaves.

Energy 179kcal/756kJ; Protein 11.6g; Carbohydrate 28g, of which sugars 0.7g; Fat 2.6g, of which saturates 0.6g; Cholesterol 113mg; Calcium 92mg; Fiber 1.1g; Sodium 225mg.

NOODLE SOUPS

Noodles are a key ingredient in many Asian soups. Beef Noodle soup, Pho, is the essence of Vietnam. This popular dish is sold as fast food on street corners and is eaten by everyone from workers to families. Thailand is represented by Thai Chicken Noodle Soup with Little Crab Cakes, and Thai Cellophane Noodle Soup. From Myanmar comes Chiang Mai Noodle Soup. And from Japan there is Tokyo-style Ramen Noodles in Soup, and Soba Noodles in Hot Soup with Tempura.

BEEF NOODLE SOUP

SOME WOULD SAY THAT THIS CLASSIC NOODLE SOUP, PHO, IS VIETNAM IN A BOWL. MADE WITH BEEF (PHO BO) OR CHICKEN (PHO GA), IT IS VIETNAMESE FAST FOOD, STREET FOOD, WORKING MEN'S FOOD AND FAMILY FOOD. IT IS CHEAP AND FILLING, AND MAKES AN INTENSELY SATISFYING MEAL AT ANY TIME OF DAY OR NIGHT. IN THE SOUTH, IN PARTICULAR, IT IS POPULAR FOR BREAKFAST. EVERYONE HAS THEIR OWN RECIPE FOR PHO, OR THEIR FAVORITE PLACE TO ENJOY IT.

SERVES 6

INGREDIENTS

9 ounces beef sirloin
1¼ pounds dried rice sticks
(vermicelli), soaked in lukewarm
water for 20 minutes
1 onion, halved and finely sliced
6–8 scallions, cut into long pieces
2 or 3 red Thai chiles, seeded and
finely sliced
4 ounces/½ cup bean sprouts
1 large bunch each fresh cilantro
and mint, stalks removed,
leaves chopped
2 limes, quartered, and hoisin sauce,
nuoc mam or *nuoc cham* to serve

For the stock
3 pounds 5 ounces oxtail, trimmed of
fat and cut into thick pieces
2¼ pounds beef shank or brisket
2 large onions, peeled and quartered
2 carrots, peeled and cut
into chunks
3-inch fresh ginger root, chopped
6 cloves
2 cinnamon sticks
6 star anise
1 teaspoon black peppercorns
30ml/2 tablespoons soy sauce
3–4 tablespoons *nuoc mam*
salt

1 To make the stock, put the oxtail into a large, deep pan and cover it with water. Bring it to the boil and blanch the meat for 10–15 minutes. Drain the meat, rinsing off any scum, and clean out the pan. Put the blanched oxtail back into the pan with the other stock ingredients, apart from the *nuoc mam* and salt, and cover with about 12 cups water. Bring it to the boil, reduce the heat and simmer, covered, for 2–3 hours.

2 Remove the lid and simmer for another hour, until the stock has reduced to about 8 cups. Skim off any fat and then strain the stock into another pan.

3 Cut the beef sirloin against the grain into very thin pieces, the size of the heel of a hand. Bring the stock to the boil once more, stir in the *nuoc mam*, season to taste with salt, then reduce the heat and leave the stock simmering gently until ready to use.

COOK'S TIPS
• The key to *pho* is a tasty, light stock flavored with ginger, cinnamon, cloves and star anise, so it is worth cooking it slowly and leaving it to stand overnight to allow the flavors to develop fully.
• The fine slices of rare, tender beef cook gently under the steaming stock that is spooned over the top. Use chopsticks to lift the noodles through the layers of flavoring and slurp them up.

4 Meanwhile, bring a pan filled with water to the boil, drain the rice sticks and add to the water. Cook for about 5 minutes or until tender—you may need to separate them with a pair of chopsticks if they look as though they are sticking together.

5 Drain the rice sticks and divide them equally among six wide soup bowls. Top each serving with the slices of beef, onions, scallions and chiles. Ladle the hot stock over the top of these ingredients, top with the bean sprouts and fresh herbs and serve with the lime wedges to squeeze over. Pass around the hoisin sauce, *nuoc mam* or *nuoc cham* for those who like a little sweetening, fish flavoring, or extra fire.

Energy 180kcal/748kJ; Protein 10.8g; Carbohydrate 4.8g, of which sugars 4.1g; Fat 4.2g, of which saturates 1.6g; Cholesterol 24mg; Calcium 35mg; Fiber 1g; Sodium 219mg.

CHICKEN AND CRAB NOODLE SOUP WITH CILANTRO OMELET

THE CHICKEN MAKES A DELICIOUS STOCK FOR THIS LIGHT NOODLE SOUP WITH ITS ELUSIVE HINT OF ENTICING AROMATIC CHINESE FLAVORS.

SERVES 6

INGREDIENTS
  2 chicken legs, skinned
  7½ cups water
  bunch of scallions
  1-inch piece fresh ginger
    root, sliced
  1 teaspoon black peppercorns
  2 garlic cloves, halved
  3 ounces rice noodles
  4 ounces fresh white crabmeat
  2 tablespoons light soy sauce
  salt and ground black pepper
  cilantro leaves, to garnish
For the omelets
  4 eggs
  2 tablespoons chopped fresh
    cilantro leaves
  1 tablespoon extra virgin olive oil

1 Put the chicken and water in a pan. Bring to the boil, reduce the heat and cook gently for 20 minutes, skimming the surface occasionally.

2 Slice half of the scallions and add to the pan with the ginger, peppercorns, garlic and salt to taste. Cover and simmer for 1½ hours.

3 Meanwhile, soak the noodles in boiling water for 4 minutes, or according to the packet instructions. Drain and refresh under cold water. Shred the remaining scallions and set aside.

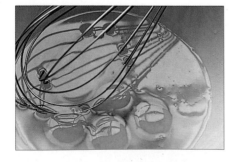

4 To make the omelets, beat the eggs with the cilantro and seasoning.

5 Heat a little of the olive oil in a small frying pan. Add a third of the egg and swirl the pan to coat the base evenly. Cook for 1 minute. Flip over and cook for 30 seconds. Turn the omelet out onto a plate and leave to cool. Repeat twice more to make three omelets.

6 Roll up the omelets tightly one at a time and slice thinly.

7 Remove the chicken from the stock and leave to cool. Put the stock through a strainer lined with cheesecloth into a clean pan. When the chicken is cool enough to handle, remove and finely shred the meat, discarding the bones.

8 Bring the stock to the boil. Add the noodles, chicken, scallions and crabmeat, then simmer for 1–2 minutes. Stir in the soy sauce and season. Ladle the soup into bowls, top each with the sliced omelet and the cilantro leaves, and serve.

Energy 159kcal/664kJ; Protein 13.5g; Carbohydrate 10.6g, of which sugars 0.4g; Fat 6.9g, of which saturates 1.7g; Cholesterol 157mg; Calcium 46mg; Fiber 0g; Sodium 526mg.

THAI CHICKEN NOODLE SOUP
WITH LITTLE CRAB CAKES

THIS SOUP IS A MEAL IN ITSELF. LOOK FOR STORES THAT SELL BUNCHES OF CILANTRO WITH THE ROOTS STILL ATTACHED, AS THEY ADD EXCELLENT FLAVOR TO THE STOCK.

SERVES 6

INGREDIENTS
  8 garlic cloves
  small bunch of cilantro, with
    roots on
  2½–3 pounds chicken
  2 star anise
  2 carrots, chopped
  2 celery sticks, chopped
  1 onion, chopped
  2 tablespoons soy sauce
  5 ounces egg noodles
  2 tablespoons vegetable oil
  4 tablespoons Thai fish sauce
  ¼ teaspoon chili powder
  5 ounces/1½ cups bean sprouts
  2 scallions, sliced
  herb sprigs, to garnish
  salt and ground black pepper
For the crab cakes
  1 teaspoon Thai red curry paste
  1 teaspoon cornstarch
  1 teaspoon Thai fish sauce
  1 small egg yolk
  1 tablespoon chopped fresh cilantro
  6 ounces white crabmeat
  2 ounces/1 cup fresh white
    bread crumbs
  2 tablespoons vegetable oil

1 Chop four of the garlic cloves, thinly slice the remainder and set aside. Cut the roots off the cilantro stems and place in a large pan with the garlic. Pick the cilantro leaves off their stems and set aside; discard the stems. Place the chicken in the pan and add the star anise, carrots, celery and onion and soy sauce. Pour in enough water to cover the chicken. Bring to the boil, reduce the heat, cover and simmer for 1 hour.

2 For the crab cakes, mix the curry paste, cornstarch, fish sauce and egg yolk in a bowl. Add the cilantro, crabmeat, bread crumbs and seasoning, then mix well. Divide the mixture into 12 portions and form each into a small cake.

3 Cook the egg noodles according to the packet instructions. Drain and set aside. Heat the oil in a small pan and fry the sliced garlic until golden brown. Drain and set aside.

4 Remove the chicken from its stock and leave until cool enough to handle. (Reserve the stock.) Discard the chicken skin, take the meat off the bones and tear it into large strips. Set aside. Strain the stock and pour 5 cups into a pan. Stir in the fish sauce, chili powder and seasoning, then bring to the boil. Reduce the heat and keep hot.

5 To cook the crab cakes, heat the vegetable oil in a large frying pan and fry the crab cakes for 2–3 minutes on each side until golden.

6 Divide the cooked noodles, fried garlic slices, bean sprouts, sliced scallions and chicken strips among six shallow soup bowls.

7 Arrange two of the crab cakes on top of the noodles, then ladle the hot chicken broth into the bowls. Sprinkle a few fresh cilantro leaves over the soups, then garnish with the herb sprigs and serve immediately.

Energy 250kcal/1049kJ; Protein 10.9g; Carbohydrate 28.8g, of which sugars 3.5g; Fat 10.9g, of which saturates 1.8g; Cholesterol 62mg; Calcium 74mg; Fiber 1.9g; Sodium 638mg.

UDON NOODLES WITH EGG BROTH AND GINGER

IN THIS DISH, CALLED ANKAKE UDON, THE SOUP FOR THE UDON IS THICKENED WITH CORNSTARCH AND RETAINS ITS HEAT FOR A LONG TIME. A PERFECT LUNCH FOR A FREEZING COLD DAY.

2 Heat at least 9 cups water in a large pan, and cook the udon for 8 minutes or according to the packet instructions. Drain under cold running water and wash off the starch with your hands. Leave in the strainer.

3 Pour the soup into a large pan and bring to the boil. Blend the cornstarch with 4 tablespoons water. Reduce the heat to medium and gradually add the cornstarch mixture to the hot soup. Stir constantly. The soup will thicken after a few minutes. Reduce the heat to low.

4 Mix the egg and scallions in a small bowl. Stir the soup once again to create a whirlpool. Pour the eggs slowly into the soup pan.

5 Reheat the udon with hot water from a kettle. Divide among four bowls and pour the soup over the top. Garnish with the ginger and serve hot.

SERVES 4

INGREDIENTS
    14 ounces dried udon noodles
    2 tablespoons cornstarch
    4 eggs, beaten
    2 scallions, finely chopped
    1-inch piece fresh ginger root,
      peeled and finely grated,
      to garnish
For the soup
    4 cups water
    1½ ounces kezuri-bushi
    1½ tablespoons mirin
    1½ tablespoons Japanese shoyu
    1½ teaspoons salt

1 To make the soup, place the water and the soup ingredients in a pan and bring to the boil on a medium heat. Remove from the heat when it starts boiling. Stand for 1 minute, then strain through cheesecloth. Check the taste and add more salt if required.

COOK'S TIPS
• You can use ready-made noodle soup, available from Japanese food stores.
• Kezuri-bushi, or shaved, dried fish, is available in various graded packets.

Energy 487kcal/2038kJ; Protein 15.5g; Carbohydrate 92.8g, of which sugars 0.6g; Fat 6.1g, of which saturates 1.6g; Cholesterol 190mg; Calcium 61mg; Fiber 0.2g; Sodium 1359mg.

POT-COOKED UDON IN MISO SOUP

UDON IS A WHITE WHEAT NOODLE EATEN WITH VARIOUS HOT AND COLD SOUPS. IN THIS DISH, KNOWN AS MISO NIKOMI UDON, THE NOODLES ARE COOKED IN A CLAY POT WITH A RICH MISO SOUP.

SERVES 4

INGREDIENTS
7-ounce chicken breast portion, boned and skinned
2 teaspoons sake
2 abura-age
3¾ cups second dashi stock, or the same amount of water and 1½ teaspoons dashi-no-moto
6 large fresh shiitake mushrooms, stalks removed, quartered
4 scallions, trimmed and chopped into ⅛-inch lengths
2 tablespoons mirin
about 3½ ounces aka miso or hatcho miso
11 ounces dried udon noodles
4 eggs
shichimi togarashi (optional)

1 Cut the chicken into bitesize pieces. Sprinkle with sake and leave to marinate for 15 minutes.

2 Put the abura-age in a strainer and thoroughly rinse with hot water from the kettle to wash off the oil. Drain on paper towels and cut each abura-age into 4 squares.

3 To make the soup, heat the second dashi stock in a large pan. When it has come to the boil, add the chicken pieces, shiitake mushrooms and abura-age and cook for 5 minutes. Remove the pan from the heat and add the scallions.

COOK'S TIPS
Look for the traditional ingredients in Japanese food stores:
• Abura-age is a thin deep-fried tofu, used in traditional Japanese soups.
• Dashi-no-moto are freeze-dried granules of dashi fish stock.
• Hatcho miso is a paste made from soybeans using traditional methods.
• Shichimi togarashi is a peppery condiment made of seven seasonings.

4 Put the mirin and miso paste into a small bowl. Scoop 2 tablespoons soup from the pan and mix this in well.

5 To cook the udon, boil at least 9 cups water in a large pan. The water should not come higher than two-thirds the depth of the pan. Cook the udon for 6 minutes and drain.

6 Put the udon in one large flameproof clay pot or casserole (or divide among four small pots). Mix the miso paste into the soup and check the taste. Add more miso if required. Ladle in enough soup to cover the udon, and arrange the soup ingredients on top of the udon.

7 Put the soup on a medium heat and put a raw egg on top. When the soup bubbles, wait for 1 minute, then cover and remove from the heat. Leave to stand for 2 minutes. Serve with shichimi togarashi, if you like.

Energy 431kcal/1819kJ; Protein 28.6g; Carbohydrate 54.7g, of which sugars 2.2g; Fat 12.6g, of which saturates 3.5g; Cholesterol 248mg; Calcium 60mg; Fiber 2.9g; Sodium 594mg.

AROMATIC BROTH <u>WITH</u> ROAST DUCK, BOK CHOY <u>AND</u> EGG NOODLES

THIS CHINESE-INSPIRED VIETNAMESE SOUP, MI VIT TIM, MAKES A DELICIOUS AUTUMN OR WINTER MEAL. IN A VIETNAMESE HOUSEHOLD, A BOWL OF FRESH OR MARINATED CHILES MIGHT BE PRESENTED AS A FIERY SIDE DISH TO CHEW ON, BUT HERE THEY ARE SLICED AND SPRINKLED OVER THE SOUP WITH HERBS. THIS RECIPE CAN BE MADE USING CHICKEN STOCK AND LEFTOVER MEAT FROM A ROASTED DUCK OR BY ROASTING A DUCK, SLICING OFF THE BREAST AND THIGH MEAT FOR THE SOUP, AND THEN USING THE MEATY CARCASS TO MAKE A STOCK.

SERVES 4

INGREDIENTS

   1 tablespoon vegetable oil
   2 shallots, thinly sliced
   1½-inch fresh ginger root, peeled
    and sliced
   1 tablespoon soy sauce
   1 teaspoon five-spice powder
   2 teaspoons sugar
   6 ounces bok choy
   1 pound fresh egg noodles
   12 ounces roast duck, thinly sliced
   sea salt
For the stock
   1 chicken or duck carcass
   2 carrots, peeled and quartered
   2 onions, peeled and quartered
   1½-inch fresh ginger root, peeled
    and cut into chunks
   2 lemongrass stalks, chopped
   2 tablespoons *nuoc mam*
   1 tablespoon soy sauce
   6 black peppercorns
For the garnish
   4 scallions, sliced
   1 or 2 red serrano chiles, sliced
   1 bunch each cilantro and
    basil leaves, chopped

1 To make the stock, put the chicken or duck carcass into a deep pan. Add all the other stock ingredients and pour in 10¼ cups water.

2 Bring to the boil and boil for a few minutes. Skim off any foam, reduce the heat and simmer gently with the lid on for 2–3 hours. Remove the lid and continue to simmer for 30 minutes to reduce the stock. Skim off any fat, season with salt, then strain the stock. Measure out 8 cups.

3 Heat the oil in a wok or deep pan and add the shallots and ginger. Stir in the soy sauce, five-spice powder, sugar and stock, and bring to the boil. Season with a little salt, reduce the heat and simmer for 10–15 minutes.

4 Cut the bok choy diagonally into wide strips and blanch in boiling water. Drain and refresh under cold running water to prevent them from cooking any further. Bring a large pan of water to the boil, then add the fresh noodles. Cook for 5 minutes, then drain well.

5 Separate the noodles into four soup bowls, lay some of the bok choy and sliced duck over them, and then ladle over generous amounts of the simmering broth. Garnish with the scallions, chiles and herbs, and serve immediately.

COOK'S TIP

If you can't find fresh egg noodles, you can use dried ones instead. Soak them in lukewarm water for about 20 minutes, then cook, one portion at a time, in a strainer lowered into boiling water. Use a chopstick to untangle the noodles as they soften.

Energy 620kcal/2616kJ; Protein 37.3g; Carbohydrate 82.9g, of which sugars 3.9g; Fat 19.7g, of which saturates 4.4g; Cholesterol 158mg; Calcium 124mg; Fiber 4.4g; Sodium 655mg.

THAI CELLOPHANE NOODLE SOUP

THE THAI NOODLES USED IN THIS SOUP GO BY VARIOUS NAMES: GLASS NOODLES, CELLOPHANE NOODLES, BEAN THREAD OR TRANSPARENT NOODLES. THEY ARE MADE FROM MUNG BEAN FLOUR, AND ARE ESPECIALLY VALUED FOR THEIR BRITTLE TEXTURE.

SERVES 4

INGREDIENTS

   4 large dried shiitake mushrooms
   ½ ounce dried lily buds
   ½ cucumber, coarsely chopped
   2 garlic cloves, halved
   3½ ounces white cabbage, chopped
   5 cups boiling water
   4 ounces cellophane noodles
   2 tablespoons soy sauce
   1 tablespoon jaggery or light
     brown sugar
   3½-ounce block silken tofu, diced
   fresh cilantro, to garnish

1 Soak the shiitake mushrooms and dried lily buds in two separate bowls of warm water for 30 minutes.

COOK'S TIP
Dried lily buds are the unopened flowers of day lilies. They must always be soaked in warm water before use.

2 Meanwhile, put the chopped cucumber, garlic and cabbage in a food processor or blender and process to a smooth paste. Scrape the mixture into a large pan and add the measured boiling water.

3 Bring to the boil, then reduce the heat and cook for 2 minutes, stirring the mixture occasionally. Strain this warm stock into another pan, return to a low heat and gently bring to simmering point.

4 Drain the soaked lily buds, rinse under cold running water, then drain again. Cut off any hard ends. Add the lily buds to the stock with the noodles, soy sauce and sugar and cook for 5 minutes more.

5 Strain the liquid from the soaked mushrooms into the soup. Discard the mushroom stems, then slice the caps. Divide them and the tofu among four bowls. Pour the soup over, garnish with fresh cilantro leaves, and serve.

Energy 143kcal/598kJ; Protein 4.9g; Carbohydrate 28.3g, of which sugars 5.6g; Fat 1.1g, of which saturates 0.1g; Cholesterol 0mg; Calcium 137mg; Fiber 0.6g; Sodium 362mg.

CHIANG MAI NOODLE SOUP

NOWADAYS A SIGNATURE DISH OF THE CITY OF CHIANG MAI, THIS DELICIOUS NOODLE SOUP ORIGINATED IN BURMA, NOW CALLED MYANMAR, WHICH LIES ONLY A LITTLE TO THE NORTH OF THE CITY. IT IS ALSO THE THAI EQUIVALENT OF THE FAMOUS MALAYSIAN "LAKSA."

SERVES 4–6

INGREDIENTS
2½ cups coconut milk
2 tablespoons Thai red curry paste
1 teaspoon ground turmeric
1 pound chicken thighs, boned and
  cut into bitesize chunks
2½ cups chicken stock
4 tablespoons Thai fish sauce
1 tablespoon dark soy sauce
juice of ½–1 lime
1 pound fresh egg noodles, blanched
  briefly in boiling water
salt and ground black pepper
To garnish
3 scallions, chopped
4 fresh red chiles, chopped
4 shallots, chopped
4 tablespoons sliced pickled mustard
  leaves, rinsed
2 tablespoons fried sliced garlic
cilantro leaves
4–6 fried noodle nests
  (optional)

1 Pour about one-third of the coconut milk into a large, heavy pan or wok. Bring to the boil over a medium heat, stirring frequently with a wooden spoon until the milk separates.

2 Add the curry paste and ground turmeric, stir to mix completely and cook until the mixture is fragrant.

3 Add the chunks of chicken and toss over the heat for about 2 minutes, making sure that all the chunks are thoroughly coated with the paste.

4 Add the remaining coconut milk, the chicken stock, fish sauce and soy sauce. Season with salt and pepper to taste. Bring to simmering point, stirring frequently, then lower the heat and cook gently for 7–10 minutes. Remove from the heat and stir in lime juice to taste.

5 Reheat the fresh egg noodles in boiling water, drain and divide among four to six warmed bowls. Divide the chunks of chicken among the bowls and ladle in the hot soup. Top each serving with scallions, chiles, shallots, pickled mustard leaves, fried garlic, cilantro leaves and a fried noodle nest, if using. Serve immediately.

Energy 679kcal/2873kJ; Protein 43.2g; Carbohydrate 88.7g, of which sugars 10.1g; Fat 19.4g, of which saturates 5.6g; Cholesterol 180mg; Calcium 95mg; Fiber 3.4g; Sodium 769mg.

TOKYO-STYLE RAMEN NOODLES IN SOUP

RAMEN IS A HYBRID CHINESE NOODLE DISH PRESENTED IN A JAPANESE WAY, AND THERE ARE MANY REGIONAL VARIATIONS FEATURING LOCAL SPECIALTIES. THIS IS A LEGENDARY TOKYO VERSION.

SERVES 4

INGREDIENTS

9 ounces dried ramen noodles

For the soup stock

   4 scallions

   3-inch fresh ginger root, quartered

   raw bones from 2 chickens, washed

   1 large onion, quartered

   4 garlic cloves, peeled

   1 large carrot, roughly chopped

   1 egg shell

   4 fluid ounces/½ cup sake

   about 4 tablespoons Japanese shoyu

   ½ teaspoon salt

For the *cha-shu* (pot-roast pork)

   1¼ pounds pork shoulder, boned

   2 tablespoons vegetable oil

   2 scallions, chopped

   1-inch fresh ginger root, peeled and sliced

   1 tablespoon sake

   3 tablespoons Japanese shoyu

   1 tablespoon superfine sugar

For the toppings

   2 hard-cooked eggs

   5 ounces menma, soaked for 30 minutes and drained

   ½ nori sheet, broken into pieces

   2 scallions, chopped

   ground white pepper

   sesame oil or chili oil

1 To make the soup stock, bruise the scallions and ginger by hitting with the side of a large knife. Pour 6¼ cups water into a wok and bring to the boil. Add the chicken bones and boil until the meat changes color. Discard the water and wash the bones.

2 Wash the wok, bring 9 cups water to the boil and add the bones and other stock ingredients, except the soy sauce and salt. Reduce the heat to low, and simmer until the water has reduced by half, skimming off any scum. Pour into a bowl through a strainer lined with cheesecloth. This will take 1–2 hours.

3 Make the *cha-shu*. Roll the meat up tightly, so that it is 3½ inches in diameter, and tie it with kitchen string.

4 Wash the wok and dry over a high heat. Heat the oil to smoking point in the wok and add the chopped scallions and ginger. Cook briefly, then add the meat. Turn often to brown the outside evenly.

5 Sprinkle with sake and add 14 fluid ounces/1⅔ cups water, the soy sauce and sugar. Boil, then reduce the heat to low and cover. Cook for 25–30 minutes, turning every 5 minutes. Remove from the heat.

6 Slice the pork into 12 fine slices. Use any leftover pork for another recipe.

7 Shell and halve the boiled eggs, and sprinkle some salt on to the yolks.

8 Pour 4 cups soup stock from the bowl into a large pan. Boil and add the soy sauce and salt. Check the seasoning; add more sauce if required.

9 Wash the wok again and bring 9 cups water to the boil. Cook the ramen noodles according to the packet instructions until just soft. Stir constantly to prevent sticking. If the water bubbles up, pour in 2 fluid ounces/¼ cup cold water. Drain well and divide among four bowls.

10 Pour the soup over the noodles to cover. Arrange half a boiled egg, pork slices, menma and nori on top, and sprinkle with scallions. Serve with pepper and sesame or chili oil. Season to taste with a little salt, if you like.

COOK'S TIPS

• Sake, made from fermented rice, can be stored in the refrigerator for at least 3 weeks in a sealed container.

• Menma are pickled bamboo shoots, and must be soaked before use.

Energy 466kcal/1947kJ; Protein 35.1g; Carbohydrate 49.9g, of which sugars 0.9g; Fat 13.9g, of which saturates 3.2g; Cholesterol 175mg; Calcium 43mg; Fiber 0.3g; Sodium 489mg.

SOBA NOODLES IN HOT SOUP WITH TEMPURA

WHEN YOU COOK JAPANESE NOODLE DISHES, EVERYONE SHOULD BE READY AT THE DINNER TABLE, BECAUSE COOKED NOODLES START TO SOFTEN AND LOSE THEIR TASTE AND TEXTURE QUITE QUICKLY.

SERVES 4

INGREDIENTS
    14 ounces dried soba noodles
    1 scallion, sliced
    shichimi togarashi (optional)
For the tempura
    16 medium jumbo shrimp, heads and
        shell removed, tails intact
    14 fluid ounces/1⅔ cups
        ice-cold water
    1 extra large egg, beaten
    7 ounces/scant 2 cups
        all-purpose flour
    vegetable oil, for deep-frying
For the soup
    ⅔ cup mirin
    ⅔ cup Japanese shoyu
    3¾ cups water
    1 ounce kezuri-bushi or
        2 packets (1 ounce)
    1 tablespoon superfine sugar
    1 teaspoon salt
    3¾ cups first dashi stock
        or the same amount of water and
        2½ teaspoons dashi-no-moto

1 To make the soup, put the mirin in a large pan. Bring to the boil, then add the rest of the soup ingredients apart from the dashi stock. Bring back to the boil, then reduce the heat to low. Skim off the scum and cook for 2 minutes. Strain the soup and put back into a clean pan with the dashi stock.

2 Remove the vein from the shrimp, then make five shallow cuts into each shrimp's belly. Clip the tip of the tail with scissors and squeeze out any moisture from the tail.

3 To make the batter, pour the ice-cold water into a bowl and mix in the beaten egg. Sift in the flour and stir briefly; it should remain fairly lumpy.

4 Heat the oil in a wok or deep-fryer to 350°F. Hold the tail of a shrimp, dunk it in the batter, then plunge it into the hot oil. Deep-fry two prawns at a time until crisp and golden. Drain on paper towels and keep warm.

5 Put the noodles in a large pan with at least 9 cups rapidly boiling water, and stir frequently to prevent them from sticking.

6 When the water foams, pour in about 2 fluid ounces/¼ cup cold water to lower the temperature. Repeat when the water foams once again. The noodles should be slightly softer than *al dente* pasta.

7 Tip the noodles into a strainer and wash under cold water with your hands to rinse off any oil.

8 Heat the soup. Warm the noodles with hot water, and divide among individual serving bowls. Place the shrimp attractively on the noodles and add the soup. Sprinkle with sliced scallion and some shichimi togarashi, if you like. Serve immediately.

COOK'S TIPS
• Shichimi togarashi is a peppery condiment made of seven seasonings.
• Kezuri-bushi is ready-shaved dried fish, one of the main ingredients used in dashi stock.
• Dashi is a fish stock that is frequently used in Japanese cooking. Freeze-dried granules are called dashi-no-moto, and these can be used to make a quick dashi.

Energy 728kcal/3053kJ; Protein 30.7g; Carbohydrate 121.8g, of which sugars 5.3g; Fat 14g, of which saturates 1.9g; Cholesterol 218mg; Calcium 173mg; Fiber 1.6g; Sodium 728mg.

SAPPORO-STYLE RAMEN NOODLES IN SOUP

THIS IS A RICH AND TANGY SOUP FROM SAPPORO, THE CAPITAL OF HOKKAIDO, WHICH IS JAPAN'S MOST NORTHERLY ISLAND. RAW GRATED GARLIC, AND CHILI OIL ARE ADDED TO WARM THE BODY.

SERVES 4

INGREDIENTS
9 ounces dried ramen noodles
For the soup stock
4 scallions
2½-inch fresh ginger root, quartered
raw bones from 2 chickens, washed
1 large onion, quartered
4 garlic cloves
1 large carrot, roughly chopped
1 egg shell
4 fluid ounces/½ cup sake
6 tablespoons miso (any color)
2 tablespoons Japanese shoyu
For the toppings
4 ounces pork loin
2-inch carrot
12 snow peas
8 baby corn cobs
1 tablespoon sesame oil
1 dried red chile, seeded
and crushed
8 ounces/1 cup bean sprouts
2 scallions, chopped
2 garlic cloves, finely grated
chili oil
salt

1 To make the soup stock, bruise the scallions and ginger by hitting with a rolling pin. Boil 6¼ cups water in a heavy pan, add the bones, and cook until the meat changes color. Discard the water and wash the bones under running water.

2 Wash the pan and boil 9 cups water, then add the bones and other stock ingredients except for the miso and soy sauce. Reduce the heat to low, and simmer for 2 hours, skimming any scum off. Pour into a bowl through a strainer lined with cheesecloth; this will take about 1–2 hours. Do not squeeze the cheesecloth.

3 Cut the pork into ¼-inch slices. Peel and halve the carrot lengthwise then cut into ⅛-inch thick, 2-inch long slices. Boil the carrot, snow peas and corn for 3 minutes in water. Drain.

4 Heat the sesame oil in a wok and fry the pork slices and chile. When the color of the meat has changed, add the beansprouts. Reduce the heat to medium and add 4 cups soup stock. Cook for 5 minutes.

5 Scoop 4 tablespoons soup stock from the wok and mix well with the miso and soy sauce in a bowl. Stir back into the soup. Reduce the heat to low.

6 Bring 9 cups water to the boil. Cook the noodles until just soft, following the instructions on the packet. Stir constantly. If the water bubbles up, pour in 2 fluid ounces/¼ cup cold water. Drain well and divide among four bowls.

7 Pour the hot soup onto the noodles and heap the bean sprouts and pork on top. Add the carrot, snow peas and corn. Sprinkle with the scallions and serve with garlic and chili oil.

Energy 365kcal/1522kJ; Protein 12.5g; Carbohydrate 54.1g, of which sugars 3.9g; Fat 10.9g, of which saturates 3.9g; Cholesterol 21mg; Calcium 43mg; Fiber 1.7g; Sodium 569mg.

PORK <u>AND</u> NOODLE BROTH <u>WITH</u> SHRIMP

THIS DELICATELY FLAVORED SOUP FROM VIETNAM IS QUICK AND EASY TO MAKE, WHILE TASTING REALLY SPECIAL. THE NOODLES MAKE THE SOUP INTO A SATISFYING AND WHOLESOME DISH.

SERVES 4–6

INGREDIENTS

12 ounces pork chops or tenderloin
8 ounces raw shrimp tails or
  cooked shrimp
5 ounces thin egg noodles
1 tablespoon vegetable oil
2 teaspoons sesame oil
4 shallots or 1 medium
  onion, sliced
1 tablespoon finely sliced fresh
  ginger root
1 garlic clove, crushed
1 teaspoon sugar
6¼ cups chicken stock
2 kaffir lime leaves
3 tablespoons Thai fish sauce
juice of ½ lime
For the garnish
4 sprigs of fresh cilantro
2 scallions, green parts only,
  chopped

1 If you are using pork chops rather than tenderloin, remove any fat and the bones. Slice and set aside.

2 If using raw shrimp tails, peel and devein the shrimp.

3 Bring a large pan of salted water to the boil and simmer the egg noodles until softened, or according to the instructions on the packet. Drain and refresh under cold running water. Set the noodles aside.

4 Pre-heat a wok. Add the vegetable and sesame oils and heat through. When the oil is hot, add the shallots or onion and stir-fry for 3–4 minutes, until evenly browned. Remove from the wok and set aside.

5 Add the ginger, garlic, sugar and chicken stock to the wok and bring to a simmer. Add the lime leaves, fish sauce and lime juice. Add the pork, then simmer for 15 minutes.

6 Add the shrimp and noodles and simmer for 3–4 minutes, or longer if using raw shrimp to ensure that they are cooked. Add the shallots or onion.

7 Serve garnished with cilantro sprigs and the green parts of the scallion.

VARIATION
This quick and delicious recipe can be made with 7 ounces boneless chicken breast instead of pork tenderloin.

COOK'S TIP
Place the pork in the freezer for 30 minutes to firm, but do not freeze it. The cold makes the meat easier to slice thinly.

Energy 223kcal/936kJ; Protein 22.2g; Carbohydrate 18.1g, of which sugars 0.7g; Fat 7.3g, of which saturates 1.8g; Cholesterol 117mg; Calcium 41mg; Fiber 0.7g; Sodium 335mg.

JAPANESE-STYLE NOODLE SOUP

THIS DELICATE, FRAGRANT SOUP IS FLAVORED WITH JUST A SUBTLE HINT OF CHILI. IT IS BEST SERVED AS A LIGHT LUNCH OR FIRST COURSE.

SERVES 4

INGREDIENTS

3 tablespoons mugi miso
7 ounces/scant 2 cups udon noodles, soba noodles or Chinese noodles
2 tablespoons sake or dry sherry
1 tablespoon rice or wine vinegar
3 tablespoons Japanese shoyu
4 ounces asparagus tips or snow peas, thinly sliced diagonally
2 ounces/scant 1 cup shiitake mushrooms, stalks removed and thinly sliced
1 carrot, sliced into julienne strips
3 scallions, thinly sliced diagonally
salt and ground black pepper
1 teaspoon dried chili flakes, to serve

1 Bring 4 cups water to the boil in a pan. Pour ⅔ cup boiling water over the miso and stir until dissolved, then set aside.

2 Meanwhile, bring another large pan of lightly salted water to the boil, add the noodles and cook until just tender.

3 Drain the noodles in a colander. Rinse under cold running water, then drain again. Set aside.

COOK'S TIPS
• Mugi miso is the fermented paste of soybeans and barley.
• If fresh shiitake mushrooms are not available, use dried ones instead. Put them in a bowl, pour over boiling water and leave to stand for 30 minutes.

4 Add the sake or sherry, rice or wine vinegar and shoyu to the pan of boiling water. Boil gently for 3 minutes or until the alcohol has evaporated, then reduce the heat and stir in the miso mixture.

5 Add the asparagus or snow peas, mushrooms, carrot and scallions, and simmer for 2 minutes until the vegetables are tender. Season to taste.

6 Divide the noodles among four warm bowls and pour the soup over the top. Sprinkle with the chili flakes to serve.

Energy 220kcal/929kJ; Protein 7.9g; Carbohydrate 39.7g, of which sugars 4.4g; Fat 4.3g, of which saturates 1.2g; Cholesterol 15mg; Calcium 37mg; Fiber 2.8g; Sodium 898mg.

NOODLE, BOK CHOY AND SALMON RAMEN

THIS LIGHTLY SPICED JAPANESE NOODLE SOUP IS ENHANCED BY SLICES OF SEARED FRESH SALMON AND CRISP VEGETABLES. THE CONTRASTS IN TEXTURE ARE AS APPEALING AS THE DELICIOUS TASTE.

SERVES 4

INGREDIENTS

6 cups good vegetable stock
1-inch piece fresh ginger root,
  finely sliced
2 garlic cloves, crushed
6 scallions, sliced
3 tablespoons soy sauce
3 tablespoons sake
1 pound salmon fillet, skinned
1 teaspoon peanut oil
12 ounces ramen or udon noodles
4 small heads bok choy,
  broken into leaves
1 fresh red chile, seeded
  and sliced
2 ounces/1 cup bean sprouts
salt and ground black pepper

1 Pour the stock into a large pan and add the ginger, garlic, and a third of the scallions.

2 Add the soy sauce and sake. Bring to the boil, then reduce the heat and simmer for 30 minutes.

3 Meanwhile, remove any pin bones from the salmon using tweezers, then cut the salmon on the slant into 12 slices, using a very sharp knife.

4 Brush a ridged griddle or frying pan with the oil and heat until very hot. Sear the salmon slices for 1–2 minutes on each side until tender and marked by the ridges of the pan. Set aside.

COOK'S TIP
To obtain the distinctive stripes on the slices of salmon, it is important that the ridged pan or griddle is very hot before they are added. Avoid moving the slices, or the stripes will become blurred.

5 Cook the ramen or udon noodles in a large pan of boiling water for 4–5 minutes or according to the instructions on the packet. Tip into a colander, drain well and refresh under cold running water. Drain again and set aside.

6 Strain the broth into a clean pan and season, then bring to the boil. Add the bok choy. Using a fork, twist the noodles into four nests and put these into deep bowls. Divide the salmon slices, scallions, chile and bean sprouts among the bowls. Ladle in the broth.

Energy 569kcal/2394kJ; Protein 34.6g; Carbohydrate 65.6g, of which sugars 4.1g; Fat 20.5g, of which saturates 4.3g; Cholesterol 83mg; Calcium 70mg; Fiber 3.5g; Sodium 746mg.

NOODLES IN SOUP

IN CHINA, NOODLES IN SOUP (TANG MEIN) ARE FAR MORE POPULAR THAN FRIED NOODLES (CHOW MEIN). YOU CAN ADAPT THIS BASIC RECIPE BY USING DIFFERENT INGREDIENTS FOR THE "DRESSING."

SERVES 4

INGREDIENTS
- 8 ounces chicken breast fillet, pork tenderloin or cooked meat
- 3 or 4 shiitake mushrooms
- 4 ounces canned sliced bamboo shoots, drained
- 4 ounces spinach leaves
- 2 scallions
- 12 ounces dried egg noodles
- 2½ cups stock
- 2 tablespoons vegetable oil
- 1 teaspoon salt
- ½ teaspoon light brown sugar
- 1 tablespoon light soy sauce
- 2 teaspoons Chinese rice wine or dry sherry
- a few drops of sesame oil
- red chili sauce, to serve

1 Place the mushrooms in a bowl and cover with boiling water. Set aside and leave to soak for 30 minutes.

2 Thinly shred the meat. Squeeze dry the shiitake mushrooms and discard any hard stalks. Then thinly shred the mushrooms, bamboo shoots, greens and scallions.

3 Cook the noodles in boiling water according to the instructions on the packet, then drain and rinse under cold water. Place in a serving bowl.

4 Bring the stock to the boil and pour over the noodles. Set aside and keep warm.

5 Heat the oil in a preheated wok, add about half of the scallions and the meat, and stir-fry for about 1 minute.

VARIATIONS
- Use lettuce hearts or Chinese cabbage in place of spinach.
- Use fresh shiitake mushrooms if they are available. They do not need to be soaked before adding to the soup.

6 Add the mushrooms, bamboo shoots and greens and stir-fry for 1 minute. Add the salt, sugar, soy sauce and rice wine or sherry and blend well.

7 Pour the "dressing" over the noodles, garnish with the remaining scallions, and sprinkle over a few drops of sesame oil. Divide between individual bowls and serve with red chili sauce.

Energy 482kcal/2032kJ; Protein 26.4g; Carbohydrate 65g, of which sugars 3.3g; Fat 13.8g, of which saturates 2.9g; Cholesterol 66mg; Calcium 87mg; Fiber 3.9g; Sodium 994mg.

SEAFOOD LAKSA

FOR A DELICIOUS MEAL, SERVE CREAMY RICE NOODLES IN A SPICY COCONUT-FLAVORED SOUP, TOPPED WITH SEAFOOD. THERE IS A FAIR AMOUNT OF WORK INVOLVED IN THE PREPARATION, BUT YOU CAN MAKE THE SOUP BASE IN ADVANCE.

SERVES 4

INGREDIENTS

   4 fresh red chiles, seeded and
     roughly chopped
   1 onion, roughly chopped
   1 piece shrimp paste, the size of a
     bouillon cube
   1 lemongrass stalk, chopped
   1-inch piece fresh ginger root, peeled
     and roughly chopped
   6 macadamia nuts or almonds
   4 tablespoons vegetable oil
   1 teaspoon paprika
   1 teaspoon ground turmeric
   16 fluid ounces/2 cups fish stock
   2½ cups coconut milk
   a dash of Thai fish sauce, to taste
   12 jumbo shrimp, peeled
     and deveined
   8 scallops
   8 ounces prepared squid, cut
     into rings
   12 ounces rice vermicelli or rice
     noodles, soaked in warm water
     until soft
   salt and ground black pepper
   lime halves, to serve
For the garnish
   ¼ cucumber, cut into matchsticks
   2 fresh red chiles, seeded and
     finely sliced
   2 tablespoons mint leaves
   2 tablespoons fried shallots or onions

1 In a blender or food processor, process the chiles, onion, shrimp paste, lemongrass, ginger and nuts until smooth in texture.

2 Heat 3 tablespoons of the oil in a large pan. Add the chili paste and fry for 6 minutes, stirring. Stir in the paprika and turmeric and fry for about 2 minutes more.

COOK'S TIP
Wear rubber gloves when preparing the chiles to prevent any juice from getting onto your hands.

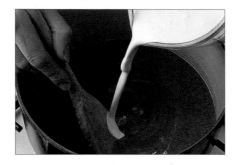

3 Add the stock and the coconut milk to the pan. Bring to the boil, then simmer gently for 15–20 minutes. Season with fish sauce.

4 Season the seafood with salt and pepper. Fry quickly in the remaining oil for 2–3 minutes until cooked.

5 Add the noodles to the soup and heat through. Divide among individual serving bowls.

6 Place the fried seafood on top, then garnish with the cucumber, chiles, mint, and fried shallots or onions. Serve with the limes.

Energy 348kcal/1456kJ; Protein 24.3g; Carbohydrate 12.8g, of which sugars 10.9g; Fat 13.1g, of which saturates 2g; Cholesterol 236mg; Calcium 111mg; Fiber 0.2g; Sodium 378mg.

NOODLE SOUP <u>WITH</u> PORK <u>AND</u> SICHUAN PICKLE

THIS SOUP IS A MEAL IN ITSELF, AND THE HOT PICKLE GIVES IT A DELICIOUS TANG.

SERVES 4

INGREDIENTS

    4 cups chicken stock
    12 ounces egg noodles
    1 tablespoon dried shrimp, soaked
      in water
    2 tablespoons vegetable oil
    8 ounces lean pork, finely shredded
    1 tablespoon yellow bean paste
    1 tablespoon soy sauce
    4 ounces Sichuan hot pickle, rinsed,
      drained and shredded
    a pinch of sugar
    2 scallions, finely sliced,
      to garnish

1 Bring the stock to the boil in a pan. Add the noodles and cook until almost tender. Drain the noodles. Drain the dried shrimp, rinse them under cold water, drain again and add to the stock.

2 Lower the heat and simmer for a further 2 minutes. Keep hot.

3 Heat the oil in a frying pan or wok. Add the pork and stir-fry over a high heat for 3 minutes.

4 Add the bean paste and soy sauce to the pork and stir-fry for 1 minute. Add the hot pickle with a pinch of sugar. Stir-fry for 1 minute further.

5 Divide the noodles and soup among individual serving bowls. Spoon the pork mixture on top, then sprinkle with the scallions and serve immediately.

Energy 480kcal/2022kJ; Protein 25.2g; Carbohydrate 64.8g, of which sugars 3.2g; Fat 15.1g, of which saturates 3.5g; Cholesterol 81mg; Calcium 81mg; Fiber 2.9g; Sodium 1023mg.

TOFU SOUPS

Nutritious and satisfying, tofu is added to Asian soups to make them into a complete meal. Tom Yam Gung with Tofu is a famous Thai speciality that is ideal as a light lunch or supper. Tofu Soup with Mushrooms, Tomato, Ginger and Cilantro is a typical Canh, or clear broth, from the north of Vietnam. Hot-and-Sour Soup is a classic Chinese dish. Japanese soups include Miso Broth with Scallions and Tofu, and Japanese Crushed Tofu Soup.

MISO BROTH <u>WITH</u> SCALLIONS <u>AND</u> TOFU

THE JAPANESE EAT MISO BROTH, A SIMPLE BUT HIGHLY NUTRITIOUS SOUP, ALMOST EVERY DAY—IT IS STANDARD BREAKFAST FARE, AND IT IS ALSO EATEN WITH RICE OR NOODLES LATER IN THE DAY.

SERVES 4

INGREDIENTS

1 bunch of scallions or
  5 baby leeks
½ ounce fresh cilantro
3 thin slices fresh ginger root
2 star anise
1 small dried red chile
5 cups dashi stock or vegetable
  stock
8 ounces bok choy or other Asian
  greens, thickly sliced
7 ounces firm tofu, cut into
  1-inch cubes
4 tablespoons red miso
2–3 tablespoons Japanese shoyu
1 fresh red chile, seeded and
  shredded (optional)

1 Cut the coarse green tops off the scallions or baby leeks and slice the rest of the scallions or leeks finely on the diagonal. Place the coarse green tops in a large pan with the cilantro stalks, fresh ginger root, star anise, dried chile and dashi or vegetable stock.

2 Heat the mixture gently until boiling, then lower the heat and simmer for 10 minutes. Strain, return to the pan and reheat until simmering. Add the green portion of the sliced scallions or leeks to the soup with the bok choy or greens and tofu. Cook for 2 minutes.

3 Mix 3 tablespoons of the miso with a little of the hot soup in a bowl, then stir it into the soup. Taste the soup and add more miso with shoyu to taste.

4 Coarsely chop the cilantro leaves and stir most of them into the soup with the white part of the scallions or leeks. Cook for 1 minute, then ladle the soup into warmed serving bowls. Sprinkle with the remaining cilantro and the fresh red chile, if using, and serve immediately.

COOK'S TIP
Dashi is available powdered in Asian and Chinese stores. Alternatively, make your own by gently simmering 4–6 inches kombu seaweed in 2 pints/5 cups water for 10 minutes. Do not boil vigorously as this makes the dashi bitter. Remove the kombu, then add ½ ounce dried bonito flakes and bring to the boil. Strain immediately through a fine strainer.

Energy 60kcal/252kJ; Protein 5.5g; Carbohydrate 4.4g, of which sugars 4.1g; Fat 2.3g, of which saturates 0.3g; Cholesterol 0mg; Calcium 294mg; Fiber 1.6g; Sodium 453mg.

HOT AND SWEET VEGETABLE AND TOFU SOUP

THIS SOOTHING, NUTRITIOUS SOUP TAKES ONLY MINUTES TO MAKE AS THE SPINACH AND SILKEN TOFU ARE SIMPLY PLACED IN BOWLS AND COVERED WITH THE FLAVORED HOT STOCK.

SERVES 4

INGREDIENTS

   5 cups vegetable stock
   1–2 teaspoons Thai red
     curry paste
   2 kaffir lime leaves, torn
   1½ ounces/3 tablespoons jaggery or
     light brown sugar
   2 tablespoons soy sauce
  juice of 1 lime
   1 carrot, cut into thin matchsticks
   2 ounces baby spinach leaves, any
     coarse stalks removed
   8-ounce block silken tofu, diced

1 Heat the stock in a large pan, then add the red curry paste. Stir constantly over a medium heat until the paste has dissolved. Add the lime leaves, jaggery or sugar and soy sauce and bring to the boil.

2 Add the lime juice and carrot to the pan. Reduce the heat and simmer for 5–10 minutes. Place the spinach and tofu in four individual serving bowls and pour the hot stock on top to serve.

Energy 105kcal/439kJ; Protein 5.3g; Carbohydrate 13.2g, of which sugars 12.8g; Fat 3.8g, of which saturates 0.5g; Cholesterol 0mg; Calcium 320mg; Fiber 0.7g; Sodium 559mg.

INDONESIAN TOFU LAKSA

THIS SPICY SOUP, WITH DEEP-FRIED TOFU, IS NOT A DISH YOU CAN THROW TOGETHER IN A FEW MINUTES, BUT IT IS MARVELOUS PARTY FOOD. GUESTS SPOON NOODLES INTO WIDE SOUP BOWLS, ADD ACCOMPANIMENTS OF THEIR CHOICE, TOP UP WITH SOUP AND TAKE SHRIMP CRACKERS TO NIBBLE.

SERVES 6

INGREDIENTS

1½ pounds small clams, scrubbed
2 cans (28 fluid ounces)
  coconut milk
2 ounces *ikan bilis* (dried anchovies)
3¾ cups water
4 ounces shallots, finely chopped
4 garlic cloves, chopped
6 macadamia nuts or blanched
  almonds, chopped
3 lemongrass stalks, root trimmed
6 tablespoons sunflower oil
½-inch cube shrimp paste
1 ounce/2 tablespoons mild
  curry powder
a few curry leaves
2 or 3 eggplants, total weight about
  1½ pounds, trimmed
1½ pounds raw peeled shrimp
2 teaspoons sugar
1 head Chinese cabbage, thinly sliced
4 ounces/2 cups bean sprouts, rinsed
2 scallions, chopped
2 ounces crispy fried onions
4 ounces deep-fried tofu
1½ pounds mixed noodles (*laksa,
  mee* and *behoon*) or one type only
shrimp crackers, to serve

1 Put the clams in a large pan with ½ inch water. Bring to the boil, cover and steam over a high heat for about 3–4 minutes, until all the clams have opened. Discard any that remain shut. Make up the coconut milk to 5 cups with water. Put the *ikan bilis* in a pan and add the water. Bring to the boil and simmer for 20 minutes.

2 Meanwhile, put the shallots, garlic and nuts into a mortar. Cut off the lower 2 inches of two of the lemongrass stalks, chop finely and add to the mortar. Pound the mixture to a paste.

3 Heat the oil in a large heavy pan, add the shallot paste and cook, stirring constantly, for 1–2 minutes, until the mixture gives off a rich aroma. Bruise the remaining lemongrass stalk and add to the pan. Toss over the heat to release its flavor. Mix the shrimp paste and curry powder to a paste with a little of the coconut milk, add to the pan and toss the mixture over the heat for 1 minute, stirring constantly, and keeping the heat low. Stir in the remaining coconut milk. Add the curry leaves and allow the mixture to simmer while you prepare the accompaniments.

VARIATION
You could substitute mussels for clams if you like. Scrub them thoroughly, removing any beards, and cook them in lightly salted water for about 5 minutes, until they open. As with clams, discard any mussels that remain closed.

4 Strain the stock into a pan. Discard the *ikan bilis*, bring to the boil, then add the eggplants. Cook for about 10 minutes, or until tender, when the skins can be peeled off easily. Lift out of the stock, peel, and cut into thick strips.

5 Arrange the eggplants on a serving platter. Sprinkle the shrimp with sugar, add to the stock and cook for about 2–4 minutes, until they have just turned pink. Remove with a slotted spoon and place next to the eggplants. Add the Chinese cabbage, bean sprouts, scallions and crispy fried onions to the platter, together with the clams.

6 Gradually stir the remaining *ikan bilis* stock into the pan of soup and bring to the boil. Rinse the fried tofu in boiling water, cool slightly and squeeze to remove excess oil. Cut each piece in half and add to the soup. Lower the heat to a very gentle simmer.

7 Cook the noodles according to the instructions of the packet, drain and pile in a dish. Remove the curry leaves and lemongrass from the soup and discard. Place the noodles, soup and the platter of seafood and vegetables on the table, along with a bowl of shrimp crackers, so that guests can help themselves to the various accompaniments.

COOK'S TIP
Dried shrimp paste, also called *blachan*, is sold in small blocks and is available from Asian supermarkets.

Energy 882kcal/3714kJ; Protein 61.5g; Carbohydrate 96.9g, of which sugars 14.9g; Fat 30.2g, of which saturates 5.3g; Cholesterol 333mg; Calcium 602mg; Fiber 7.5g; Sodium 2185mg.

THAI HOT-AND-SOUR SOUP

THIS LIGHT AND INVIGORATING SOUP, WITH ITS FINELY BALANCED COMBINATION OF FLAVORS,
IS BEST SERVED AT THE BEGINNING OF A MEAL TO STIMULATE THE APPETITE.

SERVES 4

INGREDIENTS

2 carrots
3¾ cups vegetable stock
2 Thai chiles, seeded and
  finely sliced
2 lemongrass stalks, outer leaves
  removed and each stalk cut into
  3 pieces
4 kaffir lime leaves
2 garlic cloves, finely chopped
4 scallions, finely sliced
1 teaspoon sugar
juice of 1 lime
3 tablespoons chopped fresh cilantro
4½ ounces/1 cup Japanese
  tofu, sliced
salt

1 To make carrot flowers, cut each carrot in half crosswise, then cut four V-shaped channels lengthwise. Slice into thin rounds and set aside.

2 Pour the stock into a pan. Reserve ½ teaspoon of the chiles and add the rest to the pan with the lemongrass, lime leaves, garlic and half the scallions. Bring to the boil, reduce the heat and simmer for 20 minutes.

3 Strain the stock and discard the flavorings. Return the stock to the pan, add the reserved chiles and scallions, the sugar, lime juice, cilantro and salt to taste.

4 Simmer over a gentle heat for 5 minutes, then add the carrot flowers and the tofu, and cook for a further 2 minutes until the carrot is just tender. Ladle into bowls and serve hot.

Energy 40kcal/169kJ; Protein 3.3g; Carbohydrate 3.4g, of which sugars 3.1g; Fat 1.6g, of which saturates 0.2g; Cholesterol 0mg; Calcium 197mg; Fiber 1.2g; Sodium 11mg.

JAPANESE CRUSHED TOFU SOUP

THE MAIN INGREDIENT FOR THIS TRADITIONAL JAPANESE SOUP IS CRUSHED TOFU, WHICH IS BOTH NUTRITIOUS AND SATISFYING.

SERVES 4

INGREDIENTS

    5 ounces fresh tofu, weighed
        without water
    2 dried shiitake mushrooms
    2 ounces burdock
    1 teaspoon rice vinegar
    ½ black or white konnyaku
        (about 4 ounces)
    2 tablespoons sesame oil
    4 ounces daikon, finely sliced
    2 ounces carrot, finely sliced
    3 cups kombu and bonito stock or
        instant dashi
    a pinch of salt
    2 tablespoons sake or dry white wine
    1½ teaspoons mirin
    3 tablespoons white or red miso paste
    a dash of soy sauce
    6 snow peas, trimmed, boiled and
        finely sliced, to garnish

4 Put the konnyaku in a small pan and cover with water. Bring to the boil, then drain and cool.

5 Tear the konnyaku into ¾ inch lumps: do not use a knife, as smooth cuts will prevent it from absorbing any flavor.

6 Heat the sesame oil in a deep pan. Add all the shiitake mushrooms, burdock, daikon, carrot and konnyaku. Stir-fry for 1 minute, then add the tofu and stir well.

7 Pour in the stock or dashi and add the salt, sake or wine, and mirin. Bring to the boil. Skim the broth and simmer it for 5 minutes.

8 In a small bowl, dissolve the miso paste in a little of the soup, then return it to the pan. Simmer the soup gently for 10 minutes, until the vegetables are soft. Add the soy sauce, then remove from the heat. Serve immediately, garnished with the snow peas.

1 Crush the tofu roughly by hand until it resembles lumpy scrambled egg in texture—do not crush it too finely. Wrap the tofu in a clean dish towel and put it in a strainer, then pour over plenty of boiling water. Leave the tofu to drain thoroughly for 10 minutes.

2 Soak the dried shiitake mushrooms in tepid water for 20 minutes, then drain them. Remove their stems and cut the caps into 4–6 pieces.

3 Scrub the skin off the burdock and slice it into thin shavings. Soak the shavings for 5 minutes in plenty of cold water with the vinegar added to remove any bitter taste. Drain.

Energy 85kcal/355kJ; Protein 4.8g; Carbohydrate 11.7g, of which sugars 10.9g; Fat 2.3g, of which saturates 0.5g; Cholesterol 0mg; Calcium 241mg; Fiber 3.7g; Sodium 678mg.

SPINACH <u>AND</u> TOFU SOUP

THIS IS AN EXTREMELY DELICATE AND MILD-FLAVORED SOUP, WHICH CAN BE USED TO COUNTERBALANCE THE HEAT FROM A HOT THAI CURRY.

SERVES 4–6

INGREDIENTS
    2 tablespoons dried shrimps
    4 cups chicken stock
    8 ounces fresh tofu, drained and
      cut into ¾-inch cubes
    2 tablespoons Thai fish sauce
    12 ounces fresh spinach,
      thoroughly washed
    ground black pepper
    2 scallions, finely sliced,
      to garnish

1 Rinse the dried shrimp under cold running water and drain. Combine the shrimp with the chicken stock in a large pan and bring to the boil.

2 Add the tofu and simmer for about 5 minutes. Season with fish sauce and black pepper to taste.

3 Tear the spinach leaves into pieces. Add to the soup and cook for a further 1–2 minutes.

4 Pour the soup into warmed bowls, sprinkle the chopped scallions on top to garnish, and serve.

Energy 55kcal/231kJ; Protein 7.6g; Carbohydrate 1.4g, of which sugars 1.1g; Fat 2.2g, of which saturates 0.3g; Cholesterol 25mg; Calcium 352mg; Fiber 1.3g; Sodium 300mg.

CHINESE TOFU AND LETTUCE SOUP

THIS LIGHT, CLEAR SOUP IS BRIMFUL OF COLORFUL, TASTY VEGETABLES. FOR THIS SOUP YOU NEED SMOKED OR MARINATED TOFU, WHICH HAS ADDED FLAVOR.

SERVES 4

INGREDIENTS

2 tablespoons peanut or
  sunflower oil
7 ounces smoked or marinated
  tofu, cubed
3 scallions, sliced
2 garlic cloves, cut into thin strips
1 carrot, finely sliced into rounds
4 cups vegetable stock
2 tablespoons soy sauce
1 tablespoon dry sherry or vermouth
1 teaspoon sugar
4 ounces romaine lettuce, shredded
salt and ground black pepper

1 Heat the oil in a preheated wok, then stir-fry the tofu cubes until browned, stirring continuously. Drain on paper towels and set aside.

2 Add the scallions, garlic and carrot to the wok and stir-fry for 2 minutes. Add the stock, soy sauce, sherry or vermouth, sugar, lettuce and fried tofu. Heat through gently for 1 minute, season to taste and serve.

Energy 106kcal/439kJ; Protein 4.8g; Carbohydrate 3.2g, of which sugars 2.8g; Fat 7.8g, of which saturates 1g; Cholesterol 0mg; Calcium 272mg; Fiber 0.8g; Sodium 543mg.

THAI MIXED VEGETABLE SOUP

IN THAILAND, THIS TYPE OF SOUP IS USUALLY MADE IN LARGE QUANTITIES AND THEN REHEATED FOR CONSUMPTION OVER SEVERAL DAYS. IF YOU WOULD LIKE TO DO THE SAME, DOUBLE OR TREBLE THE QUANTITIES. CHILL LEFTOVER SOUP RAPIDLY AND REHEAT THOROUGHLY BEFORE SERVING.

SERVES 4

INGREDIENTS

2 tablespoons peanut oil
1 tablespoon magic paste (see
  Cook's Tip)
3½ ounces savoy cabbage or
  Chinese cabbage, finely shredded
3½ ounces daikon, finely diced
1 medium cauliflower,
  coarsely chopped
4 celery sticks, coarsely chopped
5 cups vegetable stock
4½ ounces fried tofu, cut into
  1-inch cubes
1 teaspoon jaggery or
  light brown sugar
3 tablespoons light soy sauce

1 Heat the peanut oil in a large, heavy pan or wok. Add the magic paste and cook over a low heat, stirring frequently, until it gives off its aroma. Add the shredded savoy cabbage or Chinese cabbage, daikon, cauliflower and celery. Pour in the vegetable stock, increase the heat to medium and bring to the boil, stirring occasionally. Gently stir in the tofu cubes.

2 Add the sugar and soy sauce. Reduce the heat and simmer for 15 minutes, until the vegetables are cooked and tender. Taste and add a little more soy sauce if needed. Serve hot.

COOK'S TIP
Magic paste is a mixture of crushed garlic, white pepper and cilantro. Look for it at Thai markets.

Energy 167kcal/693kJ; Protein 10.4g; Carbohydrate 4.9g, of which sugars 4.2g; Fat 11.9g, of which saturates 0.8g; Cholesterol 0mg; Calcium 521mg; Fiber 1.9g; Sodium 832mg.

TOM YAM GUNG <u>WITH</u> TOFU

ONE OF THE MOST REFRESHING AND HEALTHY SOUPS, THIS FRAGRANT DISH IS A FAMOUS THAI SPECIALTY, AND WOULD MAKE AN IDEAL LIGHT LUNCH OR SUPPER.

SERVES 4

INGREDIENTS

    2 tablespoons peanut oil
    11 ounces firm tofu, cut into small
      bitesize pieces
    5 cups good vegetable stock
    1 tablespoon Thai chili jam (*nam
      pick pow*)
    shredded rind of 1 kaffir lime
    1 shallot, finely sliced
    1 garlic clove, peeled and
      finely chopped
    2 kaffir lime leaves, shredded
    3 red chiles, seeded and shredded
    1 lemongrass stalk,
      finely chopped
    6 shiitake mushrooms,
      thinly sliced
    4 scallions, finely shredded
    3 tablespoons Thai fish sauce
    3 tablespoons lime juice
    1 teaspoon superfine sugar
    3 tablespoons chopped fresh
      cilantro leaves
    salt and ground black pepper

2 Add the stock, chili jam, kaffir lime rind, shallot, garlic, lime leaves, two-thirds of the chiles and the lemon grass to the pan. Bring to the boil and simmer for 20 minutes.

3 Strain the stock into a clean pan. Stir in the remaining chiles, the shiitake mushrooms, scallions, fish sauce, lime juice and sugar. Simmer for 3 minutes. Add the fried tofu and heat through for 1 minute. Mix in the chopped cilantro and season to taste. Serve at once in warmed bowls.

1 Heat the oil in a wok and fry the tofu for 4–5 minutes until golden, turning occasionally to brown on all sides. Use a slotted spoon to remove the tofu and set aside. Tip the oil from the wok into a large, heavy-based pan.

COOK'S TIP
Kaffir lime leaves have a distinct citrus flavor. Fresh leaves can be bought from Asian shops, and some supermarkets sell them dried. Thai fish sauce (*nam pla*) and chilli jam (*nam pick pow*) are available from some supermarkets.

Energy 122kcal/506kJ; Protein 7.1g; Carbohydrate 3.6g, of which sugars 2.9g; Fat 8.9g, of which saturates 1.5g; Cholesterol 0mg; Calcium 395mg; Fiber 0.7g; Sodium 273mg.

CHINESE HOT-AND-SOUR SOUP

A CLASSIC CHINESE SOUP, THIS IS A WARMING AND FLAVORSOME START TO A MEAL. GARNISH IT WITH
SCALLION RINGS FOR AN ATTRACTIVE FINISH.

SERVES 4

INGREDIENTS
   ¼ ounce dried wood ears
   8 fresh shiitake mushrooms
   3 ounces tofu
   2 ounces/½ cup sliced, drained,
     canned bamboo shoots
   3¾ cups vegetable stock
   1 tablespoon superfine sugar
   3 tablespoons rice vinegar
   1 tablespoon light soy sauce
   ¼ teaspoon chili oil
   ½ teaspoon salt
   a large pinch of ground
     white pepper
   1 tablespoon cornstarch
   1 tablespoon cold water
   1 egg white
   1 teaspoon sesame oil
   2 scallions, cut into fine rings,
     to garnish

1 Soak the wood ears in hot water for 30 minutes or until soft. Drain, trim off and discard the hard base from each, and chop the wood ears roughly.

COOK'S TIPS
• To transform this tasty soup into a nutritious light lunch or supper, simply add extra mushrooms, tofu and bamboo shoots.
• Use dried shiitake mushrooms if fresh ones are not available. Soak them in boiling water for 20 minutes to reconstitute them before use.
• Use marinated deep-fried tofu if you want some extra flavor.

2 Remove and discard the stalks from the shiitake mushrooms. Cut the caps into thin strips.

3 Cut the tofu into ½-inch cubes and shred the bamboo shoots finely.

4 Place the stock, mushrooms, tofu, bamboo shoots and wood ears in a large pan. Bring the stock to the boil, lower the heat and simmer for about 5 minutes.

5 Stir in the sugar, vinegar, soy sauce, chili oil, salt and pepper.

6 Mix the cornstarch to a thin paste with the water. Add the mixture to the soup, stirring until it thickens slightly.

7 Lightly beat the egg white, then pour it slowly into the soup in a steady stream, stirring constantly. Cook, stirring, until the egg white changes color.

8 Add the sesame oil just before serving. Ladle the soup into heated bowls and garnish each portion with scallion rings.

Energy 56kcal/236kJ; Protein 2.8g; Carbohydrate 8.1g, of which sugars 4.5g; Fat 1.6g, of which saturates 0.2g; Cholesterol 0mg; Calcium 102mg; Fiber 0.2g; Sodium 286mg.

MINESTRONE WITH MARINATED FRIED TOFU

THIS SATISFYING AND APPEALING SOUP IS A MEAL IN ITSELF AND CAN BE ADAPTED TO USE WHATEVER VEGETABLES ARE AVAILABLE.

SERVES 6

INGREDIENTS

    1 tablespoon olive oil
    2 leeks, finely chopped
    2 celery sticks, finely diced
    2 garlic cloves, finely chopped
    2 zucchini, finely diced
    1 pound carrots, finely diced
    7 ounces green beans, finely sliced
    1 teaspoon dried Mediterranean herbs
    5 cups vegetable stock
    1 can (14 ounces) chopped tomatoes
    11 ounces marinated deep-fried
      tofu pieces
    ¾ ounce bunch fresh Italian parsley
      or basil, chopped
    sea salt and ground black pepper

1 Preheat the oven to 400°F. Heat the oil in a large pan then sauté the leeks, celery and garlic for 7–8 minutes, or until softened and beginning to turn golden.

2 Add the other vegetables and dried herbs. Stir to mix well, then pour over the vegetable stock and tomatoes. Bring to the boil, then simmer for 20–25 minutes, until the vegetables are tender.

3 Meanwhile, place the tofu pieces on a baking sheet and bake for 8–10 minutes to warm through.

4 Add the chopped parsley or basil to the soup and season to taste with sea salt and pepper.

5 Stir in the warmed tofu and serve immediately sprinkled with a grinding of extra black pepper.

Energy 122kcal/510kJ; Protein 7.6g; Carbohydrate 12.2g, of which sugars 10.8g; Fat 5.1g, of which saturates 0.8g; Cholesterol 0mg; Calcium 328mg; Fiber 5.2g; Sodium 36mg.

TOFU SOUP <u>WITH</u> MUSHROOMS, TOMATO, GINGER <u>AND</u> CILANTRO

THIS IS A TYPICAL CANH—A CLEAR BROTH FROM THE NORTH OF VIETNAM. IT IS DESIGNED TO BE LIGHT, TO BALANCE A MEAL THAT MAY INCLUDE SOME HEAVIER MEAT OR POULTRY DISHES.

SERVES 4

INGREDIENTS

4 ounces/scant 2 cups dried shiitake mushrooms, soaked in water for 20 minutes
1 tablespoon vegetable oil
2 shallots, halved and sliced
2 Thai chiles, seeded and sliced
1½-inch fresh ginger root, peeled and shredded or finely chopped
1 tablespoon *nuoc mam*
12 ounces tofu, rinsed, drained and cut into bitesize cubes
4 tomatoes, skinned, seeded and cut into thin strips
salt and ground black pepper
1 bunch cilantro, stalks removed, finely chopped, to garnish

For the stock

1 meaty chicken carcass or 1¼ pounds pork ribs
1 ounce dried squid or shrimp, soaked in water for 15 minutes
2 onions, peeled and quartered
2 garlic cloves, crushed
3-inch fresh ginger root, coarsely chopped
1 tablespoon *nuoc mam*
6 black peppercorns
2 star anise
4 cloves
1 cinnamon stick
sea salt

1 To make the stock, put the chicken carcass or pork ribs in a deep pan. Drain and rinse the dried squid or shrimp. Add to the pan with the remaining stock ingredients, except the salt, and pour in 8 cups water. Bring the water to the boil, and boil for a few minutes, skim off any foam, then reduce the heat and simmer gently with the lid on for 1½–2 hours. Remove the lid and continue simmering for a further 30 minutes to reduce. Skim off any fat, season with salt, strain and measure out 6¼ cups.

2 Squeeze dry the soaked shiitake mushrooms, remove the stems and slice the caps into thin strips. Heat the oil in a large pan or wok and stir in the shallots, chiles and ginger. As the fragrance begins to rise, stir in the *nuoc mam*, followed by the stock.

3 Add the tofu, mushrooms and tomatoes and bring the stock to the boil. Reduce the heat and simmer for 5–10 minutes. Season to taste and sprinkle the finely chopped fresh cilantro over the top. Serve piping hot.

Energy 127kcal/532kJ; Protein 9.9g; Carbohydrate 6.1g, of which sugars 5.1g; Fat 7.3g, of which saturates 0.9g; Cholesterol 0mg; Calcium 483mg; Fiber 2.5g; Sodium 554mg.

CHICKEN AND DUCK SOUPS

A substantial chicken soup such as Chicken, Leek and Celery Soup, Chicken Soup with Knaidlach, or Pumpkin, Rice and Chicken Soup can be a meal in itself, served with crusty bread and some fresh fruit to follow. Chicken soups from Asia are usually lighter and refreshing, often served as an appetizer or as part of a meal. Duck makes a rich soup, and there are several recipes to try, including Cream of Duck Soup with Blueberry Relish, and Duck and Nut Soup with Jujubes.

SOUTHERN AMERICAN SUCCOTASH SOUP WITH CHICKEN

BASED ON A VEGETABLE DISH FROM THE SOUTHERN STATES OF NORTH AMERICA, THIS SOUP INCLUDES SUCCULENT FRESH CORN KERNELS, WHICH GIVE IT A RICHNESS THAT COMPLEMENTS THE CHICKEN.

SERVES 4

INGREDIENTS

   3 cups chicken stock
   4 boneless, skinless chicken breasts
   2 ounces/¼ cup butter
   2 onions, chopped
   4-ounce piece rindless smoked fatty
     bacon, chopped
   1 ounce/¼ cup all-purpose flour
   4 corn cobs
   1¼ cups milk
   1 can (14 ounces) lima beans,
     drained
   3 tablespoons chopped
     fresh parsley
salt and ground black pepper

1 Bring the chicken stock to the boil in a large pan. Add the chicken breasts and bring back to the boil. Reduce the heat and cook for 12–15 minutes, until cooked through and tender. Use a slotted spoon to remove the chicken from the pan and leave to cool. Reserve the stock.

2 Melt the butter in a pan. Add the onions and cook for 4–5 minutes, until softened but not brown.

3 Add the bacon and cook for 5–6 minutes, until beginning to brown. Sprinkle in the flour and cook for 1 minute, stirring continuously.

4 Gradually stir in the hot stock and bring to the boil, stirring until thickened. Remove from the heat.

5 Using a sharp knife, remove the kernels from the corn cobs. Stir the kernels into the pan with half the milk. Return to the heat and cook, stirring occasionally, for 12–15 minutes, until the corn is tender.

VARIATION
Canned corn can be used instead of fresh corn.

6 Cut the chicken into bitesize pieces and stir into the soup. Stir in the lima beans and the remaining milk. Bring to the boil and cook for 5 minutes, then season well and stir in the parsley.

Energy 539kcal/2267kJ; Protein 51.8g; Carbohydrate 37.4g, of which sugars 11.5g; Fat 21.4g, of which saturates 10.3g; Cholesterol 155mg; Calcium 155mg; Fiber 6.4g; Sodium 1120mg.

MOROCCAN CHICKEN SOUP
WITH CHARMOULA BUTTER

THIS TASTY SOUP, INSPIRED BY THE INGREDIENTS OF NORTH AFRICA, IS SPICED WITH CHILE AND SERVED WITH A RICH AND PUNGENT LEMON BUTTER CREAMED WITH CRISP BREAD CRUMBS.

SERVES 6

INGREDIENTS
- 2 ounces/¼ cup butter
- 1 pound chicken breasts, cut into strips
- 1 onion, chopped
- 2 garlic cloves, crushed
- 1½ teaspoons all-purpose flour
- 1 tablespoon harissa
- 1¾ pints/4 cups chicken stock
- 1 can (14 ounces) chopped tomatoes
- 1 can (14 ounces) chickpeas, drained and rinsed
- salt and ground black pepper
- lemon wedges, to serve

For the charmoula
- 2 ounces/¼ cup lightly salted butter, at room temperature
- 2 tablespoons chopped fresh cilantro
- 2 garlic cloves, crushed
- 1 teaspoon ground cumin
- 1 red chile, seeded and chopped
- pinch of saffron threads
- finely grated rind of ½ lemon
- 1 teaspoon paprika
- 1 ounce/1 cup dried bread crumbs

1 Melt the butter in a large, heavy-based pan. Add the chicken strips and cook for 5–6 minutes, turning with a wooden spatula, until beginning to brown. Use a slotted spoon to remove the chicken from the pan and set aside.

2 Add the onion and garlic to the pan and cook over a gentle heat for 4–5 minutes, until softened but not brown.

3 Stir in the flour and cook for 3–4 minutes, stirring continuously, until beginning to brown.

4 Stir in the harissa and cook for a further 1 minute. Gradually pour in the stock and cook for 2–3 minutes, until slightly thickened. Stir in the tomatoes.

5 Return the chicken to the soup and add the chickpeas. Cover and cook over a low heat for 20 minutes. Season well with salt and black pepper.

6 Meanwhile, to make the charmoula, put the butter into a bowl and beat in the cilantro, garlic, cumin, chile, saffron strands, lemon rind and paprika. When the mixture is well combined, stir in the coarse bread crumbs.

7 Ladle the soup into six warmed bowls. Spoon a little of the charmoula into the center of each and leave for a few seconds to allow the butter to melt into the soup before serving with lemon wedges.

Energy 313kcal/1312kJ; Protein 25g; Carbohydrate 18.3g, of which sugars 3.3g; Fat 16.1g, of which saturates 9g; Cholesterol 88mg; Calcium 53mg; Fiber 3.6g; Sodium 207mg.

CHICKEN, LEEK AND CELERY SOUP

THIS MAKES A SUBSTANTIAL MAIN COURSE SOUP WITH FRESH CRUSTY BREAD. YOU WILL NEED NOTHING MORE THAN A SALAD AND CHEESE, OR JUST FRESH FRUIT TO FOLLOW THIS DISH.

SERVES 4–6

INGREDIENTS

3 pounds free-range chicken
1 small head of celery, trimmed
1 onion, coarsely chopped
1 fresh bay leaf
a few fresh parsley stalks
a few fresh tarragon sprigs
10 cups cold water
3 large leeks
2½ ounces/5 tablespoons butter
2 potatoes, cut into chunks
⅔ cup dry white wine
2–3 tablespoons light
   cream (optional)
salt and ground black pepper
3½ ounces pancetta, broiled until
   crisp, to garnish

1 Cut the breasts off the chicken and set aside. Chop the rest of the chicken carcass into 8–10 pieces and place in a large pan.

2 Chop 4–5 of the outer sticks of the celery and add them to the pan with the onion. Tie the bay leaf, parsley and tarragon together and add to the pan. Pour in the cold water to cover the ingredients and bring to the boil. Reduce the heat and cover the pan, then simmer for 1½ hours.

3 Remove the chicken from the pan and cut off and reserve the meat. Strain the stock, then return it to the pan and boil rapidly until it has reduced to about 6¼ cups.

4 Meanwhile, set about 5 ounces of the leeks aside. Slice the remaining leeks and the remaining celery, reserving any celery leaves. Chop the celery leaves and set aside to garnish the soup.

5 Melt half the butter in a large, heavy-based pan. Add the sliced leeks and celery, cover and cook over a low heat for about 10 minutes, or until softened but not browned. Add the potatoes, white wine and 5 cups of the stock.

6 Season well with salt and pepper, bring to the boil and reduce the heat. Part-cover the pan and simmer the soup for 15–20 minutes, or until the potatoes are cooked.

7 Meanwhile, skin the reserved chicken breasts and cut the flesh into small pieces. Melt the remaining butter in a frying pan, add the chicken and fry for 5–7 minutes, until cooked.

8 Thickly slice the remaining leeks, add to the pan and cook, stirring occasionally, for a further 3–4 minutes, until just cooked.

9 Process the soup with the cooked chicken from the stock in a blender or food processor. Taste and adjust the seasoning, and add more stock if the soup is very thick.

10 Stir in the cream, if using, and the chicken and leek mixture. Reheat gently and serve in warmed bowls. Crumble the pancetta over the soup and sprinkle with the chopped celery leaves.

Energy 294kcal/1246kJ; Protein 40.5g; Carbohydrate 22.1g, of which sugars 5.9g; Fat 2.8g, of which saturates 0.7g; Cholesterol 105mg; Calcium 69mg; Fiber 4.9g; Sodium 124mg.

COCK-A-LEEKIE WITH PUY LENTILS AND THYME

THIS ANCIENT SCOTTISH SOUP IS MADE WITH BOTH BEEF AND CHICKEN TO FLAVOR THE BROTH. THE
ADDITION OF PUY LENTILS GIVES THIS VERSION EVEN MORE EARTHINESS.

SERVES 4

INGREDIENTS

2 leeks, cut into 2-inch julienne
4 ounces/½ cup Puy lentils
1 bay leaf
a few sprigs of fresh thyme
4 ounces ground beef
2 skinless, boneless chicken breasts
3¾ cups good homemade beef stock
8 ready-to-eat prunes, cut
  into strips
salt and ground black pepper
fresh thyme sprigs, to garnish

1 Bring a small pan of salted water to the boil and cook the julienne of leeks for 1–2 minutes. Drain and refresh under cold running water. Drain again and set aside.

COOK'S TIP
To cut fine and even julienne strips, cut the leek into 2-inch lengths. Cut each piece in half lengthways, then with the cut side down, cut the leek into thin strips.

2 Pick over the lentils to check for any small stones or grit. Put into a pan with the bay leaf and thyme and cover with cold water. Bring to the boil and cook for 25–30 minutes until tender. Drain and refresh under cold water.

3 Put the ground beef and chicken breasts in a pan and pour over enough stock to cover them. Bring to the boil and cook gently for 15–20 minutes, or until tender. Using a slotted spoon, remove the chicken from the stock and leave to cool.

4 When the chicken is cool enough to handle, cut it into strips. Return it to the stock in the pan and add the lentils and the remaining stock. Bring just to the boil and add seasoning to taste.

5 Divide the leeks and prunes among four warmed bowls. Ladle over the hot chicken and lentil broth. Garnish each portion with a few fresh thyme sprigs and serve immediately.

Energy 275kcal/1160kJ; Protein 32.3g; Carbohydrate 23.5g, of which sugars 7.4g; Fat 6.4g, of which saturates 2.4g; Cholesterol 70mg; Calcium 47mg; Fiber 4.1g; Sodium 82mg.

CHICKEN AND LEEK SOUP
WITH PRUNES AND BARLEY

THIS RECIPE IS BASED ON THE TRADITIONAL SCOTTISH SOUP, COCK-A-LEEKIE. THE UNUSUAL COMBINATION OF LEEKS AND PRUNES IS SURPRISINGLY DELICIOUS.

SERVES 6

INGREDIENTS

1 chicken, weighing about
   4¼ pounds
2 pounds leeks
1 fresh bay leaf
a few fresh parsley stalks and
   thyme sprigs
1 large carrot, thickly sliced
10 cups chicken or beef stock
4 ounces/generous ½ cup
   pearl barley
14 ounces ready-to-eat prunes
salt and ground black pepper
chopped fresh parsley, to garnish

1 Cut the breasts off the chicken and set aside. Place the remaining chicken carcass in a large pan. Cut half the leeks into 2-inch lengths and add them to the pan. Tie the bay leaf, parsley and thyme into a bouquet garni and add to the pan with the carrot and the stock. Bring to the boil, then reduce the heat and cover. Simmer gently for 1 hour. Skim off any scum when the water first boils and occasionally during simmering.

2 Add the chicken breasts and cook for another 30 minutes, until they are just cooked. Leave until cool enough to handle, then strain the stock. Reserve the chicken breasts and meat from the chicken carcass. Discard all the skin, bones, cooked vegetables and herbs. Skim as much fat as you can from the stock, then return it to the pan.

3 Meanwhile, rinse the pearl barley thoroughly in a strainer under cold running water, then cook it in a large pan of boiling water for about 10 minutes. Drain, rinse well again and drain thoroughly.

4 Add the pearl barley to the stock. Bring to the boil over a medium heat, then lower the heat and cook very gently for 15 20 minutes, until the barley is just cooked and tender. Season the soup with 1 teaspoon salt and black pepper.

5 Add the prunes. Slice the remaining leeks and add them to the pan. Bring to the boil, then simmer for 10 minutes or until the leeks are just cooked.

6 Slice the chicken breasts and add them to the soup with the remaining chicken meat, sliced or cut into neat pieces. Reheat if necessary, then ladle the soup into deep plates and sprinkle with chopped parsley.

Energy 359kcal/1526kJ; Protein 41.7g; Carbohydrate 44g, of which sugars 26.9g; Fat 3g, of which saturates 0.6g; Cholesterol 105mg; Calcium 73mg; Fiber 7.4g; Sodium 104mg.

CHICKEN SOUP WITH KNAIDLACH

A BOWL OF CHICKEN SOUP CAN HEAL THE SOUL AS WELL AS THE BODY, AS ANYONE WHO HAS EVER SUFFERED FROM FLU AND BEEN COMFORTED, OR SUFFERED GRIEF AND BEEN CONSOLED, WILL KNOW. THIS SOUP IS SERVED WITH KNAIDLACH—DUMPLINGS MADE OF MATZO, EGGS AND CHICKEN FAT.

SERVES 6–8

INGREDIENTS

2¼–3¼ pounds chicken, cut
   into portions
2 or 3 onions
12–16 cups water
3–5 carrots, thickly sliced
3–5 celery sticks, thickly sliced
1 small parsnip, cut in half
2–3 tablespoons roughly chopped
   fresh parsley
2–3 tablespoons chopped fresh dill
1 or 2 pinches ground turmeric
2 chicken bouillon cubes
2 garlic cloves, finely chopped
   (optional)
salt and ground black pepper
For the knaidlach
6 ounces/¾ cup medium matzo meal
2 eggs, lightly beaten
3 tablespoons vegetable oil or
   rendered chicken fat
1 garlic clove, finely chopped (optional)
2 tablespoons chopped fresh parsley,
   plus extra to garnish
½ onion, finely grated
1 or 2 pinches of chicken bouillon
   cube or powder (optional)
about 6 tablespoons water
salt and ground black pepper

1 Put the chicken pieces in a very large pan. Keeping them whole, cut a large cross in the stem end of each onion and add to the pan with the water, carrots, celery, parsnip, parsley, half the fresh dill, the turmeric, and salt and black pepper.

2 Cover the pan and bring to the boil, then immediately lower the heat to a simmer. Skim and discard the scum that rises to the top. (Scum will continue to form but it is only the first scum that rises that will detract from the clarity and flavor of the soup.)

3 Add the crumbled bouillon cubes and simmer for 2–3 hours. When the soup is flavorful, skim off the fat. Alternatively, chill the soup and remove the layer of solid fat that forms.

4 To make the knaidlach, combine the matzo meal with the eggs, oil or fat, chopped garlic, if using, parsley, onion, salt and pepper in a large bowl. Add only a little chicken bouillon cube or powder, if using, as these are salty. Add the water and mix together until the mixture is of the consistency of a thick, soft paste.

5 Cover the matzo batter and chill for 30 minutes, during which time the mixture will become firm.

6 Bring a pan of water to the boil and have a bowl of water next to the stove. Dip two tablespoons into the water, then take a spoonful of the matzo batter. With wet hands, roll it into a ball, then slip it into the boiling water and reduce the heat so that the water simmers. Continue with the remaining matzo batter, working relatively quickly, then cover the pan and cook for 15–20 minutes.

7 Remove the knaidlach from the pan with a slotted spoon and transfer to a plate for about 20 minutes to firm up.

8 Reheat the soup, adding the remaining dill and the garlic, if using. Season to taste. Put two or three knaidlach in each bowl, pour over the soup and garnish.

VARIATIONS
• Instead of knaidlach, the soup can be served over rice or noodles.
• To make lighter knaidlach, separate the eggs and add the yolks to the matzo mixture. Whisk the whites until stiff, then fold into the mixture.

Energy 455kcal/1890kJ; Protein 26.9g; Carbohydrate 33.4g, of which sugars 10.1g; Fat 23.7g, of which saturates 5.4g; Cholesterol 173mg; Calcium 65mg; Fiber 3.9g; Sodium 136mg.

THAI CHICKEN SOUP

THIS MAKES FULL USE OF THE CHARACTERISTIC THAI FLAVORS OF GARLIC, COCONUT, LEMON, PEANUT BUTTER, FRESH CILANTRO AND CHILE.

SERVES 4

INGREDIENTS

1 tablespoon vegetable oil
1 garlic clove, finely chopped
2 skinless, boneless chicken breasts
  (6 ounces each) chopped
½ teaspoon ground turmeric
¼ teaspoon hot chili powder
3 ounces/½ cup creamed coconut
  or 4 fluid ounces/½ cup
  coconut cream
about 3½ cups hot chicken stock
2 tablespoons lemon or lime juice
2 tablespoons crunchy peanut butter
2 ounces/1 cup thread egg noodles,
  broken into small pieces
1 tablespoon chopped scallions
1 tablespoon chopped
  fresh cilantro
salt and ground black pepper
dry unsweetened shredded coconut
  and finely chopped fresh red chile,
  to garnish

1 Heat the oil in a large pan and fry the garlic for 1 minute until lightly golden. Add the chicken and spices. Stir-fry for 3–4 minutes.

2 Crumble the creamed coconut or pour the coconut cream into the hot chicken stock and stir until combined. Pour the liquid onto the chicken breasts and add the lemon or lime juice, peanut butter and thread egg noodles.

COOK'S TIP
If possible, use farm-fresh chicken and homemade chicken stock (see page 31) for the best flavor.

3 Cover the pan and simmer for 15 minutes. Add the scallions and fresh cilantro, season well with salt and ground black pepper and cook gently for a further 5 minutes.

4 Meanwhile, heat the shredded coconut and chile in a small frying pan for 2–3 minutes, stirring frequently, until the coconut is lightly browned.

5 Pour the soup into bowls and serve sprinkled with coconut and chile.

Energy 338kcal/1411kJ; Protein 25.4g; Carbohydrate 11.4g, of which sugars 2.2g; Fat 21.6g, of which saturates 13g; Cholesterol 65mg; Calcium 17mg; Fiber 0.8g; Sodium 107mg.

THAI-STYLE CHICKEN NOODLE SOUP

A FRAGRANT BLEND OF COCONUT MILK, LEMONGRASS, GINGER AND LIME MAKES A DELICIOUS SOUP, WITH JUST A HINT OF WARMING CHILE.

SERVES 4

INGREDIENTS

  1 teaspoon oil
  1 or 2 fresh red chiles, seeded
    and chopped
  2 garlic cloves, crushed
  1 large leek, finely sliced
  2½ cups chicken stock
  14 fluid ounces/1⅔ cups
    coconut milk
  1 pound skinless, boneless chicken
    thighs, cut into bitesize pieces
  2 tablespoons Thai fish sauce
  1 lemongrass stalk, split
  1-inch fresh ginger root, peeled and
    finely chopped
  1 teaspoon sugar
  4 kaffir lime leaves (optional)
  3 ounces/¾ cup frozen peas, thawed
  3 tablespoons chopped fresh cilantro

1 Heat the oil in a large pan and cook the chiles and garlic for about 2 minutes.

2 Add the sliced leek and cook for a further 2 minutes.

3 Stir in the stock and coconut milk and bring to the boil over a medium-high heat.

COOK'S TIP
• Wear rubber gloves to protect your hands when seeding and chopping fresh chiles.
• The color of Thai fish sauce can vary considerably. The lighter-colored sauces are more expensive but are considered to be better than darker versions.

4 Add the chicken, fish sauce, lemongrass, ginger, sugar and lime leaves, if using. Lower the heat and simmer, covered, for 15 minutes, until the chicken is tender, stirring occasionally.

5 Add the peas and cook for a further 3 minutes.

6 Remove the lemongrass and stir in the cilantro just before serving.

Energy 177kcal/750kJ; Protein 29.3g; Carbohydrate 9.3g, of which sugars 7.4g; Fat 2.8g, of which saturates 0.8g; Cholesterol 79mg; Calcium 50mg; Fiber 1.9g; Sodium 179mg.

CHICKEN AND ALMOND SOUP

THIS SOUP MAKES AN EXCELLENT LUNCH OR SUPPER DISH WHEN SERVED WITH NAAN BREAD. THE GROUND ALMONDS GIVE IT A LOVELY CREAMY TEXTURE.

SERVES 4

INGREDIENTS

    3 ounces/6 tablespoons
      sweet butter
    1 medium leek, chopped
    ½ teaspoon shredded fresh
      ginger root
    3 ounces/¾ cup ground almonds
    1 teaspoon salt
    ½ teaspoon crushed black
      peppercorns
    1 fresh green chile, chopped
    1 medium carrot, sliced
    2 ounces/½ cup frozen peas
    4 ounces/1 cup chicken, skinned,
      boned and cubed
    2 tablespoons chopped
      fresh cilantro
    scant 2 cups water
    8 fluid ounces/1 cup light cream
    4 sprigs of fresh cilantro

1 Melt the sweet butter in a deep, round-bottomed frying pan, and sauté the chopped leek and the ginger root until soft but only just turning brown.

2 Lower the heat and add the ground almonds, salt, peppercorns, chile, carrot, peas and chicken. Fry for about 10 minutes or until the chicken is completely cooked, stirring constantly. Add the chopped fresh cilantro.

COOK'S TIP
Ground almonds can be used as a thickener in soups, and they add extra flavor as well as texture. Their very delicate flavor blends particularly well with chicken-based soups.

3 Remove from the heat and allow to cool slightly.

4 Transfer the mixture to a food processor or blender and process for about 1½ minutes. Pour in the water and blend for a further 30 seconds.

5 Pour back into the pan and bring to the boil, stirring occasionally. Once it has boiled, lower the heat and gradually stir in the cream. Cook gently for a further 2 minutes, stirring from time to time. Serve garnished with the sprigs of fresh cilantro.

Energy 425kcal/1760kJ; Protein 14.6g; Carbohydrate 5.5g, of which sugars 3.5g; Fat 38.5g, of which saturates 18.4g; Cholesterol 94mg; Calcium 119mg; Fiber 3g; Sodium 153mg.

CHICKEN, TOMATO AND CHAYOTE SOUP

CHICKEN BREASTS AND SMOKED HADDOCK TAKE ON THE FLAVORS OF HERBS AND SPICES TO PRODUCE THIS RICH SOUP.

SERVES 4

INGREDIENTS

8 ounces skinless, boneless chicken
  breasts, diced
1 garlic clove, crushed
a pinch of freshly grated nutmeg
1 ounce/2 tablespoons butter
  or margarine
½ onion, finely chopped
1 tablespoon tomato paste
1 can (14 ounces) tomatoes, pureed
5 cups chicken stock
1 fresh chile, seeded and chopped
1 chayote, peeled and diced
  (about 12 ounces)
1 teaspoon dried oregano
½ teaspoon dried thyme
2 ounces smoked haddock fillet,
  skinned and diced
salt and ground black pepper
chopped fresh chives, to garnish

3 Add the tomato paste, puréed tomatoes, stock, chile, christophene and herbs. Bring to the boil, cover and simmer gently for 35 minutes or until the christophene is tender.

4 Add the smoked fish and simmer for a further 5 minutes or until the fish is cooked through. Adjust the seasoning and pour into warmed soup bowls. Garnish with a sprinkling of chopped fresh chives and serve piping hot.

1 Dice the chicken, place in a bowl and season with salt, pepper, garlic and nutmeg. Mix well to flavor and then set aside for about 30 minutes.

2 Melt the butter or margarine in a large pan, add the chicken and sauté over a moderate heat for 5–6 minutes. Stir in the onion and fry gently for a further 5 minutes or until the onion is slightly softened.

COOK'S TIP
This soup tastes even better using home made stock (see page 31). Once made, chicken stock will keep in an airtight container in the refrigerator for 3–4 days.

Energy 145kcal/609kJ; Protein 17.2g; Carbohydrate 5.1g, of which sugars 4.8g; Fat 6.3g, of which saturates 3.5g; Cholesterol 57mg; Calcium 53mg; Fiber 2.2g; Sodium 229mg.

PUMPKIN, RICE AND CHICKEN SOUP

THIS IS A WARM, COMFORTING SOUP WHICH, DESPITE THE SPICE AND BASMATI RICE, IS QUINTESSENTIALLY ENGLISH. FOR AN EVEN MORE SUBSTANTIAL MEAL, ADD A LITTLE MORE RICE AND MAKE SURE YOU USE ALL THE CHICKEN FROM THE STOCK.

SERVES 4

INGREDIENTS

1 wedge of pumpkin, about 1 pound
1 tablespoon sunflower oil
1 ounce/2 tablespoons butter
6 green cardamom pods
2 leeks, chopped
4 ounces/generous ½ cup basmati
  rice, soaked
12 fluid ounces/1½ cups milk
salt and ground black pepper
generous strips of pared orange rind,
  to garnish
For the chicken stock
2 chicken quarters
1 onion, quartered
2 carrots, chopped
1 celery stalk, chopped
6–8 peppercorns
3¾ cups water

1 First make the chicken stock. Place the chicken quarters, onion, carrots, celery stalk and peppercorns in a large pan. Pour in the water and slowly bring to the boil. Skim the surface of the stock if necessary, then lower the heat, cover and simmer gently for 1 hour.

2 Strain the chicken stock into a clean, large bowl, discarding the vegetables. Skin and bone one or both chicken pieces and cut the flesh into strips. (If not using both chicken pieces for the soup, reserve the other piece for another recipe.)

3 Skin the pumpkin and remove all the seeds and pith, so that you have about 12 ounces flesh. Cut the flesh into 1-inch cubes.

4 Heat the oil and butter in a pan and fry the cardamom pods for 2–3 minutes until slightly swollen. Add the leeks and pumpkin. Cook, stirring, for 3–4 minutes over a medium heat, then lower the heat, cover and sweat for 5 minutes more or until the pumpkin is quite soft, stirring once or twice.

5 Measure out 2½ cups of the stock and add to the pumpkin mixture. Bring to the boil, then lower the heat, cover, and simmer gently for 10–15 minutes, until the pumpkin is soft.

6 Pour the remaining stock into a measuring jug and combine with water to ½ pint/1¼ cups. Drain the rice and put it into a pan. Pour in the stock, bring to the boil, then simmer for about 10 minutes, until the rice is tender. Add seasoning to taste.

7 Remove the cardamom pods, then process the soup in a blender or food processor until smooth. Pour back into a clean pan and stir in the milk, chicken and rice (with any stock that has not been absorbed). Heat until simmering. Garnish with the strips of pared orange rind and freshly ground black pepper, and serve with whole-wheat bread.

COOK'S TIP
Once made, chicken stock will keep in an airtight container in the refrigerator for 3–4 days.

Energy 315kcal/1320kJ; Protein 24.6g; Carbohydrate 29.9g, of which sugars 6.3g; Fat 10.8g, of which saturates 4.9g; Cholesterol 71mg; Calcium 140mg; Fiber 2.1g; Sodium 122mg.

CHICKEN AND COCONUT SOUP

THIS RECIPE COMBINES THE ASIAN FLAVORS OF THAILAND IN A SMOOTH EUROPEAN-STYLE SOUP, AND THE FINISHED DISH IS COMPLEMENTED BY A TOPPING OF CRISP SHALLOTS.

SERVES 6

INGREDIENTS

1½ ounces/3 tablespoons butter
1 onion, finely chopped
2 garlic cloves, chopped
1-inch piece fresh ginger root,
  finely chopped
2 teaspoons Thai green curry paste
½ teaspoon turmeric
1 can (14 fluid ounces) coconut milk
16 fluid ounces/2 cups
  chicken stock
2 lime leaves, shredded
1 lemon grass stalk, finely chopped
8 skinless, boneless chicken thighs
12 ounces spinach, roughly chopped
2 teaspoons Thai fish sauce
2 tablespoons lime juice
2 tablespoons vegetable oil
2 shallots, thinly sliced
salt and ground black pepper
small handful of Thai purple
  basil leaves, to garnish

1 Melt the butter in a large, heavy pan. Add the onion, garlic and ginger. Cook for 4–5 minutes, until soft.

2 Stir in the curry paste and turmeric, and cook for a further 2–3 minutes, stirring continuously.

3 Pour in two-thirds of the coconut milk; cook for 5 minutes. Add the stock, lime leaves, lemongrass and chicken. Heat until simmering; cook for 15 minutes or until the chicken is tender.

4 Use a slotted spoon to remove the chicken thighs. Set them aside to cool.

5 Add the spinach to the pan and cook for 3–4 minutes. Stir in the remaining coconut milk and seasoning, then process the soup in a food processor or blender until almost smooth. Return the soup to the rinsed-out pan. Cut the chicken thighs into bitesize pieces and stir these into the soup with the fish sauce and lime juice.

6 Reheat the soup gently until hot, but do not let it boil. Meanwhile, heat the oil in a frying pan and cook the shallots for 6–8 minutes, until crisp and golden, stirring occasionally. Drain on paper towels. Ladle the soup into bowls, then top with the basil leaves and fried shallots, and serve.

Energy 136kcal/570kJ; Protein 14.1g; Carbohydrate 5.2g, of which sugars 4.9g; Fat 6.7g, of which saturates 3.8g; Cholesterol 49mg; Calcium 125mg; Fiber 1.4g; Sodium 344mg.

GINGER, CHICKEN AND COCONUT SOUP

THIS AROMATIC SOUP IS RICH WITH COCONUT MILK AND INTENSELY FLAVORED WITH GALANGAL,
LEMONGRASS AND KAFFIR LIME LEAVES.

SERVES 4–6

INGREDIENTS
   3 cups coconut milk
   16 fluid ounces/2 cups
     chicken stock
   4 lemongrass stalks, bruised
     and chopped
   1-inch piece galangal, finely sliced
   10 black peppercorns, crushed
   10 kaffir lime leaves, torn
   11 ounces skinless boneless chicken,
     cut into thin strips
   4 ounces white mushrooms
   2 ounces/½ cup baby corn cobs
   4 tablespoons lime juice
   3 tablespoons Thai fish sauce
For the garnish
   2 red chiles, chopped
   4 scallions, chopped
   chopped fresh cilantro

1 Bring the coconut milk and chicken stock to the boil in a pan. Add the lemongrass, galangal, peppercorns and half the kaffir lime leaves. Reduce the heat and simmer gently for 10 minutes.

2 Strain the stock into a clean pan. Return to the heat and add the chicken, mushrooms and corn. Cook for 5–7 minutes until the chicken is tender.

3 Stir in the lime juice, fish sauce to taste and the rest of the lime leaves.

4 Ladle into warm soup bowls and serve hot, garnished with red chiles, scallions and cilantro.

COOK'S TIP
Wear rubber gloves to protect your hands when handling fresh chiles.

Energy 87kcal/371kJ; Protein 13.1g; Carbohydrate 6.8g, of which sugars 6.7g; Fat 1.1g, of which saturates 0.4g; Cholesterol 35mg; Calcium 42mg; Fiber 0.3g; Sodium 620mg.

JALAPEÑO-STYLE SOUP

CHICKEN, CHILE AND AVOCADO COMBINE TO MAKE THIS SIMPLE BUT UNUSUAL SOUP. THE CHILE IS REMOVED BEFORE SERVING, LEAVING JUST A HINT OF SPICINESS.

SERVES 6

INGREDIENTS
6¼ cups chicken stock
2 cooked chicken breast fillets, skinned and cut into large strips
1 drained canned chipotle or jalapeño chile, rinsed
1 avocado

COOK'S TIPS
• When using canned chiles, it is important to rinse them thoroughly before adding them to a dish so as to remove the flavor of any pickling liquid.
• The soup tastes best if you use home made stock (see page 31). Once made, it will keep in an airtight container in the refrigerator for 3–4 days.

1 Heat the stock in a large pan and add the chicken and chile. Simmer over a very gentle heat for 5 minutes to heat the chicken through and release the flavor from the chile.

2 Cut the avocado in half, remove the stone and peel off the skin. Slice the avocado flesh neatly lengthwise.

3 Using a slotted spoon, remove the chile from the stock and discard it. Pour the soup into heated serving bowls, distributing the chicken evenly among them.

4 Carefully add a few avocado slices to each bowl and serve the soup immediately, piping hot.

Energy 95kcal/400kJ; Protein 14.7g; Carbohydrate 0.4g, of which sugars 0.1g; Fat 4g, of which saturates 0.9g; Cholesterol 41mg; Calcium 8mg; Fiber 0.6g; Sodium 134mg.

CREAM OF DUCK SOUP WITH BLUEBERRY RELISH

THIS DELICIOUS, RICH SOUP IS IDEAL FOR SMART OCCASIONS. YOU CAN USE A WHOLE DUCK, BUT COOKING WITH DUCK BREASTS AND LEGS IS EASIER.

SERVES 4

INGREDIENTS
  2 duck breasts
  4 rindless fatty bacon strips,
    chopped
  1 onion, chopped
  1 garlic clove, chopped
  2 carrots, diced
  2 celery sticks, chopped
  4 large open mushrooms,
    chopped
  1 tablespoon tomato paste
  2 duck legs
  1 tablespoon all-purpose flour
  3 tablespoons brandy
  ⅔ cup port
  1¼ cups red wine
  3¾ cups chicken stock
  1 bay leaf
  2 sprigs fresh thyme
  1 tablespoon red-currant jelly
  ⅔ cup heavy cream
  salt and ground black pepper
For the blueberry relish
  5 ounces/1¼ cups blueberries
  1 tablespoon superfine sugar
  grated rind and juice of 2 limes
  1 tablespoon chopped
    fresh parsley
  1 tablespoon balsamic vinegar

3 Remove the duck from the pan and set aside. Drain off some of the fat, leaving about 3 tablespoons in the pan.

4 Add the bacon, onion, garlic, carrots, celery and mushrooms to the pan and cook for 10 minutes, stirring occasionally. Stir in the tomato paste and cook for 2 minutes. Remove the skin and bones from the duck legs and chop the flesh. Add to the pan and cook for 5 minutes.

5 Stir in the flour and cook for 1 minute. Gradually stir in the brandy, port, wine and stock and bring to the boil, stirring. Add the bay leaf, thyme and red-currant jelly, then stir until the jelly melts. Reduce the heat and simmer for 1 hour.

6 Meanwhile, make the relish. Put the blueberries, sugar, lime rind and juice, parsley and vinegar in a small bowl. Very lightly bruise the blueberries with a fork, leaving some of the berries whole. Set aside until required.

7 Strain the soup through a colander, then through a fine strainer into a clean pan. Bring to the boil, reduce the heat and simmer for 10 minutes.

8 Meanwhile, remove and discard the skin and fat from the duck breasts and cut the meat into thin strips. Add the meat strips to the soup with the heavy cream and season well. Bring just to boiling point.

9 Ladle the soup into warmed bowls and top each serving with a dollop of the blueberry relish. Serve piping hot.

1 Use a sharp knife to score the skin and fat on the duck breasts.

2 Preheat a heavy pan. Place the duck breasts in the pan, skin-sides down, and cook for 8–10 minutes, until golden. Turn and cook for a further 5–6 minutes.

Energy 642kcal/2673kJ; Protein 39.2g; Carbohydrate 14.2g, of which sugars 13.6g; Fat 35g, of which saturates 17.2g; Cholesterol 252mg; Calcium 83mg; Fiber 2.8g; Sodium 384mg.

DUCK BROTH <u>WITH</u> ORANGE SPICED DUMPLINGS

USING A DELICATE TOUCH WHEN BRINGING TOGETHER THE MIXTURE FOR THE DUMPLINGS WILL CREATE A LIGHT TEXTURE TO MATCH THEIR DELICIOUS FLAVOR.

SERVES 4

INGREDIENTS

  1 duckling, about 4–4½ pounds,
    with liver
  1 large onion, peeled
    and halved
  2 carrots, peeled and
    thickly sliced
  ½ garlic bulb
  bouquet garni
  3 cloves
  2 tablespoons chopped chives,
    to garnish
For the spiced dumplings
  2 thick slices white bread
  4 tablespoons milk
  2 strips rindless fatty bacon
  1 shallot, finely chopped
  1 garlic clove, crushed
  1 egg yolk, beaten
  grated rind of 1 orange
  ½ teaspoon paprika
  2 ounces /½ cup all-purpose flour
  salt and ground black pepper

1 Set the duck liver aside. Using a sharp knife, cut off the breasts from the duckling and set them aside.

2 Put the carcass into a large, heavy-based pan and pour in enough water to cover the carcass. Bring to the boil and skim the scum off the surface.

3 Add the onion, carrots, garlic, bouquet garni and cloves. Reduce the heat and cover the pan, then simmer for 2 hours, skimming occasionally to remove scum.

4 Lift the carcass from the broth and leave to cool. Strain the broth, and skim it to remove any fat. Return the broth to the pan and simmer gently, uncovered, until reduced to 5 cups.

5 Remove all the meat from the duck carcass and shred it finely. Set aside.

6 For the dumplings, soak the bread in the milk for 5 minutes. Remove the skin and fat from the duck breasts. Grind the meat with the liver and bacon. Squeeze the milk from the bread, then add the bread to the meat with the shallot, garlic, egg yolk, orange rind, paprika, flour and seasoning, and mix.

7 Form a spoonful of the mixture into a ball, a little smaller than a walnut. Repeat with the remaining mixture to make 20 small dumplings.

8 Bring a large pan of lightly salted water to the boil and poach the dumplings for 4–5 minutes, until they are just tender.

9 Bring the duck broth back to the boil and add the dumplings.

10 Divide the shredded duck meat between four warmed bowls and ladle in the broth and dumplings. Garnish with chives.

Energy 289kcal/1214kJ; Protein 29.9g; Carbohydrate 19g, of which sugars 2.8g; Fat 13g, of which saturates 3.1g; Cholesterol 196mg; Calcium 63mg; Fiber 1.3g; Sodium 373mg.

DUCK AND PRESERVED LIME SOUP

THIS RICH CAMBODIAN SOUP, SAMLAW TIAH, ORIGINATES IN THE CHIU CHOW REGION OF SOUTHERN CHINA. THIS RECIPE IS ADAPTED FROM THE WONDERFUL BOOK ESSENTIALS OF ASIAN CUISINE, *WRITTEN BY CORINNE TRANG WHOSE CAMBODIAN GRANDMOTHER WAS OF CHIU CHOW ANCESTRY.*

SERVES 4–6

INGREDIENTS
    1 lean duck, weighing roughly
        3 pounds 5 ounces
    2 preserved limes
    1 ounce fresh ginger root,
        thinly sliced
    sea salt and ground black pepper
For the garnish
    vegetable oil, for frying
    1 ounce fresh root ginger, thinly
        sliced into strips
    2 garlic cloves, thinly sliced
        into strips
    2 scallions, finely sliced

COOK'S TIP
Preserved limes have a distinctive bitter flavor. Look out for them in Asian markets.

1 Place the duck in a large pan with enough water to cover. Season with salt and pepper and bring the water to the boil. Reduce the heat, cover the pot, and simmer for 1½ hours.

2 Add the preserved limes and ginger to the cooking liquid. Continue to simmer for another hour, skimming off the fat from time to time, until the liquid has reduced a little and the duck is so tender, it almost falls off the bone.

3 Meanwhile heat some vegetable oil in a wok. Stir in the ginger and garlic strips and fry until gold and crispy. Drain well on paper towels and keep aside for garnishing.

4 Transfer the duck to a large dish and shred the meat into individual bowls. Check the broth for seasoning, then ladle it over the duck. Sprinkle the scallions with the fried ginger and garlic over the top and serve immediately.

Energy 114kcal/479kJ; Protein 14g; Carbohydrate 0.4g, of which sugars 0.4g; Fat 6.4g, of which saturates 1.7g; Cholesterol 75mg; Calcium 11mg; Fiber 0.1g; Sodium 78mg.

DUCK AND NUT SOUP WITH JUJUBES

THIS NORTHERN VIETNAMESE DISH IS RICH AND DELICIOUS. PACKED WITH NUTS AND SWEETENED WITH JUJUBES (DRIED CHINESE RED DATES), IT RESEMBLES NEITHER A SOUP NOR A STEW, BUT SOMETHING IN BETWEEN. SERVED ON ITS OWN, OR WITH RICE AND PICKLES, IT IS A MEAL IN ITSELF.

SERVES 4

INGREDIENTS

  2–3 tablespoons vegetable oil
  4 duck legs, split into thighs
    and drumsticks
  juice of 1 coconut
  4 tablespoons *nuoc mam*
  4 lemongrass stalks, bruised
  12 chestnuts, peeled
  3½ ounces unsalted cashew nuts,
    roasted
  3½ ounces unsalted almonds,
    roasted
  3½ ounces unsalted peanuts, roasted
  12 jujubes
  sea salt and ground black pepper
  a small bunch of fresh basil leaves,
    to garnish

1 Heat the oil in a heavy pan. Brown the duck pieces in the oil and drain on paper towels.

2 Bring 7¾ cups water to the boil. Reduce the heat and add the coconut juice, *nuoc mam*, lemongrass and duck legs. Cover the pan and simmer over a gentle heat for 2–3 hours.

3 Add the nuts and jujubes and cook for 40–45 minutes, until the chestnuts are soft and the duck is tender. Skim off any fat, season to taste. Sprinkle the basil leaves over the top to serve.

COOK'S TIP
To extract the coconut juice, pierce the eyes on top and turn the coconut upside down over a bowl.

Energy 664kcal/2767kJ; Protein 36.1g; Carbohydrate 29.3g, of which sugars 15.4g; Fat 47.2g, of which saturates 7.4g; Cholesterol 110mg; Calcium 112mg; Fiber 5.5g; Sodium 731mg.

MEAT SOUPS

Nourishing meaty soups are just the thing for warming you up on cold winter days. This section includes soups from all around the world—Irish Kidney and Bacon Soup, Mediterranean Sausage and Pesto Soup, Chinese Pork and Rice Porridge, and Japanese Miso Soup with Pork and Vegetables. For a special occasion, serve the delicious traditional Khmer dish, Spicy Beef and Eggplant Soup, or exotic Vietnamese Pork and Lotus Root Broth.

SPICY BEEF AND EGGPLANT SOUP

A WONDERFUL KHMER DISH, THIS SOUP, SAMLAW MACHOU KROEUNG, IS SWEET, SPICY AND TANGY. THE FLAVOR IS MAINLY DERIVED FROM THE CAMBODIAN HERBAL CONDIMENT, KROEUNG, AND THE FERMENTED FISH EXTRACT, TUK TREY.

SERVES 6

INGREDIENTS
For the stock
   2¼ pounds beef shanks or brisket
   2 large onions, quartered
   2–3 carrots, cut into chunks
   3½ ounces fresh ginger root, sliced
   2 cinnamon sticks
   4 star anise
   1 teaspoon black peppercorns
   2 tablespoons soy sauce
   3–4 tablespoons *tuk trey*
For the soup
   4 dried New Mexico chiles
   1 tablespoon vegetable oil
   5 tablespoons *kroeung*
   2 or 3 fresh or dried red
    Thai chiles
   5 tablespoons tamarind extract
   1–2 tablespoons *tuk trey*
   2 tablespoons jaggery
   12 Thai eggplants, stems removed,
    cut into bitesize chunks
   a bunch of watercress, trimmed
   a handful of fresh curry leaves
   sea salt and ground black pepper

1 To make the stock, put the beef shanks into a deep pan with all the other stock ingredients, apart from the soy sauce and *tuk trey*. Cover with 12 cups water and bring to the boil. Reduce the heat and simmer, covered, for 2–3 hours.

COOK'S TIP
Thai chiles and eggplants, and also tamarind extract and *tuk trey*, can be found in Southeast Asian markets.

2 Soak the New Mexico chiles in water for 30 minutes. Split them open, remove the seeds and scrape out the pulp with a teaspoon.

3 Take the lid off the stock and stir in the remaining two ingredients. Bring back to the boil and simmer, uncovered, for another hour, until the stock has reduced to about 7¾ cups.

4 Skim off any fat, strain the stock into a bowl and put aside. Lift the meat onto a plate, tear it into thin strips and put half of it aside for the soup.

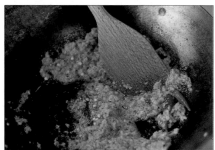

5 Heat the oil in a heavy pan. Stir in the *kroeung* along with the pulp from the New Mexico chiles and the whole Thai chiles. Stir the spicy paste as it sizzles, until it begins to darken. Add the tamarind extract, *tuk trey*, sugar and the reserved stock. Stir well and bring the liquid to the boil.

6 Reduce the heat and add the reserved beef, eggplants and watercress. Cook for about 20 minutes to allow the flavors to mingle.

7 Meanwhile, dry-fry the curry leaves. Heat a small heavy pan over a high heat, add the curry leaves and cook them until they begin to crackle. Transfer them to a plate and set aside.

8 Season the soup to taste. Stir in half the curry leaves and ladle the soup into individual bowls. Sprinkle the remaining curry leaves over the top and serve.

Energy 303kcal/1276kJ; Protein 37g; Carbohydrate 16.5g, of which sugars 14.5g; Fat 10.6g, of which saturates 4.2g; Cholesterol 90mg; Calcium 35mg; Fiber 2.4g; Sodium 0.3mg.

BEEF AND BARLEY SOUP

THIS TRADITIONAL IRISH FARMHOUSE SOUP MAKES A WONDERFULLY RESTORATIVE DISH ON A COLD DAY. THE FLAVORS DEVELOP PARTICULARLY WELL IF IT IS MADE IN ADVANCE AND REHEATED.

SERVES 6–8

INGREDIENTS

1–1½ pounds rib steak, or other
  stewing beef on the bone
2 large onions
2 ounces/¼ cup pearl barley
2 ounces/¼ cup green split peas
3 large carrots, chopped
2 white turnips, peeled and diced
3 celery sticks, chopped
1 large or 2 medium leeks, thinly
  sliced and thoroughly washed in
  cold water
sea salt and ground black pepper
chopped fresh parsley, to serve

1 Bone the meat and put the bones and half an onion, roughly sliced, into a large pan. Cover with cold water, season and bring to the boil. Skim if necessary, then simmer until needed.

2 Meanwhile, trim any fat or gristle from the meat and cut into small pieces. Chop the remaining onions finely. Drain the stock from the bones, make it up with water to 9 cups, and return to the rinsed pan with the meat, onions, barley and split peas.

3 Season, bring to the boil, and skim if necessary. Reduce the heat, cover and simmer for about 30 minutes.

4 Add the rest of the vegetables and simmer for 1 hour, or until the meat is tender. Check the seasoning.

5 Serve in large warmed bowls, generously sprinkled with parsley.

Energy 167kcal/705kJ; Protein 16g; Carbohydrate 21.4g, of which sugars 7.8g; Fat 2.6g, of which saturates 0.8g; Cholesterol 34mg; Calcium 54mg; Fiber 3.6g; Sodium 58mg.

ROAST LAMB SHANKS IN BARLEY BROTH

SUCCULENT ROASTED LAMB SHANKS STUDDED WITH GARLIC AND ROSEMARY MAKE A FABULOUS MEAL WHEN SERVED IN A HEARTY VEGETABLE, BARLEY AND TOMATO BROTH.

SERVES 4

INGREDIENTS
    4 small lamb shanks
    4 garlic cloves, cut into slivers
    handful of fresh rosemary sprigs
    2 tablespoons olive oil
    2 carrots, diced
    2 celery sticks, diced
    1 large onion, chopped
    1 bay leaf
    few sprigs of fresh thyme
    5 cups lamb stock
    2 ounces pearl barley
    1 pound tomatoes, peeled and
      roughly chopped
    grated rind of 1 large lemon
    2 tablespoons chopped
      fresh parsley
    salt and ground black pepper

4 Remove the lamb shanks from the casserole using a slotted spoon.

5 Skim the fat from the surface of the roasted vegetables, then add them to the broth. Stir in the tomatoes, lemon rind and parsley.

6 Bring the soup back to the boil. Reduce the heat and simmer for 5 minutes. Add the lamb shanks and heat through, then season. Put a lamb shank into each of four large bowls, then ladle the barley broth over the meat, and serve at once.

1 Preheat the oven to 300°F. Make small cuts all over the lamb and insert slivers of garlic and sprigs of rosemary into them.

2 Heat the oil in a flameproof casserole and brown the shanks two at a time. Remove and set aside. Add the carrots, celery and onion in batches and cook until lightly browned. Put all the vegetables in the casserole with the bay leaf and thyme. Pour in stock to cover, place the lamb shanks on top and roast for 2 hours.

3 Meanwhile, pour the remaining stock into a large pan. Add the pearl barley, then bring to the boil. Reduce the heat, cover and simmer for 1 hour, or until the barley is tender.

Energy 287kcal/1199kJ; Protein 22.5g; Carbohydrate 19.5g, of which sugars 7.6g; Fat 13.7g, of which saturates 0.9g; Cholesterol 0mg; Calcium 35mg; Fiber 2.3g; Sodium 24mg.

SOUR BROTH WITH WATER SPINACH AND BEEF

WATER SPINACH IS A POPULAR VEGETABLE IN VIETNAM. WHEN COOKED, THE STEMS REMAIN CRUNCHY WHILE THE LEAVES SOFTEN, LENDING A CONTRAST OF TEXTURE. SERVED AS AN APPETIZER, OR PALATE CLEANSER, THIS IS A LIGHT SOUP WITH TENDER BITES OF RARE BEEF AND SOUR NOTES OF LEMON.

SERVES 4–6

INGREDIENTS
    2 tablespoons *nuoc mam*
    1 teaspoon sugar
    6 ounces beef tenderloin, finely
      sliced against the grain into
      1-inch strips
    5 cups beef or chicken stock
    6 ounces water spinach,
      trimmed, rinsed, leaves and
      stalks separated
    juice of 1 lemon
    ground black pepper
    1 red or green chile, seeded and
      finely sliced, to garnish

1 Stir the *nuoc mam* with the sugar, toss in the beef and marinate for 30 minutes.

2 Bring the stock to the boil, reduce the heat and add the water spinach. Stir in the lemon juice and season with pepper.

3 Place the meat strips in individual bowls and ladle the piping hot broth over the top. (The meat will cook in the hot broth.) Garnish each serving with sliced chiles, and serve.

Energy 61kcal/254kJ; Protein 7.4g; Carbohydrate 1.2g, of which sugars 1.1g; Fat 3g, of which saturates 1.1g; Cholesterol 17mg; Calcium 51mg; Fiber 0.6g; Sodium 0.06mg.

PORK AND LOTUS ROOT BROTH

THIS VIETNAMESE SOUP IS FROM THE CENTRAL REGION OF THE COUNTRY WHERE THE LOTUS, OR WATER LILY, IS USED IN MANY DISHES. IN THIS CLEAR BROTH, WHICH IS SERVED AS AN APPETIZER, THE THIN, ROUND SLICES OF FRESH LOTUS ROOT LOOK LIKE PRETTY, DELICATE FLOWERS FLOATING IN WATER.

SERVES 4–6

INGREDIENTS
For the stock
  1 pound pork ribs
  1 onion, quartered
  2 carrots, cut into chunks
  1 ounce dried squid or dried shrimp,
    soaked in water for 30 minutes,
    rinsed and drained
  1 tablespoon *nuoc mam*
  1 tablespoon soy sauce
  6 black peppercorns
  sea salt
For the broth
  1 pound fresh lotus roots, peeled and
    thinly sliced
  ground black pepper
  1 red chile, seeded and finely sliced,
    and a small bunch of basil leaves,
    to garnish

1 Put the ribs into a deep pan and cover with water. Add the other stock ingredients and bring to the boil. Reduce the heat and simmer for 1 hour.

2 Take off the lid and simmer for a further 30 minutes to reduce the stock. Strain the stock—you should have roughly 5 cups—and shred the meat off the pork ribs.

3 Pour the stock back into the pan and bring it to the boil. Reduce the heat and add the lotus root. Partially cover the pan and simmer gently for 30–40 minutes, until the lotus root is tender.

4 Stir in the shredded meat and season the broth with salt and pepper. Ladle into warmed serving bowls and garnish with the chile and basil leaves.

Energy 181kcal/756kJ; Protein 23.8g; Carbohydrate 4g, of which sugars 3.1g; Fat 7.8g, of which saturates 2.7g; Cholesterol 74mg; Calcium 65mg; Fiber 1.4g; Sodium 0.27mg.

MISO SOUP WITH PORK AND VEGETABLES

THIS IS QUITE A RICH AND FILLING SOUP. ITS JAPANESE NAME, TANUKI JIRU, MEANS RACCOON SOUP FOR HUNTERS, BUT AS RACCOONS ARE NOT EATEN NOWADAYS, PORK IS USED INSTEAD.

SERVES 4

INGREDIENTS

7 ounces lean boneless pork
6-inch piece burdock or 1 parsnip
2 ounces daikon
4 fresh shiitake mushrooms
½ konnyaku or 4½ ounces tofu
a little sesame oil, for stir-frying
2½ cups second dashi stock, or
  the same amount of water and
  2 teaspoons dashi-no-moto
4½ tablespoons miso
2 scallions, chopped
1 teaspoon sesame seeds

1 Press the meat down on a chopping board using the palm of your hand and slice horizontally into very thin long strips, then cut the strips crosswise into stamp-size pieces. Set the pork aside.

2 Peel the burdock, if using, with a potato peeler, then cut diagonally into ½-inch thick slices. Quickly plunge the slices into a bowl of cold water to prevent them from discoloring. If you are using parsnip, peel, cut it in half lengthwise, then cut it into ½-inch thick half-moon-shaped slices.

3 Peel and slice the daikon into ⅔-inch thick disks. Cut the disks into ⅔-inch cubes. Remove the shiitake stalks and cut the caps into quarters.

4 Place the konnyaku, if using, in a pan of boiling water and cook for 1 minute. Drain and cool. Cut in quarters lengthwise, then crosswise into ⅛-inch thick pieces.

5 Heat a little sesame oil in a heavy cast-iron or enamel pan until purple smoke rises. Stir-fry the pork, then add the konnyaku or tofu and all the vegetables except for the scallions. When the color of the meat has changed, add the stock.

6 Bring to the boil over a medium heat, and skim off the foam until the soup looks fairly clear. Reduce the heat, cover and simmer for 15 minutes.

7 Put the miso in a small bowl and mix with 60ml/4 tablespoons hot stock to make a smooth paste. Stir one-third of the miso into the soup; taste and add more if required. Add the scallions and remove from the heat. Serve very hot in individual soup bowls, sprinkled with sesame seeds.

COOK'S TIPS
• Burdock can be substituted with parsnip in this recipe.
• Daikon, also known as mooli, is a long, white vegetable which is a member of the radish family.
• Konnyaku is a gelatinous cake made from a relative of the sweet potato.

Energy 110kcal/459kJ; Protein 16g; Carbohydrate 1.3g, of which sugars 0.9g; Fat 4.5g, of which saturates 1g; Cholesterol 32mg; Calcium 295mg; Fiber 0.4g; Sodium 573mg.

SWEET-AND-SOUR PORK SOUP

THIS VERY QUICK, SHARP AND TANGY SOUP IS PERFECT FOR AN INFORMAL SUPPER. IT CAN ALSO BE MADE WITH SHREDDED CHICKEN BREAST INSTEAD OF PORK.

SERVES 6–8

INGREDIENTS

2 pounds pork tenderloin, trimmed
1 unripe papaya, halved, seeded, peeled and shredded
3 shallots, chopped
5 garlic cloves, chopped
1 teaspoon crushed black peppercorns
1 tablespoon shrimp paste
2 tablespoons vegetable oil
6¼ cups chicken stock
1-inch piece fresh ginger root, grated
4 fluid ounces/½ cup tamarind water
1 tablespoon honey
juice of 1 lime
2 small red chiles, seeded and sliced
4 scallions, sliced
salt and ground black pepper

1 Cut the pork into very fine strips, 2 inches long. Mix with the papaya and set aside. Process the shallots, garlic, peppercorns and shrimp paste in a food processor or blender to form a paste.

2 Heat the oil in a heavy pan and fry the paste for 1–2 minutes. Add the stock and bring to the boil. Reduce the heat. Add the pork and papaya, ginger, and tamarind water.

3 Simmer the soup for 7–8 minutes, until the pork is tender.

4 Stir in the honey, lime juice, and most of the sliced chiles and scallions. Season to taste with salt and ground black pepper.

5 Ladle the soup into bowls and serve immediately, garnished with the remaining chiles and onions.

Energy 229kcal/963kJ; Protein 32.8g; Carbohydrate 11.1g, of which sugars 10.9g; Fat 6.2g, of which saturates 2.1g; Cholesterol 95mg; Calcium 37mg; Fiber 2.3g; Sodium 111mg.

PORK AND RICE PORRIDGE

Originating in China, this dish has now spread throughout the whole of Southeast Asia and is loved for its comforting blandness. It is invariably served with a few strongly flavored accompaniments.

2 Pour the stock into a large pan. Bring to the boil and add the rice. Season the ground pork. Add it by taking small teaspoons and tapping the spoon on the side of the pan so that the meat falls into the soup in small lumps.

3 Stir in the fish sauce and pickled garlic and simmer for 10 minutes, until the pork is cooked. Stir in the celery.

4 Serve the rice porridge in individual warmed bowls. Sprinkle the prepared garlic and shallots on top and season with plenty of ground pepper.

COOK'S TIP
Pickled garlic has a distinctive flavor and is available from Asian food stores.

SERVES 2

INGREDIENTS
 3¾ cups vegetable stock
 7 ounces/1¾ cups cooked rice
 8 ounces ground pork
 1 tablespoon Thai fish sauce
 2 heads pickled garlic,
  finely chopped
 1 celery stick, finely diced
 salt and ground black pepper
To garnish
 2 tablespoons peanut oil
 4 garlic cloves, thinly sliced
 4 small red shallots, finely sliced

1 Make the garnishes by heating the peanut oil in a frying pan and cooking the garlic and shallots over a low heat until brown. Drain on paper towels and reserve.

Energy 375kcal/1574kJ; Protein 26.8g; Carbohydrate 31.1g, of which sugars 0.2g; Fat 16.8g, of which saturates 4g; Cholesterol 71mg; Calcium 32mg; Fiber 0.3g; Sodium 89mg.

MEDITERRANEAN SAUSAGE *AND* PESTO SOUP

THIS DELICIOUS SOUP MAKES A SATISFYING ONE~POT MEAL THAT BRINGS THE SUMMERY FLAVOR OF BASIL TO MIDWINTER MEALS. THE LENTILS ENHANCE THE FLAVOR OF THE SMOKED SAUSAGE. THICK SLICES OF WARM CRUSTY BREAD MAKE THE PERFECT ACCOMPANIMENT.

SERVES 4

INGREDIENTS

 1 tablespoon olive oil, plus extra
  for frying
 1 red onion, chopped
 1 pound smoked pork sausages
 8 ounces/1 cup red lentils
 1 can (14 ounces) chopped tomatoes
 4 cups water
 oil, for deep-frying
 salt and ground black pepper
 4 tablespoons pesto and fresh basil
  sprigs, to garnish

1 Heat the oil in a large pan and cook the onion until softened. Coarsely chop all but one of the sausages and add them to the pan. Cook for 5 minutes, stirring, or until the sausages are cooked.

2 Stir in the lentils, tomatoes and water, and bring to the boil. Reduce the heat, cover and simmer for about 20 minutes. Cool the soup slightly before pureeing it in a blender. Return the soup to the rinsed pan.

3 Cook the remaining sausage in a little oil in a small frying pan, turning it often, for 10 minutes, or until lightly browned and firm. Transfer to a chopping board or plate and leave to cool slightly, then slice thinly.

4 Heat the oil for deep-frying to 375°F or until a cube of day-old bread browns in about 60 seconds. Deep-fry the sausage slices and basil briefly until the sausages are brown and the basil leaves are crisp.

5 Lift them out using a slotted spoon and drain on paper towels.

6 Reheat the soup, add seasoning to taste, then ladle into warmed individual soup bowls. Sprinkle with the deep-fried sausage slices and basil and swirl a little pesto through each portion. Serve with warm crusty bread.

Energy 656kcal/2741kJ; Protein 30.9g; Carbohydrate 46.7g, of which sugars 8.2g; Fat 39.7g, of which saturates 13.1g; Cholesterol 75mg; Calcium 250mg; Fiber 4.8g; Sodium 1109mg.

LAMB AND VEGETABLE BROTH

THIS IS A GOOD MODERN ADAPTATION OF THE TRADITIONAL RECIPE FOR IRISH MUTTON BROTH, KNOWN LOCALLY AS BRACHÁN CAOIREOLA, AND IS DELICIOUS SERVED WITH WHOLE-WHEAT BREAD TO MAKE A FILLING LUNCH DISH ON A COLD WINTER'S DAY.

SERVES 6

INGREDIENTS

1½ pounds lamb cross rib
1 large onion
2 bay leaves
3 carrots, chopped
½ white turnip, diced
½ small white cabbage, shredded
2 large leeks, thinly sliced
1 tablespoon tomato paste
2 tablespoons chopped fresh parsley
salt and ground black pepper

COOK'S TIP
Cross rib is the rib joint between the middle neck and loin. It is the best cut to use for this soup.

1 Trim any excess fat from the meat. Chop the onion, and put the lamb and bay leaves in a large pan. Add 6¼ cups water and bring to the boil. Skim the surface and then simmer for about 1½–2 hours. Remove the lamb onto a board and leave to cool until ready to handle.

2 Remove the meat from the bones and cut into small pieces. Discard the bones and return the meat to the broth. Add the vegetables, tomato paste and parsley, and season well. Simmer for another 30 minutes, until the vegetables are just tender. Ladle into warmed soup bowls and serve piping hot.

Energy 167kcal/696kJ; Protein 14.6g; Carbohydrate 10.5g, of which sugars 9g; Fat 7.6g, of which saturates 3.4g; Cholesterol 48mg; Calcium 58mg; Fiber 3.7g; Sodium 81mg.

BEEF AND LAMB STEW

THIS TRADITIONAL JEWISH CHAMIM IS MADE WITH SAVORY MEATS AND CHICKPEAS, BAKED IN A VERY LOW OVEN FOR SEVERAL HOURS. A PARCEL OF RICE IS OFTEN ADDED TO THE BROTH PART WAY THROUGH COOKING, WHICH PRODUCES A LIGHTLY PRESSED RICE WITH A SLIGHTLY CHEWY TEXTURE.

SERVES 8

INGREDIENTS

9 ounces/1 cup chickpeas, soaked overnight
3 tablespoons olive oil
1 onion, chopped
10 garlic cloves, chopped
1 parsnip, sliced
3 carrots, sliced
1–2 teaspoons ground cumin
½ teaspoon ground turmeric
1 tablespoon chopped fresh ginger root
8 cups beef stock
1 potato, peeled and cut into chunks
½ large zucchini, sliced or cut into chunks
14 ounces fresh or canned tomatoes, diced
3–4 tablespoons brown or green lentils
2 bay leaves
9 ounces salted meat such as corned beef (or double the quantity of lamb)
9 ounces piece of lamb
½ large bunch fresh cilantro, chopped
7 ounces /1 cup long grain rice
1 lemon, cut into wedges, and a spicy sauce or finely chopped fresh chiles, to serve

1 Preheat the oven to 250ºF. Drain the chickpeas.

2 Heat the oil in a large flameproof casserole, add the onion, garlic, parsnip, carrots, cumin, turmeric and ginger and cook for 2–3 minutes. Add the chickpeas, stock, potato, zucchini, tomatoes, lentils, bay leaves, salted meat, lamb and cilantro. Cover and cook in the oven for about 3 hours.

COOK'S TIP
Add 1 or 2 pinches of baking soda to the soaking chickpeas to make them tender, but do not add too much, as it can make them mushy.

3 Put the rice on a double thickness of cheesecloth and tie together at the corners, allowing enough room for the rice to expand while it is cooking.

4 Two hours before the end of cooking, remove the casserole from the oven. Place the rice parcel in the casserole, anchoring the edge of the cheesecloth parcel under the lid so that the parcel is held above the soup and allowed to steam. Return the casserole to the oven and continue cooking for a further 2 hours.

5 Carefully remove the lid and the rice. Skim any fat off the top of the soup and ladle the soup into bowls with a scoop of the rice and one or two pieces of meat. Serve with lemon wedges and a spoonful of hot sauce or chopped fresh chiles.

Energy 385kcal/1621kJ; Protein 25.6g; Carbohydrate 48.6g, of which sugars 5.3g; Fat 10.8g, of which saturates 2.7g; Cholesterol 24mg; Calcium 116mg; Fiber 5.4g; Sodium 54mg.

THREE-DELICACY SOUP

THIS DELICIOUS SOUP COMBINES THREE INGREDIENTS—CHICKEN, HAM AND SHRIMP. THEIR DIFFERENT FLAVORS ARE RETAINED IN THE SIMPLE CHICKEN STOCK.

SERVES 4

INGREDIENTS

4 ounces chicken breast fillet
4 ounces honey-roast ham
4 ounces peeled shrimp
3 cups chicken stock
salt
chopped scallions,
   to garnish

1 Thinly slice the chicken breast and ham into small pieces. If the shrimp are large, cut them in half lengthwise.

COOK'S TIP
Fresh, uncooked shrimp impart the best flavor. If unavailable, use ready-cooked shrimp. Add towards the end of cooking, to prevent over-cooking.

2 In a wok or large pan, bring the stock to a rolling boil and add the chicken, ham and shrimp. Bring back to the boil, add salt to taste and simmer for a further 1 minute.

3 Ladle into individual soup bowls. Serve hot, garnished with chopped scallions.

LAMB AND CUCUMBER SOUP

THIS IS A VERY SIMPLE SOUP TO PREPARE, BUT IT TASTES DELICIOUS NEVERTHELESS. YOU CAN USE EITHER CHICKEN OR VEGETABLE STOCK.

SERVES 4

INGREDIENTS

8 ounces lamb steak
1 tablespoon light soy sauce
2 teaspoons Chinese rice wine
½ teaspoon sesame oil
3-inch piece cucumber
3 cups chicken or vegetable stock
1 tablespoon rice vinegar
salt and ground white pepper

COOK'S TIPS
• If Chinese rice wine is not available, use dry sherry instead.
• Vegetable or chicken stock may be used for this dish. Homemade stock (see pages 30 and 31) tastes much better than a bouillon cube. Once made, it can be kept in the refrigerator for 3–4 days, or frozen for longer storage.

1 Using a sharp knife, trim off any excess fat from the lamb steaks. Thinly slice the lamb into small pieces.

2 Combine the soy sauce, wine or sherry and sesame oil in a small bowl. Add the sliced lamb and marinate for 25–30 minutes. Discard the marinade.

3 Halve the cucumber piece lengthwise (do not peel it), then cut into thin slices diagonally.

4 In a wok or large pan, bring the stock to a rolling boil, add the lamb and stir to separate the slices.

5 Return to the boil, then add the cucumber slices, vinegar and seasoning. Bring back to the boil and serve immediately.

Top: Energy 83kcal/351kJ; Protein 17.7g; Carbohydrate 0.3g, of which sugars 0.3g; Fat 1.7g, of which saturates 0.5g; Cholesterol 93mg; Calcium 27mg; Fiber 0g; Sodium 781mg.
Bottom: Energy 105kcal/438kJ; Protein 11.2g; Carbohydrate 0.4g, of which sugars 0.3g; Fat 6.6g, of which saturates 3g; Cholesterol 43mg; Calcium 6mg; Fiber 0g; Sodium 316mg.

INDIAN LAMB SOUP with RICE and COCONUT

THIS MEATY SOUP THICKENED WITH LONG GRAIN RICE AND FLAVORED WITH CUMIN AND CORIANDER SEEDS IS BASED ON THE CLASSIC INDIAN MULLIGATAWNY SOUP.

SERVES 6

INGREDIENTS

  2 onions, chopped
  6 garlic cloves, crushed
  2-inch piece fresh ginger
    root, grated
  6 tablespoons olive oil
  2 tablespoons black poppy seeds
  1 teaspoon cumin seeds
  1 teaspoon coriander seeds
  ½ teaspoon ground turmeric
  1 pound boneless lamb chump
    chops, trimmed and cut into
    bitesize pieces
  ¼ teaspoon cayenne pepper
  5 cups lamb stock
  2 ounces/generous ⅓ cup long
    grain rice
  2 tablespoons lemon juice
  4 tablespoons coconut milk
  salt and ground black pepper
  fresh cilantro sprigs and
    toasted flaked coconut,
    to garnish

1 Process the onions, garlic, ginger and 1 tablespoon of the oil in a food processor or blender to form a paste. Set aside.

2 Heat a small, heavy frying pan. Add the poppy, cumin and coriander seeds and toast for a few seconds, shaking the pan, until they begin to release their aroma.

3 Transfer the toasted seeds to a mortar and grind them to a powder with a pestle. Stir in the ground turmeric. Set aside.

4 Heat the rest of the oil in a heavy pan. Fry the lamb in batches over a high heat for about 4–5 minutes, until browned all over. Remove the lamb and set aside.

5 Add the onion, garlic and ginger paste to the pan and cook for 1–2 minutes, stirring continuously. Stir in the ground spices and cook for 1 minute. Return the meat to the pan with any meat juices that have seeped out while it has been standing. Add the cayenne, stock and seasoning.

6 Bring to the boil, cover and simmer for 30–35 minutes or until the lamb is tender.

7 Stir in the rice, then cover and cook for a further 15 minutes.

8 Add the lemon juice and coconut milk and simmer for a further 2 minutes.

9 Ladle the soup into six warmed bowls and garnish with sprigs of cilantro and lightly toasted flaked coconut. Serve piping hot.

Energy 249kcal/1036kJ; Protein 15.8g; Carbohydrate 7.5g, of which sugars 0.8g; Fat 17.3g, of which saturates 4.5g; Cholesterol 56mg; Calcium 14mg; Fiber 0.2g; Sodium 64mg.

BULGARIAN SOUR LAMB SOUP

THIS TRADITIONAL SOUR SOUP USES LAMB, THOUGH PORK AND POULTRY ARE POPULAR ALTERNATIVES. THE PAPRIKA BUTTER MAKES AN UNUSUAL GARNISH.

SERVES 4–5

INGREDIENTS

   2 tablespoons oil
   1 pound lean lamb, trimmed
     and cubed
   1 onion, diced
   2 tablespoons all-purpose flour
   1 tablespoon paprika
   4 cups hot lamb stock
   3 sprigs of fresh parsley
   4 scallions
   4 sprigs of fresh dill
   1 ounce/scant ¼ cup long
     grain rice
   2 eggs, beaten
   2–3 tablespoons vinegar or
     lemon juice
   salt and ground black pepper
For the garnish
   1 ounce/2 tablespoons butter, melted
   1 teaspoon paprika
   a little fresh parsley or lovage
     and dill

1 In a large pan heat the oil and fry the meat until brown. Add the onion and cook until it has softened. Sprinkle in the flour and paprika. Stir well, add the stock and cook for 10 minutes.

2 Tie the parsley, scallions and dill together with string and add to the large pan with the rice and seasoning. Bring to the boil, then simmer for about 30–40 minutes, or until the lamb is tender.

COOK'S TIP
Add extra vinegar or lemon juice if you want a more piquant flavor.

3 Remove the pan from the heat and stir in the eggs. Add the vinegar or lemon juice. Discard the tied herbs and season to taste.

4 For the garnish, melt the butter in a pan and add the paprika. Ladle the soup into warmed serving bowls. Garnish with the herbs and a little red paprika butter.

Energy 314kcal/1309kJ; Protein 21.6g; Carbohydrate 10.1g, of which sugars 1.2g; Fat 21.1g, of which saturates 8.4g; Cholesterol 155mg; Calcium 49mg; Fiber 0.8g; Sodium 139mg.

SOUP OF TOULOUSE SAUSAGE WITH BORLOTTI BEANS AND BREAD CRUMBS

A BIG-FILLER SOUP, THIS RECIPE IS BASED LOOSELY ON CASSOULET. FRENCH SAUSAGES AND ITALIAN BEANS CONTRIBUTE FLAVOR AND SUBSTANCE, AND THE SOUP IS TOPPED WITH GOLDEN BREAD CRUMBS.

SERVES 6

INGREDIENTS
9 ounces/generous 1¼ cups
  borlotti beans
4 ounces piece pancetta,
  finely chopped
6 Toulouse sausages, thickly sliced
1 large onion, finely chopped
2 garlic cloves, chopped
2 carrots, finely diced
2 leeks, finely chopped
6 tomatoes, peeled, seeded
  and chopped
2 tablespoons tomato paste
5⅔ cups vegetable stock
6 ounces collards, roughly shredded
1 ounce/2 tablespoons butter
4 ounces/2 cups fresh white
  bread crumbs
2 ounces/⅔ cup freshly grated
  Parmesan cheese
salt and ground black pepper

1 Put the borlotti beans in a large bowl, cover with plenty of cold water and leave to soak overnight.

2 Next day, place the beans in a pan, cover with plenty of cold water and bring to the boil, then boil for 10 minutes. Drain well.

3 Heat a large pan and dry fry the pancetta until browned, when the fat runs. Add the sausages and cook for 4–5 minutes, stirring occasionally, until beginning to brown.

4 Add the onion and garlic and cook for 3–4 minutes until softened. Add the beans, carrots, leeks, tomatoes and tomato paste, then add the stock. Stir, bring to the boil and cover. Simmer for about 1¼ hours or until the beans are tender, then stir in the collards and cook for 12–15 minutes more. Season well.

5 Meanwhile, melt the butter in a frying pan and fry the bread crumbs, stirring, for 4–5 minutes, until golden, then stir in the Parmesan.

6 Ladle the soup into six warmed bowls. Sprinkle the fried bread crumb mixture over each portion. Serve with some warm crusty bread.

VARIATION
Toulouse sausage, which is flavored with garlic, can be substituted with Polish kielbasa or Italian sweet sausage.

Energy 574kcal/2405kJ; Protein 29g; Carbohydrate 47.7g, of which sugars 10.2g; Fat 31g, of which saturates 12.5g; Cholesterol 75mg; Calcium 284mg; Fiber 10.7g; Sodium 1179mg.

BRAISED CABBAGE SOUP WITH BEEF AND HORSERADISH CREAM

THIS BRILLIANT WINTER SOUP REALLY IS A COMPLETE MAIN COURSE IN A BOWL. THE JOINT OF BEEF CAN BE COOKED AS RARE OR AS WELL DONE AS YOU LIKE.

SERVES 6

INGREDIENTS
2 pounds red cabbage, hard core discarded and leaves shredded
2 onions, finely sliced
1 large cooking apple, peeled, cored and chopped
3 tablespoons soft light brown sugar
2 garlic cloves, crushed
¼ teaspoon grated nutmeg
½ teaspoon caraway seeds
3 tablespoons red wine vinegar
4 cups beef stock
1½ pounds sirloin joint
2 tablespoons olive oil
salt and ground black pepper
watercress, to garnish
For the horseradish cream
1–2 tablespoons fresh horseradish
2 teaspoons wine vinegar
½ teaspoon Dijon mustard
⅔ cup heavy cream

1 Preheat the oven to 300°F. Mix together the first eight ingredients and 3 tablespoons of the stock. Add plenty of seasoning, then put into a large buttered casserole and cover with a tight-fitting lid.

2 Bake for 2½ hours, checking every 30 minutes or so to ensure that the cabbage is not becoming too dry. If necessary, add a few more tablespoons of the stock. Remove the casserole from the oven and set aside. Increase the oven temperature to 450°F.

3 Trim off most of the fat from the sirloin, leaving a thin layer. Tie the joint with string. Heat the oil in a heavy frying pan until smoking. Add the beef and cook until well browned all over.

4 Transfer to a roasting pan and roast for about 15–20 minutes for medium-rare or 25–30 minutes for well-done beef.

5 For the horseradish cream, grate the horseradish and mix with the wine vinegar, mustard and seasoning into 3 tablespoons of the cream. Lightly whip the remaining cream and fold in the horseradish mixture. Chill until required.

6 Spoon the braised cabbage into a pan and pour in the remaining stock. Bring just to boiling point.

7 Remove the beef from the oven and leave to rest for 5 minutes, then remove the string and carve into slices.

8 Ladle the soup into bowls and divide the beef among them, resting on the cabbage. Spoon a little horseradish cream onto each serving of beef, and garnish with small bunches of watercress. Serve at once.

Energy 395kcal/1645kJ; Protein 29.4g; Carbohydrate 19.4g, of which sugars 18.5g; Fat 22.5g, of which saturates 11.1g; Cholesterol 92mg; Calcium 104mg; Fiber 3.8g; Sodium 97mg.

IRISH BACON BROTH

A HEARTY MEAL IN A SOUP BOWL. THE BACON HOCK CONTRIBUTES FLAVOR AND SOME MEAT TO THIS DISH, BUT IT MAY BE SALTY SO REMEMBER TO TASTE AND ADD EXTRA SALT ONLY IF REQUIRED.

SERVES 6–8

INGREDIENTS

1 bacon hock, about 2 pounds
3 ounces/⅓ cup pearl barley
3 ounces/⅓ cup lentils
2 leeks, sliced, or onions, diced
4 carrots, diced
7 ounces rutabaga, diced
3 potatoes, diced
small bunch of herbs (thyme, parsley, bay leaf)
1 small cabbage, trimmed and quartered or sliced
salt and ground black pepper
chopped fresh parsley, to garnish
brown bread, to serve

COOK'S TIP

Traditionally, the cabbage is simply trimmed and quartered, although it may be sliced if you prefer.

1 Soak the bacon in cold water overnight. Next morning, drain, put into a large pan and cover with cold water. Bring to the boil and skim off any scum. Add the barley and lentils. Bring back to the boil and simmer for 15 minutes.

2 Add the vegetables, some black pepper and the herbs. Bring back to the boil, reduce the heat and simmer gently for 1½ hours, or until the meat is tender.

3 Lift the bacon hock from the pan with a slotted spoon. Remove the skin, then take the meat off the bones and break it into bitesize pieces. Return to the pan with the cabbage. Discard the herbs and cook for a little longer until the cabbage is cooked to your liking.

4 Adjust the seasoning and ladle into serving bowls, garnish with parsley and serve with freshly baked brown bread.

IRISH KIDNEY AND BACON SOUP

ALTHOUGH THERE IS A MODERN TWIST IN THE SEASONINGS, THE TWO MAIN INGREDIENTS OF THIS MEATY SOUP ARE STILL VERY TRADITIONALLY IRISH.

SERVES 4–6

INGREDIENTS

8 ounces beef kidney
1 tablespoon vegetable oil
4 fatty bacon strips, chopped
1 large onion, chopped
2 garlic cloves, finely chopped
1 tablespoon all-purpose flour
6¼ cups water
a good dash of Worcestershire sauce
a good dash of soy sauce
1 tablespoon chopped fresh thyme,
  or 1 teaspoon dried
3 ounces/¾ cup grated cheese
4–6 slices French bread, toasted
salt and ground black pepper

1 Wash the kidney in cold, salted water. Drain, dry well on paper towels and chop into small pieces.

COOK'S TIP
Beef kidneys are tougher than veal or lamb, so need to be cooked more slowly.

2 Heat the vegetable oil in a large pan over a medium heat. Add the chopped bacon and sauté for a few minutes. Add the prepared kidney and continue cooking until nicely browned. Stir in the chopped onion and chopped garlic, and cook until the onion is just soft but not browned.

3 Add the flour and cook for 2 minutes. Gradually add the water, stirring constantly. Add the sauces, thyme and seasoning to taste. Reduce the heat and simmer gently for 30–35 minutes.

4 Sprinkle the cheese onto the toast and broil until it is bubbling. Pour the soup into bowls, and top with the bread.

Energy 379kcal/1592kJ; Protein 23.7g; Carbohydrate 34g, of which sugars 3.2g; Fat 17g, of which saturates 7.1g; Cholesterol 184mg; Calcium 225mg; Fiber 1.6g; Sodium 1167mg.

GOLDEN CHORIZO AND CHICKPEA SOUP

THIS HEARTY SPANISH SOUP IS SUBSTANTIAL ENOUGH TO MAKE A COMPLETE MEAL. SMALL UNCOOKED CHORIZO SAUSAGES ARE AVAILABLE FROM SPANISH DELICATESSENS, BUT READY-TO-EAT CHORIZO CAN BE CUT INTO CHUNKS AND USED INSTEAD.

SERVES 4

INGREDIENTS
    4 ounces/⅔ cup dried chickpeas
pinch of saffron strands
3 tablespoons olive oil
1 pound uncooked mini
    chorizo sausages
1 teaspoon dried chili flakes
6 garlic cloves, finely chopped
1 pound tomatoes, roughly chopped
12 ounces new potatoes, quartered
2 bay leaves
scant 2 cups water
4 tablespoons chopped fresh parsley
salt and ground black pepper
2 tablespoons extra virgin olive oil,
    to garnish
crusty bread, to serve

1 Put the chickpeas in a large bowl, cover with plenty of cold water and leave to soak overnight.

2 Next day, drain and place in a large pan. Cover with plenty of fresh water and bring to the boil, skimming off any scum as it forms. Cover and simmer for 2–3 hours, until tender. Add more boiling water, if necessary, to keep the chickpeas well covered during cooking. Drain, reserving the cooking liquid.

3 Heat the oil in a large, deep frying pan. Add the chorizo sausages and fry over a medium heat for 5 minutes, until a lot of oil has seeped out of the sausages and they are pale golden brown. Drain and set aside.

4 Soak the saffron strands in a little warm water.

5 Add the chili flakes and garlic to the fat in the frying pan and cook for a few seconds. Stir in the saffron with its soaking water, the chopped tomatoes, chickpeas, potatoes, chorizo sausages and bay leaves. Pour in scant 2 cups of the chickpea cooking liquor and the water, and stir in salt and pepper to taste.

6 Bring to the boil, then reduce the heat and simmer for 45–50 minutes, stirring gently occasionally, until the potatoes are tender and the soup has thickened slightly.

7 Add the chopped parsley to the soup and adjust the seasoning. Ladle the soup into four large, warmed soup plates and drizzle a little extra virgin olive oil over each portion. Serve with crusty bread.

Energy 642kcal/2674kJ; Protein 21.7g; Carbohydrate 42.3g, of which sugars 8.1g; Fat 44g, of which saturates 12.5g; Cholesterol 68mg; Calcium 174mg; Fiber 6.1g; Sodium 997mg.

KALE, CHORIZO ᴬᴺᴰ POTATO SOUP

THIS HEARTY WINTER SOUP HAS A SPICY KICK TO IT, WHICH COMES FROM THE CHORIZO SAUSAGE.
THE SOUP BECOMES MORE POTENT IF CHILLED OVERNIGHT. IT IS WORTH BUYING THE BEST POSSIBLE
CHORIZO SAUSAGE TO IMPROVE THE FLAVOR.

SERVES 6–8

INGREDIENTS
    8 ounces kale, stems removed
    8 ounces chorizo sausage
    1½ pounds red potatoes
    7½ cups vegetable stock
    1 teaspoon ground black pepper
    pinch cayenne pepper (optional)
    12 slices French bread, broiled
    salt and ground black pepper

1 Process the kale in a food processor for a few seconds to chop it finely.

2 Prick the sausages and place in a pan with enough water to cover. Simmer for 15 minutes. Drain and cut into thin slices.

3 Cook the potatoes in lightly salted boiling water for about 15 minutes or until tender. Drain and place in a bowl, then mash, adding a little of the cooking liquid to form a thick paste.

COOK'S TIP
Chorizo sausage is usually sold whole or cut into lengths or rounds.

4 Bring the vegetable stock to the boil and add the kale. Add the chorizo and simmer for 5 minutes. Add the paste gradually, and simmer for 20 minutes. Season with black pepper and cayenne.

5 Place bread slices in each bowl, and pour over the soup. Serve, generously sprinkled with pepper.

Energy 411kcal/1740kJ; Protein 13.2g; Carbohydrate 69.3g, of which sugars 6.2g; Fat 11g, of which saturates 4.1g; Cholesterol 15mg; Calcium 140mg; Fiber 4g; Sodium 812mg.

CELERIAC SOUP WITH CABBAGE, BACON AND HERBS

VERSATILE, YET OFTEN OVERLOOKED, CELERIAC IS A WINTER VEGETABLE THAT MAKES EXCELLENT SOUP. IT TASTES WONDERFUL TOPPED WITH A COMPLEMENTARY SEASONAL VERSION OF A SALSA.

SERVES 4

INGREDIENTS

2 ounces butter
2 onions, chopped
1½ pounds celeriac,
  roughly diced
1 pound potatoes, roughly diced
5 cups vegetable stock
⅔ cup light cream
salt and ground black pepper
sprigs of fresh thyme,
  to garnish
For the cabbage and bacon topping
1 small savoy cabbage
2 ounces/¼ cup butter
6 ounces rindless fatty bacon,
  roughly chopped
1 tablespoon chopped fresh thyme
1 tablespoon chopped
  fresh rosemary

1 Melt the butter in a pan. Add the onions and cook for 4–5 minutes, until softened. Add the celeriac. Cover the vegetables with a wet piece of baking parchment, then put a lid on the pan and cook gently for 10 minutes.

2 Remove the paper. Stir in the potatoes and stock, bring to the boil, reduce the heat and simmer for 20 minutes. Leave to cool slightly. Using a slotted spoon, remove half the celeriac and potatoes from the soup and set them aside.

3 Puree the soup in a food processor or blender. Return the soup to the pan with the reserved celeriac and potatoes.

4 Prepare the cabbage and bacon mixture. Discard the tough outer leaves from the cabbage. Roughly tear the remaining leaves, discarding any hard stalks, and blanch them in boiling salted water for 2–3 minutes. Refresh under cold running water and drain.

5 Melt the butter in a large frying pan and cook the bacon for 3–4 minutes. Add the cabbage, thyme and rosemary, and stir-fry for 5–6 minutes, until tender. Season well.

6 Add the cream to the soup and season it well, then reheat gently until piping hot.

7 Ladle the soup into warmed bowls and pile the cabbage mixture in the center of each portion. Garnish with sprigs of fresh thyme.

VARIATION
Savoy cabbage is used for the topping in this dish, but other greens, such as kale or collards, would also be suitable.

Energy 462kcal/1919kJ; Protein 12.3g; Carbohydrate 24.3g, of which sugars 7.3g; Fat 35.7g, of which saturates 20.4g; Cholesterol 97mg; Calcium 144mg; Fiber 4.3g; Sodium 954mg.

BACON AND CHICKPEA SOUP WITH TORTILLA CHIPS

THIS SILKY-SMOOTH NUTTY SOUP IS ABSOLUTELY DELICIOUS AND SO EASY TO MAKE. TAKE IT TO THE SOFA WITH A BOWL OF WARM AND SPICY TORTILLA CHIPS AND DIP, CRUNCH AND SLURP YOUR WAY THROUGH YOUR FAVORITE TELEVISION FIX.

SERVES 4–6

INGREDIENTS
    14 ounces/2 cups dried chickpeas, soaked overnight in cold water
    4 ounces/½ cup butter
    5 ounces pancetta or fatty bacon, roughly chopped
    2 onions, finely chopped
    1 carrot, chopped
    1 celery stick, chopped
    1 tablespoon chopped fresh rosemary
    2 fresh bay leaves
    2 garlic cloves, halved
For the tortilla chips
    3 ounces/6 tablespoons butter
    ½ teaspoon sweet paprika
    ¼ teaspoon ground cumin
    6 ounces plain tortilla chips
    salt and ground black pepper

1 Drain the chickpeas, put them in a large pan and cover with plenty of cold water. Bring to the boil and simmer for about 20 minutes. Strain and set aside.

2 Melt the butter in a large pan and add the pancetta or bacon. Fry over a medium heat until just beginning to turn golden. Add the chopped vegetables and cook for 5–10 minutes until soft.

COOK'S TIP
Packets of diced bacon are available in most supermarkets, and these are ideal for adding to soups.

3 Add the chickpeas to the pan with the rosemary, bay leaves, garlic cloves and enough water to cover completely. Bring to the boil, half cover, turn down the heat and simmer for 45–60 minutes, stirring occasionally. (The chickpeas should start to disintegrate and will thicken the soup.)

4 Allow the soup to cool slightly, then pour it into a blender or food processor and process until smooth. Return the soup to the rinsed-out pan, taste and season with salt and plenty of black pepper. Reheat gently.

5 To make the tortilla chips, preheat the oven to 350°F. Melt the butter with the paprika and cumin in a pan, then lightly brush the mixture over the tortilla chips. Reserve any leftover spiced butter.

6 Spread the chips out on a baking sheet and warm through in the oven for 5 minutes.

7 Ladle the soup into bowls, pour some of the reserved spiced butter over each and sprinkle with a little paprika. Serve with the warm tortilla chips.

Energy 996kcal/4154kJ; Protein 31.4g; Carbohydrate 80.1g, of which sugars 6.6g; Fat 63.3g, of which saturates 30.1g; Cholesterol 126mg; Calcium 252mg; Fiber 14.3g; Sodium 1186mg.

INDIAN BEEF <u>AND</u> BERRY SOUP

THE FRESH BERRIES GIVE THIS UNUSUAL SOUP A PLEASANT KICK. THIS IS AN IDEAL SOUP TO SERVE ON A REALLY COLD DAY, AS IT IS WARMING AND FILLING WITH A COMFORTING SWEETNESS.

SERVES 4

INGREDIENTS

2 tablespoons vegetable oil
1 pound tender beef steak
2 medium onions, finely sliced
1 ounce/2 tablespoons butter
4 cups good beef stock
  or bouillon
½ teaspoon salt
4 ounces/1 cup fresh huckleberries,
  blueberries or blackberries,
  lightly mashed
1 tablespoon honey

1 Heat the oil in a heavy pan until almost smoking. Add the steak and brown on both sides over a medium-high heat. Remove the steak from the pan and set aside.

2 Reduce the heat to low and add the sliced onions and butter to the pan. Stir well, scraping up the meat juices. Cook over a low heat until the onions are soft.

3 Add the beef stock or bouillon and salt and bring to the boil, stirring well. Mix in the mashed berries and the honey. Simmer for 20 minutes.

4 Meanwhile, cut the steak into thin, bitesize slivers. Taste the soup and add more salt or honey if necessary. Add the steak to the pan. Cook gently for 30 seconds, stirring, then serve hot.

COOK'S TIP
For best results, use a good homemade beef stock (see page 32).

Energy 338kcal/1404kJ; Protein 26.8g; Carbohydrate 10.3g, of which sugars 8.6g; Fat 21.3g, of which saturates 8.2g; Cholesterol 79mg; Calcium 38mg; Fiber 2g; Sodium 113mg.

TOMATO AND BEEF SOUP

*FRESH TOMATOES AND SCALLIONS GIVE THIS LIGHT BEEF BROTH A SUPERB FLAVOR AND APPEARANCE.
GARNISH THE SOUP WITH SHREDDED SCALLIONS.*

SERVES 4

INGREDIENTS
  3 ounces round steak, trimmed
    of fat
  3¾ cups beef stock
  2 tablespoons tomato paste
  6 tomatoes, halved, seeded
    and chopped
  2 teaspoons superfine sugar
  1 tablespoon cornstarch
  1 tablespoon cold water
  1 egg white
  ½ teaspoon sesame oil
  2 scallions, shredded
  salt and ground black pepper

1 Cut the beef into thin strips and place it in a pan. Pour over boiling water to cover. Cook for 2 minutes, then drain thoroughly and set aside.

2 Bring the stock to the boil in a clean pan. Stir in the tomato paste, then the tomatoes and sugar. Add the beef, allow the stock to boil again, then lower the heat and simmer for 2 minutes.

3 Mix the cornstarch to a thin paste with the cold water. Add the paste to the soup, stirring constantly until it thickens slightly but does not become lumpy.

4 Lightly beat the egg white in a small bowl.

5 Pour the egg white into the soup in a steady stream, stirring all the time. As soon as the egg white changes color, add salt and pepper, stir the soup and pour it into heated bowls.

6 Drizzle sesame oil on each portion, sprinkle with scallions and serve.

Energy 79kcal/337kJ; Protein 6.2g; Carbohydrate 11.1g, of which sugars 7.6g; Fat 1.5g, of which saturates 0.5g; Cholesterol 11mg; Calcium 16mg; Fiber 1.5g; Sodium 58mg.

CLEAR SOUP WITH MEATBALLS

A CHINESE-STYLE SOUP, IN WHICH TINY MEATBALLS ARE COMBINED WITH LIGHTLY COOKED VEGETABLES IN A TASTY AND FRAGRANT STOCK.

SERVES 8

INGREDIENTS

4–6 Chinese mushrooms,
  soaked in warm water for
  30 minutes
2 tablespoons peanut oil
1 large onion, peeled and
  finely chopped
2 garlic cloves, finely crushed
½-inch piece fresh ginger
  root, bruised
9 cups beef or chicken stock,
  including soaking liquid from
  the mushrooms
2 tablespoons soy sauce
4 ounces curly kale, spinach or
  Chinese cabbage, shredded
For the meatballs
6 ounces/¾ cup finely ground beef
1 small onion, finely chopped
1 or 2 garlic cloves, crushed
1 tablespoon cornstarch
a little egg white, lightly beaten
salt and ground black pepper

1 First prepare the meatballs. Mix the beef with the onion, garlic, cornstarch and seasoning in a food processor and then bind with sufficient egg white to make a firm mixture. With wet hands, roll into tiny, bitesize balls and set aside.

2 Drain the mushrooms. Add the soaking liquid to the stock. Trim off and discard the stalks. Slice the caps finely and set aside.

3 Heat a wok or large pan and add the oil. Fry the onion, garlic and ginger for 2–3 minutes to bring out the flavor, but do not allow to brown.

4 When the onion is soft, pour in the stock. Bring to the boil, then stir in the soy sauce and mushroom slices and simmer for 10 minutes.

5 Add the meatballs and cook for a further 10 minutes.

6 Just before serving, remove the ginger. Stir in the shredded curly kale, spinach or Chinese cabbage. Heat through for 1 minute only—no longer or the leaves will be overcooked. Ladle the soup into warmed bowls and serve immediately, piping hot.

Energy 102kcal/423kJ; Protein 5.4g; Carbohydrate 5.8g, of which sugars 3g; Fat 6.5g, of which saturates 1.9g; Cholesterol 13mg; Calcium 39mg; Fiber 0.9g; Sodium 307mg.

SPINACH AND LEMON SOUP WITH MEATBALLS

THIS SOUP, KNOWN AS AARSHE SAAK, IS ALMOST STANDARD FARE IN MANY PARTS OF THE MIDDLE EAST. IN GREECE, IT IS MADE WITHOUT THE MEATBALLS AND IS SIMPLY CALLED AVGOLEMONO.

SERVES 6

INGREDIENTS

2 large onions
3 tablespoons oil
1 tablespoon ground turmeric
4 ounces/½ cup yellow split peas
5 cups water
8 ounces ground lamb
1 pound spinach, chopped
2 ounces/½ cup rice flour
juice of 2 lemons
1 or 2 garlic cloves, finely chopped
2 tablespoons chopped fresh mint
4 eggs
salt and ground black pepper
sprigs of fresh mint, to garnish

1 Chop one of the onions and fry in 2 tablespoons of the oil in a large pan until golden. Add the turmeric, peas and water and bring to the boil. Simmer for 20 minutes.

2 Grate the other onion into a bowl, add the lamb and seasoning and mix well. Using your hands, form the mixture into small balls, about the size of walnuts. Carefully add to the pan and simmer for 10 minutes, then add the spinach, cover and simmer for 20 minutes.

3 Mix the flour with about 8 fluid ounces/1 cup cold water to make a smooth paste, then slowly add to the pan, stirring all the time. Add the lemon juice, season and cook over a gentle heat for 20 minutes.

4 Meanwhile, heat the remaining oil in a small pan and fry the garlic briefly until golden. Stir in the mint and remove the pan from the heat.

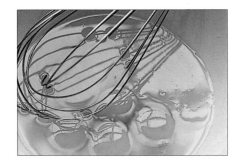

5 Break the eggs into a small bowl and beat with an egg whisk.

6 Remove the soup from the heat and stir in the beaten eggs. Ladle into warmed soup bowls.

7 Sprinkle the prepared garlic and mint mixture over the soup, garnish with mint sprigs and serve immediately.

Energy 316kcal/1318kJ; Protein 19.8g; Carbohydrate 25.7g, of which sugars 6.3g; Fat 15.3g, of which saturates 4.1g; Cholesterol 156mg; Calcium 203mg; Fiber 3.9g; Sodium 189mg.

ONION <u>AND</u> PANCETTA SOUP

THIS SOUP COMES FROM UMBRIA, WHERE IT IS SOMETIMES THICKENED WITH BEATEN EGGS AND PLENTY OF GRATED PARMESAN CHEESE. IT IS THEN SERVED ON TOP OF HOT TOASTED CROUTES.

SERVES 4

INGREDIENTS

    4 ounces pancetta strips, rinds
      removed, roughly chopped
    2 tablespoons olive oil
    ½ ounce/1 tablespoon butter
    1½ pounds onions, finely sliced
    2 teaspoons sugar
    5 cups chicken stock
    12 ounces ripe Italian plum
      tomatoes, peeled and
      roughly chopped
    a few fresh basil leaves, shredded
    salt and ground black pepper
    grated Parmesan cheese,
      to serve

1 Put the chopped pancetta in a large pan and heat gently, stirring constantly, until the fat runs. Increase the heat to medium, add the oil, butter, sliced onions and sugar and stir well to mix all the ingredients.

2 Half-cover the pan and cook the onions gently for about 20 minutes until golden. Stir frequently and lower the heat if necessary.

3 Add the stock, tomatoes and salt and pepper and bring to the boil, stirring. Lower the heat, half-cover the pan and simmer, stirring occasionally, for about 30 minutes.

4 Check the consistency of the soup and add a little more stock or water if it is too thick.

5 Just before serving, stir in most of the basil and adjust the seasoning to taste. Serve hot, garnished with the remaining shredded basil. Hand round the freshly grated Parmesan separately.

COOK'S TIP
Look for Vidalia onions to make this soup. They are available at large supermarkets, and have a sweet flavor and attractive, yellowish flesh.

BEEF CHILE SOUP

THIS IS A HEARTY DISH BASED ON A TRADITIONAL CHILE RECIPE. IT IS IDEAL SERVED WITH FRESH, CRUSTY BREAD AS A WARMING START TO ANY MEAL.

SERVES 4

INGREDIENTS

1 tablespoon oil
1 onion, chopped
6 ounces/¾ cup ground beef
2 garlic cloves, chopped
1 fresh red chile, sliced
1 ounce/¼ cup all-purpose flour
1 can (14 ounces) chopped
  tomatoes
2½ cups beef stock
8 ounces/2 cups canned kidney
  beans, drained
2 tablespoons chopped
  fresh parsley
salt and ground black pepper
crusty bread, to serve

1 Heat the oil in a large pan. Fry the onion and ground beef for 5 minutes until brown and sealed.

2 Add the garlic, chile and flour. Cook for 1 minute. Add the tomatoes and pour in the stock. Bring to the boil.

COOK'S TIPS
• For a milder flavor, remove the seeds from the chile after slicing it. Wear rubber gloves to protect your skin when handling chiles.
• You can use dried red kidney beans instead of canned ones, but they must be soaked overnight in cold water. Next day, boil them rapidly for 15 minutes before reducing the heat and simmering for at least an hour until tender.
• Use homemade beef stock (see page 32) for a better flavor.

3 Stir in the drained kidney beans and add salt and pepper to taste. Cook for 20 minutes.

4 Add the chopped parsley, reserving a little to garnish the finished dish. Pour the soup into warm bowls, sprinkle with the reserved parsley and serve with crusty bread.

Energy 226kcal/946kJ; Protein 14.2g; Carbohydrate 19.4g, of which sugars 6.2g; Fat 10.7g, of which saturates 3.5g; Cholesterol 26mg; Calcium 79mg; Fiber 5.3g; Sodium 267mg.

WONTON SOUP

IN CHINA, WONTON SOUP IS SERVED AS A SNACK, OR DIM SUM, RATHER THAN AS A SOUP COURSE DURING A LARGE MEAL. IT IS A FRESH-TASTING, DELICATELY FLAVORED SOUP.

2 Place about 1 teaspoon of the pork and shrimp mixture in the center of each wonton wrapper.

3 Wet the edges of each filled wonton wrapper with a little water and press them together with your fingers to seal. Fold each wonton parcel over.

4 To cook, bring the stock to a rolling boil in a wok, add the wontons and cook for 4–5 minutes. Season with the soy sauce and add the scallions.

5 Ladle into warmed individual soup bowls and serve hot.

SERVES 4

INGREDIENTS

   6 ounces pork, not too lean,
     roughly chopped
   2 ounces peeled shrimp,
     finely chopped
   1 teaspoon light brown sugar
   1 tablespoon Chinese rice wine
     or dry sherry
   1 tablespoon light soy sauce
   1 teaspoon finely chopped scallions
   1 teaspoon finely chopped fresh
     ginger root
   24 ready-made wonton wrappers
   about 3 cups stock
   1 tablespoon light soy sauce
   finely chopped scallions,
     to garnish

1 In a bowl, thoroughly mix the chopped pork and shrimp with the sugar, rice wine or sherry, soy sauce, scallions and ginger. Set aside for 25–30 minutes for the flavors to blend.

COOK'S TIP
Use a vegetable or light chicken stock (see pages 30–1) for this soup.

Energy 134kcal/568kJ; Protein 13.6g; Carbohydrate 16.3g, of which sugars 1.9g; Fat 2.1g, of which saturates 0.7g; Cholesterol 52mg; Calcium 42mg; Fiber 0.6g; Sodium 589mg.

PORK AND VEGETABLE SOUP

THE UNUSUAL INGREDIENTS IN THIS INTERESTING JAPANESE SOUP ARE AVAILABLE FROM SPECIALIST FOOD STORES AND JAPANESE SUPERMARKETS.

SERVES 4

INGREDIENTS

2 ounces burdock (optional)
1 teaspoon rice vinegar
½ black konnyaku (about 4 ounces)
2 teaspoons oil
7 ounces pork loin, cut into thin
  1¼–½-inch-long strips
4 ounces daikon, peeled and
  thinly sliced
2 ounces carrot, thinly sliced
1 medium potato, thinly sliced
4 shiitake mushrooms, stems
  removed and thinly sliced
3½ cups kombu and bonito stock or
  instant dashi
1 tablespoon *sake* or dry white wine
3 tablespoons red or white
  miso paste
For the garnish
  2 scallions, thinly sliced
  seven-spice flavor (shichimi)

1 Scrub the skin off the burdock, if using, with a vegetable brush. Slice the vegetable into fine shavings. Soak the prepared burdock for 5 minutes in plenty of water with the vinegar added to remove any bitter taste, then drain.

2 Put the piece of konnyaku in a small pan and add enough water just to cover it. Bring to the boil over a moderate heat, then drain and allow to cool. This removes any bitter taste.

3 Using your hands, tear the konnyaku into ¾-inch lumps. Do not use a knife as a smooth cut surface will not absorb any flavor.

4 Heat the oil in a large pan and quickly stir-fry the pork. Add the burdock, if using, daikon, carrot, potato, shiitake mushrooms and konnyaku, then stir-fry for 1 minute. Pour in the stock and sake or wine.

5 Bring the soup to the boil, then skim it and simmer for 10 minutes, until the vegetables have softened.

6 Ladle a little of the soup into a small bowl and dissolve the miso paste in it. Pour back into the pan and bring to the boil once more. Do not continue to boil or the flavor will be lost. Remove from the heat, then pour into individual warmed serving bowls.

7 Sprinkle with the scallions and seven-spice flavor (shichimi) and serve.

Energy 245kcal/1017kJ; Protein 9.7g; Carbohydrate 8.8g, of which sugars 2.2g; Fat 19g, of which saturates 6.8g; Cholesterol 36mg; Calcium 19mg; Fiber 1.6g; Sodium 51mg.

FISH SOUP <u>WITH</u> ROUILLE

MAKING THIS SOUP IS SIMPLICITY ITSELF, YET THE FLAVOR SUGGESTS IT IS THE PRODUCT OF PAINSTAKING PREPARATION AND COOKING.

<u>SERVES 6</u>

INGREDIENTS
   2¼ pounds mixed fish
   2 tablespoons extra virgin
      olive oil
   1 onion, peeled and finely
      chopped
   1 carrot, chopped
   1 leek, chopped
   2 large ripe tomatoes, chopped
   1 red bell pepper, seeded
      and chopped
   2 garlic cloves, peeled
   5 ounces/⅔ cup tomato paste
   1 large fresh bouquet garni
   1¼ cups dry white wine
   salt and ground black pepper
For the *rouille*
   2 garlic cloves, roughly chopped
   1 teaspoon coarse salt
   1 thick slice of white bread, crust
      removed, soaked in water and
      squeezed dry
   1 fresh red chile, seeded and
      roughly chopped
   3 tablespoons olive oil
   salt and cayenne pepper
For the garnish
   12 slices of baguette, toasted in
      the oven
   2 ounces Gruyère cheese,
      finely grated

1 Cut the fish into 3-inch chunks, removing any obvious bones. Heat the oil in a large pan, then add the fish and chopped vegetables. Stir until these begin to color.

2 Add all the other soup ingredients, then pour in just enough cold water to cover the mixture. Season well and bring to just below boiling point, then lower the heat to a bare simmer, cover and cook for 1 hour.

3 Meanwhile, make the *rouille*. Put the garlic and coarse salt in a mortar and crush to a paste with a pestle. Add the soaked bread and chile and pound until smooth, or puree in a food processor. Whisk in the olive oil, a drop at a time, to make a smooth, shiny sauce that resembles mayonnaise. Season with salt and add a pinch of cayenne if you like a fiery taste. Set the *rouille* aside.

4 Lift out and discard the bouquet garni from the soup. Puree the soup in batches in a food processor, then put through a fine strainer placed over a clean pan, pushing the solids through with the back of a ladle.

5 Reheat the soup without letting it boil. Check the seasoning and ladle into individual bowls. Top each serving with two slices of toasted baguette, a spoonful of rouille and some grated Gruyère.

COOK'S TIP
Any firm fish can be used for this recipe. If you use whole fish, include the heads, which enhance the flavor of the soup.

Energy 518kcal/2179kJ; Protein 41.5g; Carbohydrate 49g, of which sugars 10.8g; Fat 14.9g, of which saturates 3.6g; Cholesterol 85mg; Calcium 193mg; Fiber 4.3g; Sodium 665mg.

THAI FISH BROTH

LEMONGRASS, CHILES AND GALANGAL ARE AMONG THE FLAVORINGS USED IN THIS FRAGRANT SOUP.

SERVES 2–3

INGREDIENTS

    4 cups fish or light chicken stock
    4 lemongrass stalks
    3 limes
    2 small fresh hot red chiles,
      seeded and thinly sliced
    ¾-inch piece fresh galangal, peeled
      and thinly sliced
    6 cilantro stalks and leaves
    2 kaffir lime leaves, coarsely
      chopped (optional)
    12 ounces monkfish fillet, skinned
      and cut into 1-inch pieces
    1 tablespoon rice vinegar
    3 tablespoons Thai fish sauce
    2 tablespoons chopped cilantro
      leaves, to garnish

1 Pour the stock into a pan and bring it to the boil. Meanwhile, slice the bulb end of each lemongrass stalk diagonally into pieces about ⅛ inch thick. Peel off four wide strips of lime rind with a potato peeler, taking care to avoid the white pith underneath, which would make the soup bitter. Squeeze the limes and reserve the juice.

2 Add the sliced lemongrass, lime rind, chiles, galangal and cilantro stalks to the stock, with the kaffir lime leaves, if using. Simmer for 1–2 minutes.

VARIATIONS

• Shrimp, scallops, squid or sole can be substituted for the monkfish.
• If you use kaffir lime leaves, you will need the juice of only 2 limes.

3 Add the monkfish, rice vinegar and fish sauce, with half the reserved lime juice. Simmer for about 3 minutes, until the fish is just cooked. Lift out and discard the cilantro stalks, taste the broth and add more lime juice if necessary; the soup should taste quite sour. Sprinkle with the cilantro leaves and serve very hot.

Energy 124kcal/529kJ; Protein 28.3g; Carbohydrate 0.7g, of which sugars 0.6g; Fat 1g, of which saturates 0.2g; Cholesterol 25mg; Calcium 64mg; Fiber 1.3g; Sodium 40mg.

PAD THAI RED MONKFISH SOUP

THIS LIGHT COCONUT SOUP IS BASED ON THAILAND'S CLASSIC STIR-FRIED NOODLE DISH.

SERVES 4

INGREDIENTS

6 ounces flat rice noodles
2 tablespoons vegetable oil
2 garlic cloves, peeled and
  chopped
1 tablespoon red curry paste
1 pound monkfish tail, cut into
  bitesize pieces
1¼ cups coconut cream
3 cups hot chicken stock
3 tablespoons Thai fish sauce
1 tablespoon jaggery
4 tablespoons roughly chopped
  roasted peanuts
4 scallions, shredded lengthwise
2 ounces bean sprouts
large handful of fresh Thai
  basil leaves
salt and ground black pepper
1 red chile, seeded and cut
  lengthwise into slivers,
  to garnish

1 Soak the noodles in boiling water for 10 minutes, or according to the packet instructions. Drain.

2 Heat the oil in a wok or pan over a high heat. Add the garlic and cook for 2 minutes. Stir in the curry paste and cook for 1 minute.

COOK'S TIP
Thai fish sauce (*nam pla*) is made from salted, fermented fish. The color of the sauce can vary considerably. Look for a light-colored sauce, as it is considered better than the darker version.

3 Add the monkfish and stir-fry over a high heat for 4–5 minutes, until just tender. Pour in the coconut cream and stock. Stir in the fish sauce and sugar, and bring just to the boil. Add the drained noodles and cook for 1–2 minutes, until tender.

4 Stir in half the peanuts, half the scallions, half the bean sprouts, the basil and seasoning. Ladle the soup into deep bowls and sprinkle over the remaining peanuts. Garnish with the rest of the scallions and bean sprouts, and the red chile.

Energy 379kcal/1589kJ; Protein 25.5g; Carbohydrate 41.2g, of which sugars 4.7g; Fat 12g, of which saturates 2g; Cholesterol 18mg; Calcium 49mg; Fiber 0.9g; Sodium 111mg.

SALMON CHOWDER

DILL IS THE PERFECT PARTNER FOR SALMON IN THIS CREAMY SOUP FROM THE USA. IT TAKES ITS INSPIRATION FROM THE SATISFYING SOUPS THAT ARE TYPICAL OF THE EASTERN SEABOARD OF THE COUNTRY, AND IS BEST SERVED IMMEDIATELY AFTER COOKING, WHEN THE SALMON IS JUST TENDER.

SERVES 4

INGREDIENTS

- ¾ ounce/1½ tablespoons butter
- 1 onion, finely chopped
- 1 leek, finely chopped
- 1 small fennel bulb, finely chopped
- 1 ounce/¼ cup all-purpose flour
- 7 cups fish stock
- 2 medium potatoes, cut into ½-inch cubes
- 1 pound salmon fillet, skinned and cut into ¾-inch cubes
- 6 fluid ounces/¾ cup milk
- 4 fluid ounces/½ cup whipping cream
- 2 tablespoons chopped fresh dill

salt and ground black pepper

1 Melt the butter in a large pan. Add the onion, leek and chopped fennel and cook for 6 minutes until softened.

2 Stir in the flour. Reduce the heat to low and cook for 3 minutes, stirring occasionally with a wooden spoon.

3 Add the fish stock and potatoes to the mixture in the pan. Season with a little salt and ground black pepper. Bring to the boil, then reduce the heat, cover and simmer gently for about 20 minutes or until the potatoes are tender when tested with a fork.

4 Add the cubed salmon fillet and simmer gently for 3–5 minutes until it is just cooked.

5 Stir the milk, cream and chopped dill into the contents of the pan. Cook until just warmed through, stirring occasionally, but do not allow to boil. Adjust the seasoning to taste, then ladle into warmed soup bowls to serve.

Energy 464kcal/1934kJ; Protein 27.9g; Carbohydrate 22.1g, of which sugars 6.5g; Fat 30g, of which saturates 12.9g; Cholesterol 101mg; Calcium 131mg; Fiber 3.1g; Sodium 122mg.

CURRIED SALMON SOUP

A HINT OF MILD CURRY PASTE REALLY ENHANCES THE FLAVOR OF THIS SOUP, WITHOUT MAKING IT TOO SPICY. COCONUT CREAM ADDS A LUXURY TOUCH, WHILE HELPING TO AMALGAMATE THE FLAVORS. SERVED WITH CHUNKS OF WARM BREAD, THIS MAKES A SUBSTANTIAL APPETIZER.

SERVES 4

INGREDIENTS

2 ounces/¼ cup butter
2 onions, peeled and roughly
   chopped
2 teaspoons mild curry paste
16 fluid ounces/2 cups water
⅔ cup white wine
1¼ cups heavy cream
4 fluid ounces/½ cup coconut
   cream
2 potatoes, about 12 ounces,
   peeled and cubed
1 pound salmon fillet, skinned
   and cut into bitesize pieces
4 tablespoons chopped fresh
   Italian parsley
salt and ground black pepper

1 Melt the butter in a large pan, add the onions and cook for 3–4 minutes, until beginning to soften. Stir in the curry paste. Cook for 1 minute more.

2 Add the water, wine, cream and coconut cream, with seasoning. Bring to the boil, stirring until the coconut has dissolved.

3 Add the potatoes to the pan. Simmer, covered, for about 15 minutes or until they are almost tender. Do not allow them to break down into the mixture.

4 Add the fish gently so as not to break it up. Simmer for 2–3 minutes until just cooked. Add the parsley and adjust the seasoning. Serve immediately.

Energy 837kcal/3466kJ; Protein 26.3g; Carbohydrate 16.6g, of which sugars 3.6g; Fat 71.8g, of which saturates 41.2g; Cholesterol 186mg; Calcium 74mg; Fiber 0.9g; Sodium 158mg.

SALMON SOUP <u>WITH</u> SALSA <u>AND</u> ROUILLE

THIS SMART FISH SOUP IS THE PERFECT CHOICE FOR SUMMER ENTERTAINING. SORREL IS A GOOD PARTNER FOR SALMON, BUT DILL OR FENNEL ARE EQUALLY DELICIOUS ALTERNATIVES.

SERVES 4

INGREDIENTS
   6 tablespoons extra virgin
     olive oil
   1 onion, peeled and roughly
     chopped
   1 leek, chopped
   1 celery stick, chopped
   1 fennel bulb, roughly chopped
   1 red bell pepper, seeded
     and sliced
   3 garlic cloves, chopped
   grated rind and juice of 2 oranges
   1 bay leaf
   1 can (14 ounces) chopped tomatoes
   5 cups fish stock
   pinch of cayenne pepper
   1¾ pounds salmon fillet, skinned
   1¼ cups heavy cream
   salt and ground black pepper
   4 thin slices baguette, to serve
For the ruby salsa
   2 tomatoes, peeled, seeded
     and diced
   ½ small red onion, very
     finely chopped
   1 tablespoon cod's roe
   1 tablespoon chopped fresh sorrel
For the *rouille*
   4 fluid ounces/½ cup mayonnaise
   1 garlic clove, crushed
   1 teaspoon sun-dried
     tomato paste

1 Heat the oil in a large pan and add the chopped onion, leek, celery, fennel, pepper and garlic. Cover the pan and cook gently for 20 minutes or until all the vegetables have softened. Do not allow the onion and garlic to brown.

2 Add the orange rind and juice, bay leaf and tomatoes. Cover and cook for 4–5 minutes, stirring occasionally. Add the stock and cayenne, cover the pan and simmer for 30 minutes.

3 Add the salmon and cook gently for 8–10 minutes, until just cooked. Using a slotted spoon, remove the salmon and place it on a large plate.

4 Flake the salmon into large pieces, and remove any bones that were missed when the fish was originally filleted. Put the flaked salmon in a dish and set it aside.

COOK'S TIP
For a smart presentation, choose wide, shallow soup plates, so that there is plenty of room for the *rouille*-topped toast on top of the flaked salmon. The ruby salsa adds the finishing touch.

5 Meanwhile, make the salsa. Put the tomatoes in a bowl and add the finely chopped red onion. Stir in the cod's roe and the chopped fresh sorrel. Transfer the mixture to a serving dish and set it aside.

6 To make the *rouille* to top the toast, mix the mayonnaise with the crushed garlic and the sun-dried tomato paste in a bowl.

7 Leave the soup to cool slightly, then remove and discard the bay leaf. Puree the soup in a food processor or blender until smooth, then press it through a fine strainer into the rinsed pan.

8 Stir in the cream and season well, then add the flaked salmon. Toast the baguette slices under a hot broiler on both sides and set aside.

9 Reheat the soup gently without letting it boil. Ladle it into bowls and float the toasted baguette slices on top. Add a spoonful of *rouille* to each slice of baguette and spoon some ruby salsa on top. Serve immediately.

Energy 1153kcal/4772kJ; Protein 44.9g; Carbohydrate 13.7g, of which sugars 12.5g; Fat 102.5g, of which saturates 34.9g; Cholesterol 225mg; Calcium 127mg; Fiber 4.7g; Sodium 268mg.

MATELOTE

THIS FISHERMEN'S CHUNKY SOUP IS TRADITIONALLY MADE FROM FRESHWATER FISH, INCLUDING EEL. ANY FIRM FISH CAN BE USED, BUT TRY TO INCLUDE AT LEAST SOME EEL, AND USE A ROBUST DRY WHITE OR RED WINE FOR EXTRA FLAVOR.

SERVES 6

INGREDIENTS
2¼ pounds mixed fish, including
  1 pound conger eel if possible
2 ounces/¼ cup butter
1 onion, thickly sliced
2 celery sticks, thickly sliced
2 carrots, thickly sliced
1 bottle dry white or red wine
fresh bouquet garni containing
  parsley, bay leaf and chervil
2 cloves
6 black peppercorns
beurre manié for thickening,
  see Cook's Tip
salt and cayenne pepper
For the garnish
1 ounce/2 tablespoons butter
12 baby onions, peeled
12 white mushrooms
chopped Italian parsley

1 Cut all the fish into thick slices, removing any obvious bones. Melt the butter in a large pan, put in the fish and sliced vegetables and stir over a medium heat until lightly browned. Pour in the wine and enough cold water to cover. Add the bouquet garni and spices and season. Bring to the boil, lower the heat and simmer gently for 20–30 minutes, until the fish is tender, skimming the surface occasionally.

2 Meanwhile, prepare the garnish. Heat the butter in a deep frying pan and sauté the baby onions until golden and tender. Add the mushrooms and fry until golden. Season and keep hot.

3 Pour the soup through a large strainer into a clean pan. Discard the herbs and spices in the strainer, then divide the fish among deep soup plates (you can skin the fish if you wish, but this is not essential) and keep hot.

4 Reheat the soup until it boils. Lower the heat and whisk in the *beurre manié* little by little until the soup thickens. Season it and pour over the fish. Garnish each portion with the fried baby onions and mushrooms and sprinkle with chopped parsley.

COOK'S TIP
To make the *beurre manié* for thickening, mix ½ ounce/1 tablespoon softened butter with 1 tablespoon all-purpose flour. Add to the boiling soup a pinch at a time, whisking all the time.

Energy 323kcal/1346kJ; Protein 31.4g; Carbohydrate 2.3g, of which sugars 1.9g; Fat 11.6g, of which saturates 6.7g; Cholesterol 103mg; Calcium 35mg; Fiber 0.8g; Sodium 192mg.

SMOKED MACKEREL AND TOMATO SOUP

ALL THE INGREDIENTS FOR THIS UNUSUAL SOUP ARE COOKED IN A SINGLE PAN, SO IT IS NOT ONLY QUICK AND EASY TO PREPARE, BUT REDUCES THE CLEARING UP. SMOKED MACKEREL GIVES THE SOUP A ROBUST FLAVOR, BUT THIS IS TEMPERED BY THE CITRUS TONES IN THE LEMONGRASS AND TAMARIND.

SERVES 4

INGREDIENTS
  7 ounces smoked mackerel fillets
  4 tomatoes
  4 cups vegetable stock
  1 lemongrass stalk, finely chopped
  2-inch piece fresh galangal,
    finely diced
  4 shallots, finely chopped
  2 garlic cloves, finely chopped
  ½ teaspoon dried chilli flakes
  1 tablespoon Thai fish sauce
  1 teaspoon jaggery or light
    brown sugar
  3 tablespoons thick tamarind juice,
    made by mixing tamarind paste
    with warm water
small bunch of fresh chives or
    scallions, to garnish

1 Prepare the smoked mackerel fillets. Remove and discard the skin, if necessary, then chop the flesh into large pieces. Remove any stray bones with your fingers or a pair of tweezers.

2 Cut the tomatoes in half, squeeze out most of the seeds with your fingers, then finely dice the flesh with a sharp knife. Set aside.

3 Pour the stock into a large pan and add the lemongrass, galangal, shallots and garlic. Bring to the boil, reduce the heat and simmer for 15 minutes.

4 Add the fish, tomatoes, chili flakes, fish sauce, sugar and tamarind juice. Simmer for 4–5 minutes, until the fish and tomatoes are heated through. Serve garnished with chives or scallions.

Energy 203kcal/845kJ; Protein 10.3g; Carbohydrate 5.3g, of which sugars 5g; Fat 15.8g, of which saturates 3.3g; Cholesterol 53mg; Calcium 21mg; Fiber 1.2g; Sodium 385mg.

CARIBBEAN SALT COD AND OKRA SOUP

INSPIRED BY INGREDIENTS POPULARLY USED IN CARIBBEAN COOKING, THIS COLORFUL, CHUNKY SOUP IS SERVED IN DEEP BOWLS AROUND A CHIVE-FLAVORED SWEET YAM MASH. OKRA GIVES THE DISH A FLAVOR THAT IS A CROSS BETWEEN ASPARAGUS AND EGGPLANT.

2 Heat the oil in a heavy-based pan. Add the garlic, onion and chile, and cook for 4–5 minutes until softened.

3 Add the salt cod and cook for 3–4 minutes, until it begins to color. Stir in the tomatoes, wine and bay leaves and bring to the boil. Pour in the water, bring to the boil, reduce the heat and simmer for 10 minutes.

4 Meanwhile, trim the stalk ends off the okra and cut the pods into chunks. Add to the soup and cook for 10 minutes. Stir in the callaloo or spinach and cook for 5 minutes, until the okra is tender.

5 Meanwhile, prepare the creamed yam. Peel the yam and cut it into large dice, then place in a pan with the lemon juice and add cold water to cover. Bring to the boil and cook for 15–20 minutes, until tender. Drain well, then return the yam to the pan and dry it out over the heat for a few seconds. Mash with the butter and cream, and season well. Stir in the chives.

6 Season the soup and stir in the chopped parsley. Spoon portions of creamed yam into the centers of six soup bowls and ladle the soup around it. Serve immediately.

SERVES 6

INGREDIENTS

    7 ounces salt cod, soaked for
       24 hours, changing the water
       several times
    1 tablespoon olive oil
    1 garlic clove, chopped
    1 onion, chopped
    1 green chile, seeded and chopped
    6 plum tomatoes, peeled and
       chopped
    8 fluid ounces/1 cup white wine
    2 bay leaves
    3¾ cups water
    8 ounces okra
    8 ounces callaloo or spinach
    2 tablespoons chopped
       fresh parsley
    salt and ground black pepper
For the creamed yam
    1½ pounds yam
    juice of 1 lemon
    2 ounces/¼ cup butter
    2 tablespoons heavy cream
    1 tablespoon chopped
       fresh chives

1 Drain and skin the salt cod, then rinse it under cold running water. Cut the flesh into bitesize pieces, removing any bones, and set aside.

Energy 322kcal/1352kJ; Protein 10.7g; Carbohydrate 36.7g, of which sugars 5.3g; Fat 12.8g, of which saturates 6.6g; Cholesterol 40mg; Calcium 159mg; Fiber 4.6g; Sodium 137mg.

COD, FAVA BEAN <u>AND</u> SPINACH CHOWDER

FRESH COD AND VEGETABLES ARE ABUNDANT IN THIS THICK AND CREAMY SOUP, WHICH IS FINISHED WITH CRISP WHOLE-WHEAT CROUTONS TO SOAK UP THE DELICIOUS LIQUID. MAKE IT EARLY IN THE SUMMER TO TAKE ADVANTAGE OF THE YOUNGEST, SWEETEST FRESH BEANS.

SERVES 6

INGREDIENTS

    4 cups milk
    ⅔ cup heavy cream
    1½ pounds cod fillet, skinned
       and boned
    3 tablespoons extra virgin
       olive oil
    1 onion, sliced
    2 garlic cloves, finely chopped
    1 pound potatoes, peeled and
       thickly sliced
    1 pound fresh fava beans,
       podded
    8 ounces baby spinach leaves
    pinch of grated nutmeg
    2 tablespoons chopped
       fresh chives
    salt and ground black pepper
    fresh chives, to garnish
For the croutons
    4 tablespoons olive oil
    6 slices whole-wheat bread,
       crusts removed, cut into
       large cubes

1 Pour the milk and cream into a large pan and bring to the boil. Add the cod and bring back to the boil. Reduce the heat and simmer for 2–3 minutes, then remove from the heat and leave to stand for about 6 minutes, until the fish is just cooked. Use a slotted spoon to remove the fish from the cooking liquid.

2 Using a fork, flake the cooked cod into chunky pieces, removing any bones or skin, then cover and set aside.

3 Heat the olive oil in a large pan and add the onion and garlic. Cook for about 5 minutes, until softened, stirring occasionally. Add the potatoes, stir in the milk mixture and bring to the boil. Reduce the heat and cover the pan. Cook for 10 minutes. Add the fava beans; cook for 10 minutes more or until the beans are tender and the potatoes just begin to break up.

4 Meanwhile, to make the croutons, heat the oil in a frying pan and add the bread cubes. Cook over a medium heat, stirring often, until golden all over. Remove using a slotted spoon and leave to drain on paper towels.

5 Add the cod to the soup and heat through gently. Just before serving, add the spinach and stir for 1–2 minutes, until wilted. Season the soup well and stir in the nutmeg and chives.

6 Ladle the soup into six warmed soup bowls and pile the croutons on top. Garnish with fresh chives and serve immediately.

COOK'S TIP
When fresh fava beans are out of season, frozen beans are acceptable as an alternative. Make sure that you cook them for the time recommended on the packet.

Energy 603kcal/2525kJ; Protein 37.9g; Carbohydrate 44.7g, of which sugars 12.2g; Fat 31.6g, of which saturates 12.4g; Cholesterol 96mg; Calcium 398mg; Fiber 7.6g; Sodium 375mg.

CAMBODIAN BAMBOO, FISH AND RICE SOUP

THIS IS A REFRESHING KHMER SOUP MADE WITH FRESHWATER FISH. A SPECIALTY OF PHNOM PENH, SAMLAW TRAPEANG IS FLAVORED WITH COCONUT MILK, THE FERMENTED FISH EXTRACT, TUK PRAHOC, LEMONGRASS AND GALANGAL—SOME OF CAMBODIA'S PRINCIPAL INGREDIENTS.

SERVES 4

INGREDIENTS

For the stock
- 1½ pounds pork ribs
- 1 onion, quartered
- 8 ounces carrots, cut into chunks
- 1 ounce dried squid or dried shrimp, soaked in water for 30 minutes, rinsed and drained
- 1 tablespoon *nuoc mam*
- 1 tablespoon soy sauce
- 6 black peppercorns
- salt

For the soup
- 3 ounces/scant ½ cup long grain rice, well rinsed
- 8 fluid ounces/1 cup coconut milk
- 2 tablespoons *tuk prahoc*
- 2 lemongrass stalks, trimmed and crushed
- 1 ounce galangal, thinly sliced
- 2 or 3 Thai chiles
- 4 garlic cloves, crushed
- 1 tablespoon jaggery
- 1 fresh bamboo shoot, peeled, boiled in water for 10 minutes, and sliced
- 1 pound freshwater fish fillets, such as carp or catfish, skinned and cut into bitesize pieces
- a small bunch fresh basil leaves
- a small bunch fresh cilantro, finely chopped, and 1 green chile, finely sliced, to garnish
- rice or noodles, to serve

1 To prepare the stock, put the ribs in a large pan and cover with 10 cups of cold water. Bring the water to the boil, skim off any fat, and add the remaining stock ingredients. Cover the pan and simmer for 1 hour, then skim off any foam or fat.

2 Continue to simmer the stock for a further 1–1½ hours, until it has reduced. Check and add more seasoning if necessary and strain the stock into another pan. There should be approximately 7¾ cups of stock.

3 Bring the pan of stock to the boil. Stir in the rice and reduce the heat. Add the coconut milk, *tuk prahoc*, lemongrass, galangal, chiles, garlic and sugar. Simmer for about 10 minutes to let the flavors mingle.

4 Add the bamboo shoot and fish. Simmer for about 5 minutes, until the fish is cooked. Check the seasoning and stir in the basil. Ladle the soup into individual bowls, garnish with the chopped cilantro and sliced chile, and serve with the rice or noodles.

Energy 181kcal/763kJ; Protein 22.8g; Carbohydrate 19.6g, of which sugars 4.3g; Fat 1.3g, of which saturates 0.2g; Cholesterol 52mg; Calcium 64mg; Fiber 0.9g; Sodium 145mg.

JAMAICAN RICE AND PEA SOUP WITH SALT COD

BASED ON THE CLASSIC CARIBBEAN DISH OF RICE AND PEAS, THIS RECIPE IS MADE WITH BLACK-EYED PEAS, BUT KIDNEY BEANS OR, MORE TRADITIONALLY, PIGEON PEAS CAN BE USED INSTEAD. THIS IS A VERY HEARTY SOUP THAT CAN BE SERVED AS A COMPLETE MEAL.

SERVES 6

INGREDIENTS

1 tablespoon sunflower oil
3 ounces/6 tablespoons butter
4 ounces thick rindless bacon strips,
    cut into lardons
1 onion, chopped
2 garlic cloves, chopped
1 red chile, seeded and chopped
8 ounces/generous 1 cup long
    grain rice
2 fresh thyme sprigs
1 cinnamon stick
1 can (14 ounces) black-eyed peas,
    drained and rinsed
3¾ cups water
12 ounces salt cod, soaked for
    24 hours, changing the water
    several times
all-purpose flour, for dusting
1 can (14 ounces) coconut milk
6 ounces baby spinach leaves
2 tablespoons chopped fresh parsley
salt and ground black pepper

1 Heat the oil and 1 ounce/2 tablespoons of the butter in a large, heavy pan. Add the bacon strips and cook for 3–4 minutes, until golden. Stir in the onion, garlic and chile and cook for a further 4–5 minutes.

2 Stir in the rice. Cook for 1–2 minutes, until the grains are translucent. Stir in the thyme, cinnamon stick and black-eyed peas and cook for 1–2 minutes. Pour in the water and bring to the boil. Reduce the heat to low and cook for 25–30 minutes.

3 Meanwhile, wash the soaked salt cod under cold running water. Pat dry with paper towels and remove the skin. Cut into large bitesize pieces and toss in the flour until evenly coated. Shake off the excess flour.

4 Melt the remaining butter in a large, heavy frying pan. Add the cod, in batches if necessary, and cook for 4–5 minutes until tender and golden. Remove the cod and set aside.

5 Stir the coconut milk into the cooked rice and peas. Remove the cinnamon stick and cook for 2–3 minutes. Stir in the spinach and cook for a further 2–3 minutes. Add the cod and chopped parsley, season and heat through. Ladle the soup into bowls and serve.

COOK'S TIP
Lardons are thicker and slightly longer than matchsticks. Cut them from thick bacon or smoked ham.

Energy 443kcal/1852kJ; Protein 30g; Carbohydrate 43.2g, of which sugars 5.1g; Fat 16.8g, of which saturates 8.3g; Cholesterol 71mg; Calcium 105mg; Fiber 3.8g; Sodium 999mg.

SMOKED COD AND POTATO SOUP

THIS THICK, CREAMY SOUP HAS A RICH, SMOKY FISH FLAVOR. USE FLOURY POTATOES THAT WILL DISINTEGRATE EASILY AND THICKEN THE SOUP.

SERVES 6

INGREDIENTS
   12 ounces smoked cod fillet
   1 onion, chopped
   bouquet garni
   3¾ cups water
   1¼ pounds floury potatoes,
      quartered
   2½ cups milk
   1½ ounces/3 tablespoons butter
   salt and ground black pepper
   chopped chives, to garnish
   crusty bread, to serve

1 Put the fish fillet, chopped onion, bouquet garni and water into a large, heavy pan and bring to the boil. Skim the scum from the surface of the liquid, then cover, reduce the heat and poach gently for 10–15 minutes, until the fish flakes easily.

2 Lift the cod from the pan, cool slightly, then remove the skin and bones. Flake the flesh and put aside. Return the skin and bones to the pan and simmer for 30 minutes.

3 Strain the fish stock and return to the pan, then add the potatoes and simmer for about 25 minutes. Remove the potatoes from the pan. Add the milk to the pan and bring to the boil.

4 Mash the potatoes with the butter, then whisk into the soup. Add the flaked fish to the pan and heat through. Season. Ladle into soup bowls, sprinkle with chives, and serve with crusty bread.

Energy 205kcal/864kJ; Protein 16.1g; Carbohydrate 19g, of which sugars 6.4g; Fat 7.8g, of which saturates 4.7g; Cholesterol 41mg; Calcium 142mg; Fiber 1g; Sodium 536mg.

BOURRIDE OF RED MULLET AND FENNEL

THIS FISH SOUP FROM PROVENCE IN FRANCE IS MADE WITH FRESH MAYONNAISE. THE SECRET OF SUCCESS IS TO COOK THE SOUP GENTLY.

SERVES 4

INGREDIENTS

1½ tablespoons olive oil
1 onion, chopped
3 garlic cloves, chopped
2 fennel bulbs, halved, cored and
  thinly sliced
4 tomatoes, chopped
1 bay leaf
1 fresh thyme sprig
5 cups fish stock
1½ pounds red mullet or snapper
8 baguette slices
1 garlic clove
2 tablespoons sun-dried
  tomato paste
12 black olives, pitted and
  quartered
salt and ground black pepper
fresh fennel fronds, to garnish
For the mayonnaise
  2 egg yolks
  2 teaspoons white wine vinegar
  1¼ cups extra virgin olive oil

1 Heat the olive oil in a large, heavy pan. Add the onion and garlic and cook for 5 minutes, until softened. Add the fennel and cook for a further 2–3 minutes. Stir in the tomatoes, bay leaf, thyme and fish stock. Bring the mixture to the boil, then reduce the heat and simmer for 30 minutes.

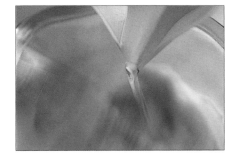

2 Meanwhile, make the mayonnaise. Put the egg yolks and vinegar in a bowl. Season and whisk well. Whisk in the oil, a little at a time, increasing the speed from a few drops at a time to a slow trickle. Transfer to a bowl and set aside.

3 Scale and fillet the mullet. Cut each fillet into two or three pieces, then add them to the soup and cook gently for 5 minutes. Use a slotted spoon to remove the mullet, and set aside.

4 Put the cooking liquid through a fine strainer, pressing the vegetables with a ladle to extract as much of the flavor as possible.

5 Whisk about a ladleful of the soup into the mayonnaise, then whisk in the remaining soup all at once.

6 Return the soup to a clean pan and cook very gently, whisking continuously, until the mixture is slightly thickened. Add the fish to the soup and set aside.

7 Toast the baguette slices on both sides. Rub each slice with the clove of garlic and spread with sun-dried tomato paste. Divide the olives among the toasted bread slices.

8 Reheat the soup, but do not allow it to boil. Ladle it into bowls and top each with two toasts. Garnish with fennel.

Energy 322kcal/1354kJ; Protein 35.3g; Carbohydrate 17.5g, of which sugars 6.4g; Fat 12.9g, of which saturates 1g; Cholesterol 0mg; Calcium 173mg; Fiber 4.4g; Sodium 299mg.

FISH <u>AND</u> SWEET POTATO SOUP

*THE SUBTLE SWEETNESS OF THE POTATO, COMBINED WITH THE FISH AND THE AROMATIC FLAVOR OF
OREGANO, MAKES THIS AN APPETIZING SOUP.*

SERVES 4

INGREDIENTS
½ onion, chopped
6 ounces sweet potato, peeled
and diced
6 ounces boneless white fish fillet,
skinned
2 ounces carrot, chopped
1 teaspoon chopped fresh oregano
or ½ teaspoon dried oregano
½ teaspoon ground cinnamon
6¼ cups fish stock
5 tablespoons light cream
chopped fresh parsley, to garnish

VARIATION
Garnish with chopped fresh tarragon
instead of parsley.

1 Put the chopped onion, diced sweet
potato, white fish, chopped carrot,
oregano, cinnamon and half the fish
stock in a pan. Bring to the boil, then
simmer for 20 minutes or until the
potato is cooked.

2 Allow to cool, then process in a
blender or food processor until smooth.

3 Return the soup to the pan, then add
the remaining fish stock and gently
bring to the boil. Reduce the heat to
low and add the cream, then gently
heat through without boiling, stirring
occasionally.

4 Serve hot in warmed soup bowls,
garnished with chopped fresh parsley.

Energy 119kcal/501kJ; Protein 9.4g; Carbohydrate 11.9g, of which sugars 4.7g; Fat 4.1g, of which saturates 2.4g; Cholesterol 30mg; Calcium 38mg; Fiber 1.6g; Sodium 53mg.

FISHERMAN'S SOUP

THERE IS SOMETHING TRULY DELICIOUS ABOUT THE COMBINED FLAVORS OF BACON AND FISH. THIS HEARTY SOUP IS IDEAL FOR A WINTER LUNCH OR SUPPER.

SERVES 4

INGREDIENTS

6 fatty bacon strips, chopped
½ ounce/1 tablespoons butter
1 large onion, chopped
1 garlic clove, finely chopped
2 tablespoons chopped
  fresh parsley
1 teaspoon fresh thyme leaves or
  ½ teaspoon dried thyme
1 pound tomatoes, peeled, seeded
  and chopped
⅔ cup dry vermouth or
  white wine
scant 2 cups fish stock
11 ounces potatoes, diced
1½–2 pounds skinless white fish
  fillets, cut into large chunks
salt and ground black pepper
fresh Italian parsley, to garnish

1 Fry the bacon in a large pan over moderate heat until lightly browned but not crisp. Remove from the pan and drain on paper towels.

2 Add the butter to the pan and cook the onion, stirring occasionally, for 3–5 minutes until soft. Add the garlic and herbs and continue cooking for 1 minute, stirring. Add the tomatoes, vermouth or wine and stock and bring to the boil.

3 Reduce the heat, cover and simmer the stew for 15 minutes. Add the potatoes, cover again and simmer for a further 10–12 minutes or until the potatoes are almost tender.

4 Add the chunks of fish and the bacon pieces. Simmer gently, uncovered, for 5 minutes or until the fish is just cooked and the potatoes are tender. Adjust the seasoning, garnish with Italian parsley and serve.

COOK'S TIP
In winter, when fresh tomatoes are lacking in flavor, you can substitute canned chopped tomatoes.

Energy 368kcal/1543kJ; Protein 39.1g; Carbohydrate 17g, of which sugars 5.6g; Fat 13.7g, of which saturates 5.4g; Cholesterol 110mg; Calcium 38mg; Fiber 2.1g; Sodium 617mg.

TOMATO SOUP <u>WITH</u> CHILE SQUID

ASIAN-STYLE SEARED SQUID MINGLES WITH THE PUNGENT TOMATO AND GARLIC FLAVORS OF THE MEDITERRANEAN IN THIS SUPERLATIVE SOUP.

3 Heat 2 tablespoons of the oil in a pan. Add the shallots and garlic, and cook for 4–5 minutes, until just softened. Stir in the tomatoes and tomato paste, and season. Cover and cook for 3 minutes. Add half the stock and simmer for 5 minutes, until the tomatoes are very soft.

4 Cool the soup, then rub it through a strainer and return it to the rinsed-out pan. Stir in the remaining stock and the sugar, and reheat gently.

5 Meanwhile, heat the remaining oil in a large frying pan. Add the squid rings and tentacles, and the chiles. Cook for 4–5 minutes, stirring continuously, then remove from the heat and stir in the chopped tarragon.

6 Taste the soup and adjust the seasoning if necessary. If the soup tastes slightly sharp, add a little extra sugar. Ladle the soup into four bowls and spoon the chile squid in the center. Serve immediately with crusty bread.

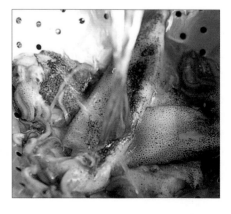

SERVES 4

INGREDIENTS

   4 small squid (or 1 or 2 large squid)
   4 tablespoons olive oil
   2 shallots, chopped
   1 garlic clove, crushed
   2½ pounds ripe tomatoes,
     roughly chopped
   1 tablespoon sun-dried
     tomato paste
   scant 2 cups vegetable stock
   about ½ teaspoon sugar
   2 red chiles, seeded and chopped
   2 tablespoons chopped fresh tarragon
   salt and ground black pepper
   crusty bread, to serve

1 To clean the squid, grasp the head and tentacles in one hand and pull the body away with the other. Discard the intestines that come away with the head. Cut the tentacles away from the head in one piece and reserve them; discard the head. Pull the plastic-like quill out of the main body and remove any roe that may be present. Pull off the fins from either side of the body pouch and rub off the semi-transparent, mottled skin. Wash the prepared squid under cold running water.

2 Cut the squid into rings and set these aside with the tentacles.

Energy 186kcal/777kJ; Protein 8.1g; Carbohydrate 10.9g, of which sugars 10.2g; Fat 12.6g, of which saturates 2g; Cholesterol 84mg; Calcium 30mg; Fiber 3.2g; Sodium 69mg.

SEAFARER'S STEW

ANY VARIETY OF FIRM FISH MAY BE USED IN THIS RECIPE, BUT BE SURE TO USE SMOKED HADDOCK AS WELL; IT IS ESSENTIAL FOR ITS DISTINCTIVE FLAVOR.

SERVES 4

INGREDIENTS

  8 ounces undyed smoked
    haddock fillet
  8 ounces fresh monkfish fillet
  20 mussels, scrubbed
  2 fatty bacon strips
  1 tablespoon extra virgin
    olive oil
  1 shallot, finely chopped
  8 ounces carrots, peeled and
    coarsely grated
  ⅔ cup light or heavy cream
  4 ounces cooked peeled shrimp
  salt and ground black pepper
  2 tablespoons chopped fresh parsley,
    to garnish

5 Stir in the cream together with the haddock, monkfish, mussels and shrimp and heat gently, without boiling. Season and serve in large bowls, garnished with parsley.

1 In a large, heavy pan, simmer the haddock and monkfish in 5 cups water for 5 minutes, then add the mussels and cover the pan.

2 Cook for a further 5 minutes or until all the mussels have opened. Discard any that have not. Drain, reserving the liquid. Return the liquid to the rinsed pan and set aside.

3 Flake the haddock, removing any skin and bones, then cut the monkfish into large chunks. Cut the bacon into strips.

4 Heat the oil in a heavy frying pan and fry the shallot and bacon for 3–4 minutes or until the shallot is soft and the bacon lightly browned. Add to the strained fish broth, bring to the boil, then add the grated carrots and cook for 10 minutes.

Energy 255kcal/1070kJ; Protein 31.3g; Carbohydrate 7.1g, of which sugars 5.8g; Fat 11.5g, of which saturates 5.9g; Cholesterol 123mg; Calcium 101mg; Fiber 1.6g; Sodium 748mg.

SMOKED HADDOCK CHOWDER

BASED ON A TRADITIONAL SCOTTISH RECIPE, THIS SOUP HAS AMERICAN-STYLE SWEETNESS FROM THE SWEET POTATOES AND BUTTERNUT SQUASH, AND IS FLAVORED WITH A HINT OF THAI BASIL.

SERVES 6

INGREDIENTS

14 ounces sweet potatoes
  (pink-fleshed variety)
8 ounces butternut squash
2 ounces /¼ cup butter
1 onion, chopped
1 pound smoked haddock fillets
1¼ cups water
2½ cups milk
small handful of Thai basil leaves
4 tablespoons heavy cream
salt and ground black pepper

3 Use a sharp knife to skin the smoked haddock fillets.

4 Add the fillets and water to the pan. Bring to the boil, reduce the heat and simmer for 10 minutes, until the fish is cooked. Use a slotted spoon to lift the fish out of the pan, and leave to cool. Set the cooking liquid aside.

5 When cool enough to handle, carefully break the flesh into large flakes, discarding the skin and bones. Set the fish aside.

6 Press the sweet potatoes through a strainer and beat in the remaining butter with seasoning to taste. Strain the reserved fish cooking liquid and return it to the rinsed pan, then whisk in the sweet potato. Stir in the milk and bring to the boil. Simmer for about 2–3 minutes.

7 Stir in the butternut squash, fish, Thai basil leaves and cream. Season the soup to taste and heat through without boiling. Ladle the soup into six warmed soup bowls and serve immediately.

1 Peel the sweet potatoes and butternut squash and cut into small, bitesize pieces. Cook them separately in boiling salted water for 15 minutes or until just tender. Drain both well.

2 Melt half the butter in a large, heavy pan. Add the onion and cook for 4–5 minutes, until soft.

COOK'S TIP
The best type of smoked fish to use in this recipe is Finnan haddock, but other types of smoked haddock can be used with almost equal success.

Energy 285kcal/1196kJ; Protein 19.1g; Carbohydrate 20.7g, of which sugars 9.9g; Fat 14.7g, of which saturates 8.9g; Cholesterol 64mg; Calcium 166mg; Fiber 2.1g; Sodium 173mg.

SOUP NIÇOISE WITH SEARED TUNA

INGREDIENTS FOR THE FAMOUS SALAD FROM NICE IN THE SOUTH OF FRANCE ARE TRANSFORMED INTO A SIMPLE, YET ELEGANT, SOUP BY ADDING A HOT GARLIC-INFUSED STOCK.

SERVES 4

INGREDIENTS
  12 bottled anchovy fillets, drained
  2 tablespoons milk
  4 ounces green beans, halved
  4 plum tomatoes
  16 black olives, pitted
  1¾ pints/4 cups good
    vegetable stock
  3 garlic cloves, crushed
  2 tablespoons lemon juice
  1 tablespoon olive oil
  4 tuna steaks, about 3 ounces each
  small bunch of scallions,
    shredded lengthwise
  handful of fresh basil leaves,
    finely shredded
  salt and ground black pepper
  fresh crusty bread, to serve

1 Soak the anchovies in the milk for 10 minutes. Drain well and dry on paper towels.

2 Cook the green beans in boiling salted water for 2–3 minutes. Drain, refresh under cold running water and drain. Split any thick beans diagonally lengthwise. Wash the olives to remove any oil, then cut into quarters.

3 Peel, halve and seed the tomatoes, then cut into wedges. Set all the prepared ingredients aside.

4 Bring the stock to the boil in a large, heavy pan. Add the garlic, reduce the heat and simmer for 10 minutes. Season the stock well and add the lemon juice.

5 Meanwhile, brush a griddle pan or frying pan with the oil and heat until very hot. Season the tuna and cook for about 2 minutes on each side. Do not overcook the tuna or it will become dry.

6 Gently toss together the green beans, tomatoes, scallions, anchovies, black olives and shredded basil leaves.

7 Put the seared tuna steaks into four bowls and pile the vegetable mixture on top. Carefully ladle the hot garlic stock around the ingredients. Serve at once, with crusty bread.

COOK'S TIP
Buy anchovy fillets that have been bottled in extra virgin olive oil if you can, as they have a far superior flavor to the smaller anchovy fillets.

Energy 217kcal/909kJ; Protein 27.4g; Carbohydrate 3g, of which sugars 2.7g; Fat 10.7g, of which saturates 2.2g; Cholesterol 34mg; Calcium 76mg; Fiber 2g; Sodium 829mg.

CULLEN SKINK

THIS IS A TRADITIONAL SCOTTISH SOUP. A CULLEN IS A SEATOWN OR PORT DISTRICT OF A TOWN, WHILE SKINK MEANS STOCK OR BROTH.

3 Pour the stock through a strainer and return to the pan.

4 Add the potatoes and simmer for about 25 minutes, or until tender. Remove the potatoes from the pan using a slotted spoon.

5 Add the milk to the pan and bring to the boil.

6 Meanwhile, mash the potatoes with the butter, then whisk into the liquid in the pan until thick and creamy. Add the flaked fish to the pan and adjust the seasoning. Sprinkle with chives and serve immediately.

SERVES 6

INGREDIENTS
    1 Finnan haddock, about 12 ounces
    1 onion, chopped
    bouquet garni
    3¾ cups water
    1¼ pounds potatoes, quartered
    2½ cups milk
    1½ ounces/3 tablespoons butter
    salt and ground black pepper
    chopped fresh chives, to garnish

1 Put the haddock, onion, bouquet garni and water into a pan and bring to the boil. Reduce the heat, cover and poach for 10–15 minutes.

2 Lift the cooked haddock from the pan, using a fish slice, and remove the skin and bones. Flake the flesh and reserve. Return the skin and bones to the pan and simmer, uncovered, for 30 minutes.

Energy 205kcal/864kJ; Protein 16.1g; Carbohydrate 19g, of which sugars 6.4g; Fat 7.8g, of which saturates 4.7g; Cholesterol 41mg; Calcium 137mg; Fiber 1g; Sodium 132mg.

SMOKED COD AND OKRA SOUP

*THE INSPIRATION FOR THIS SOUP CAME FROM A GHANAIAN RECIPE FOR OKRA SOUP. HERE IT IS
ENHANCED BY THE ADDITION OF SMOKED FISH.*

SERVES 4

INGREDIENTS
  2 green bananas
  2 ounces/4 tablespoons butter
    or margarine
  1 onion, finely chopped
  2 tomatoes, peeled and finely chopped
  4 ounces okra, trimmed
  8 ounces smoked cod fillet, cut into
    bitesize pieces
  3¾ cups fish stock
  1 fresh chile, seeded and chopped
  salt and ground black pepper
  sprigs of fresh parsley, to garnish

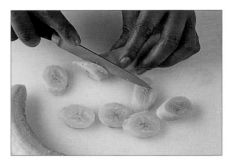

3 Add the cod, fish stock, chile and
seasoning. Bring to the boil, then
reduce the heat and simmer for about
20 minutes or until the cod is cooked
through and flakes easily.

4 Peel the cooked bananas and cut into
slices. Stir into the soup, heat through
for a few minutes, and ladle into
warmed soup bowls. Garnish with sprigs
of parsley and serve piping hot.

1 Slit the skins of the green bananas
and place in a large pan. Cover with
water, bring to the boil and cook over a
moderate heat for 25 minutes, until the
bananas are tender. Transfer to a plate
and leave to cool.

2 Melt the butter or margarine in a
large pan and sauté the onion for about
5 minutes until soft. Stir in the chopped
tomatoes and okra and fry gently for a
further 10 minutes.

Energy 230kcal/963kJ; Protein 12.6g; Carbohydrate 20.9g, of which sugars 18.6g; Fat 11.3g, of which saturates 6.8g; Cholesterol 53mg; Calcium 65mg; Fiber 2.6g; Sodium 741mg.

FISH BALL SOUP

THE JAPANESE NAME FOR THIS SOUP IS TSUMIRE-JIRU. TSUMIRE MEANS, QUITE LITERALLY, SARDINE BALLS, AND THESE ARE ADDED TO THIS DELICIOUS SOUP TO IMPART THEIR ROBUST FLAVOR.

SERVES 4

INGREDIENTS

3½ fluid ounces/generous ⅓ cup
   sake or dry white wine
5 cups instant dashi
4 tablespoons white miso paste
5 ounces shimeji mushrooms or
   6 shiitake mushrooms
1 leek or large scallion
For the fish balls
   ¾ ounce fresh ginger root
   1¾ pounds fresh sardines, gutted
     and heads removed
   2 tablespoons white miso paste
   1 tablespoon sake or dry
     white wine
   1½ teaspoons sugar
   1 egg
   2 tablespoons cornstarch

1 First make the fish balls. To do this, grate the ginger and squeeze it well to yield 1 teaspoon ginger juice.

2 Rinse the sardines, then cut in half along the backbone. Remove all the bones. To skin a boned sardine, lay it skin-side down, then run a sharp knife along the skin from tail to head.

3 Coarsely chop the sardines and process with the ginger juice, miso, sake or wine, sugar and egg to a thick paste in a food processor or blender. Transfer to a bowl and mix in the cornstarch until thoroughly blended.

4 Trim the shimeji mushrooms, or either separate each stem or remove the stems from the shiitake mushrooms. Shred the mushrooms. Cut the leek or scallion into 1½-inch strips.

5 Bring the ingredients for the soup to the boil. Use two wet spoons to shape small portions of the sardine mixture into bitesize balls and drop them into the soup. Add the prepared mushrooms and leek or scallion.

6 Simmer the soup until the sardine balls float to the surface. Ladle the soup into individual, deep soup bowls, and serve immediately.

COOK'S TIP
If fresh shimeji or shiitake mushrooms are not available, use dried ones instead. Put them in a bowl, pour over boiling water and leave to stand for 30 minutes.

Energy 322kcal/1348kJ; Protein 33.9g; Carbohydrate 10.6g, of which sugars 3.3g; Fat 14.4g, of which saturates 4.1g; Cholesterol 48mg; Calcium 176mg; Fiber 1.3g; Sodium 462mg.

CREAMY FISH CHOWDER

A TRADITIONAL SOUP THAT NEVER FAILS TO PLEASE, WHETHER IT IS MADE WITH MILK OR, MORE LUXURIOUSLY, WITH A GENEROUS AMOUNT OF CREAM.

SERVES 4

INGREDIENTS
   3 thick-cut bacon strips
   1 large onion
   1½ pounds potatoes
   4 cups fish stock
   1 pound skinless haddock, cut into
     1-inch cubes
   2 tablespoons chopped fresh parsley
   1 tablespoon chopped fresh chives
   1¼ cups whipping cream or whole
     milk
   salt and ground black pepper

1 Remove the rind from the bacon and discard it; then cut the bacon into small pieces. Chop the onion and cut the potatoes into ¾-inch cubes.

2 Fry the bacon in a deep pan until the fat is rendered. Add the onion and potatoes and cook over low heat, without browning, for about 10 minutes. Season to taste.

3 Pour off excess bacon fat from the pan. Add the fish stock and bring to a boil. Simmer until the vegetables are tender, about 15–20 minutes.

4 Stir in the cubes of fish, the parsley and chives. Simmer for about 3–4 minutes, until the fish is just cooked.

5 Stir the cream or milk into the chowder and reheat gently, but do not bring to the boil. Season to taste.

6 Ladle into warmed soup bowls and serve immediately.

Energy 329kcal/1386kJ; Protein 30.3g; Carbohydrate 34.5g, of which sugars 8.4g; Fat 8.6g, of which saturates 3.7g; Cholesterol 63mg; Calcium 128mg; Fiber 2.4g; Sodium 364mg.

SMOKED COD CHOWDER

THE SHARP FLAVOR OF THE SMOKED COD CONTRASTS WELL WITH THE CREAMY SOUP. SERVE THIS SOUP AS A SUBSTANTIAL APPETIZER BEFORE A LIGHT MAIN COURSE. WARM, CRUSTY WHOLE-WHEAT BREAD GOES WELL WITH IT.

SERVES 4–6

INGREDIENTS
    12 ounces smoked cod fillet
    1 small onion, finely chopped
    1 bay leaf
    4 black peppercorns
    3¾ cups milk
    2 teaspoons cornstarch
    2 teaspoons cold water
    1 can (7 ounces) corn kernels
    1 tablespoon chopped fresh parsley
    crusty whole-wheat bread,
        to serve

2 Bring to the boil. Reduce the heat and simmer very gently for 12–15 minutes, or until the fish is just cooked.

5 Drain the corn and add to the pan together with the flaked fish and chopped fresh parsley.

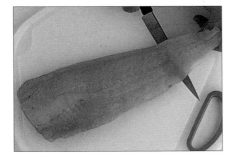

1 Skin the fish with a knife and put it into a large pan with the onion, bay leaf, black peppercorns and milk.

COOK'S TIP
The flavor of the chowder improves if it is made a day in advance. Chill in the refrigerator until required, then reheat gently to prevent the fish disintegrating.

3 Using a slotted spoon, lift out the fish and flake it into large chunks. Remove and discard the bay leaf and peppercorns.

4 Blend the cornstarch with the water carefully until it forms a smooth paste, and add to the pan. Bring to the boil and simmer until slightly thickened.

VARIATION
Haddock fillets would be equally good in this chowder, or try smoked fillets for a stronger taste.

6 Reheat the soup until it is piping hot, but do not boil, taking care that the fish does not disintegrate.

7 Ladle into warmed soup bowls and serve immediately with plenty of warm crusty whole-wheat bread.

Energy 166kcal/702kJ; Protein 16.9g; Carbohydrate 18.2g, of which sugars 10.8g; Fat 3.4g, of which saturates 1.7g; Cholesterol 36mg; Calcium 189mg; Fiber 0.6g; Sodium 191mg.

ARUGULA SOUP WITH KILN-SMOKED SALMON

KILN-SMOKED SALMON HAS ACTUALLY BEEN "COOKED" DURING THE SMOKING PROCESS, PRODUCING A DELICIOUS FLAKY TEXTURE. THIS IS IN CONTRAST TO TRADITIONAL COLD-SMOKED SALMON, WHICH IS NOT ACTUALLY COOKED BUT DOES NOT SPOIL BECAUSE IT HAS BEEN PRESERVED FIRST IN BRINE.

2 Add the cream and stock, stir in gently and bring slowly to the boil. Allow to simmer gently for about 5 minutes.

3 Add the arugula, reserving a few leaves to garnish, and the basil, then return the soup briefly to the boil and turn off the heat. Add a little cold water and allow to cool for a few minutes.

4 Puree in a blender until smooth, adding a little salt and pepper to taste. When ready to serve, reheat gently but do not allow to boil.

5 Serve in warmed bowls with a few flakes of salmon, a leaf or two of arugula and a drizzle of virgin olive oil over the top.

SERVES 4

INGREDIENTS
  1 tablespoon olive oil
  1 small onion, sliced
  1 garlic clove, crushed
  ⅔ cup heavy cream
  12 fluid ounces/1½ cups
    vegetable stock
  12 ounces arugula
  4 fresh basil leaves
  salt and ground black pepper
  flaked kiln-smoked salmon and virgin
    olive oil, to garnish

1 Put the olive oil in a high-sided pan over medium heat and allow to heat up. Add the sliced onion and sweat for a few minutes, stirring continuously. Add the garlic and continue to sweat gently until soft and transparent, although you should not allow the onion to color.

VARIATION
Cold-smoked salmon is also very good with this soup, and can be used if you can't find the kiln-smoked variety. Simply cut a few slices into medium to thick strips and add to the hot soup. Warming the smoked salmon for a few minutes increases the flavor.

Energy 258kcal/1063kJ; Protein 6.8g; Carbohydrate 3.2g, of which sugars 2.8g; Fat 24.3g, of which saturates 13.1g; Cholesterol 56mg; Calcium 174mg; Fiber 2.1g; Sodium 395mg.

HOT-AND-SOUR FISH SOUP

THIS UNUSUAL TANGY SOUP, CANH CHUA CA, CAN BE FOUND THROUGHOUT SOUTHEAST ASIA— WITH THE BALANCE OF HOT, SWEET AND SOUR FLAVORS VARYING FROM CAMBODIA TO THAILAND TO VIETNAM. CHILES PROVIDE THE HEAT, TAMARIND PRODUCES THE TARTNESS.

SERVES 4

INGREDIENTS

1 catfish, sea bass or red snapper, about 2¼ pounds, filleted
1 ounce dried squid, soaked in water for 30 minutes
1 tablespoon vegetable oil
2 scallions, sliced
2 shallots, sliced
1½-inch fresh ginger root, peeled and chopped
2 or 3 lemongrass stalks, cut into strips and crushed
2 tablespoons tamarind paste
2 or 3 Thai chiles, seeded and sliced
1 tablespoon sugar
2–3 tablespoons *nuoc mam*
8 ounces fresh pineapple, peeled and diced
3 tomatoes, skinned, seeded and roughly chopped
2 ounces canned sliced bamboo shoots, drained
1 small bunch fresh cilantro, stalks removed, leaves finely chopped
salt and ground black pepper
4 ounces/½ cup bean sprouts and 1 bunch dill, fronds roughly chopped, to garnish
lime quarters, to serve
For the marinade
2 tablespoons *nuoc mam*
2 garlic cloves, finely chopped

1 Cut the fish into bitesize pieces. Reserve the head, tail and bones for the stock. In a bowl, mix together the marinade ingredients and add the fish pieces. Toss until well coated, cover and set aside. Drain and rinse the soaked dried squid.

COOK'S TIP
Depending on your mood, or your palate, you can adjust the balance of hot and sour by adding more chile or tamarind to taste. Enjoyed as a meal in itself, the soup is usually served with plain steamed rice.

2 Heat the oil in a deep pan and stir in the scallions, shallots, ginger, lemongrass and dried squid. Add the reserved fish head, tail and bones, and sauté for 1 minute. Add 5 cups water and bring to the boil. Reduce the heat and simmer for 30 minutes.

3 Strain the stock into another deep pan and bring the clear broth to the boil. Stir in the tamarind paste, chiles, sugar and *nuoc mam*, and simmer for 2–3 minutes.

4 Add the pineapple, tomatoes and bamboo shoots, and simmer for a further 2–3 minutes.

5 Finally stir in the fish pieces and the chopped fresh cilantro, and cook until the fish turns opaque.

6 Season to taste and ladle the soup into hot bowls. Garnish with bean sprouts and dill, and serve with the lime quarters to squeeze over.

Energy 335kcal/1415kJ; Protein 44g; Carbohydrate 24g, of which sugars 19g; Fat 7g, of which saturates 1g; Cholesterol 108mg; Calcium 138mg; Fiber 2.3g; Sodium 1.2g.

SEAFOOD SOUP <u>WITH</u> ROUILLE

THIS IS A REALLY CHUNKY, AROMATIC MIXED FISH SOUP FROM FRANCE, FLAVORED WITH PLENTY OF SAFFRON AND HERBS. ROUILLE, A FIERY HOT PASTE, IS SERVED SEPARATELY FOR EVERYONE TO SWIRL INTO THEIR SOUP TO FLAVOR.

SERVES 6

INGREDIENTS

- 3 gurnard or red mullet, scaled and gutted
- 12 large shrimp
- 1½ pounds white fish, such as cod, haddock, halibut or monkfish
- 8 ounces mussels
- 1 onion, quartered
- 5 cups water
- 1 teaspoon saffron threads
- 5 tablespoons olive oil
- 1 fennel bulb, roughly chopped
- 4 garlic cloves, crushed
- 3 strips pared orange rind
- 4 sprigs of thyme
- 1½ pounds tomatoes or 1 can (14 ounces) chopped tomatoes
- 2 tablespoons sun-dried tomato paste
- 3 bay leaves
- salt and ground black pepper

For the *rouille*

- 1 red bell pepper, seeded and roughly chopped
- 1 fresh red chile, seeded and sliced
- 2 garlic cloves, chopped
- 5 tablespoons olive oil
- ½ ounce/¼ cup fresh bread crumbs

1 To make the *rouille*, process the pepper, chile, garlic, oil and bread crumbs in a blender or food processor until smooth. Transfer to a serving dish and chill until required.

2 Fillet the gurnard or mullet by cutting away the flesh from the backbone. Reserve the heads and bones. Cut the fillets into small chunks. Shell half the shrimp and reserve the trimmings to make the stock. Skin the white fish, discarding any bones, and cut into large chunks. Scrub the mussels well, discarding any that are open.

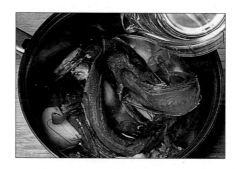

3 Put the fish trimmings and shrimp trimmings in a pan with the onion and water. Bring to the boil, then simmer gently for 30 minutes. Cool slightly and strain.

4 Soak the saffron threads in 1 tablespoon boiling water.

5 Heat 2 tablespoons of the oil in a large sauté pan. Add the gurnard or mullet and white fish and fry over a high heat for 1 minute. Drain.

6 Heat the remaining oil and fry the fennel, garlic, orange rind and thyme until beginning to color. Make up the strained stock to about 5 cups with water.

7 If using fresh tomatoes, plunge them into boiling water for 30 seconds, then refresh in cold water. Peel and chop. Add the stock to the pan with the saffron, tomatoes, tomato puree and bay leaves. Season, bring almost to the boil, then simmer gently, covered, for 20 minutes.

8 Stir in the gurnard or mullet, white fish, shelled and non-shelled shrimp and mussels. Cover the pan and cook for 3–4 minutes. Discard any mussels that do not open.

9 Ladle the soup into warmed bowls and serve hot with the *rouille* in a separate serving dish.

Energy 349kcal/1462kJ; Protein 45.4g; Carbohydrate 9.6g, of which sugars 6.5g; Fat 14.5g, of which saturates 1.7g; Cholesterol 100mg; Calcium 117mg; Fiber 2.6g; Sodium 318mg.

SHELLFISH SOUPS

If you like shellfish, you will find some of the most delicious and luxurious soups in this section. Clam Chowder is a classic recipe from New England, while Soft-shell Crab, Shrimp and Corn Bisque is a favorite Louisiana dish. Or you could try traditional Mussel and Fennel Bree, or Shore Crab Soup, both from Scotland. From China there is Wonton and Shrimp Tail Soup, and from Thailand comes Coconut and Seafood Soup, as well as Thai Shrimp and Squash Soup.

SEAFOOD CHOWDER

CHOWDER TAKES ITS NAME FROM THE FRENCH WORD FOR CAULDRON—CHAUDIÈRE—THE TYPE OF POT TRADITIONALLY USED FOR SOUPS AND STEWS. LIKE MOST CHOWDERS, THIS IS A SUBSTANTIAL DISH, WHICH COULD EASILY BE SERVED WITH CRUSTY BREAD FOR A LUNCH OR SUPPER.

SERVES 4–6

INGREDIENTS

7 ounces/generous 1 cup drained,
    canned corn kernels
2½ cups milk
½ ounce/1 tablespoon butter
1 small leek, sliced
1 small garlic clove, crushed
2 rindless smoked fatty bacon
    strips, chopped
1 small green bell pepper, seeded
    and diced
1 celery stalk, chopped
4 ounces/generous ½ cup white
    long grain rice
1 teaspoon all-purpose flour
scant 2 cups hot chicken or
    vegetable stock
4 large scallops, preferably
    with corals
4 ounces white fish fillet, such
    as monkfish or plaice
1 tablespoon finely chopped
    fresh parsley
a good pinch of cayenne pepper
2–3 tablespoons light cream
    (optional)
salt and ground black pepper

1 Place half the corn kernels in a food processor or blender. Add a little of the milk and process until thick and creamy.

VARIATION
Instead of monkfish or plaice, try this chowder with haddock or cod, which go well with cream, if you are using it.

2 Melt the butter in a large pan and gently fry the leek, garlic and bacon for 4–5 minutes until the leek has softened but not browned. Add the diced green pepper and chopped celery and sweat over a very gentle heat for 3–4 minutes more, stirring frequently.

3 Stir in the rice and cook for a few minutes until the grains begin to swell. Sprinkle over the flour. Cook, stirring occasionally, for about 1 minute, then gradually stir in the remaining milk and the stock.

4 Bring the mixture to the boil over a medium heat, then lower the heat and stir in the creamed corn mixture, with the whole corn kernels. Season well.

5 Cover the pan and simmer the chowder very gently for 20 minutes or until the rice is tender, stirring occasionally, and adding a little more chicken stock or water if the mixture thickens too quickly or the rice begins to stick to the bottom of the pan.

6 Pull the corals away from the scallops and slice the white flesh into ¼-inch pieces. Cut the fish fillet into bitesize chunks.

7 Stir the scallops and fish into the chowder, cook for 4 minutes, then stir in the corals, parsley and cayenne. Cook for a few minutes to heat through, then stir in the cream, if using. Adjust the seasoning and serve.

Energy 361kcal/1520kJ; Protein 21.9g; Carbohydrate 47.1g, of which sugars 13.6g; Fat 10.1g, of which saturates 4.9g; Cholesterol 41mg; Calcium 213mg; Fiber 2.1g; Sodium 437mg.

WONTON AND SHRIMP TAIL SOUP

A WELL-FLAVORED CHICKEN STOCK OR BROTH IS A MUST FOR THIS CLASSIC CHINESE SNACK, WHICH IS POPULAR ON FAST-FOOD STALLS IN TOWNS AND CITIES THROUGHOUT SOUTHERN CHINA. SERVE IT AS AN APPETIZER OR PART OF A MAIN MEAL.

SERVES 4

INGREDIENTS

    7 ounces ground pork
    7 ounces cooked, peeled shrimp,
      thawed if frozen
    2 teaspoons rice wine or
      dry sherry
    2 teaspoons light soy sauce
    1 teaspoon sesame oil
    24 thin wonton wrappers
    5 cups chicken stock
    12 jumbo shrimp, shelled, with
      tails still on
    12 ounces bok choy,
      coarsely shredded
    salt and ground black pepper
    4 scallions, sliced, and ½-inch piece
      fresh ginger root, finely shredded,
      to garnish

1 Put the pork, shrimp, rice wine or sherry, soy sauce and sesame oil in a large bowl. Add plenty of seasoning and mix the ingredients thoroughly.

2 Put about 2 teaspoons of pork mixture in the center of each wonton wrapper. Bring up the sides of the wrapper and pinch them together to seal the filling in a small bundle.

3 Bring a large pan of water to the boil. Add the wontons and cook for 3 minutes, then drain well and set aside.

4 Pour the stock into a pan and bring to the boil. Season to taste. Add the jumbo shrimp and cook for 2–3 minutes, until just tender. Add the wontons and bok choy and cook for 1–2 minutes. Garnish with scallions and ginger to serve.

Energy 208kcal/874kJ; Protein 26.8g; Carbohydrate 11.8g, of which sugars 2.2g; Fat 6.2g, of which saturates 2g; Cholesterol 179mg; Calcium 234mg; Fiber 2.4g; Sodium 655mg.

CRAB AND ASPARAGUS SOUP WITH NUOC CHAM

IN THIS DELICIOUS VIETNAMESE SOUP, THE RECIPE HAS CLEARLY BEEN ADAPTED FROM THE CLASSIC FRENCH ASPARAGUS VELOUTÉ TO PRODUCE A MEATIER VERSION THAT HAS MORE TEXTURE, AND THE VIETNAMESE STAMP OF NUOC CHAM, A CHILLI DIPPING SAUCE.

SERVES 4

INGREDIENTS
 1 tablespoon vegetable oil
 2 shallots, finely chopped
 2 garlic cloves, finely chopped
 1 tablespoon rice flour
   or cornstarch
 8 ounces /1⅓ cups cooked crab
   meat, chopped into small pieces
 1 pound preserved asparagus, finely
   chopped, or 1 pound fresh
   asparagus, trimmed and steamed
 salt and ground black pepper
 basil and cilantro leaves,
   to garnish
 nuoc cham, to serve
For the stock
 1 meaty chicken carcass
 1 ounce dried shrimp, soaked in
   water for 30 minutes, rinsed
   and drained
 2 onions, peeled and quartered
 2 garlic cloves, crushed
 1 tablespoon *nuoc mam*
 6 black peppercorns
 sea salt

1 To make the stock, put the chicken carcass into a deep pan. Add all the other stock ingredients, except the salt, and pour in 8 cups water. Boil for a few minutes, skim off any foam, then reduce the heat and simmer gently with the lid on for 1½–2 hours. Remove the lid and simmer for a further 30 minutes to reduce the stock. Skim off any fat, season with salt, then strain the stock and measure out roughly 6¼ cups.

2 Heat the oil in a deep pan or wok. Stir in the shallots and garlic, until they begin to color. Remove from the heat, stir in the flour, and then pour in the stock. Put the pan back over the heat and bring the liquid to the boil, stirring constantly, until smooth.

COOK'S TIPS
• You can increase the quantity of crabmeat as much as you like, to make a soup that is very rich and filling.
• Jars of asparagus preserved in brine are used for this recipe, or fresh asparagus that has been steamed until very soft and tender. It is best to avoid canned asparagus, because it tends to have a metallic taste.

3 Add the crabmeat and asparagus, reduce the heat and leave to simmer for 15–20 minutes. Season to taste with salt and pepper, then ladle the soup into bowls, garnish with fresh basil and cilantro leaves, and serve with a splash of *nuoc cham*.

Energy 142kcal/590kJ; Protein 17.1g; Carbohydrate 6.9g, of which sugars 3g; Fat 5.1g, of which saturates 0.6g; Cholesterol 72mg; Calcium 177mg; Fiber 2.1g; Sodium 584mg.

MUSSEL AND FENNEL BREE

Bree is the Scottish word for a soup or broth, most often associated with shellfish rather like a bisque or bouillabaisse. Mussels are particularly good partners for the anise flavor of Pernod or Ricard. Try to get the native Scottish mussels that are smaller with a good flavor. You will need two pans for this dish, one to cook the mussels in and one for the bree.

SERVES 4

INGREDIENTS

2¼ pounds fresh mussels
1 fennel bulb
4 fluid ounces/½ cup dry
  white wine
1 leek, finely sliced
olive oil
1 ounce/2 tablespoons butter
splash of Pernod or Ricard
⅔ cup heavy cream
1 ounce fresh parsley, chopped

2 Strip off the coarse outer leaves of the fennel and roughly chop them. Set to one side. Then take the central core of the fennel and chop it very finely. Set the chopped core aside in a separate dish or bowl.

3 Place the roughly chopped fennel leaves, the mussels and the wine in a large pan, cover and cook gently until all the mussels open, for about 5 minutes. Discard any mussels that remain closed.

6 Strain the liquor onto the leek mixture and bring to the boil. Add a little water and the pastis, and simmer for a few minutes.

7 Add the cream and parsley and bring back to the boil.

8 Place the mussels in a serving tureen and pour over the soup. Serve piping hot with crusty bread for mopping up the juices.

COOK'S TIP
Farmed or "rope-grown" mussels are easier to clean. If you use mussels with lots of barnacles you will need to remove these first.

1 Clean the mussels thoroughly, removing any beards and scraping off any barnacles. Discard any that are broken or open.

4 In a second pan, heat the oil and butter, add the leek and finely chopped core of the fennel, and cook gently, stirring continuously, until soft.

5 Meanwhile remove the mussels from the first pan and either leave in the shell or remove and discard the shells. Set aside while you make the bree.

Energy 392kcal/1624kJ; Protein 13.4g; Carbohydrate 5.7g, of which sugars 3g; Fat 33g, of which saturates 16.9g; Cholesterol 105mg; Calcium 95mg; Fiber 2.8g; Sodium 297mg.

THAI SHRIMP AND SQUASH SOUP

THIS SQUASH SOUP COMES FROM NORTHERN THAILAND. IT IS QUITE HEARTY, SOMETHING OF A CROSS BETWEEN A SOUP AND A STEW. THE BANANA FLOWER ISN'T ESSENTIAL—YOU MAY FIND IT DIFFICULT TO OBTAIN—BUT IT DOES ADD A UNIQUE AND AUTHENTIC FLAVOR.

SERVES 4

INGREDIENTS
  1 butternut squash, about 11 ounces
  4 cups vegetable stock
  3½ ounces/scant 1 cup green beans,
    cut into 1-inch pieces
  1¾ ounces dried banana
    flower (optional)
  1 tablespoon Thai fish sauce
  8 ounces raw shrimp
  small bunch fresh basil
  cooked rice, to serve
For the chili paste
  4 ounces shallots, sliced
  10 drained bottled green peppercorns
  1 small fresh green chile, seeded
    and finely chopped
  ½ teaspoon shrimp paste

1 Peel the butternut squash and cut it in half. Scoop out the seeds with a teaspoon and discard, then cut the flesh into neat cubes. Set aside.

2 Make the chili paste by pounding the shallots, peppercorns, chile and shrimp paste together using a mortar and pestle or pureeing them in a spice blender.

3 Heat the stock gently in a large pan, then stir in the chili paste. Add the squash, beans and banana flower, if using. Bring to the boil and cook for 15 minutes.

4 Add the fish sauce, shrimp and basil. Bring to simmering point, then simmer for 3 minutes. Serve in warmed bowls, accompanied by rice.

Energy 64kcal/271kJ; Protein 11.3g; Carbohydrate 3.4g, of which sugars 2.8g; Fat 0.7g, of which saturates 0.2g; Cholesterol 110mg; Calcium 82mg; Fiber 1.7g; Sodium 199mg.

SHORE CRAB SOUP

THESE LITTLE CRABS HAVE A VELVET FEEL TO THEIR SHELL. THEY ARE MOSTLY CAUGHT OFF THE WEST COAST OF SCOTLAND, AND CAN BE QUITE DIFFICULT TO FIND AT THE SUPERMARKET. IF YOU HAVE TROUBLE FINDING THEM, YOU CAN ALSO USE COMMON OR BROWN CRABS FOR THIS RECIPE.

SERVES 4

INGREDIENTS
  2¼ pounds shore or velvet crabs
  2 ounces/¼ cup butter
  2 ounces leek, washed and chopped
  2 ounces carrot, chopped
  2 tablespoons brandy
  8 ounces ripe tomatoes, chopped
  1 tablespoon tomato paste
  4 fluid ounces/½ cup dry
    white wine
  6¼ cups fish stock
  sprig of fresh tarragon
  4 tablespoons heavy cream
  lemon juice

1 Bring a large pan of water to a rolling boil and plunge the live crabs into it. They will be killed very quickly, and the bigger the pan and the more water there is, the better. Once the crabs are dead—a couple of minutes at most—take them out of the water, place in a large bowl and smash them up. This can be done with either a wooden mallet or the end of a rolling pin.

2 Melt the butter in a heavy pan, add the leek and carrot and cook gently until soft but not colored.

COOK'S TIP
If you don't have fish stock then water will do, or you could use some of the water used to boil the crabs initially.

VARIATION
Crème fraîche may be used in place of heavy cream, if you prefer.

3 Add the crabs and continue cooking. When very hot, pour in the brandy, stirring to allow the flavor to pervade the whole pan.

4 Add the tomatoes, tomato paste, wine, stock and tarragon. Bring to the boil and simmer gently for about 30 minutes.

5 Push the soup through a metal strainer, forcing as much of the tomato mixture through as possible. (If you like you could remove the big claws and puree the remains in a blender.)

6 Return to the heat, simmer for a few minutes then season to taste. Add the cream and lemon juice, and serve.

Energy 419kcal/1741kJ; Protein 35.1g; Carbohydrate 3.8g, of which sugars 3.6g; Fat 25.7g, of which saturates 15.1g; Cholesterol 196mg; Calcium 252mg; Fiber 1.1g; Sodium 1122mg.

CLAM CHOWDER

IF FRESH CLAMS ARE HARD TO FIND, USE FROZEN OR CANNED CLAMS FOR THIS CLASSIC RECIPE FROM NEW ENGLAND. LARGE CLAMS SHOULD BE CUT INTO CHUNKY PIECES. RESERVE A FEW CLAMS IN THEIR SHELLS TO GARNISH, IF YOU LIKE. TRADITIONALLY, THE SOUP IS SERVED WITH SALTINE CRACKERS. YOU SHOULD BE ABLE TO FIND THESE IN ANY GOOD SUPERMARKET.

SERVES 4

INGREDIENTS

3¾ ounces salt pork or thinly sliced
   unsmoked bacon, diced
1 large onion, chopped
2 potatoes, peeled and cut into cubes
1 bay leaf
1 fresh thyme sprig
1¼ cups milk
14 ounces cooked clams, cooking
   liquid reserved
⅔ cup heavy cream
salt, ground white pepper and
   cayenne pepper
finely chopped fresh parsley,
   to garnish

1 Put the salt pork or unsmoked bacon in a pan, and heat gently, stirring frequently, until the fat runs and the meat is starting to brown. Add the chopped onion and fry over a low heat until softened but not browned.

2 Add the cubed potatoes, the bay leaf and thyme sprig, stir well to coat with fat, then pour in the milk and reserved clam liquid and bring to the boil. Lower the heat and simmer for about 10 minutes, until the potatoes are tender but still firm. Lift out the bay leaf and thyme sprig and discard.

3 Remove the shells from most of the clams. Add all the clams to the pan and season to taste with salt, pepper and cayenne. Simmer gently for 5 minutes more, then stir in the cream. Heat until the soup is very hot, but do not allow it to boil. Pour into a tureen, garnish with the chopped parsley, and serve.

CHINESE CRAB <u>AND</u> CORN SOUP

FROZEN WHITE CRABMEAT WORKS AS WELL AS FRESH IN THIS DELICATELY FLAVORED SOUP.

SERVES 4

INGREDIENTS

2½ cups fish or chicken stock
1-inch fresh ginger root, peeled and
   very finely sliced
1 can (14 ounces) creamed corn
5 ounces cooked white crab meat
1 tablespoon arrowroot or cornstarch
1 tablespoon rice wine or dry sherry
1–2 tablespoons light soy sauce
1 egg white
salt and ground white pepper
shredded scallions, to garnish

1 Put the stock and ginger in a large pan and bring to the boil. Stir in the creamed corn and bring back to the boil.

2 Switch off the heat and add the crabmeat. Put the arrowroot or cornstarch in a cup and stir in the rice wine or sherry to make a smooth paste; stir this into the soup. Cook over a low heat for about 3 minutes until the soup has thickened and is slightly glutinous in consistency. Add light soy sauce, salt and white pepper to taste.

3 In a bowl, whisk the egg white to a stiff foam. Gradually fold it into the soup. Ladle the soup into heated bowls, garnish each portion with scallions and serve.

COOK'S TIP

This soup can be made with whole kernel corn, but creamed corn gives a better texture. If you can't find it in a can, use thawed frozen creamed corn instead; the result will be just as good.

VARIATION

To make shrimp and corn soup, substitute 5 ounces cooked peeled shrimp for the crabmeat. Chop the peeled shrimp roughly and add to the soup at the beginning of step 2.

Top: Energy 392kcal/1631kJ; Protein 24.3g; Carbohydrate 15.3g, of which sugars 5.7g; Fat 26.3g, of which saturates 15.1g; Cholesterol 136mg; Calcium 191mg; Fiber 0.7g; Sodium 1632mg.
Bottom: Energy 184kcal/779kJ; Protein 10.6g; Carbohydrate 33.8g, of which sugars 9.9g; Fat 1.6g, of which saturates 0.3g; Cholesterol 27mg; Calcium 51mg; Fiber 1.4g; Sodium 762mg.

SCALLOP <u>AND</u> JERUSALEM ARTICHOKE SOUP

THE SUBTLE SWEETNESS OF SCALLOPS COMBINES WELL WITH THE FLAVOR OF JERUSALEM ARTICHOKES IN THIS ATTRACTIVE AND SATISFYING GOLDEN SOUP.

SERVES 6

INGREDIENTS

2¼ pounds Jerusalem artichokes
juice of ½ lemon
4 ounces/½ cup butter
1 onion, peeled and finely
  chopped
2½ cups fish stock
1¼ cups milk
generous pinch of saffron threads
6 large or 12 small scallops, with
  their corals
⅔ cup whipping cream
salt and ground white pepper
3 tablespoons flaked almonds and
  1 tablespoon finely chopped
  fresh chervil, to garnish

1 Working quickly, scrub and peel the Jerusalem artichokes, cut them into ¾-inch chunks and drop them into a bowl of cold water which has been acidulated with the lemon juice. This will prevent the prepared artichokes from discoloring.

2 Melt half the butter in a pan, add the onion and cook over a low heat until softened. Drain the artichokes and add them to the pan. Cook gently for 5 minutes, stirring frequently. Pour in the stock and milk, add the saffron and bring to the boil. Lower the heat and simmer until the artichokes are tender but not mushy.

3 Meanwhile, carefully separate the scallop corals from the white flesh. Prick the corals and slice each scallop in half horizontally. Heat half the remaining butter in a frying pan, add the scallops and corals and cook very briefly (for about 1 minute) on each side. Dice the scallops and corals, keeping them separate, and set them aside until needed.

4 When the artichokes are cooked, tip the contents of the pan into a blender or food processor. Add half the white scallop meat and puree until very smooth. Return the soup to the clean pan, season with salt and white pepper, and keep hot over a low heat while you prepare the garnish.

5 Heat the remaining butter in a frying pan, add the almonds and toss over a medium heat until golden brown. Add the diced corals and cook for about 30 seconds.

6 Stir the cream into the soup and add the remaining diced white scallop meat. Ladle the soup into individual bowls and garnish each serving with the almonds, scallop corals and a sprinkling of chervil.

Energy 408kcal/1691kJ; Protein 12.8g; Carbohydrate 18.8g, of which sugars 16.4g; Fat 31.9g, of which saturates 17.5g; Cholesterol 86mg; Calcium 150mg; Fiber 4.7g; Sodium 247mg.

CRAB, COCONUT AND CILANTRO SOUP

QUICK AND EASY TO PREPARE, THIS SOUP HAS ALL THE FLAVORS ASSOCIATED WITH THE BAHIA REGION OF BRAZIL: CREAMY COCONUT, PALM OIL, FRAGRANT CILANTRO AND CHILE.

SERVES 4

INGREDIENTS

2 tablespoons olive oil
1 onion, finely chopped
1 celery stick, finely chopped
2 garlic cloves, crushed
1 fresh red chile, seeded
  and chopped
1 large tomato, peeled and chopped
3 tablespoons chopped fresh cilantro
4 cups fresh crab or
  fish stock
1¼ pounds crabmeat
8 fluid ounces/1 cup coconut milk
2 tablespoons palm oil
juice of 1 lime
salt
hot chili oil and lime wedges,
  to serve

1 Heat the olive oil in a pan over a low heat. Stir in the onion and celery, and sauté gently for 5 minutes, until softened and translucent. Stir in the garlic and chile and cook for a further 2 minutes.

2 Add the tomato and half the cilantro and increase the heat. Cook, stirring, for 3 minutes, then add the stock. Bring to the boil, then simmer for 5 minutes.

3 Stir the crab, coconut milk and palm oil into the pan and simmer over a very low heat for a further 5 minutes. The consistency should be thick, but not stew-like, so add some water if needed.

4 Stir in the lime juice and remaining cilantro, then season with salt to taste. Serve in heated bowls with the chili oil and lime wedges on the side.

Energy 228kcal/951kJ; Protein 23.6g; Carbohydrate 5.4g, of which sugars 5g; Fat 12.6g, of which saturates 3.7g; Cholesterol 90mg; Calcium 199mg; Fiber 1.1g; Sodium 767mg.

THAI FISH SOUP

THAI FISH SAUCE, OR NAM PLA, IS RICH IN B VITAMINS AND IS USED EXTENSIVELY IN THAI COOKING. IT IS AVAILABLE FROM THAI OR INDONESIAN STORES AND GOOD SUPERMARKETS.

3 Prepare the scallops by cutting them in half, leaving the corals attached to one half.

4 Return the stock to a clean pan, add the shrimp, mussels, monkfish and scallops and cook for 3 minutes. Remove from the heat and add the lime juice and fish sauce.

5 Serve garnished with the shredded lime leaf and finely sliced red chile.

SERVES 4

INGREDIENTS

12 ounces raw large shrimp
1 tablespoon peanut oil
5 cups well-flavored chicken or
  fish stock
1 lemongrass stalk, bruised and cut
  into 1-inch lengths
2 kaffir lime leaves, torn into pieces
juice and finely grated rind of 1 lime
½ fresh green chile, seeded and
  finely sliced
4 scallops
24 mussels, scrubbed
4 ounces monkfish fillet, cut into
  ¾-inch chunks
2 teaspoons Thai fish sauce
For the garnish
  1 kaffir lime leaf, shredded
  ½ fresh red chile, finely sliced

1 Peel the shrimp, reserving the shells, and remove the black vein running along their backs.

2 Heat the oil in a pan and fry the shrimp shells until pink. Add the stock, lemongrass, lime leaves, lime rind and green chile. Bring to the boil, simmer for 20 minutes, then pour through a strainer, reserving the liquid.

Energy 197kcal/830kJ; Protein 34.9g; Carbohydrate 3g, of which sugars 0.3g; Fat 5.1g, of which saturates 0.8g; Cholesterol 217mg; Calcium 108mg; Fiber 0g; Sodium 701mg.

SOFT-SHELL CRAB, SHRIMP AND CORN GUMBO

A WELL-FLAVORED CHICKEN AND SHELLFISH STOCK GIVES THIS DISH THE AUTHENTIC TASTE OF A TRADITIONAL LOUISIANA GUMBO. SERVE WITH SPOONS AND FORKS TO EAT THE CHUNKY CORN.

SERVES 6

INGREDIENTS
  2 tablespoons vegetable oil
  1 onion, peeled and finely
    chopped
  1 garlic clove, peeled and chopped
  4 ounces rindless fatty
    bacon, chopped
  1½ ounces/⅓ cup all-purpose flour
  1 celery stick, chopped
  1 red bell pepper, seeded
    and chopped
  1 red chile, seeded and chopped
  1 pound plum tomatoes, chopped
  2 large corn cobs
  4 soft-shell crabs, washed well
  2 tablespoons chopped
    fresh parsley
  small bunch of scallions,
    roughly chopped
  salt and ground black pepper
For the stock
  12 ounces whole uncooked shrimp
  2 large chicken wings
  1 carrot, thickly sliced
  3 celery sticks, sliced
  1 onion, peeled and sliced
  handful of parsley stalks
  2 bay leaves
  6¼ cups water

1 To make the stock, peel the shrimp and put the shells in a pan. Set the shrimp aside. Add the remaining ingredients to the pan. Bring to the boil and skim. Cover and cook for 1 hour.

2 To make the gumbo, heat the oil in a large pan, add the onion and garlic and cook for 3–4 minutes. Add the bacon and cook for 3 minutes. Stir in the flour and cook for 3–4 minutes.

3 When the mixture is turning golden, strain in the stock, stirring continuously. Add the celery, pepper, chile and tomatoes, bring to the boil and simmer for 5 minutes.

4 Cut the corn cobs into 1-inch slices, and add to the gumbo.

5 To prepare the crabs, cut off the eyes and mouth, cut across the face and hook out the stomach with your fingers. Pull off the tail flap and pull out the gills, or dead man's fingers. Quarter the crabs, then add to the gumbo with the shrimp.

6 Simmer for 15 minutes until the crabs and corn are cooked. Season, then stir in the parsley and scallions. Serve in deep bowls.

Energy 166kcal/694kJ; Protein 10.2g; Carbohydrate 11.1g, of which sugars 5.5g; Fat 9.3g, of which saturates 2.2g; Cholesterol 37mg; Calcium 94mg; Fiber 2.2g; Sodium 1280mg.

SAFFRON SEAFOOD SOUP

FILLING YET NOT TOO RICH, THIS GOLDEN SOUP WILL MAKE A DELICIOUS MEAL ON EARLY SUMMER
EVENINGS, SERVED WITH LOTS OF HOT FRESH BREAD AND A GLASS OF FRUITY, DRY WHITE WINE.
WHEN MUSSELS ARE NOT AVAILABLE USE SHRIMP IN THEIR SHELLS INSTEAD.

SERVES 4

INGREDIENTS

1 parsnip, quartered
2 carrots, quartered
1 onion, quartered
2 celery sticks, quartered
2 smoked bacon strips,
  rinds removed
juice of 1 lemon
pinch of saffron threads
1 pound fish heads
1 pound fresh mussels, scrubbed
1 leek, shredded
2 shallots, finely chopped
2 tablespoons chopped dill, plus
  extra sprigs to garnish
1 pound haddock, skinned and boned
3 egg yolks
2 tablespoons heavy cream
salt and ground black pepper

1 Put the parsnip, carrots, onion, celery, bacon, lemon juice, saffron threads and fish heads in a large pan with 3¾ cups water and bring to the boil. Boil gently for about 20 minutes or until reduced by half.

COOK'S TIP
Fish stock freezes well and will keep for up to 6 months.

2 Discard any mussels that are open and don't close when tapped sharply. Add the rest to the pan of stock. Cook for about 4 minutes, until they have opened. Strain the soup and return the liquid to the pan. Discard any unopened mussels, then remove the remaining ones from their shells and set aside.

3 Add the leeks and shallots to the soup, bring to the boil and cook for 5 minutes. Add the dill and haddock, and simmer for a further 5 minutes until the fish is tender. Remove the haddock, using a slotted spoon, then flake it into a bowl, using a fork.

4 In another bowl, whisk together the eggs and heavy cream. Whisk in a little of the hot soup, then whisk the mixture back into the hot but not boiling liquid. Continue to whisk for several minutes as it heats through and thickens slightly, but do not let it boil.

5 Add the flaked haddock and mussels to the soup and check the seasoning. Garnish with tiny sprigs of dill and serve piping hot.

Energy 278kcal/1167kJ; Protein 33.2g; Carbohydrate 9.8g, of which sugars 8.5g; Fat 12.1g, of which saturates 4.8g; Cholesterol 222mg; Calcium 147mg; Fiber 3.4g; Sodium 377mg.

SAFFRON-FLAVORED MUSSEL SOUP

THERE'S A FRAGRANT TASTE OF THE SEA OFF THE SPANISH COAST IN THIS CREAMY SOUP FILLED WITH THE JET BLACK SHELLS OF PLUMP MUSSELS. SAFFRON GOES WELL WITH SHELLFISH, AND GIVES THE SOUP A LOVELY PALE YELLOW COLOR.

SERVES 4

INGREDIENTS
 3–3½ pounds fresh mussels
 2½ cups white wine
 a few fresh parsley stalks
 2 ounces/¼ cup butter
 2 leeks, finely chopped
 2 celery sticks, finely chopped
 1 carrot, chopped
 2 garlic cloves, peeled and
  chopped
 large pinch of saffron threads
 2½ cups heavy cream
 3 tomatoes, peeled, seeded
  and chopped
 salt and ground black pepper
 2 tablespoons chopped fresh chives,
  to garnish

1 Clean the mussels and pull away the beards. Put into a large pan with the wine and parsley stalks. Cover, bring to the boil and cook for 4–5 minutes, shaking the pan occasionally, until the mussels have opened. Discard the stalks and any unopened mussels.

2 Drain the mussels over a large bowl, reserving the cooking liquid. When cool enough to handle, remove about half of the cooked mussels from their shells. Set aside with the remaining mussels in their shells.

COOK'S TIP
The most efficient way to clean fresh mussels is to scrub them under cold running water, using a stiff brush to remove any sand or dirt.

3 Melt the butter in a large pan, add the leeks, celery, carrot and garlic, and cook for 5 minutes until softened. Put the reserved mussel cooking liquid through a fine strainer or cheesecloth. Add to the pan and cook over a high heat for 8–10 minutes to reduce the liquid slightly. Strain into a clean pan, add the saffron threads and cook for 1 minute.

4 Add the cream and bring back to the boil. Season well. Add all the mussels and the tomatoes and heat gently to warm through. Ladle the soup into four bowls, then sprinkle with the chopped chives and serve immediately.

Energy 1054kcal/4359kJ; Protein 22.8g; Carbohydrate 7.5g, of which sugars 7.4g; Fat 93.4g, of which saturates 57.1g; Cholesterol 277mg; Calcium 327mg; Fiber 1.4g; Sodium 372mg.

SHRIMP BISQUE

THE CLASSIC FRENCH METHOD FOR MAKING A BISQUE INVOLVES PUSHING THE SHELLFISH THROUGH A TAMIS, OR DRUM SIEVE. THIS RECIPE IS SIMPLER AND THE RESULT IS JUST AS SMOOTH.

SERVES 6–8

INGREDIENTS
1½ pounds small or
  medium cooked shrimp in
  their shells
1½ tablespoons vegetable oil
2 onions, peeled, halved
  and sliced
1 large carrot, sliced
2 celery sticks, sliced
9 cups water
a few drops of lemon juice
2 tablespoons tomato paste
bouquet garni
2 ounces/4 tablespoons butter
2 ounces/⅓ cup all-purpose flour
3–4 tablespoons brandy
⅔ cup whipping cream

1 Remove the heads from the shrimp and peel away the shells. Reserve the heads and shells for the stock. Place the shrimp in a covered bowl and place in the refrigerator.

2 Heat the oil in a large pan, add the heads and shells and cook over a high heat, stirring, until they start to brown.

3 Reduce the heat to medium, add the vegetables and fry, stirring occasionally, for 5 minutes until the onions are soft but not browned.

4 Add the water, lemon juice, tomato paste and bouquet garni. Bring to the boil, then reduce the heat, cover and simmer gently for 25 minutes. Remove from the heat and put the stock through a strainer.

5 Melt the butter in a heavy pan over a medium heat. Stir in the flour and cook until just golden, stirring occasionally to prevent it sticking to the base.

6 Add the brandy. Gradually pour in half the shrimp stock, whisking vigorously until smooth, then whisk in the remaining liquid. Season if necessary.

7 Reduce the heat, cover and simmer for 5 minutes, stirring frequently.

8 Strain the soup into a clean pan. Add the cream and a little extra lemon juice to taste, then stir in most of the reserved shrimp and cook over a medium heat, stirring frequently, until hot. Serve at once, garnished with the remaining reserved shrimp.

COOK'S TIP
If you prefer, you may leave the brandy out of this dish, and it will still taste delicious.

Energy 220kcal/915kJ; Protein 9g; Carbohydrate 9.7g, of which sugars 4g; Fat 15g, of which saturates 8.3g; Cholesterol 122mg; Calcium 73mg; Fiber 1.1g; Sodium 566mg.

SHRIMP AND CORN BISQUE

HOT PEPPER SAUCE BRINGS A TOUCH OF SPICE TO THIS MILD, CREAMY SOUP. IT LOOKS VERY ATTRACTIVE GARNISHED WITH SPRIGS OF FRESH DILL.

SERVES 4

INGREDIENTS

2 tablespoons olive oil
1 onion, very finely chopped
2 ounces/4 tablespoons butter
  or margarine
1 ounce/¼ cup flour
3 cups fish stock
8 fluid ounces/1 cup milk
4 ounces/1 cup peeled cooked
  small shrimps, deveined
  if necessary
8 ounces/1½ cups corn kernels
½ teaspoon chopped fresh dill
  or thyme
hot pepper sauce
4 fluid ounces/½ cup light cream
salt
sprigs of fresh dill, to garnish

1 Heat the olive oil in a large heavy pan. Add the onion and cook over a low heat for 8–10 minutes until softened but not browned.

2 Meanwhile, melt the butter or margarine in a medium pan. Add the flour and cook for 1–2 minutes, stirring. Stir in the stock and milk, bring to the boil and cook for 5–8 minutes, stirring frequently.

3 Cut each shrimp into two or three pieces and add to the onion with the corn and dill or thyme. Cook for 2–3 minutes, then remove from the heat and set aside.

4 Add the sauce mixture to the shrimp and corn mixture, and mix well.

5 Remove 3 cups of the soup and puree it in a blender or food processor. Return the paste to the rest of the soup in the pan and stir well. Season with salt and hot pepper sauce to taste.

6 Add the cream and stir to blend. Heat the soup almost to boiling point, stirring frequently.

7 Divide into individual soup bowls and serve hot, garnished with sprigs of dill.

Energy 358kcal/1494kJ; Protein 12.4g; Carbohydrate 24.7g, of which sugars 10g; Fat 24.1g, of which saturates 11.9g; Cholesterol 84mg; Calcium 211mg; Fiber 1.2g; Sodium 1368mg.

CORN AND CRABMEAT SOUP

THIS SOUP ORIGINATED IN THE U.S.A. BUT IT HAS SINCE BEEN INTRODUCED INTO CHINA. YOU MUST USE CREAMED CORN IN THE RECIPE TO ACHIEVE THE RIGHT CONSISTENCY.

SERVES 4

INGREDIENTS
4 ounces crabmeat
½ teaspoon finely chopped fresh
   ginger root
2 tablespoons milk
1 tablespoon cornstarch
2 egg whites
2½ cups vegetable stock
1 can (8 ounces) creamed corn
salt and ground black pepper
chopped scallions, to garnish

1 Flake the crabmeat and mix with the ginger in a bowl. In another bowl, mix the milk and cornstarch until smooth.

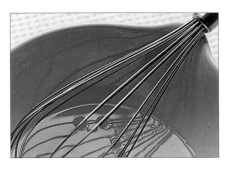

2 Beat the egg whites until frothy.

3 Add the milk and cornstarch mixture and beat again until smooth. Blend with the crabmeat.

4 In a wok or large pan, bring the vegetable stock to the boil. Add the creamed corn and bring back to the boil once more.

5 Stir in the crabmeat and egg white mixture, adjust the seasoning and stir gently until well blended. Serve garnished with chopped scallions.

VARIATION
You can use coarsely chopped chicken breast instead of crabmeat.

Energy 115kcal/486kJ; Protein 8.6g; Carbohydrate 18.8g, of which sugars 5.8g; Fat 1.1g, of which saturates 0.2g; Cholesterol 21mg; Calcium 47mg; Fiber 0.8g; Sodium 346mg.

CORN AND SCALLOP CHOWDER

FRESH CORN IS IDEAL FOR THIS CHOWDER, ALTHOUGH CANNED OR FROZEN CORN ALSO WORKS WELL.
THIS SOUP IS ALMOST A MEAL IN ITSELF AND MAKES A PERFECT LUNCH DISH.

SERVES 4–6

INGREDIENTS

2 corn cobs or 7 ounces/
  generous 1 cup frozen or
  canned corn
2½ cups milk
½ ounce butter or margarine
1 small leek or onion, chopped
1½ ounces/¼ cup smoked fatty
  bacon, finely chopped
1 small garlic clove, peeled
  and crushed
1 small green bell pepper, seeded
  and diced
1 celery stick, chopped
1 medium potato, diced
1 tablespoon all-purpose flour
1¼ cups chicken or
  vegetable stock
4 scallops
4 ounces cooked fresh mussels
a pinch of paprika
⅔ cup light cream (optional)
salt and ground black pepper

1 Using a sharp knife, slice down the corn cobs, if using, to remove the kernels. Place half the kernels in a food processor or blender and process with a little of the milk. Set the other half aside.

2 Melt the butter or margarine in a large pan and gently fry the leek or onion, bacon and garlic for 4–5 minutes, until the leek is soft but not browned. Add the green pepper, celery and potato and sweat over a gentle heat for a further 3–4 minutes, stirring frequently.

3 Stir in the flour and cook for about 1–2 minutes, until golden and frothy. Stir in a little milk and the corn mixture, then add the stock, the remaining milk and corn kernels and seasoning.

4 Bring to the boil, and then simmer, partially covered, for 15–20 minutes until the vegetables are tender.

5 Pull the corals away from the scallops and slice the white flesh into ¼-inch slices. Stir the scallops into the soup, cook for 4 minutes and then stir in the corals, mussels and paprika. Heat through for a few minutes and then stir in the cream, if using. Check the seasoning and serve.

Energy 200kcal/845kJ; Protein 13g; Carbohydrate 23.6g, of which sugars 10.5g; Fat 6.7g, of which saturates 3.2g; Cholesterol 31mg; Calcium 150mg; Fiber 1.8g; Sodium 326mg.

CLAM AND CORN CHOWDER

THIS IS A RICH, CREAMY CHOWDER, MADE WITH HEAVY CREAM. IT USES WHOLE BABY CORN, BABY NEW POTATOES AND ONIONS, AND SMALL CLAMS. SERVE IT WITH LIME WEDGES, IF YOU LIKE.

SERVES 4

INGREDIENTS

1¼ cups heavy cream
3 ounces/6 tablespoons
  sweet butter
1 small onion, finely chopped
1 apple, cored and sliced
1 garlic clove, crushed
3 tablespoons mild curry powder
12 ounces/3 cups baby
  corn cobs
8 ounces cooked new potatoes
24 boiled baby onions
2½ cups fish stock
40 small clams
salt and ground black pepper

1 Pour the cream into a small pan and cook over a high heat, stirring continuously, until it is reduced by half.

2 In a larger pan, melt half the butter. Add the onion, apple, garlic and curry powder. Sauté until the onion is translucent. Add the reduced cream and stir well.

3 In another pan, melt the remaining butter and add the baby corn, potatoes and baby onions. Cook for 5 minutes. Increase the heat and add the cream mixture and stock. Bring to the boil.

4 Add the clams. Cover and cook until the clams have opened. Discard any that do not open.

5 Season well to taste with salt and freshly ground black pepper. Ladle into soup bowls and serve piping hot.

COOK'S TIPS
• Canned or bottled clams in brine, once drained, can be used as an alternative to fresh ones in their shells. Discard any shells that remain closed during cooking, as this means they were already dead when they were canned or bottled.
• Serve lime wedges with the soup as a garnish, if you like.

Energy 676kcal/2798kJ; Protein 18.2g; Carbohydrate 24.2g, of which sugars 11.3g; Fat 56.9g, of which saturates 35g; Cholesterol 193mg; Calcium 136mg; Fiber 3.8g; Sodium 2038mg.

LOBSTER BISQUE

BISQUE IS A LUXURIOUS, VELVETY SOUP THAT CAN BE MADE WITH ANY CRUSTACEANS, SUCH AS CRAB OR SHRIMP. IF LOBSTER IS YOUR FAVORITE SHELLFISH, THIS VERSION IS FOR YOU.

SERVES 6

INGREDIENTS

1¼ pounds fresh lobster
3 ounces/6 tablespoons butter
1 onion, chopped
1 carrot, diced
1 celery stick, diced
3 tablespoons brandy
8 fluid ounces/1 cup dry white wine
4 cups fish stock
1 tablespoon tomato paste
3 ounces/scant ½ cup long grain rice
fresh bouquet garni
⅔ cup heavy cream, plus extra
    to garnish
salt, ground white pepper and
    cayenne pepper

1 Cut the lobster into pieces. Melt half the butter in a large pan, add the vegetables and cook over a low heat until soft. Put in the lobster and stir gently until the shells turn red.

2 Pour over the brandy and set it alight. When the flames die down, add the wine and boil until reduced by half. Pour in the fish stock and simmer for 2–3 minutes. Remove the lobster.

3 Stir in the tomato paste and rice, add the bouquet garni and cook until the rice is tender, about 15 minutes. Meanwhile, remove the lobster meat from the shell and return the shells to the pan. Dice the meat and set it aside.

COOK'S TIP
It is best to buy a live lobster, chilling it in the freezer until it is comatose and then killing it just before cooking. If you can't face the procedure, use a cooked lobster; take care not to overcook the flesh. Stir for only 30–60 seconds.

4 When the rice is cooked, discard all the larger bits of shell. Put the mixture in a blender or food processor and whizz to a paste. Press the paste through a fine strainer over the clean pan. Stir the mixture, then heat until almost boiling. Season with salt, pepper and cayenne, then lower the heat and stir in the cream. Dice the remaining butter and whisk it into the bisque. Add the diced lobster meat and serve at once. If you like, pour a small spoonful of brandy into each soup bowl and swirl in a little extra cream.

Energy 347kcal/1438kJ; Protein 8.5g; Carbohydrate 12.9g, of which sugars 2.6g; Fat 24.3g, of which saturates 15g; Cholesterol 94mg; Calcium 48mg; Fiber 0.6g; Sodium 195mg.

CHILE CLAM BROTH

THIS SOUP OF SUCCULENT CLAMS IN A TASTY STOCK COULD NOT BE EASIER TO PREPARE. POPULAR IN COASTAL AREAS OF COLOMBIA, IT MAKES THE PERFECT LUNCH ON A HOT SUMMER'S DAY.

SERVES 6

INGREDIENTS

2 tablespoons olive oil
1 onion, finely chopped
3 garlic cloves, crushed
2 fresh red chiles, seeded and finely chopped
8 fluid ounces/1 cup dry white wine
1 can (14 fluid ounces) plum tomatoes, drained
1 large potato, about 9 ounces, peeled and diced
14 fluid ounces/1⅔ cups fish stock
3 pounds fresh clams
1 tablespoon chopped fresh cilantro
1 tablespoon chopped fresh Italian parsley
salt
lime wedges, to garnish

1 Heat the oil in a pan. Add the onion and sauté for 5 minutes over a low heat. Stir in the garlic and chiles and cook for a further 2 minutes. Pour in the wine and bring to the boil, then simmer for 2 minutes.

2 Add the tomatoes, diced potato and stock. Bring to the boil, cover and lower the heat so that the soup simmers.

3 Season with salt and cook for 15 minutes, until the potatoes are beginning to break up and the tomatoes have made a rich sauce.

4 Meanwhile, wash the clams thoroughly under cold running water. Gently tap any that are open, and discard them if they do not close.

5 Add the clams to the soup, cover the pan and cook for about 3–4 minutes, or until the clams have opened, then stir in the chopped herbs. Season with salt to taste.

6 Check over the clams and throw away any that have failed to open. Ladle the soup into warmed bowls. Offer the lime wedges separately, to be squeezed over the soup just before eating.

Energy 290kcal/1217kJ; Protein 36.2g; Carbohydrate 14.1g, of which sugars 3.5g; Fat 7.2g, of which saturates 1.3g; Cholesterol 145mg; Calcium 184mg; Fiber 1.5g; Sodium 2614mg.

SPICED MUSSEL SOUP

CHUNKY AND COLORFUL, THIS TURKISH FISH SOUP IS LIKE A CHOWDER IN ITS CONSISTENCY.
IT IS FLAVORED WITH HARISSA SAUCE, WHICH IS MORE FAMILIAR IN NORTH AFRICAN COOKING.

SERVES 6

INGREDIENTS
    3–3½ pounds fresh mussels
    ⅔ cup white wine
    2 tablespoons olive oil
    1 onion, finely chopped
    2 garlic cloves, crushed
    2 celery sticks, finely sliced
    bunch of scallions finely sliced
    1 potato, diced
    1½ teaspoons harissa sauce
    3 tomatoes, peeled and diced
    3 tablespoons chopped fresh parsley
    ground black pepper
    thick plain yogurt, to serve (optional)

1 Scrub the mussels, discarding any damaged ones or any open ones that do not close when tapped with a knife.

2 Bring the wine to the boil in a large pan. Add the mussels and cover with a lid. Cook for 4–5 minutes until the mussels have opened wide. Discard any that remain closed.

3 Drain the mussels, reserving the cooking liquid. Reserve a few mussels in their shells to use as a garnish, and shell the rest.

4 Heat the oil in a pan and fry the onion, garlic, celery and scallions for 5 minutes.

5 Add the shelled mussels, reserved liquid, potato, harissa sauce and tomatoes. Bring to the boil, reduce the heat and cover. Simmer gently for 25 minutes or until the potatoes are breaking up.

6 Stir in the parsley and pepper and add the reserved mussels in their shells. Heat through for 1 minute. Serve hot with a spoonful of yogurt, if you like.

Energy 153kcal/644kJ; Protein 14.5g; Carbohydrate 7.8g, of which sugars 3.2g; Fat 5.6g, of which saturates 0.9g; Cholesterol 30mg; Calcium 178mg; Fiber 1.5g; Sodium 175mg.

EGG AND CHEESE SOUPS

Omelets are often used to add protein to light Asian soups, and in this section you will find several examples, such as Thai Omelet Soup, Shrimp and Egg-knot Soup, and Egg Flower Soup. Eggs are also an ingredient in many Mediterranean soups, for example Portuguese Garlic Soup and Greek Avgolemono. Cheese may also be included for added protein and flavor, as in the classic Roman Egg and Cheese Soup, and Irish Leek and Blue Cheese Soup.

PORTUGUESE GARLIC SOUP

THIS RECIPE IS BASED ON THE WONDERFUL BREAD SOUPS OR AÇORDAS OF PORTUGAL. BEING A SIMPLE SOUP IT SHOULD BE MADE WITH THE BEST INGREDIENTS—PLUMP GARLIC, FRESH CILANTRO, HIGH-QUALITY CRUSTY COUNTRY BREAD AND EXTRA VIRGIN OLIVE OIL.

SERVES 6

INGREDIENTS

  1 ounce fresh cilantro, leaves and
    stalks chopped separately
  6¼ cups vegetable or chicken stock,
    or water
  5 or 6 plump garlic cloves, peeled
  6 eggs
  10 ounces day-old bread, most
    of the crust removed, torn into
    bitesize pieces
  salt and ground black pepper
  6 tablespoons extra virgin olive oil,
    plus extra to serve

1 Place the cilantro stalks in a pan. Add the stock or water and bring to the boil. Lower the heat and simmer for 10 minutes, then process in a blender or food processor and strain back into the pan.

2 Crush the garlic with 1 teaspoon salt, then stir in 4 fluid ounces/½ cup hot soup. Return the mixture to the pan.

3 Meanwhile, poach the eggs in a frying pan of simmering water for about 3–4 minutes, until just set. Use a slotted spoon to remove them from the pan and transfer to a warmed plate. Trim off any untidy bits of white.

4 Bring the soup back to the boil and add seasoning. Stir in the chopped cilantro leaves and remove from the heat.

5 Place the bread in six soup plates or bowls and drizzle the oil over it. Ladle in the soup and stir. Add a poached egg to each bowl and serve immediately, offering olive oil at the table so that it can be drizzled over the soup to taste.

Energy 299kcal/1249kJ; Protein 11.6g; Carbohydrate 24.6g, of which sugars 2.8g; Fat 18g, of which saturates 3.1g; Cholesterol 190mg; Calcium 170mg; Fiber 3g; Sodium 323mg.

THAI OMELET SOUP

THIS IS A SURPRISINGLY SATISFYING SOUP FROM THAILAND THAT IS VERY QUICK AND EASY TO PREPARE. IT IS A VERSATILE RECIPE, TOO, IN THAT YOU CAN VARY THE VEGETABLES YOU USE ACCORDING TO WHAT IS SEASONALLY AVAILABLE.

SERVES 4

INGREDIENTS

   1 egg
   1 tablespoon peanut oil
   3¾ cups vegetable stock
   2 large carrots, finely diced
   4 outer leaves savoy
     cabbage, shredded
   2 tablespoons soy sauce
   ½ teaspoon granulated sugar
   ½ teaspoon ground black pepper
   fresh cilantro leaves, to garnish

VARIATION
Use bok choy instead of savoy cabbage, if you like. In Thailand there are about forty different types of bok choy, including miniature versions.

1 Put the egg in a bowl and beat lightly with a fork. Heat the oil in a small frying pan until it is hot, but not smoking. Pour in the egg and swirl the pan so that it coats the base evenly. Cook over a medium heat until the omelet has set and the underside is golden. Slide it out of the pan and roll it up like a pancake. Slice into ¼-inch rounds and set aside for the garnish.

2 Put the stock into a large pan. Add the carrots and cabbage and bring to the boil. Reduce the heat and simmer for 5 minutes, then add the soy sauce, sugar and pepper.

3 Stir well, then pour into warmed bowls. Lay a few omelet rounds on the surface of each portion and complete the garnish with the cilantro leaves.

Energy 64kcal/264kJ; Protein 2.3g; Carbohydrate 4.3g, of which sugars 4.1g; Fat 4.3g, of which saturates 0.7g; Cholesterol 48mg; Calcium 27mg; Fiber 1.1g; Sodium 560mg.

FRENCH ONION SOUP
WITH GRUYÈRE CROUTES

THIS IS PERHAPS THE MOST FAMOUS OF ALL ONION SOUPS. TRADITIONALLY, IT WAS SERVED AS A SUSTAINING EARLY MORNING MEAL TO THE PORTERS AND WORKERS OF LES HALLES MARKET IN PARIS.

SERVES 6

INGREDIENTS

2 ounces/¼ cup butter
1 tablespoon olive oil
4½ pounds yellow onions, peeled and sliced
1 teaspoon chopped fresh thyme
1 teaspoon superfine sugar
1 tablespoon sherry vinegar
6¼ cups good beef, chicken or duck stock
1½ tablespoons all-purpose flour
⅔ cup dry white wine
3 tablespoons brandy
salt and ground black pepper
For the croutes
6–12 thick slices day-old French stick or baguette, about 1 inch thick
1 garlic clove, halved
1 tablespoon French mustard
4 ounces/1 cup coarsely grated Gruyère cheese

1 Melt the butter with the oil in a large pan. Add the onions and stir to coat them in the fat. Cook over a medium heat for 5–8 minutes, stirring once or twice, until the onions begin to soften. Stir in the thyme.

2 Reduce the heat to very low, cover the pan and cook the onions for 20–30 minutes, stirring frequently, until they are very soft and golden yellow.

3 Uncover the pan and increase the heat slightly. Stir in the sugar and cook for 5–10 minutes, until the onions start to brown. Add the sherry vinegar and increase the heat again, then continue cooking, stirring frequently, until the onions turn a deep, golden brown— this could take up to 20 minutes.

COOK'S TIP
The long slow cooking of the onions is the key to success with this soup. If the onions brown too quickly the soup will be bitter.

4 Meanwhile, bring the stock to the boil in another pan. Stir the flour into the onions and cook for about 2 minutes, then gradually pour in the hot stock. Add the wine and brandy and season the soup to taste with salt and pepper. Simmer for 10–15 minutes.

5 For the croutes, preheat the oven to 300°F. Place the slices of bread on a greased baking tray and bake for 15–20 minutes, until dry and lightly browned. Rub the bread with the cut surface of the garlic and spread with the mustard, then sprinkle the grated Gruyère cheese over the slices.

6 Preheat the broiler on the hottest setting. Ladle the soup into a large flameproof pan or six flameproof bowls. Float the croutes on the soup, then grill until the cheese melts, bubbles and browns. Serve immediately.

Energy 484kcal/2030kJ; Protein 15.3g; Carbohydrate 67.2g, of which sugars 21.5g; Fat 15.1g, of which saturates 8.7g; Cholesterol 36mg; Calcium 314mg; Fiber 6.4g; Sodium 611mg.

AVGOLEMONO

THIS IS A GREAT FAVORITE IN GREECE AND IS A FINE EXAMPLE OF HOW JUST A FEW INGREDIENTS CAN MAKE A MARVELOUS DISH IF CAREFULLY CHOSEN AND COOKED. IT IS ESSENTIAL TO USE A WELL-FLAVORED STOCK. ADD AS LITTLE OR AS MUCH RICE AS YOU LIKE.

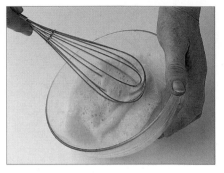

2 Whisk the egg yolks in a bowl, then add about 2 tablespoons of the lemon juice, whisking constantly until the mixture is smooth and bubbly. Add a ladleful of soup and whisk again.

3 Remove the soup from the heat and slowly add the egg mixture, whisking all the time. The soup will turn a pretty lemon color and will thicken slightly.

4 Taste and add more lemon juice if necessary. Stir in the parsley. Serve at once, without reheating, garnished with lemon slices and parsley sprigs.

SERVES 4

INGREDIENTS
3¾ cups chicken stock, preferably homemade
2 ounces/generous ⅓ cup long grain rice
3 egg yolks
2–4 tablespoons lemon juice
2 tablespoons finely chopped fresh parsley
salt and ground black pepper
lemon slices and fresh parsley sprigs, to garnish

1 Pour the stock into a pan, bring to simmering point, then add the drained rice. Half cover and cook for about 12 minutes until the rice is just tender. Season with salt and pepper.

COOK'S TIP
The trick here is to add the egg mixture to the soup without it curdling. Avoid whisking the mixture into boiling liquid. It is safest to remove the soup from the heat entirely and then whisk in the mixture in a slow but steady stream. Do not reheat as curdling would be almost inevitable.

Energy 96kcal/404kJ; Protein 3.3g; Carbohydrate 10.9g, of which sugars 0.2g; Fat 4.7g, of which saturates 1.2g; Cholesterol 151mg; Calcium 39mg; Fiber 0.4g; Sodium 10mg.

SPICY TOMATO AND EGG DROP SOUP

POPULAR IN SOUTHERN VIETNAM AND CAMBODIA, THIS SPICY TOMATO SOUP WITH EGGS IS PROBABLY ADAPTED FROM THE TRADITIONAL CHINESE EGG DROP SOUP. ACCOMPANIED BY JASMINE OR GINGER RICE, THIS IS A TASTY DISH FOR A LIGHT LUNCH OR SUPPER.

SERVES 4

INGREDIENTS

    2 tablespoons peanut or
      vegetable oil
    3 shallots, finely sliced
    2 garlic cloves, finely chopped
    2 Thai chiles, seeded and
      finely sliced
    1 ounce galangal, shredded
    8 large, ripe tomatoes, skinned,
      seeded and finely chopped
    1 tablespoon sugar
    2 tablespoons *nuoc mam* or
      tuk trey
    4 lime leaves
    3¾ cups chicken stock
    1 tablespoon wine vinegar
    4 eggs
    sea salt and ground black pepper
For the garnish
    chili oil, for drizzling
    a small bunch of fresh cilantro,
      finely chopped
    a small bunch of fresh mint leaves,
      finely chopped

3 Stir the water clockwise with a spoon and drop an egg into the center of the swirl. Follow with the others, or poach two at a time and keep the water boiling to throw the whites up over the yolks. Turn off the heat, cover the pan and leave to poach until firm enough to lift.

4 Using a slotted spoon, lift the eggs out of the water and slip them into the hot soup.

5 Drizzle a little chili oil over the eggs, sprinkle with the cilantro and mint, and serve piping hot.

1 Heat the oil in a wok or heavy pan. Stir in the shallots, garlic, chiles and galangal and cook until golden and fragrant. Add the tomatoes with the sugar, *nuoc mam* and lime leaves. Pour in the stock and bring to the boil. Reduce the heat and simmer for 30 minutes. Season to taste.

2 Just before serving, bring a wide pan of water to the boil. Add the vinegar and a little salt. Break the eggs into individual cups or small bowls.

Energy 175kcal/732kJ; Protein 7.8g; Carbohydrate 10.9g, of which sugars 10.6g; Fat 11.6g, of which saturates 2.4g; Cholesterol 190mg; Calcium 47mg; Fiber 2.1g; Sodium 88mg.

EGG FLOWER SOUP

THIS SIMPLE, HEALTHY SOUP IS FLAVORED WITH FRESH GINGER ROOT AND CHINESE FIVE-SPICE POWDER. IT IS QUICK AND DELICIOUS AND CAN BE MADE AT THE LAST MINUTE.

SERVES 4

INGREDIENTS

    5 cups fresh chicken or
      vegetable stock
    2 teaspoons peeled, grated fresh
      root ginger
    2 teaspoons light soy sauce
    1 teaspoon sesame oil
    1 teaspoon Chinese five-spice powder
    1 tablespoon cornstarch
    2 eggs
    salt and ground black pepper
    1 scallion, very finely sliced
      diagonally, and 1 tablespoon
      roughly chopped cilantro or Italian
      parsley, to garnish

COOK'S TIP
This soup is a good way of using up leftover egg yolks or whites which have been stored in the freezer.

1 Put the chicken or vegetable stock into a large pan with the ginger, soy sauce, oil and five-spice powder. Bring to the boil and allow to simmer gently for about 10 minutes.

2 Blend the cornstarch in a measuring cup with 4–5 tablespoons water and stir into the stock. Cook, stirring constantly, until slightly thickened. Season to taste with salt and pepper.

3 In a pitcher, beat the eggs together with 2 tablespoons cold water until the mixture becomes frothy.

4 Bring the soup back just to the boil and drizzle in the egg mixture, stirring vigorously with chopsticks. Choose a pitcher with a fine spout to form a very thin drizzle. Serve at once, sprinkled with the sliced scallions and chopped cilantro or parsley.

Energy 71kcal/298kJ; Protein 3.3g; Carbohydrate 7.1g, of which sugars 0.2g; Fat 3.6g, of which saturates 0.9g; Cholesterol 95mg; Calcium 16mg; Fiber 0g; Sodium 217mg.

SHRIMP AND EGG-KNOT SOUP

OMELETS AND PANCAKES ARE OFTEN USED TO ADD PROTEIN TO LIGHT ORIENTAL SOUPS. IN THIS RECIPE, THIN OMELETS ARE TWISTED INTO LITTLE KNOTS AND ADDED AT THE LAST MINUTE.

SERVES 4

INGREDIENTS

    1 scallion, shredded
    3½ cups well-flavored stock or
      instant dashi
    1 teaspoon soy sauce
    dash of sake or dry white wine
    pinch of salt
For the shrimp balls
    7 ounces /generous 1 cup raw large
      prawns, shelled, thawed if frozen
    2½ ounces cod fillet, skinned
    1 teaspoon egg white
    1 teaspoon sake or dry white wine,
      plus a dash extra
    4½ teaspoons cornstarch or
      potato flour
    2 or 3 drops soy sauce
    pinch of salt
For the omelet
    1 egg, beaten
    dash of mirin
    pinch of salt
    oil, for cooking

1 To make the shrimp balls, use a pin to remove the black vein running down the back of each shrimp. Place the shrimp, cod, egg white, sake or dry white wine, cornstarch or potato flour, soy sauce and a pinch of salt in a food processor or blender and process to a thick, sticky paste. Shape the mixture into 4 balls, place in a steaming basket and steam over a pan of vigorously boiling water for about 10 minutes.

2 To make the garnish, soak the scallion shreds in iced water for about 5 minutes, until they curl, then drain.

3 To make the omelet, mix the egg with the mirin and salt. Heat a little oil in a frying pan and pour in the egg mixture, coating the pan evenly. When the omelet has set, turn it over and cook for 30 seconds. Leave to cool.

4 Cut the omelet into strips and tie each in a knot. Heat the stock or dashi, then add the soy sauce, sake or wine and salt. Divide the shrimp balls and egg-knots among 4 bowls and add the soup. Garnish with the scallion.

Energy 98kcal/412kJ; Protein 13.6g; Carbohydrate 7.1g, of which sugars 0.2g; Fat 1.9g, of which saturates 0.5g; Cholesterol 153mg; Calcium 51mg; Fiber 0.1g; Sodium 218mg.

EGG <u>AND</u> CHEESE SOUP

IN THIS CLASSIC ROMAN SOUP, EGGS AND CHEESE ARE BEATEN INTO HOT SOUP, PRODUCING THE SLIGHTLY SCRAMBLED TEXTURE THAT IS CHARACTERISTIC OF THIS DISH.

SERVES 6

INGREDIENTS
3 eggs
3 tablespoons fine semolina
6 tablespoons freshly grated
 Parmesan cheese
pinch of nutmeg
6¼ cups cold meat or chicken stock
salt and ground black pepper
12 rounds of rustic bread or ciabatta,
 to serve

COOK'S TIP
Once added to the hot soup, the egg will begin to cook and the soup will become less smooth. Try not to overcook the soup at this stage because it may cause the egg to curdle.

1 Beat the eggs in a bowl, then beat in the semolina and the cheese. Add the nutmeg and beat in 8 fluid ounces/ 1 cup of the meat or chicken stock. Pour the mixture into a measuring cup.

2 Pour the remaining stock into a large pan and bring to a gentle simmer, stirring occasionally.

3 A few minutes before you are ready to serve the soup, whisk the egg mixture into the hot stock. Raise the heat slightly, and bring it barely to the boil. Season and cook for 3–4 minutes.

4 To serve, toast the rounds of rustic bread or ciabatta, place two in each soup plate and ladle on the hot soup. Serve immediately.

Energy 245kcal/1030kJ; Protein 14.1g; Carbohydrate 27.5g, of which sugars 1.3g; Fat 9.4g, of which saturates 4.1g; Cholesterol 110mg; Calcium 246mg; Fiber 1.1g; Sodium 424mg.

GARLIC SOUP WITH EGG AND CROUTONS

SPANISH SOUP AND ITALIAN POLENTA MARRY WONDERFULLY WELL IN THIS RECIPE. THE DELICIOUS GARLIC SOUP ORIGINATES FROM ANDALUSIA IN SPAIN.

SERVES 4

INGREDIENTS
  1 tablespoon extra virgin
    olive oil
  1 garlic bulb, unpeeled and broken
    into cloves
  4 slices day-old ciabatta bread,
    broken into pieces
  5 cups chicken stock
  pinch of saffron
  1 tablespoon white wine vinegar
  4 eggs
  salt and ground black pepper
  chopped fresh parsley,
    to garnish
For the polenta
  3 cups milk
  6 ounces/1 cup quick-cook polenta
  2 ounces/¼ cup butter

1 Preheat the oven to 400°F. Brush the oil over a roasting pan, then add the garlic and bread, and roast for about 20 minutes, until the garlic is soft and the bread is dry. Leave until cool enough to handle.

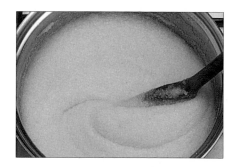

2 Meanwhile, make the polenta. Bring the milk to the boil in a large, heavy pan and gradually pour in the polenta, stirring constantly. Cook for about 5 minutes, or according to the packet instructions, stirring frequently, until the polenta begins to come away from the side of the pan.

3 Spoon the polenta onto a chopping board and spread out to about ½-inch thick. Allow to cool and set, then cut into ½-inch dice.

4 Squeeze the garlic cloves from their skins into a food processor or blender. Add the bread and 1¼ cups of the stock, then process until smooth. Pour into a pan. Pound the saffron in a mortar and stir in a little of the remaining stock, then add to the soup with enough of the remaining stock to thin the soup as required.

5 Melt the butter in a frying pan and cook the diced polenta over a high heat for 1–2 minutes, tossing until beginning to brown. Drain on paper towels.

6 Season the soup and reheat gently. Bring a large frying pan of water to the boil. Add the vinegar and reduce the heat to a simmer. Crack an egg onto a saucer. Swirl the water with a knife and drop the egg into the middle of the swirl. Repeat with the remaining eggs and poach for 2–3 minutes until set. Lift out the eggs using a draining spoon, then place one in each of four bowls.

7 Ladle the soup over the poached eggs, sprinkle polenta croutons and parsley on top and serve.

Energy 415kcal/1731kJ; Protein 13.4g; Carbohydrate 43.9g, of which sugars 0.9g; Fat 20.8g, of which saturates 8.6g; Cholesterol 217mg; Calcium 57mg; Fiber 1.9g; Sodium 247mg.

CREAMY ZUCCHINI AND DOLCELATTE SOUP

THE BEAUTY OF THIS SOUP IS ITS DELICATE COLOR, ITS CREAMY TEXTURE AND ITS SUBTLE TASTE.
GARNISH IT WITH SOME SPRIGS OF FRESH OREGANO. IF YOU PREFER A MORE PRONOUNCED CHEESE
FLAVOR, USE GORGONZOLA INSTEAD OF DOLCELATTE.

2 Add the zucchini and oregano, with salt and pepper to taste. Cook over a medium heat for 10 minutes, stirring frequently to prevent sticking.

3 Pour in the stock and bring to the boil, stirring frequently. Lower the heat, half-cover the pan and simmer gently, stirring occasionally, for about 30 minutes.

4 Add the diced dolcelatte, stirring until it is melted.

5 Process the soup in a blender or food processor until smooth, then press through a strainer into a clean pan.

6 Add two-thirds of the cream and stir over a low heat until hot, but not boiling. Check the consistency and add some more stock if the soup is too thick. Taste and adjust the seasoning if necessary.

7 Pour into heated bowls. Swirl in the remaining cream, garnish with fresh oregano and extra Dolcelatte cheese, crumbled, and serve.

SERVES 4–6

INGREDIENTS
   2 tablespoons olive oil
   ½ ounce/1 tablespoon butter
   1 medium onion, roughly chopped
   2 pounds zucchini, trimmed
     and sliced
   1 teaspoon dried oregano
   about 2½ cups vegetable stock
   4 ounces dolcelatte cheese, diced
   1¼ cups light cream
   salt and ground black pepper
To garnish
   sprigs of fresh oregano
   extra dolcelatte cheese

1 Heat the oil and butter in a large pan until foaming. Add the chopped onion and cook gently for about 5 minutes, stirring frequently, until the onion is softened but not brown.

Energy 250kcal/1031kJ; Protein 8.6g; Carbohydrate 5.8g, of which sugars 5.1g; Fat 21.5g, of which saturates 11.7g; Cholesterol 47mg; Calcium 182mg; Fiber 1.7g; Sodium 266mg.

IRISH LEEK AND BLUE CHEESE SOUP

THE BLUE CHEESE IS AN INTEGRAL PART OF THIS SUBSTANTIAL SOUP, WHICH MAKES FULL USE OF INGREDIENTS THAT HAVE ALWAYS BEEN IMPORTANT IN IRISH COOKING. IT CAN BE A GOOD WAY TO USE UP CHEESES LEFT OVER FROM THE CHEESEBOARD. SERVE WITH FRESHLY BAKED BROWN BREAD.

SERVES 6

INGREDIENTS

3 large leeks
2 ounces /¼ cup butter
2 tablespoons oil
4 ounces Irish blue cheese,
  such as Cashel Blue
½ ounce/2 tablespoons
  all-purpose flour
1 tablespoon whole-grain Irish
  mustard, or to taste
6¼ cups chicken stock
ground black pepper
2 ounces/½ cup grated cheese and
  chopped chives or scallion greens,
  to garnish

VARIATION

Any melting blue-veined cheese can be used in this recipe, such as Cabrales, Gorgonzola or Picon.

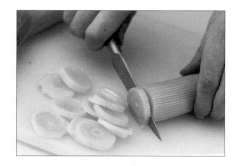

1 Slice the leeks thinly. Heat the butter and oil together in a large heavy pan and gently cook the leeks in it, covered, for 10–15 minutes, or until just softened but not brown.

2 Grate the cheese coarsely and add it to the pan, stirring over a low heat until it is melted. Add the flour and cook for 2 minutes, stirring constantly with a wooden spoon, then add ground black pepper and mustard to taste.

3 Gradually add the stock, stirring constantly and blending it in well; bring the soup to the boil.

4 Reduce the heat, cover and simmer very gently for about 15 minutes. Check the seasoning.

5 Serve the soup garnished with the extra grated cheese and the chopped chives or scallion greens, and hand fresh bread around separately.

Energy 205kcal/852kJ; Protein 8.2g; Carbohydrate 7.9g, of which sugars 2.2g; Fat 15.7g, of which saturates 9.9g; Cholesterol 40mg; Calcium 188mg; Fiber 2.2g; Sodium 347mg.

EGGPLANT SOUP WITH MOZZARELLA AND GREMOLATA

GREMOLATA, A CLASSIC ITALIAN MIXTURE OF GARLIC, LEMON AND PARSLEY, ADDS A FLOURISH OF FRESH FLAVOR TO THIS RICH CREAM SOUP.

SERVES 6

INGREDIENTS

2 tablespoons olive oil
2 shallots, chopped
2 garlic cloves, chopped
2¼ pounds eggplants, trimmed and
   roughly chopped
4 cups chicken stock
⅔ cup heavy cream
2 tablespoons chopped
   fresh parsley
6 ounces buffalo mozzarella,
   thinly sliced
salt and ground black pepper

For the gremolata
2 garlic cloves, finely chopped
grated rind of 2 lemons
1 tablespoon chopped fresh parsley

1 Heat the oil in a large pan and add the shallots and garlic. Cook for 4–5 minutes, until soft. Add the eggplants and cook for about 25 minutes, stirring occasionally, until soft and browned.

2 Pour in the stock and cook for about 5 minutes. Leave the soup to cool slightly, then puree in a food processor or blender until smooth. Return to the rinsed pan and season. Add the cream and parsley and bring to the boil.

3 Mix the ingredients for the gremolata in a small bowl.

4 Ladle the soup into bowls and lay the mozzarella on top. Sprinkle with the gremolata and serve.

Energy 261kcal/1079kJ; Protein 7.5g; Carbohydrate 4.9g, of which sugars 4.3g; Fat 23.7g, of which saturates 13.1g; Cholesterol 51mg; Calcium 137mg; Fiber 3.5g; Sodium 124mg.

BUTTERNUT SQUASH AND BLUE CHEESE RISOTTO SOUP

THIS IS, IN FACT, A VERY WET RISOTTO, BUT IT BEARS MORE THAN A PASSING RESEMBLANCE TO SOUP AND MAKES A VERY ELEGANT FIRST COURSE FOR A DINNER PARTY.

SERVES 4

INGREDIENTS

1 ounce/2 tablespoons butter
2 tablespoons olive oil
2 onions, finely chopped
½ celery stick, finely sliced
1 small butternut squash, peeled, seeded and cut into small cubes
1 tablespoon chopped sage
11 ounces/1½ cups risotto rice
5 cups hot chicken stock
2 tablespoons heavy cream
4 ounces blue cheese, finely diced
2 tablespoons olive oil
4 large sage leaves
salt and ground black pepper

1 Place the butter in a large pan with the oil and heat gently. Add the onions and celery, and cook for 4–5 minutes, until softened.

2 Stir in the butternut squash and cook for 3–4 minutes, then add the sage.

3 Add the rice and cook for 1–2 minutes, stirring, until the grains are slightly translucent. Add the chicken stock a ladleful at a time.

4 Cook until each ladleful of stock has been absorbed before adding the next. Continue adding the stock in this way until you have a very wet rice mixture. Season and stir in the cream.

5 Meanwhile, heat the oil in a frying pan and fry the sage leaves for a few seconds until crisp. Drain.

6 Stir the blue cheese into the risotto soup and ladle it into bowls. Garnish with a fried sage leaf.

Energy 505kcal/2100kJ; Protein 9.2g; Carbohydrate 63.7g, of which sugars 5.7g; Fat 23g, of which saturates 8.3g; Cholesterol 26mg; Calcium 110mg; Fiber 2.7g; Sodium 91mg.

BROCCOLI AND STILTON SOUP

THIS IS A REALLY EASY BUT RICH SOUP—CHOOSE SOMETHING SIMPLE TO FOLLOW, SUCH AS PLAINLY ROASTED OR BROILED MEAT, POULTRY OR FISH.

2 Melt the butter in a large pan and cook the onion and leek until soft but not colored. Add the broccoli and potato, then pour in the stock. Cover and simmer for 15–20 minutes, until the vegetables are tender.

3 Cool slightly then pour into a blender or food processor and puree until smooth. Pour the mixture through a strainer back into the rinsed pan.

4 Add the milk and double cream to the pan. Season to taste with salt and ground black pepper. Reheat gently. At the last minute add the cheese, stirring until it just melts. Do not allow to boil.

5 Meanwhile, blanch the reserved broccoli florets and cut them vertically into thin slices. Ladle the soup into warmed bowls, and garnish with the sliced broccoli and a generous grinding of black pepper.

COOK'S TIP
Choose broccoli that has bright, compact florets. Yellowing florets and a pungent smell are an indication of overmaturity.

SERVES 4

INGREDIENTS
  12 ounces broccoli
  1 ounce/2 tablespoons butter
  1 onion, chopped
  1 leek, white part only, chopped
  1 small potato, cut into chunks
  2½ cups hot chicken stock
  1¼ cups milk
  3 tablespoons heavy cream
  4 ounces Stilton cheese, rind removed, crumbled
  salt and ground black pepper

1 Cut the broccoli into florets, discarding any tough stems. Set aside two small florets to garnish the finished dish.

Energy 316kcal/1314kJ; Protein 14.7g; Carbohydrate 11.8g, of which sugars 7.2g; Fat 23.4g, of which saturates 14.7g; Cholesterol 60mg; Calcium 255mg; Fiber 3.7g; Sodium 310mg.

TOMATO AND BLUE CHEESE SOUP

THE CONCENTRATED FLAVOR OF ROASTED TOMATOES STRIKES A GREAT BALANCE WITH THE STRONG BLUE CHEESE AND THE BACON GARNISH.

SERVES 4

INGREDIENTS

3 pounds ripe tomatoes, peeled, quartered and seeded
2 garlic cloves, crushed
2 tablespoons vegetable oil or butter
1 leek, chopped
1 carrot, chopped
5 cups chicken stock
4 ounces blue cheese, crumbled
3 tablespoons whipping cream
several large fresh basil leaves, or 1 or 2 fresh parsley sprigs, plus extra to garnish
6 ounces bacon, cooked and crumbled, to garnish
salt and ground black pepper

3 Stir in the stock and baked tomatoes. Bring to the boil, then lower the heat, cover and simmer for about 20 minutes, until all the vegetables are soft.

4 Add the blue cheese, cream and basil or parsley. Transfer to a food processor or blender and process until smooth. Taste and adjust the seasoning. Reheat the soup, but do not boil. Garnish with bacon and a sprig of fresh parsley.

1 Preheat the oven to 400°F. Spread the tomatoes in a shallow ovenproof dish. Sprinkle with the garlic and some salt and pepper. Place in the oven and bake for 35 minutes.

2 Heat the oil or butter in a large pan. Add the leek and carrot and season lightly with salt and pepper. Cook over low heat, stirring often, for about 10 minutes, until softened.

Energy 365kcal/1519kJ; Protein 16.8g; Carbohydrate 14.7g, of which sugars 14.3g; Fat 27g, of which saturates 12.1g; Cholesterol 57mg; Calcium 191mg; Fiber 5.2g; Sodium 1067mg.

CAULIFLOWER <u>AND</u> BROCCOLI SOUP <u>WITH</u> CHEDDAR CHEESE CROUTES

CREAMY CAULIFLOWER SOUP IS GIVEN REAL BITE BY ADDING CHUNKY CAULIFLOWER AND BROCCOLI FLORETS AND CRUSTY BREAD PILED HIGH WITH MELTING CHEDDAR CHEESE.

SERVES 4

INGREDIENTS

2 ounces /¼ cup butter
1 onion, peeled and roughly
  chopped
1 garlic clove, peeled and chopped
2 cauliflowers
1 large potato, cut into bitesize
  chunks
3¾ cups chicken stock
8 ounces broccoli
⅔ cup heavy cream
6 rindless fatty bacon strips
1 small baguette
8 ounces/2 cups sharp grated
  Cheddar cheese
salt and ground black pepper
chopped fresh parsley,
  to garnish

1 Melt the butter in a large pan and add the onion and garlic. Cook for 4–5 minutes, until softened.

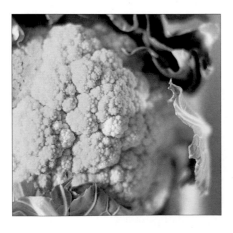

2 Break the cauliflowers into florets and add about half and all the potato to the pan. Pour in the chicken stock and bring to the boil. Reduce the heat and simmer for 20 minutes, until very soft.

3 Meanwhile, cook the rest of the cauliflower in boiling salted water for about 6 minutes, or until just tender. Remove from the pan and refresh under cold running water, then drain well.

4 Chop the broccoli into florets and add to the boiling salted water. Cook for 3–4 minutes, until just tender. Drain and refresh under cold water. Add to the cauliflower and set aside.

5 Cool the soup slightly, then process it in a food processor or blender until smooth. Return the soup to the rinsed-out pan. Add the cream and salt and pepper to taste, then heat gently until piping hot. Add the blanched cauliflower and broccoli and heat through but do not boil.

6 Meanwhile, preheat the broiler to high. Broil the bacon until very crisp, then leave to cool slightly.

7 Ladle the soup into flameproof bowls. Tear the baguette into four ragged pieces and place one in the center of each bowl. Sprinkle grated cheese over the bread and stand the bowls on one or two baking trays. Grill for 2–3 minutes, until the cheese is melted and bubbling. Take care when serving the hot bowls.

8 Roughly chop the bacon and sprinkle it over the melted cheese, then sprinkle the chopped parsley over the top and serve immediately.

Energy 737kcal/3071kJ; Protein 34.8g; Carbohydrate 45.5g, of which sugars 9.2g; Fat 46.2g, of which saturates 26.4g; Cholesterol 121mg; Calcium 589mg; Fiber 6.6g; Sodium 1206mg.

ONE-POT MEALS

A soup can be substantial enough to be a complete, one-pot meal, and in this section there are exciting dishes to serve on their own for lunch or supper. Gumbo is just such a dish, and here you will find recipes for Seafood and Sausage Gumbo, Louisiana Seafood Gumbo and Green Herb Gumbo. In Asian countries a laksa makes a complete meal — Malaysian Shrimp Laksa is a good example. From the Mediterranean come Provençal Fish Soup with Pasta, and classic Bouillabaisse.

SEAFOOD AND SAUSAGE GUMBO

GUMBO IS A SOUP, BUT IS OFTEN SERVED OVER RICE AS A MAIN COURSE. THIS RECIPE IS ENOUGH FOR TEN TO TWELVE PEOPLE—SERVE IT FOR AN INFORMAL LUNCH OR SUPPER PARTY.

SERVES 10–12

INGREDIENTS

3 pounds raw shrimp in the shell
6¼ cups water
4 medium onions, 2 of them quartered
4 bay leaves
6 fluid ounces/¾ cup vegetable oil
4 ounces/1 cup flour
5 tablespoons margarine or butter
2 green bell peppers, seeded and finely chopped
4 celery sticks, finely chopped
1½ pounds Polish or andouille sausage, cut into ½-inch slices
1 pound fresh okra, cut into ½-inch slices
3 garlic cloves, crushed
½ teaspoon fresh or dried thyme leaves
2 teaspoons salt
½ teaspoon ground black pepper
½ teaspoon white pepper
1 teaspoon cayenne pepper
2 tablespoons hot pepper sauce (optional)
6 ounces/2 cups chopped, peeled, fresh or canned plum tomatoes
1 pound fresh crabmeat
boiled rice, to serve

1 Peel and devein the shrimp; reserve the heads and shells. Cover and chill the shrimp while you make the sauce.

2 Place the shrimp heads and shells in a pan with the water, quartered onion and 1 bay leaf. Bring to the boil, then partly cover and simmer for 20 minutes. Strain and set aside.

3 To make a Cajun roux, heat the oil in a heavy frying pan. When the oil is hot, add the flour, a little at a time, and blend to a smooth paste.

4 Cook over a medium-low heat, stirring constantly for 25–40 minutes until the roux reaches the color of peanut butter. Remove the pan from the heat and continue stirring until the roux has cooled and stopped cooking.

5 Melt the margarine or butter in a large, heavy pan or flameproof casserole. Finely chop the remaining onions and add to the pan with the chopped peppers and celery. Cook over medium-low heat for 6–8 minutes, until the onions are softened, stirring occasionally.

6 Add the sausage and mix well. Cook for 5 minutes more. Add the okra and garlic, stir, and cook until the okra stops producing white "threads."

7 Add the remaining bay leaves, the thyme, salt, the black and the white peppers, cayenne pepper, and hot pepper sauce to taste, if using. Mix thoroughly. Stir in 6 cups of the shrimp stock and the chopped tomatoes. Bring to the boil, partly cover the pan, lower the heat and simmer for about 20 minutes.

8 Whisk in the Cajun roux. Increase the heat and bring to the boil, whisking well. Lower the heat again and simmer, uncovered, for a further 40–45 minutes, stirring occasionally.

9 Gently stir in the shrimp and crabmeat. Cook for 3–4 minutes until the shrimp turn pink.

10 To serve, put a mound of hot boiled rice in each serving bowl and ladle on the gumbo, making sure each person gets some shrimp, some crabmeat and some sausage.

Energy 481kcal/2001kJ; Protein 28.7g; Carbohydrate 22.9g, of which sugars 8.8g; Fat 31.1g, of which saturates 6.6g; Cholesterol 96mg; Calcium 279mg; Fiber 4.1g; Sodium 1954mg.

LOUISIANA SEAFOOD GUMBO

GUMBO IS A SOUP, BUT IS SERVED OVER RICE AS A MAIN COURSE. IN LOUISIANA, OYSTERS ARE CHEAP AND PROLIFIC, AND WOULD BE USED HERE INSTEAD OF MUSSELS.

SERVES 6

INGREDIENTS

1 pound fresh mussels
1 pound shrimp, in the shell
1 cooked crab, about 2¼ pounds
a small bunch of parsley, leaves
  chopped and stalks reserved
⅔ cup vegetable oil
4 ounces/1 cup all-purpose flour
1 green bell pepper, chopped
1 large onion, chopped
2 celery sticks, sliced
3 garlic cloves, finely chopped
3 ounces smoked spiced sausage,
  skinned and sliced
10 ounces/1½ cups white long
  grain rice
6 scallions, shredded
cayenne pepper and
  Tabasco sauce
salt

1 Wash the mussels in several changes of cold water, pulling away the black "beards." Discard any mussels that are broken or do not close when you tap them firmly.

2 Bring 8 fluid ounces/1 cup water to the boil in a deep pan. Add the mussels, cover tightly and cook over a high heat, shaking frequently, for 3 minutes. As the mussels open, lift them out with tongs into a strainer set over a bowl. Discard any that fail to open. Shell the mussels, discarding the shells. Return the liquid from the bowl to the pan and increase the quantity up to 8 cups with water.

3 Peel the shrimp and set them aside, reserving a few for the garnish. Put the shells and heads into the pan.

4 Remove all the meat from the crab, separating the brown and white meat. Add all the pieces of shell to the pan with 2 teaspoons salt.

5 Bring the shellfish stock to the boil, skimming it regularly. When there is no more froth on the surface, add the parsley stalks and simmer for 15 minutes. Cool the stock, then strain it into a measuring cup and increase to 8 cups with water.

6 Heat the oil in a heavy pan and stir in the flour. Stir constantly over a medium heat with a wooden spoon or whisk until the roux reaches a golden-brown color. Immediately add the pepper, onion, celery and garlic. Continue cooking for about 3 minutes until the onion is soft. Stir in the sausage. Reheat the stock.

7 Stir the brown crabmeat into the roux, then ladle in the hot stock a little at a time, stirring constantly until it has all been smoothly incorporated. Bring to a low boil, partially cover the pan, then simmer the gumbo for 30 minutes.

8 Meanwhile, cook the rice in plenty of lightly salted boiling water until the grains are tender.

9 Add the shrimp, mussels, white crabmeat and scallions to the gumbo. Return to the boil and season with salt, if necessary, cayenne and a dash or two of Tabasco sauce. Simmer for a further minute, then add the chopped parsley leaves. Serve immediately, ladling the soup over the hot rice in soup plates.

COOK'S TIP
It is vital to stir constantly to darken the roux without burning. Should black specks appear at any stage of cooking, discard the roux and start again. Have the onion, green bell pepper and celery ready to add to the roux the minute it reaches the correct golden-brown stage, as this arrests its darkening.

Energy 518kcal/2161kJ; Protein 23.6g; Carbohydrate 54.8g, of which sugars 2.1g; Fat 22.9g, of which saturates 3.7g; Cholesterol 55mg; Calcium 143mg; Fiber 1.5g; Sodium 728mg.

MALAYSIAN SHRIMP LAKSA

THIS SPICY SHRIMP AND NOODLE SOUP TASTES JUST AS GOOD WHEN MADE WITH FRESH CRABMEAT OR ANY FLAKED COOKED FISH INSTEAD OF THE SHRIMP. IF YOU ARE SHORT OF TIME, BUY READYMADE LAKSA PASTE, WHICH YOU WILL FIND IN ORIENTAL STORES.

SERVES 2–3

INGREDIENTS
    4 ounces rice vermicelli or stir-fry
      rice noodles
    1 tablespoon vegetable or
      peanut oil
    2½ cups fish stock
    14 fluid ounces/1⅔ cups thin
      coconut milk
    2 tablespoons Thai fish sauce
    ½ lime
    16–24 cooked peeled shrimp
    salt
    cayenne pepper
    4 tablespoons fresh cilantro
      sprigs and leaves, chopped,
      to garnish
For the spicy paste
    2 lemongrass stalks,
      finely chopped
    2 fresh red chiles, seeded
      and chopped
    1-inch fresh ginger root, peeled
      and sliced
    ½ teaspoon shrimp paste
    2 garlic cloves, peeled and
      chopped
    ½ teaspoon ground turmeric
    2 tablespoons tamarind paste

1 Cook the rice vermicelli or stir-fry rice noodles in a large pan of boiling salted water for 3–4 minutes, or according to the instructions on the packet.

2 Transfer the noodles to a large strainer or colander, then rinse under cold water and drain. Set aside.

3 To make the spicy paste, place all the prepared ingredients in a mortar and pound with a pestle. Alternatively, put the ingredients in a food processor until a smooth paste is formed.

4 Heat the vegetable or peanut oil in a large pan, add the spicy paste and fry, stirring constantly, for a few moments to release all the flavors. Be careful not to let it burn.

5 Add the fish stock and coconut milk and bring to the boil. Stir in the fish sauce, then simmer for 5 minutes. Season with salt and cayenne to taste, adding a squeeze of lime. Add the shrimp and heat through for a few seconds.

6 Divide the noodles between two or three soup plates. Pour over the soup. Garnish each portion with fresh cilantro and serve piping hot.

Energy 436kcal/1830kJ; Protein 36.9g; Carbohydrate 55.3g, of which sugars 10.2g; Fat 7.6g, of which saturates 1.2g; Cholesterol 341mg; Calcium 239mg; Fiber 0.8g; Sodium 562mg.

PROVENÇAL FISH SOUP

THE ADDITION OF RICE MAKES THIS A SUBSTANTIAL MAIN-MEAL SOUP. BASMATI OR THAI RICE HAVE THE BEST FLAVOR, BUT ANY LONG GRAIN RICE COULD BE USED. IF YOU PREFER A STRONGER TOMATO FLAVOR, REPLACE THE WHITE WINE WITH EXTRA BOTTLED TOMATOES.

SERVES 4–6

INGREDIENTS

  1 pound fresh mussels
  about 8 fluid ounces/1 cup white wine
  1½–2 pounds mixed white fish
    fillets, such as monkfish, plaice,
    flounder, cod or haddock
  6 large scallops
  2 tablespoons olive oil
  3 leeks, chopped
  1 garlic clove, crushed
  1 red bell pepper, seeded and cut
    into 1-inch pieces
  1 yellow bell pepper, seeded and cut
    into 1-inch pieces
  6 ounces fennel bulb, cut into
    1½-inch pieces
  1 can (14 ounces) chopped tomatoes
  ⅔ cup bottled strained tomatoes
  about 1¾ pints/4 cups well-flavored
    fish stock
  generous pinch of saffron threads,
    soaked in 1 tablespoon hot water
  6 ounces/scant 1 cup basmati
    rice, soaked
  8 large raw shrimp, peeled and
    deveined
  salt and ground black pepper
  2–3 tablespoons fresh dill,
    to garnish

1 Clean the mussels, discarding any that do not close when tapped with a knife. Place them in a heavy pan. Add 6 tablespoons of the wine, cover, bring to the boil over a high heat and cook for about 3 minutes or until all the mussels have opened.

2 Strain, reserving the liquid. Discard any mussels that have not opened. Set aside half the mussels in their shells for the garnish; shell the rest and put them in a bowl.

3 Cut the fish into 1-inch cubes. Detach the corals from the scallops and slice the white flesh into three or four pieces. Add the scallops to the fish and the corals to the shelled mussels.

4 Heat the olive oil in a pan and fry the leeks and garlic for 3–4 minutes, until softened. Add the pepper chunks and fennel, and fry for 2 minutes more, until just softened.

COOK'S TIP
To make your own fish stock, place about 1 pound white fish trimmings—bones, heads, but not gills—in a large pan. Add a chopped onion, carrot, bay leaf, parsley sprig, 6 peppercorns and a piece of pared lemon rind. Pour in 5 cups water, bring to the boil, then simmer gently for 25–30 minutes. Strain through cheesecloth.

5 Add all of the tomatoes, stock, saffron water, mussel liquid and wine. Season and cook for 5 minutes. Drain the rice, stir it into the mixture, cover and simmer for 10 minutes.

6 Carefully stir in the white fish and cook over a low heat for 5 minutes. Add the shrimp, cook for 2 minutes, then add the scallop corals and shelled mussels and cook for 2–3 minutes more, until all the fish is tender. Add a little extra white wine or stock if needed. Spoon into warmed soup dishes, top with mussels in their shells and sprinkle with the dill. Serve immediately.

Energy 568kcal/2385kJ; Protein 59.9g; Carbohydrate 50.5g, of which sugars 12.9g; Fat 9.7g, of which saturates 1.6g; Cholesterol 163mg; Calcium 182mg; Fiber 5.9g; Sodium 418mg.

CHICKEN SOUP <u>WITH</u> VERMICELLI

IN MOROCCO, THE COOK—WHO IS ALMOST ALWAYS THE MOST SENIOR FEMALE OF THE HOUSEHOLD—WOULD USE A WHOLE CHICKEN FOR THIS NOURISHING SOUP, TO SERVE TO HER FAMILY.

SERVES 4–6

INGREDIENTS

2 tablespoons sunflower oil
½ ounce/1 tablespoon butter
1 onion, chopped
2 chicken legs or breast pieces,
  halved or quartered
flour, for dusting
2 carrots, cut into 1½-inch pieces
1 parsnip, cut into 1½-inch pieces
6¼ cups chicken stock
1 cinnamon stick
a good pinch of paprika
a pinch of saffron
2 egg yolks
juice of ½ lemon
2 tablespoons chopped fresh cilantro
2 tablespoons chopped fresh parsley
5 ounces vermicelli
salt and ground black pepper

1 Heat the oil and butter in a pan or flameproof casserole, and fry the onion for 3–4 minutes until softened. Dust the chicken pieces in seasoned flour and fry gently until they are evenly browned.

2 Transfer the chicken to a plate and add the carrots and parsnip to the pan. Cook over a gentle heat for 3–4 minutes, stirring frequently. Return the chicken to the pan. Add the stock, cinnamon stick and paprika and season well.

3 Bring the soup to the boil, cover and simmer for 1 hour until the vegetables are very tender.

4 Meanwhile, blend the saffron in 2 tablespoons boiling water. Beat the egg yolks with the lemon juice in a separate bowl and add the cilantro and parsley. When the saffron water has cooled, stir into the egg and lemon mixture.

5 When the vegetables are tender, transfer the chicken to a plate. Increase the heat and stir in the noodles. Cook for 5–6 minutes until tender. Remove the skin and bones from the chicken and chop the flesh into bitesize pieces.

6 When the vermicelli is cooked, stir in the chicken pieces and the egg, lemon and saffron mixture. Cook over a low heat for 1–2 minutes, stirring all the time. Adjust the seasoning and serve.

Energy 236kcal/984kJ; Protein 15.8g; Carbohydrate 24.1g, of which sugars 3.3g; Fat 8.5g, of which saturates 2.5g; Cholesterol 108mg; Calcium 40mg; Fiber 1.6g; Sodium 60mg.

CHICKEN MINESTRONE

THIS IS A SPECIAL MINESTRONE MADE WITH FRESH CHICKEN. SERVED WITH CRUSTY ITALIAN BREAD, IT MAKES A HEARTY MEAL IN ITSELF.

SERVES 4–6

INGREDIENTS

1 tablespoon olive oil
2 chicken thighs
3 rindless fatty bacon strips,
  chopped
1 onion, finely chopped
a few fresh basil leaves, shredded
a few fresh rosemary leaves,
  finely chopped
1 tablespoon chopped fresh
  Italian parsley
2 potatoes, cut into ½-inch cubes
1 large carrot, cut into ½-inch cubes
2 small zucchini, cut into
  ½-inch cubes
1 or 2 celery sticks, cut into
  ½-inch cubes
4 cups chicken stock
7 ounces/1¾ cups frozen peas
3½ ounces/scant 1 cup stellette or
  other small soup pasta
salt and ground black pepper
Parmesan cheese shavings,
  to serve

1 Heat the oil in a large frying pan, add the chicken thighs and fry for about 5 minutes on each side. Remove with a slotted spoon and set aside.

2 Add the bacon, onion and herbs to the pan and cook gently, stirring constantly, for about 5 minutes. Add the potatoes, carrot, zucchini and celery and cook for 5–7 minutes more.

COOK'S TIP
This soup has more flavor if you use homemade chicken stock (see page 31).

3 Return the chicken thighs to the pan, add the stock and bring to the boil. Cover and cook over a low heat for 35–40 minutes, stirring the soup occasionally to prevent sticking.

4 Remove the chicken thighs with a slotted spoon and place them on a board. Stir the peas and pasta into the soup and bring back to the boil. Simmer, stirring, for 7–8 minutes or according to the instructions on the packet, until the pasta is just *al dente*.

5 Meanwhile, remove and discard the chicken skin, then remove the meat from the chicken bones and cut it into small (½-inch) pieces.

6 Return the chicken meat to the soup, stir well and heat through. Taste and add more salt and ground black pepper if necessary.

7 Ladle into warmed soup plates or bowls, top with Parmesan shavings and serve piping hot.

Energy 198kcal/833kJ; Protein 15.6g; Carbohydrate 23.3g, of which sugars 3.9g; Fat 5.4g, of which saturates 1.4g; Cholesterol 30mg; Calcium 31mg; Fiber 3.2g; Sodium 224mg.

GENOESE MINESTRONE

IN GENOA, THEY OFTEN MAKE MINESTRONE LIKE THIS, WITH PESTO STIRRED IN TOWARDS THE END OF COOKING. IT IS PACKED FULL OF VEGETABLES AND HAS A STRONG, HEADY FLAVOR, MAKING IT AN EXCELLENT VEGETARIAN SUPPER DISH WHEN SERVED WITH BREAD.

SERVES 4–6

INGREDIENTS

3 tablespoons olive oil
1 onion, finely chopped
2 celery sticks, finely chopped
1 large carrot, finely chopped
5 ounces green beans, cut into
   2-inch pieces
1 zucchini, finely sliced
1 potato, cut into ½-inch cubes
¼ savoy cabbage, shredded
1 small eggplant, cut into
   ½-inch cubes
1 can (7 ounces) cannellini beans,
   drained and rinsed
2 Italian plum tomatoes, chopped
5 cups vegetable stock
3½ ounces spaghetti or vermicelli
salt and ground black pepper
For the pesto
   about 20 fresh basil leaves
   1 garlic clove
   2 teaspoons pine nuts
   1 tablespoon freshly grated
      Parmesan cheese
   1 tablespoon freshly grated
      Pecorino cheese
   2 tablespoons extra virgin
      olive oil

1 Heat the oil in a large pan, add the onion, celery and carrot, and cook over a low heat, stirring, for 5–7 minutes.

2 Mix in the green beans, zucchini, potato and cabbage. Stir-fry over a medium heat for 3 minutes. Add the eggplant, cannellini beans and plum tomatoes and stir-fry for 2–3 minutes.

3 Pour in the stock with salt and pepper to taste. Bring to the boil. Stir well, cover and lower the heat. Simmer for 40 minutes, stirring occasionally.

4 Meanwhile, put all the pesto ingredients in a food processor and process until the mixture forms a smooth sauce, adding 1–3 tablespoons water through the feeder tube if the sauce seems too thick.

5 Break the pasta into small pieces and add it to the soup. Simmer, stirring frequently, for 5 minutes. Add the pesto sauce and stir it in well, then simmer for 2–3 minutes more, or until the pasta is *al dente*.

6 Check the seasoning and serve hot, in warmed soup plates or bowls.

Energy 222kcal/927kJ; Protein 8.2g; Carbohydrate 27.4g, of which sugars 6.6g; Fat 9.2g, of which saturates 2.1g; Cholesterol 5mg; Calcium 129mg; Fiber 4.9g; Sodium 203mg.

BEAN AND PASTA SOUP

THIS HEARTY, MAIN-MEAL SOUP SOMETIMES GOES BY THE SIMPLER NAME OF PASTA E FAGIOLI, WHILE SOME ITALIANS REFER TO IT AS MINESTRONE DI PASTA E FAGIOLI. TRADITIONAL RECIPES USE DRIED BEANS AND A HAM BONE.

SERVES 4–6

INGREDIENTS

    2 tablespoons olive oil
    4 ounces/⅔ cup pancetta or rindless
      smoked fatty bacon, diced
    1 onion
    1 carrot
    1 celery stick
    7½ cups beef stock
    1 cinnamon stick or a good pinch of
      ground cinnamon
    3½ ounces/scant 1 cup small
      pasta shapes, such as conchiglie
      or coralini
    1 can (14 ounces) borlotti beans,
      rinsed and drained
    1 thick slice cooked ham (about
      8 ounces), diced
    salt and ground black pepper
    Parmesan cheese shavings,
      to serve

1 Heat the oil in a large pan, add the pancetta or bacon and cook, stirring, until lightly colored.

2 Finely chop the vegetables, add to the pan and cook for about 10 minutes, stirring frequently, until lightly colored.

3 Pour in the stock, add the cinnamon with salt and pepper to taste and bring to the boil. Cover and simmer gently for 15–20 minutes.

COOK'S TIP
This soup will have the best flavor if you use a good homemade beef stock (see page 32).

4 Add the pasta shapes. Bring back to the boil, lower the heat and simmer, stirring frequently, for 5 minutes. Add the borlotti beans and diced ham and simmer for 2–3 minutes, until the pasta is *al dente*.

5 Remove the cinnamon stick, if used, taste the soup and adjust the seasoning.

6 Spoon into warmed bowls and serve hot, sprinkled with Parmesan shavings.

VARIATIONS
• If you prefer, you can use spaghetti or tagliatelle instead of the small pasta shapes, breaking it into small pieces over the pan.
• Use cannellini or white navy beans instead of the borlotti. Add them to the pan after the stock in step 1. If you like, add 1 tablespoon tomato paste along with the beans.

Energy 240kcal/1010kJ; Protein 16.7g; Carbohydrate 25.1g, of which sugars 4.8g; Fat 8.8g, of which saturates 2.2g; Cholesterol 32mg; Calcium 60mg; Fiber 5g; Sodium 1009mg.

BACON AND LENTIL SOUP

SERVE THIS HEARTY AND FLAVORSOME SOUP FOR A FAMILY LUNCH OR SUPPER WITH CHUNKS OF WARM, CRUSTY BREAD. IT'S JUST THE THING FOR A COLD WINTER'S DAY.

SERVES 4

INGREDIENTS

1 pound thick-sliced bacon, cubed
1 onion, roughly chopped
1 small turnip, roughly chopped
1 celery stick, chopped
1 potato, roughly chopped
1 carrot, sliced
3 ounces/scant ½ cup lentils
bouquet garni
ground black pepper
fresh Italian parsley, to garnish

COOK'S TIP

Use green or brown lentils for this soup as they retain their disk shape when cooked and do not disintegrate.

1 Heat a large pan and add the bacon. Cook for a few minutes, allowing the fat to run out.

2 Add the chopped onion, turnip, celery and potato and the sliced carrot. Cook for 4 minutes, stirring from time to time.

3 Add the lentils, bouquet garni, seasoning and enough water to cover. Bring to the boil and simmer for 1 hour or until the lentils are tender.

4 Ladle the soup into warm bowls and serve garnished with Italian parsley.

Energy 359kcal/1500kJ; Protein 24.5g; Carbohydrate 23.5g, of which sugars 4.6g; Fat 19.2g, of which saturates 7.1g; Cholesterol 60mg; Calcium 42mg; Fiber 2.8g; Sodium 1759mg.

GALICIAN BROTH

THIS DELICIOUS MAIN-MEAL SOUP IS VERY SIMILAR TO THE WARMING, CHUNKY MEAT AND POTATO BROTHS OF COOLER CLIMATES.

SERVES 4

INGREDIENTS

1 pound piece smoked or
   cured ham
2 bay leaves
2 onions, peeled and
   finely sliced
6¼ cups cold water
2 teaspoons paprika
1½ pounds potatoes, cut into
   large chunks
8 ounces collards
1 can (14 ounces) navy or cannellini
   beans, drained
salt and ground black pepper

1 Soak the smoked or cured ham overnight in cold water.

2 Next day, drain the gammon and put it in a large pan with the bay leaves and onions. Pour the water on top.

3 Bring to the boil, then reduce the heat and simmer for about 1½ hours until the meat is tender. Keep an eye on the pan to make sure it doesn't boil over.

4 Drain the meat, reserving the cooking liquid, and leave to cool slightly. Discard the skin and any excess fat from the meat then cut into small chunks. Return to the pan with the cooking liquid, paprika and potatoes. Cover and simmer gently for 20 minutes.

5 Cut away the cores from the collards. Roll up the leaves and cut into thin shreds. Add to the pan with the beans and simmer for about 10 minutes. Season with salt and freshly ground black pepper to taste, ladle into warmed soup bowls and serve piping hot.

COOK'S TIP
Bacon knuckles can be used instead of smoked or cured ham. The bones will give the juices a delicious flavor.

Energy 419kcal/1763kJ; Protein 32.1g; Carbohydrate 52.7g, of which sugars 11.5g; Fat 10.3g, of which saturates 3.2g; Cholesterol 26mg; Calcium 226mg; Fiber 10.9g; Sodium 1412mg.

IRISH COUNTRY SOUP

TRADITIONALLY, BUTTERED CHUNKS OF BROWN BREAD, OR IRISH SODA BREAD, WOULD BE SERVED WITH THIS HEARTY ONE-POT MEAL, WHICH IS BASED ON THE CLASSIC IRISH STEW.

SERVES 4

INGREDIENTS

1 tablespoon vegetable oil
1½ pounds boneless lamb chump
    chops, trimmed and cut into
    small cubes
2 small onions, quartered
2 leeks, thickly sliced
4 cups water
2 large potatoes, cut into chunks
2 carrots, thickly sliced
sprig of fresh thyme, plus extra
    to garnish
½ ounce/1 tablespoon butter
2 tablespoons chopped fresh parsley
salt and ground black pepper
brown or Irish soda bread, to serve

VARIATION

The vegetables can be varied according
to the season. Rutabaga, turnip, celeriac
and even cabbage could be added in
place of some of those listed.

1 Heat the oil in a large pan, add
the lamb in batches and fry, turning
occasionally, until well browned all over.
Use a slotted spoon to remove the lamb
from the pan and set aside.

2 When all the lamb has been browned,
add the onions to the pan and cook
for 4–5 minutes, until the onions are
browned. Return the meat to the pan
and add the leeks. Pour in the water,
then bring to the boil. Reduce the heat,
then cover and simmer for about 1 hour.

3 Add the potatoes, carrots and fresh
thyme, and cook for 40 minutes, until
the lamb is tender. Remove from the
heat and leave to stand for 5 minutes,
then skim off the fat.

4 Pour off the stock into a clean pan
and whisk the butter into it. Stir in the
parsley and season well, then pour the
liquid back over the soup ingredients.

5 Ladle the soup into warmed bowls
and garnish with sprigs of fresh thyme.

Energy 453kcal/1893kJ; Protein 36.5g; Carbohydrate 20.5g, of which sugars 6.2g; Fat 25.6g, of which saturates 11.3g; Cholesterol 136mg; Calcium 53mg; Fiber 3.7g; Sodium 185mg.

MOROCCAN HARIRA

THIS IS A HEARTY MAIN-COURSE MEAT AND VEGETABLE SOUP, EATEN DURING THE MONTH OF RAMADAN, WHEN THE MUSLIM POPULATION FASTS BETWEEN SUNRISE AND SUNSET.

SERVES 4

INGREDIENTS

1 pound well-flavored tomatoes
8 ounces lamb, cut into pieces
½ teaspoon ground turmeric
½ teaspoon ground cinnamon
1 ounce/2 tablespoons butter
4 tablespoons chopped
  fresh cilantro
2 tablespoons chopped
  fresh parsley
1 onion, chopped
2 ounces/¼ cup split red lentils
3 ounces/½ cup dried chickpeas,
  soaked overnight in cold water
2½ cups water
4 pearl onions or shallots
1 ounce/¼ cup fine noodles
salt and ground black pepper
fresh cilantro, lemon slices
  and ground cinnamon, to garnish

COOK'S TIPS
• Most of the vitamins in fruits and vegetables are just under the skin. So, if you wish to improve the nutritional content, or simply save some time, the skins of the tomatoes can be left on.
• For maximum cinnamon flavor, grind a broken cinnamon stick in a spice grinder or a coffee grinder kept especially for spices.

1 Plunge the tomatoes into boiling water for 30 seconds, then refresh in cold water. Peel off the skins. Cut into quarters and remove the seeds. Chop the flesh roughly.

2 Put the pieces of lamb, ground turmeric, cinnamon, butter, fresh cilantro, parsley and onion into a large pan, and cook over a medium heat, stirring, for 5 minutes.

3 Add the chopped tomatoes and continue to cook for 10 minutes, stirring the mixture frequently.

4 Rinse the lentils under running water and drain them well. Stir them into the contents of the pan, with the drained chickpeas and the measured water. Season with salt and pepper. Bring to the boil, lower the heat, cover, and simmer gently for 1½ hours.

5 Add the onions or shallots. Cook for 25 minutes. Add the noodles and cook for 5 minutes more. Spoon into bowls and garnish with the cilantro, lemon slices and cinnamon.

Energy 294kcal/1234kJ; Protein 19.7g; Carbohydrate 25.2g, of which sugars 4.9g; Fat 13.5g, of which saturates 6.6g; Cholesterol 58mg; Calcium 55mg; Fiber 4g; Sodium 119mg.

Scotch Broth

Sustaining and warming, Scotch broth is custom-made for the chilly Scottish weather, and makes a delicious winter soup anywhere. Traditionally, a large pot of it is made, and this is dipped into throughout the next few days, the flavor improving all the time.

SERVES 6–8

INGREDIENTS

2¼ pounds lean shoulder or
   breast of lamb, cut into large,
   even-size chunks
7½ cups cold water
1 large onion, chopped
2 ounces/¼ cup pearl barley
bouquet garni
1 large carrot, chopped
1 turnip, chopped
3 leeks, chopped
1 small white cabbage,
   finely shredded
salt and ground black pepper
chopped fresh parsley, to garnish

1 Put the lamb and water in a large pan over a medium heat and gently bring to the boil. Skim off the scum that rises to the top with a spoon.

2 Add the onion, pearl barley and bouquet garni, and stir in thoroughly.

3 Bring the soup back to the boil, then reduce the heat, partly cover the pan and simmer gently for a further 1 hour. Make sure that it does not boil dry.

4 Add the remaining vegetables to the pan and season with salt and ground black pepper. Bring to the boil, partly cover again and simmer for about 35 minutes, until the vegetables are tender.

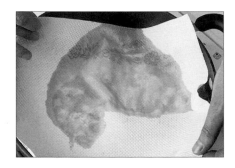

5 Remove the surplus fat from the top of the soup with paper towels. Serve the soup hot, garnished with chopped parsley, and accompanied by chunks of fresh bread.

Energy 387kcal/1619kJ; Protein 36.2g; Carbohydrate 17.7g, of which sugars 9.1g; Fat 19.5g, of which saturates 8.8g; Cholesterol 127mg; Calcium 86mg; Fiber 4.3g; Sodium 157mg.

CLAM AND PASTA SOUP

THIS SOUP IS A VARIATION OF THE TRADITIONAL PASTA DISH, SPAGHETTI ALLE VONGOLE, USING PANTRY INGREDIENTS. SERVE IT WITH HOT FOCACCIA OR CIABATTA FOR AN INFORMAL SUPPER WITH FRIENDS.

<u>SERVES 4</u>

INGREDIENTS
2 tablespoons olive oil
1 large onion, finely chopped
2 garlic cloves, crushed
1 can (14 ounces) chopped tomatoes
1 tablespoon sun-dried tomato paste
1 teaspoon granulated sugar
1 teaspoon dried mixed herbs
about 3 cups fish or vegetable
  stock
⅔ cup red wine
2 ounces/½ cup small pasta shapes
1 jar or can (5 ounces) clams in
  natural juice
2 tablespoons finely chopped fresh
  Italian parsley, plus a few whole
  leaves to garnish
salt and ground black pepper

1 Heat the oil in a large pan. Add the garlic, tomatoes, tomato paste, sugar, herbs, stock and wine, with salt and pepper to taste. Bring to the boil. Lower the heat, half-cover the pan and simmer for 10 minutes. Cook the onion gently for 5 minutes until softened.

2 Add the pasta and simmer, uncovered, for about 10 minutes or until *al dente*. Stir occasionally to prevent the pasta shapes from sticking together.

COOK'S TIP
Use whichever small pasta shapes you have in the pantry, or spaghetti broken into small pieces.

3 Add the clams and their juice to the soup and heat through for 3–4 minutes, adding more stock if required. Do not allow it to boil, or the clams will become tough. Remove from the heat, stir in the chopped parsley and adjust the seasoning. Serve hot, sprinkled with coarsely ground black pepper and parsley leaves.

Energy 196kcal/821kJ; Protein 9.3g; Carbohydrate 20.2g, of which sugars 8.9g; Fat 6.5g, of which saturates 1g; Cholesterol 25mg; Calcium 67mg; Fiber 2.6g; Sodium 466mg.

SQUASH, BACON AND SWISS CHEESE SOUP

THIS IS A LIGHTLY SPICED SQUASH SOUP, ENRICHED WITH PLENTY OF CREAMY MELTING CHEESE. SERVE IT WITH CRUSTY BREAD FOR LUNCH OR SUPPER.

SERVES 4

INGREDIENTS

2 pounds butternut squash
8 ounces smoked lean back bacon
1 tablespoon oil
8 ounces onions, roughly chopped
2 garlic cloves, crushed
2 teaspoons ground cumin
1 tablespoon ground coriander
10 ounces potatoes, cut into
  small chunks
3¾ cups vegetable stock
2 teaspoons cornstarch
2 tablespoons crème fraîche
Tabasco sauce, to taste
salt and freshly ground
  black pepper
6 ounces/1½ cups Gruyère cheese,
  grated, to serve
crusty bread, to serve

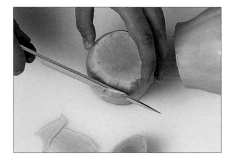

1 Cut the squash into large pieces. Using a sharp knife, carefully remove the skin, wasting as little of the flesh as possible.

2 Scoop out and discard the seeds. Chop the squash into small chunks. Remove all the fat from the bacon and roughly chop it into small pieces.

3 Heat the oil in a large pan and cook the onions and garlic for 3 minutes, or until beginning to soften.

4 Add the bacon and cook for about 3 minutes. Stir in the spices and cook on a low heat for a further minute.

COOK'S TIPS
• Pumpkin can be used in place of butternut squash and is equally delicious.
• The soup will have a superior flavor if you make your own vegetable stock (see page 30).

5 Add the chopped squash, potatoes and stock. Bring to the boil and simmer for 15 minutes, or until the squash and potatoes are tender.

6 Blend the cornstarch with 2 tablespoons water and add to the soup with the crème fraîche. Bring to the boil and simmer, uncovered, for 3 minutes. Adjust the seasoning and add Tabasco sauce to taste.

7 Ladle the soup into bowls and sprinkle the cheese on top. Serve with crusty bread to scoop up the melted cheese.

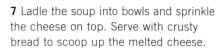

Energy 438kcal/1823kJ; Protein 24g; Carbohydrate 23g, of which sugars 8.1g; Fat 27.4g, of which saturates 15.3g; Cholesterol 81mg; Calcium 414mg; Fiber 3.7g; Sodium 1195mg.

LAMB, PEA AND PUMPKIN SOUP

THIS IS A HEARTY SOUP TO WARM THE COCKLES OF THE HEART IN EVEN THE CHILLIEST WEATHER.
THE CARAWAY SEEDS AND CHILE ADD A SPICY FLAVOR.

SERVES 4

INGREDIENTS

4 ounces/⅔ cup split black-eyed
  peas, soaked for 1–2 hours
  or overnight
1½ pounds shoulder or
  breast of lamb, cut into
  medium-size chunks
1 teaspoon chopped fresh thyme or
  ½ teaspoon dried thyme
2 bay leaves
5 cups stock or water
1 onion, peeled and sliced
8 ounces pumpkin, cut into
  1-inch dice
2 black cardamom pods
1½ teaspoons ground turmeric
1 tablespoon chopped
  fresh cilantro
½ teaspoon caraway seeds
1 fresh green chile, seeded
  and chopped
2 green bananas
1 carrot
salt and ground black pepper

1 Drain the black-eyed peas, place them in a pan and cover with fresh cold water.

2 Bring the peas to the boil, boil rapidly for 10 minutes and then reduce the heat and simmer, covered, for about 40–50 minutes until tender, adding more water if necessary. Remove the pan from the heat and set aside to cool.

COOK'S TIP
Wear rubber gloves to protect your hands when preparing the green chilli.

3 Meanwhile, put the lamb in a large pan, add the thyme, bay leaves and stock or water and bring to the boil. Cover and simmer over a moderate heat for 1 hour, until tender.

4 Add the onion, pumpkin, cardamom, turmeric, cilantro, caraway, chile and seasoning and stir.

5 Bring back to a simmer and cook, uncovered, for 15 minutes, stirring occasionally, until the pumpkin is tender.

6 When the beans are cool, spoon into a blender or food processor with their liquid and blend to a smooth paste.

7 Peel the bananas and cut into medium slices. Cut the carrot into thin slices. Stir into the soup with the bean paste and cook for 10–12 minutes, until the carrot is tender. Adjust the seasoning and serve immediately.

Energy 469kcal/1971kJ; Protein 41g; Carbohydrate 34g, of which sugars 19.6g; Fat 19.7g, of which saturates 9g; Cholesterol 128mg; Calcium 72mg; Fiber 6.6g; Sodium 156mg.

LAMB AND LENTIL SOUP

LAMB AND LENTILS GO TOGETHER SO WELL, THEY ALMOST SEEM TO HAVE BEEN MADE FOR ONE ANOTHER. THIS IS A GREAT DISH TO SERVE FOR A WINTER LUNCH.

SERVES 4

INGREDIENTS

6¼ cups water or stock
2 pounds shoulder or breast of lamb,
  cut into chops
½ onion, peeled and finely
  chopped
1 garlic clove, peeled and crushed
1 bay leaf
1 clove
2 sprigs fresh thyme
8 ounces potatoes, cut into
  1-inch pieces
6 ounces/¾ cup red lentils
salt and ground black pepper
chopped fresh parsley

2 Add the potato and lentils to the pan and season with a little salt and plenty of black pepper. Pour the remaining stock or water to come just above surface of the meat and vegetables— add more if the soup becomes too thick.

3 Cover and allow to simmer for 25 minutes or until the lentils are cooked and well blended into the soup.

4 Check the seasoning and adjust as necessary. Stir in the parsley and serve.

1 Put about 5 cups of the stock or water and the meat in a large pan with the onion, garlic, bay leaf, clove and sprigs of thyme. Bring to the boil and simmer for about 1 hour until the lamb is tender.

COOK'S TIP
Red lentils do not need soaking before they are cooked; simply pick them over and remove any pieces of grit and debris, then rinse well.

Energy 587kcal/2465kJ; Protein 55.7g; Carbohydrate 34.9g, of which sugars 2.6g; Fat 26g, of which saturates 11.9g; Cholesterol 171mg; Calcium 48mg; Fiber 2.9g; Sodium 216mg.

CHUNKY BEAN AND VEGETABLE SOUP

A SUBSTANTIAL SOUP, NOT UNLIKE MINESTRONE, USING A SELECTION OF VEGETABLES, WITH CANNELLINI BEANS FOR EXTRA PROTEIN AND FIBER. SERVE WITH A HUNK OF WHOLE-WHEAT BREAD.

SERVES 4

INGREDIENTS

2 tablespoons olive oil
2 celery sticks, chopped
2 leeks, sliced
3 carrots, sliced
2 garlic cloves, crushed
1 can (14 ounces) chopped tomatoes
  with basil
5 cups vegetable stock
1 can (14 ounces) cannellini beans
  (or mixed beans), drained
1 tablespoon pesto sauce
salt and ground black pepper
Parmesan cheese shavings,
  to serve

1 Heat the olive oil in a large pan. Add the celery, leeks, carrots and garlic and cook for about 5 minutes until softened.

2 Stir in the tomatoes and stock. Bring to the boil, then cover and cook gently for 15 minutes.

3 Stir in the beans and pesto, with salt and pepper to taste. Heat through for a further 5 minutes.

4 Serve in warmed bowls, sprinkled with shavings of Parmesan cheese.

COOK'S TIP
Extra vegetables can be added to the soup to make it even more substantial. For example, add some thinly sliced zucchini or finely shredded cabbage for the last 5 minutes of the cooking time. Or, stir in some small whole-wheat pasta shapes, if you like. Add them at the same time as the tomatoes, as they will take 10–15 minutes to cook.

Energy 204kcal/857kJ; Protein 10.6g; Carbohydrate 23.6g, of which sugars 8.8g; Fat 8.1g, of which saturates 1.9g; Cholesterol 4mg; Calcium 150mg; Fiber 9.3g; Sodium 451mg.

CARIBBEAN VEGETABLE SOUP

THIS VEGETABLE SOUP FROM THE CARIBBEAN IS REFRESHING AND FILLING, AND A GOOD CHOICE FOR A MAIN LUNCH DISH.

SERVES 4

INGREDIENTS

1 ounce/2 tablespoons butter
  or margarine
1 onion, chopped
1 garlic clove, crushed
2 carrots, sliced
6¼ cups vegetable stock
2 bay leaves
2 sprigs fresh thyme
1 celery stick, finely chopped
2 green bananas, peeled and cut into
  4 pieces
6 ounces white yam or eddoe, peeled
  and cubed
1 ounce/2 tablespoons red lentils
1 chayote, peeled and chopped
1 ounce/2 tablespoons macaroni (optional)
salt and ground black pepper
chopped scallions, to garnish

1 Melt the butter or margarine and fry the onion, garlic and carrots for a few minutes, stirring occasionally, until beginning to soften. Add the stock, bay leaves and thyme and bring to the boil.

COOK'S TIP
Use other root vegetables or potatoes if yam or *eddoes* are not available. Add more stock if you want a thinner soup.

2 Add the celery, green bananas, white yam or eddoe, lentils, chayote and macaroni, if using. Season with salt and ground black pepper and simmer for 25 minutes or until all the vegetables are cooked.

3 Spoon the soup into warmed bowls and serve garnished with chopped scallions.

Energy 214kcal/903kJ; Protein 3.8g; Carbohydrate 39g, of which sugars 21.4g; Fat 5.9g, of which saturates 3.4g; Cholesterol 13mg; Calcium 55mg; Fiber 3.6g; Sodium 61mg.

BEEF AND HERB SOUP WITH YOGURT

THIS CLASSIC IRANIAN SOUP, AASHE MASTE, IS A MEAL IN ITSELF AND IS A POPULAR COLD-WEATHER DISH. SERVE IT WITH WARMED NAAN BREAD.

SERVES 4

INGREDIENTS
 2 large onions
 2 tablespoons oil
 1 tablespoon ground turmeric
 3½ ounces/scant ½ cup yellow
  split peas
 5 cups water
 8 ounces ground beef
 7 ounces/1 cup rice
 3 tablespoons each chopped fresh
  parsley, cilantro and chives
 ½ ounce/1 tablespoons butter
 1 large garlic clove, finely chopped
 4 tablespoons chopped fresh mint
 2 or 3 saffron threads dissolved in
  1 tablespoon boiling water (optional)
salt and ground black pepper
plain yogurt and naan bread,
  to serve
fresh mint, to garnish

1 Chop one of the onions. Heat the oil in a pan and fry the chopped onion until golden brown. Add the turmeric, split peas and water, bring to the boil, reduce the heat and simmer for 20 minutes.

2 Shred the other onion into a bowl, add the ground beef and seasoning and mix well. Form the mixture into small balls about the size of walnuts. Carefully add to the pan and simmer for 10 minutes.

3 Add the rice, parsley, cilantro and chives. Simmer for 30 minutes until the rice is tender, stirring frequently.

4 Melt the butter in a small pan and fry the garlic. Stir in the mint and sprinkle over the soup with the saffron, if using.

5 Spoon the soup into warmed serving dishes. Garnish with mint and serve with yogurt and warm naan bread.

Energy 497kcal/2074kJ; Protein 21.9g; Carbohydrate 61g, of which sugars 6.6g; Fat 18.7g, of which saturates 6.6g; Cholesterol 42mg; Calcium 87mg; Fiber 3.4g; Sodium 85mg.

VEGETABLE BROTH WITH GROUND BEEF

THIS IS A VERITABLE CORNUCOPIA OF FLAVORS, COMBINING TO PRODUCE A RICH AND SATISFYING BROTH THAT IS PERFECT FOR LUNCH OR SUPPER.

SERVES 6

INGREDIENTS

2 tablespoons peanut oil
4 ounces finely ground beef
1 large onion, grated or
  finely chopped
1 garlic clove, crushed
1 or 2 fresh chiles, seeded
  and chopped
½-inch cube shrimp paste, prepared
3 macadamia nuts or 6 almonds,
  finely ground
1 carrot, finely grated
1 teaspoon soft brown sugar
4 cups chicken stock
2 ounces dried shrimps, soaked in
  warm water for 10 minutes
8 ounces spinach, finely shredded
8 ears of baby corn, sliced, or
  7 ounces canned corn kernels
1 large tomato, chopped
juice of ½ lemon
salt

3 Pour in the stock and bring the mixture gently to the boil.

4 Reduce the heat to a simmer. and then add the soaked shrimp, together with their soaking liquid. Simmer for about 10 minutes.

5 A few minutes before serving, add the spinach, corn, tomato and lemon juice. Simmer for 1–2 minutes, to heat through. Do not overcook at this stage because this will spoil both the appearance and the taste of the end result. Ladle into warmed bowls and serve immediately.

1 Heat the oil in a pan. Add the beef, onion and garlic and cook, stirring, until the meat changes color.

2 Add the chiles, shrimp paste, macadamia nuts or almonds, carrot, sugar and salt to taste.

COOK'S TIP
To make this broth very hot and spicy, add the seeds from the chiles.

Energy 187kcal/780kJ; Protein 11.7g; Carbohydrate 12g, of which sugars 6.1g; Fat 10.6g, of which saturates 2.2g; Cholesterol 54mg; Calcium 183mg; Fiber 2.1g; Sodium 524mg.

MULLIGATAWNY SOUP

*MULLIGATAWNY (WHICH LITERALLY MEANS "PEPPER WATER") WAS INTRODUCED INTO ENGLAND IN THE
LATE EIGHTEENTH CENTURY BY MEMBERS OF THE COLONIAL SERVICES RETURNING HOME FROM INDIA.*

SERVES 4

INGREDIENTS
  2 ounces/4 tablespoons butter or
    4 tablespoons oil
  2 large chicken joints (about
    12 ounces each)
  1 onion, chopped
  1 carrot, chopped
  1 small turnip, chopped
  about 1 tablespoon curry powder,
    to taste
  4 cloves
  6 black peppercorns, lightly crushed
  2 ounces/¼ cup lentils
  3¾ cups chicken stock
  1½ ounces/¼ cup golden raisins
  salt and ground black pepper

1 Melt the butter or heat the oil in a
large pan, then brown the chicken over
a brisk heat. Transfer the chicken to a
plate and set aside.

2 Add the onion, carrot and turnip to
the pan and cook, stirring occasionally,
until lightly colored.

3 Stir in the curry powder, cloves and
crushed peppercorns and cook for
1–2 minutes, then add the lentils.

4 Pour the stock into the pan, bring
to the boil, then add the golden raisins,
the chicken and any juices from the
plate. Cover the pan and simmer gently
for about 1¼ hours.

5 Remove the chicken from the pan
and discard the skin and bones. Chop
the flesh, return to the soup and reheat.
Check the seasoning before serving the
soup piping hot.

COOK'S TIP
Choose red split lentils for the best color,
although either green or brown lentils
could also be used.

Energy 347kcal/1447kJ; Protein 28.7g; Carbohydrate 16g, of which sugars 9.6g; Fat 19.1g, of which saturates 8.9g; Cholesterol 142mg; Calcium 54mg; Fiber 2.1g; Sodium 160mg.

SMOKED TURKEY AND LENTIL SOUP

LENTILS SEEM TO ENHANCE THE FLAVOR OF SMOKED TURKEY, AND COMBINED WITH FOUR TASTY VEGETABLES THEY MAKE A FINE MEAL-IN-A-POT.

SERVES 4

INGREDIENTS

   1 ounce/2 tablespoons butter
   1 large carrot, chopped
   1 onion, chopped
   1 leek, white part only, chopped
   1 celery stick, chopped
   4 ounces/1½ cups mushrooms,
     chopped
   2 fluid ounces/¼ cup dry
     white wine
   5 cups chicken stock
   2 teaspoons dried thyme
   1 bay leaf
   4 ounces/½ cup green lentils
   3 ounces smoked turkey meat, diced
   salt and ground black pepper

1 Melt the butter in a large pan. Add the carrot, onion, leek, celery and mushrooms. Cook for 3–5 minutes until golden.

2 Stir in the wine and chicken stock. Bring to the boil and skim off any foam that rises to the surface. Add the thyme and bay leaf. Lower the heat, cover and simmer gently for 30 minutes.

3 Add the lentils and continue cooking, covered, for a further 30–40 minutes until they are just tender. Stir the soup occasionally.

4 Add the turkey and season to taste with salt and pepper. Cook until just heated through. Ladle into warmed bowls and serve hot.

Energy 201kcal/844kJ; Protein 15g; Carbohydrate 20.4g, of which sugars 4.1g; Fat 6.3g, of which saturates 3.5g; Cholesterol 27mg; Calcium 39mg; Fiber 3.4g; Sodium 73mg.

PROVENÇAL FISH SOUP WITH PASTA

THIS COLORFUL SOUP HAS ALL THE FLAVORS OF THE MEDITERRANEAN. SERVE IT AS A MAIN COURSE FOR A DELICIOUSLY FILLING LUNCH.

SERVES 4

INGREDIENTS

 2 tablespoons olive oil
 1 onion, sliced
 1 garlic clove, crushed
 1 leek, sliced
 4 cups water
 1 can (8 ounces) chopped
   plum tomatoes
 a pinch of Mediterranean herbs
 ¼ teaspoon saffron strands (optional)
 4 ounces small pasta
 about 8 live mussels in the shell
 1 pound white fish, filleted
   and skinned
 salt and ground black pepper
For the *rouille*
 2 garlic cloves, crushed
 1 canned pimiento, drained
   and chopped
 1 tablespoon fresh white
   bread crumbs
 4 tablespoons mayonnaise
 toasted French bread, to serve

1 Heat the oil in a large pan and add the onion, garlic and leek. Cover and cook gently for about 5 minutes, stirring occasionally, until the vegetables are softened.

2 Add the water, tomatoes, herbs, saffron, if using, and pasta. Season with salt and pepper and continue cooking for a further 15–20 minutes.

COOK'S TIP
Any type of white fish, such as cod, haddock, plaice or monkfish, can be used for this dish.

3 Scrub the mussels and pull off the "beards." Discard any that do not close when sharply tapped.

4 Cut the fish into bitesize chunks and add to the soup, placing the mussels on top. Simmer for 5–10 minutes until the mussels open and the fish is cooked. Discard any unopened mussels.

5 To make the *rouille*, pound together the garlic, canned pimiento and bread crumbs in a pestle and mortar (or in a blender or food processor). Stir in the mayonnaise and season well.

6 Spread the toasted French bread with the *rouille*. Ladle the soup into warmed bowls and serve with the French bread.

Energy 386kcal/1618kJ; Protein 27g; Carbohydrate 28.9g, of which sugars 4.8g; Fat 18.8g, of which saturates 2.8g; Cholesterol 67mg; Calcium 45mg; Fiber 2.7g; Sodium 195mg.

SHRIMP CREOLE

RAW SHRIMP ARE COMBINED WITH CHOPPED FRESH VEGETABLES AND CAYENNE PEPPER TO MAKE THIS TASTY SOUP. SERVED WITH BOILED RICE IT MAKES A FILLING MEAL.

SERVES 4

INGREDIENTS

1½ pounds raw shrimp in the shell, with heads, if available
16 fluid ounces/2 cups water
3 tablespoons olive or vegetable oil
6 ounces/1½ cups onions, very finely chopped
3 ounces/½ cup celery, very finely chopped
3 ounces/½ cup green bell pepper, very finely chopped
1 ounce/½ cup chopped fresh parsley
1 garlic clove, crushed
1 tablespoon Worcestershire sauce
¼ teaspoon cayenne pepper
4 fluid ounces/½ cup dry white wine
2 ounces/1 cup chopped peeled plum tomatoes
1 teaspoon salt
1 bay leaf
1 teaspoon sugar
fresh parsley, to garnish

4 Increase the heat to medium. Stir in the wine and simmer for 3–4 minutes.

5 Add the tomatoes, reserved shrimp stock, salt, bay leaf and sugar and bring to the boil. Stir well, then reduce the heat to low and simmer for about 30 minutes, until the tomatoes have fallen apart and the sauce has reduced slightly. Remove from the heat and leave to cool slightly.

6 Discard the bay leaf. Pour the sauce into a food processor or blender and puree until quite smooth. Taste and adjust the seasoning as necessary.

7 Return the tomato sauce to the pan and bring to the boil. Add the shrimp and simmer for 4–5 minutes, until they turn pink. Ladle into individual soup bowls and garnish with fresh parsley.

1 Peel and devein the shrimp, reserving the heads and shells. Set aside in a covered bowl in the refrigerator.

2 Put the shrimp heads and shells in a pan with the water. Bring to the boil and simmer for 15 minutes. Strain and reserve 12 fluid ounces/1½ cups of stock.

3 Heat the oil in a heavy pan. Add the onions and cook over a low heat for 8–10 minutes until softened. Add the celery and green pepper and cook for 5 minutes further. Stir in the parsley, garlic, Worcestershire sauce and cayenne. Cook for another 5 minutes.

Energy 250kcal/1044kJ; Protein 30.8g; Carbohydrate 5.6g, of which sugars 4.5g; Fat 9.6g, of which saturates 1.2g; Cholesterol 329mg; Calcium 170mg; Fiber 1.6g; Sodium 830mg.

GREEN HERB GUMBO

TRADITIONALLY SERVED AT THE END OF LENT, THIS IS A JOYFUL, SWEETLY SPICED AND REVITALIZING DISH, EVEN IF YOU HAVEN'T BEEN FASTING.

SERVES 6–8

INGREDIENTS

12 ounces piece raw smoked or
   cured ham
2 tablespoons lard or cooking oil
1 large Bermuda onion, peeled and
   roughly chopped
2 or 3 garlic cloves, peeled and
   crushed
1 teaspoon dried oregano
1 teaspoon dried thyme
2 bay leaves
2 cloves
2 celery sticks, finely sliced
1 green bell pepper, seeded
   and chopped
½ medium green cabbage, stalked
   and finely shredded
9 cups light stock or water
7 ounces collards or kale,
   finely shredded
7 ounces Chinese mustard cabbage,
   finely shredded
7 ounces spinach, shredded
1 bunch of watercress, shredded
6 scallions, finely shredded
1 ounce/½ cup chopped fresh parsley
½ teaspoon ground allspice
¼ nutmeg, grated
a pinch of cayenne pepper
salt and ground black pepper
warm French or garlic bread,
   to serve

1 Dice the smoked or cured ham quite small, keeping any fat and rind in one separate piece. Put the fat with the lard or oil in a deep pan and heat through until it sizzles. Stir in the diced ham, onion, garlic, oregano and thyme and cook over a medium heat for 5 minutes, stirring occasionally.

2 Add the bay leaves, cloves, celery and green pepper and stir over a medium heat for 2–3 minutes, then add the cabbage and stock or water. Bring to the boil and simmer for 5 minutes.

3 Add the collards or kale and mustard cabbage, boil for a further 2 minutes, then add the spinach, watercress and scallions. Return to the boil, then lower the heat and simmer for 1 minute. Add the parsley, allspice and nutmeg, salt, black pepper and cayenne to taste.

4 Remove the piece of ham fat and, if you can find them, the cloves. Ladle into individual soup bowls and serve immediately, with warm French bread or garlic bread.

Energy 138kcal/573kJ; Protein 10.7g; Carbohydrate 8.8g, of which sugars 7.8g; Fat 6.8g, of which saturates 1.5g; Cholesterol 10mg; Calcium 129mg; Fiber 3.6g; Sodium 440mg.

CHUNKY CHICKEN SOUP

THIS THICK CHICKEN AND VEGETABLE SOUP IS GARNISHED WITH GARLIC-FLAVORED FRIED CROUTONS. SERVE IT FOR AN INFORMAL LUNCH OR SUPPER.

SERVES 4

INGREDIENTS
   4 skinless, boneless chicken thighs
   ½ ounce/1 tablespoon butter
   2 small leeks, finely sliced
   1 ounce/2 tablespoons long
     grain rice
   3¾ cups chicken stock
   1 tablespoon chopped mixed fresh
     parsley and mint
   salt and ground black pepper
For the garlic croutons
   2 tablespoons olive oil
   1 garlic clove, crushed
   4 slices bread, cut into cubes

1 Cut the chicken into ½-inch cubes. Melt the butter in a pan, add the leeks and cook until tender. Add the rice and chicken and cook for 2 minutes.

2 Add the stock, then cover the pan and simmer gently for 15–20 minutes until tender.

COOK'S TIP
The croutons can be made from plain or flavored bread, but it's best if the bread is a few days old rather than fresh.

3 To make the garlic croutons, heat the oil in a large frying pan. Add the crushed garlic clove and bread cubes and cook until the bread is golden brown, stirring all the time to prevent burning. Drain on paper towels and sprinkle with a pinch of salt.

4 Add the chopped parsley and mint to the soup. Taste and adjust the seasoning.

5 Ladle the soup into warmed bowls and serve piping hot, garnished with the garlic croutons.

Energy 276kcal/1158kJ; Protein 27.4g; Carbohydrate 18.8g, of which sugars 1.8g; Fat 10.4g, of which saturates 3.1g; Cholesterol 78mg; Calcium 46mg; Fiber 1.5g; Sodium 214mg.

BEEF BROTH WITH CASSAVA

THIS "BIG" SOUP IS ALMOST LIKE A STEW. THE ADDITION OF WINE IS NOT TRADITIONAL, BUT IT ENHANCES THE RICHNESS OF THE BROTH.

SERVES 4

INGREDIENTS

1 pound stewing beef, cubed

5 cups beef stock

1¼ cups white wine

1 tablespoon soft brown sugar

1 onion, finely chopped

1 bay leaf

bouquet garni

1 sprig fresh thyme

1 tablespoon tomato paste

1 large carrot, sliced

10 ounces cassava or yam, cubed

2 ounces spinach, chopped

a little hot pepper sauce, to taste

salt and ground black pepper

1 Put the beef, stock, wine, sugar, onion, bay leaf, bouquet garni, thyme and tomato paste in a large pan, bring to the boil and then cover and simmer for about 1¼ hours, until the beef is tender.

2 Add the carrot, cassava or yam, spinach, a few drops of hot pepper sauce, salt and pepper, and simmer for a further 15 minutes until both the meat and vegetables are tender. Ladle into warmed bowls and serve.

Energy 308kcal/1295kJ; Protein 27.4g; Carbohydrate 26.7g, of which sugars 7.4g; Fat 10.9g, of which saturates 4.4g; Cholesterol 65mg; Calcium 49mg; Fiber 1.9g; Sodium 105mg.

CORN CHOWDER <u>WITH</u> CONCHIGLIETTE

CORN KERNELS COMBINE WITH SMOKED TURKEY AND PASTA TO MAKE THIS SATISFYING AND FILLING ONE-POT MEAL, PERFECT FOR A HUNGRY FAMILY OR FOR GUESTS.

SERVES 6–8

INGREDIENTS

  1 small green bell pepper
  1 pound potatoes, peeled and cut
    into ½-inch dice
  12 ounces/2 cups canned or
    frozen corn kernels
  1 onion, chopped
  1 celery stick, chopped
  bouquet garni
  2½ cups chicken stock
  1¼ cups skimmed milk
  2 ounces conchigliette
  oil, for frying
  5 ounces smoked turkey
    strips, diced
  salt and ground black pepper
  bread sticks, to serve

3 Add the milk and salt and pepper. Process half of the soup in a food processor or blender and return to the pan with the pasta. Simmer for 10 minutes or until the pasta is *al dente*.

4 Heat the oil in a non-stick frying pan and fry the turkey strips quickly for 2–3 minutes. Stir into the soup. Ladle the soup into warmed bowls and serve hot with bread sticks.

1 Seed the green pepper and cut into dice. Cover with boiling water and leave to stand for 2 minutes. Drain and rinse.

2 Put the potatoes into a pan with the corn, onion, celery, diced pepper, bouquet garni and stock. Bring to the boil, cover and simmer for 20 minutes.

Energy 169kcal/716kJ; Protein 8.4g; Carbohydrate 29.1g, of which sugars 8.7g; Fat 2.9g, of which saturates 1.1g; Cholesterol 6mg; Calcium 59mg; Fiber 1.9g; Sodium 495mg.

BOUILLABAISSE

PERHAPS THE MOST FAMOUS OF ALL MEDITERRANEAN FISH SOUPS, THIS RECIPE, ORIGINATING FROM MARSEILLES IN THE SOUTH OF FRANCE, IS A RICH AND COLORFUL MIXTURE OF FISH AND SHELLFISH, FLAVORED WITH TOMATOES, SAFFRON AND ORANGE.

SERVES 6

INGREDIENTS
3–3½ pounds mixed fish and
    8 ounces well-flavored tomatoes
a pinch of saffron threads
6 tablespoons olive oil
1 onion, sliced
1 leek, sliced
1 celery stick, sliced
2 garlic cloves, crushed
bouquet garni
1 strip orange rind
½ teaspoon fennel seeds
1 tablespoon tomato paste
2 teaspoons Pernod
salt and ground black pepper
6 slices French bread and 3 tablespoons
    chopped fresh parsley, to serve

1 Remove the heads, tails and fins from the fish and set the fish aside. Put the trimmings in a large pan with 5 cups water. Bring to the boil and simmer for 15 minutes. Strain and reserve the liquid.

2 Scald the tomatoes, then drain and refresh in cold water. Peel them and chop roughly.

3 Cut the fish into large chunks. Leave the shellfish in their shells.

4 Soak the saffron in 1–2 tablespoons hot water.

5 Heat the oil in a large pan, add the onion, leek and celery and cook until softened. Add the garlic, bouquet garni, orange rind, fennel seeds and chopped tomatoes. Stir in the saffron and soaking liquid, and the reserved fish stock. Season, then bring to the boil and simmer for 30–40 minutes.

6 Add the shellfish and boil for about 6 minutes. Add the fish and cook for 6–8 minutes more, until it flakes easily.

7 Using a slotted spoon, transfer the fish to a warmed serving platter. Keep the liquid boiling, to allow the oil to emulsify with the broth. Add the tomato paste and Pernod, then check the seasoning.

8 Ladle the soup into warm bowls, sprinkle with chopped parsley and serve with French bread.

COOK'S TIPS
• Choose fish such as red mullet, monkfish, red snapper and whiting, and large raw shrimp and clams.
• Saffron comes from the orange and red stigmas of a type of crocus, which must be harvested by hand, and is extremely expensive. Its flavor is unique and cannot be replaced by any other spice. It is an essential ingredient in traditional bouillabaisse and should not be omitted.

Energy 321kcal/1344kJ; Protein 46.8g; Carbohydrate 3.2g, of which sugars 2.8g; Fat 13g, of which saturates 1.9g; Cholesterol 115mg; Calcium 38mg; Fiber 1.3g; Sodium 163mg.

PLANTAIN AND CORN SOUP

HERE THE SWEETNESS OF THE CORN AND PLANTAINS IS OFFSET BY A LITTLE CHILE TO CREATE AN UNUSUAL SOUP.

SERVES 4

INGREDIENTS
    1 ounce/2 tablespoons butter
      or margarine
    1 onion, finely chopped
    1 garlic clove, crushed
    10 ounces yellow plantains, peeled
      and sliced
    1 large tomato, peeled and
      roughly chopped
    6 ounces/1 cup corn kernels
    1 teaspoon dried tarragon,
      crushed
    3¾ cups vegetable or chicken stock
    1 fresh green chile, seeded
      and chopped
    a pinch of freshly grated nutmeg
    salt and ground black pepper

1 Melt the butter or margarine in a pan over a moderate heat, add the onion and garlic and fry for a few minutes until the onion is soft.

2 Add the plantains, tomato and corn kernels, and cook for a further 5 minutes.

3 Add the tarragon, stock, green chile and salt and freshly ground black pepper, then simmer for 10 minutes or until the plantain is tender.

4 Stir in the grated nutmeg. Ladle the soup into warmed bowls and serve immediately, piping hot.

PEANUT SOUP

PEANUTS (OR GROUNDNUTS) ARE WIDELY USED IN SAUCES IN AFRICAN COOKING—HERE THEY MAKE A WONDERFULLY RICH SOUP FLAVORED WITH GINGER AND CHILE. WHITE YAM AND OKRA COMPLETE THE AFRICAN EXPERIENCE.

SERVES 4

INGREDIENTS
    3 tablespoons peanut paste
    6¼ cups stock or water
    2 tablespoons tomato paste
    1 onion, chopped
    2 slices fresh ginger root
    ¼ teaspoon dried thyme
    1 bay leaf
    chili powder
    8 ounces white yam, diced
    10 small okras, trimmed (optional)
    salt

COOK'S TIP
Peanut paste should be available in health food stores, but if it is unobtainable you could use peanut butter instead.

1 Place the peanut paste in a bowl, add 1¼ cups of the stock or water and the tomato paste. Using a wooden spoon, blend together to make a smooth paste.

2 Spoon the nut mixture into a pan and add the onion, ginger, thyme, bay leaf, chili powder, salt to taste, and the remaining stock.

3 Heat gently until simmering, then cook for 1 hour, whisking from time to time to prevent the nut mixture from sticking to the base of the pan.

4 Add the white yam, cook for a further 10 minutes, and then add the okra, if using, and simmer until both vegetables are tender.

5 Ladle into warmed bowls and serve immediately, piping hot.

Top: Energy 190kcal/803kJ; Protein 2.4g; Carbohydrate 33.8g, of which sugars 9.8g; Fat 6g, of which saturates 3.4g; Cholesterol 13mg; Calcium 15mg; Fiber 2g; Sodium 162mg.
Bottom: Energy 144kcal/604kJ; Protein 4g; Carbohydrate 19.6g, of which sugars 3.1g; Fat 6.1g, of which saturates 1.5g; Cholesterol 0mg; Calcium 19mg; Fiber 1.8g; Sodium 59mg.

SOUPS FOR ENTERTAINING

Soups can be made in advance and reheated, which makes them the ideal appetizer when entertaining. This section contains luxurious and creative recipes for elegant dinner parties. Impress your friends with Oyster Soup, Winter Melon Soup with Tiger Lilies, or Mediterranean Seafood Soup with Saffron Rouille. Adding a little liqueur or spirits makes a soup really special. Try Iced Tomato and Vodka Soup, or Chilled Vegetable Soup with Pastis.

SHERRIED ONION <u>AND</u> ALMOND SOUP <u>WITH</u> SAFFRON

THE SPANISH COMBINATION OF ONIONS, SHERRY AND SAFFRON GIVES THIS PALE YELLOW SOUP A BEGUILING FLAVOR THAT IS PERFECT AS THE OPENING COURSE OF A SPECIAL MEAL.

2 Add the saffron threads and cook, uncovered, for 3–4 minutes, then add the ground almonds and cook, stirring constantly, for another 2–3 minutes. Pour in the stock and sherry and stir in 1 teaspoon salt. Season with plenty of black pepper. Bring to the boil, then lower the heat and simmer gently for about 10 minutes.

SERVES 4

INGREDIENTS

   1½ ounces/3 tablespoons butter
   2 large yellow onions, thinly sliced
   1 small garlic clove, finely chopped
   good pinch of saffron threads
     (about 12 threads)
   2 ounces blanched almonds,
     toasted and finely ground
   3 cups good chicken or
     vegetable stock
   3 tablespoons dry sherry
   salt and ground black pepper
   2 tablespoons flaked or slivered
     almonds, toasted and chopped,
     and fresh parsley, to garnish

1 Melt the butter in a heavy pan over a low heat. Add the onions and garlic, stirring to coat them thoroughly in the butter, and then cover the pan and cook very gently, stirring frequently, for 15–20 minutes, until the onions are a soft texture and golden yellow in color.

VARIATION
This soup is also delicious served chilled. Use olive oil rather than butter and add a little more chicken or vegetable stock to make a slightly thinner soup, then leave to cool and chill for at least 4 hours. Just before serving, taste for seasoning. Float 1–2 ice cubes in each bowl.

3 Process the soup in a blender or food processor until smooth, then return it to the rinsed pan. Reheat slowly, stirring occasionally, but do not allow the soup to boil. Taste for seasoning, adding more salt and pepper if required.

4 Ladle the soup into heated bowls, garnish with the toasted flaked or slivered almonds and a little parsley, and serve immediately.

Energy 255kcal/1054kJ; Protein 5.8g; Carbohydrate 11.5g, of which sugars 8.1g; Fat 19.6g, of which saturates 6.1g; Cholesterol 21mg; Calcium 82mg; Fiber 3.2g; Sodium 68mg.

VERMOUTH SOUP WITH SEARED SCALLOPS, ARUGULA OIL AND CAVIAR

SEARED SCALLOPS FORM AN ELEGANT TOWER IN THE CENTER OF THIS CRÈME DE LA CRÈME OF FINE SOUPS. THE CAVIAR GARNISH LOOKS—AND TASTES—SUPERB.

SERVES 4

INGREDIENTS

   1 ounce/2 tablespoons butter
   5 shallots, sliced
   ½ pint/1¼ cups dry
     white wine
   ½ pint/1¼ cups vermouth
   1½ pints/3¾ cups fish stock
   ½ pint/1¼ cups heavy cream
   ½ pint/1¼ cups light cream
   1 tablespoon olive oil
   12 large scallops
   salt and ground black pepper
   1 tablespoon caviar
     and chopped chives,
     to garnish
For the arugula oil
   4 ounces arugula leaves
   4 fluid ounces/½ cup
     olive oil

1 Prepare the arugula oil first. Process the arugula leaves and olive oil in a food processor or blender for 1–2 minutes to give a green paste. Line a small bowl with a piece of cheesecloth and scrape the paste into it. Gather up the cheesecloth and squeeze it well to extract the green, arugula-flavored oil from the paste. Set aside.

2 Melt the butter in a large pan. Add the shallots and cook over a gentle heat for 8–10 minutes, until soft but not browned. Add the wine and vermouth and boil for 8–10 minutes, until the liquid is reduced to about a quarter of the volume.

3 Add the stock and bring back to the boil. Boil until reduced by half. Pour in the heavy and light creams, and return to the boil. Reduce the heat and simmer gently for 12–15 minutes, until just thick enough to coat the back of a spoon.

4 Pour through a fine strainer into the rinsed pan, and set aside.

5 Heat a ridged griddle or frying pan. Brush the scallops with oil, add them to the pan and sear for 1–2 minutes on each side, until just cooked, when they will be white and tender.

6 Reheat the soup gently, then check and adjust the seasoning to taste.

7 Arrange three scallops, one on top of the other, in the center of each of four warmed, shallow soup plates. Ladle the hot soup around the scallops and top them with a little of the caviar. Drizzle some arugula oil over the surface of the soup, then sprinkle with chopped chives.

Energy 557kcal/2303kJ; Protein 13.1g; Carbohydrate 4.7g, of which sugars 2.6g; Fat 48.9g, of which saturates 28.9g; Cholesterol 140mg; Calcium 63mg; Fiber 0.2g; Sodium 148mg.

TORTILLA TOMATO SOUP

THERE ARE SEVERAL TORTILLA SOUPS. THIS ONE IS AN AGUADA—OR LIQUID—VERSION, AND IS INTENDED FOR SERVING AS AN APPETIZER OR LIGHT MEAL. IT IS VERY EASY AND QUICK TO PREPARE, OR MAKE IT IN ADVANCE AND FRY THE TORTILLA STRIPS AS IT REHEATS. THE CRISP TORTILLA PIECES ADD INTEREST AND GIVE THE SOUP AN UNUSUAL TEXTURE.

SERVES 4

INGREDIENTS

4 corn tortillas
1 tablespoon vegetable oil, plus extra
   for frying
1 small onion, chopped
2 garlic cloves, crushed
12 ounces ripe plum tomatoes
1 can (14 ounces) plum tomatoes, drained
4 cups chicken stock
small bunch of fresh cilantro
2 ounces/½ cup grated mild
   Cheddar cheese
salt and ground black pepper

1 Using a sharp knife, cut each tortilla into four or five strips, each measuring about ¾ inch wide. Pour vegetable oil to a depth of ¾ inch into a frying pan. Heat until a small piece of tortilla, added to the oil, floats on the top and bubbles at the edges.

2 Add a few tortilla strips to the hot oil and fry until crisp and golden brown.

3 Remove the tortilla chips with a slotted spoon and drain on paper towels. Cook the remaining tortilla strips in the same way.

4 Heat the 1 tablespoon vegetable oil in a large pan. Add the onion and garlic and cook over a medium heat for 2–3 minutes, until the onion is soft and translucent. Do not let the garlic turn brown or it will give the soup a bitter taste.

5 Skin the fresh tomatoes by plunging them into boiling water for 30 seconds, refreshing them in cold water, draining them and then peeling off the skins with a sharp knife.

6 Chop the fresh and canned tomatoes and add them to the onion mixture. Pour in the chicken stock. Bring to the boil, then lower the heat and simmer for 10 minutes, until the liquid has reduced slightly. Stir the mixture occasionally.

7 Roughly chop or tear the cilantro into pieces. Add it to the soup and season with salt and ground black pepper to taste.

8 Place a few of the crisp tortilla pieces in each of four large heated soup bowls. Ladle the soup on top. Sprinkle each portion with some of the grated mild Cheddar cheese and serve immediately.

COOK'S TIP
An easy way to chop fresh herbs is to put them in a mug and snip with a pair of scissors. Hold the scissors vertically with one hand on each handle and work the blades back and forth until the herbs are finely and evenly chopped. If you are using woody herbs, such as rosemary or thyme, remember to strip the leaves from the stalks before putting them in the mug. They are then ready to be chopped.

Energy 270kcal/1135kJ; Protein 8.3g; Carbohydrate 36.9g, of which sugars 7.2g; Fat 10.7g, of which saturates 3.6g; Cholesterol 12mg; Calcium 164mg; Fiber 3.3g; Sodium 248mg.

ICED TOMATO <u>AND</u> VODKA SOUP

THIS FRESH-FLAVORED SOUP PACKS A PUNCH LIKE A FROZEN BLOODY MARY. IT IS DELICIOUS SERVED AS AN IMPRESSIVE FIRST COURSE FOR A SUMMER'S DINNER PARTY, WITH SUN-DRIED TOMATO BREAD.

SERVES 4

INGREDIENTS

1 pound ripe, well-flavored tomatoes, halved or roughly chopped

2½ cups jellied beef stock or consommé

1 small red onion, halved

2 celery sticks, cut into large pieces

1 garlic clove, roughly chopped

1 tablespoon tomato paste

2 teaspoons lemon juice

2 teaspoons Worcestershire sauce

a handful of small fresh basil leaves

2 tablespoons vodka

salt and ground black pepper

crushed ice, 4 small celery sticks and sun-dried tomato bread, to serve

1 Put the halved or chopped tomatoes, jellied stock or consommé, onion and celery in a blender or food processor. Add the garlic, then spoon in the tomato paste. Pulse until all the vegetables are finely chopped, then process to a smooth paste.

2 Press the mixture through a strainer into a large bowl and stir in the lemon juice, Worcestershire sauce, basil leaves and vodka.

3 Add salt and pepper to taste. Cover and chill. Serve the soup with a little crushed ice and place a celery stick in each bowl.

COOK'S TIPS

• Canned beef consommé is ideal for this recipe, but vegetable stock, for vegetarians, will work well too.

• If you or your guests are fond of celery, you can stand more celery sticks in a pitcher of iced water on the table for people to help themselves. The celery sticks can be used as additional edible stirrers and taste delicious after being dipped into the soup.

• Making your own sun-dried tomato bread is easy and is bound to impress your guests. If you don't have time, however, look out for tomato-flavored ciabatta or focaccia.

Energy 46kcal/194kJ; Protein 1.3g; Carbohydrate 5.5g, of which sugars 5.2g; Fat 0.4g, of which saturates 0.1g; Cholesterol 0mg; Calcium 22mg; Fiber 1.6g; Sodium 44mg.

TOMATO AND PEACH JUS WITH SHRIMP

AMERICAN-STYLE SOUPS, MADE FROM THE CLEAR JUICES EXTRACTED FROM VEGETABLES OR FRUITS AND REFERRED TO AS "WATER" SOUPS BY CHEFS, PROVIDE THE INSPIRATION FOR THIS RECIPE.

SERVES 6

INGREDIENTS
- 3–3½ pounds ripe peaches
- 2½ pounds beef tomatoes
- 2 tablespoons white wine vinegar
- 1 lemongrass stalk, crushed and chopped
- 1-inch fresh ginger root, grated
- 1 bay leaf
- ⅔ cup water
- 18 jumbo shrimp, shelled with tails on and deveined
- olive oil, for brushing
- salt and ground black pepper
- fresh cilantro leaves and 2 vine-ripened tomatoes, peeled, seeded and diced, to garnish

1 Peel the tomatoes and peaches and cut into chunks. Put into a food processor and puree them. Stir in the vinegar and seasoning.

2 Line a large bowl with cheesecloth. Pour the puree into the bowl, gather up the ends of the cheesecloth and tie tightly. Suspend over the bowl and leave at room temperature for 3 hours or until about 5 cups juice have drained through.

3 Meanwhile, put the lemongrass, ginger and bay leaf into a pan with the water, and simmer for 5–6 minutes. Set aside to cool.

4 When the mixture is cool, strain into the tomato and peach juice and chill in the refrigerator for at least 4 hours.

5 Using a sharp knife, slit the shrimp down their curved sides, cutting about three-quarters of the way through and keeping their tails intact. Open the shrimp out flat.

6 Heat a griddle or frying pan and brush with a little oil. Sear the shrimp for 1–2 minutes on each side, until tender and slightly charred. Pat dry on paper towels to remove any remaining oil. Cool, but do not chill.

7 When ready to serve, ladle the soup into bowls and place three shrimp in each portion.

8 Add some torn cilantro leaves and diced tomato to each bowl, to garnish.

Energy 188kcal/797kJ; Protein 12.7g; Carbohydrate 25.2g, of which sugars 25.2g; Fat 4.8g, of which saturates 0.8g; Cholesterol 98mg; Calcium 71mg; Fiber 5.8g; Sodium 116mg.

CORN <u>AND</u> CRAB BISQUE

THIS IS A LOUISIANA CLASSIC, WHICH IS CERTAINLY LUXURIOUS ENOUGH FOR A DINNER PARTY AND IS THEREFORE WELL WORTH THE EXTRA TIME REQUIRED TO PREPARE THE FRESH CRAB. THE CRAB SHELLS, TOGETHER WITH THE CORN COBS, FROM WHICH THE KERNELS ARE STRIPPED, MAKE A FINE-FLAVORED STOCK. SERVE THE SOUP WITH HOT FRENCH BREAD OR GRISSINI BREADSTICKS.

SERVES 8

INGREDIENTS
    4 large corn cobs
    2 bay leaves
    1 cooked crab (about 2¼ pounds)
    1 ounce/2 tablespoons butter
    2 tablespoons all-purpose flour
    1¼ cups whipping cream
    6 scallions, shredded
    a pinch of cayenne pepper
    salt and ground black and
        white pepper
    hot French bread or grissini
        breadsticks, to serve

1 Pull away the outer husks and silk from the cobs of corn and strip off the kernels.

2 Keep the corn kernels on one side and put the stripped cobs into a deep pan or flameproof casserole with about 12½ cups cold water, the bay leaves and 2 teaspoons salt. Bring to the boil and leave to simmer while you prepare the crab.

3 Pull away the two flaps between the big claws of the crab, stand it on its "nose," where the flaps were, and bang down firmly with the heel of your hand on the rounded end.

4 Separate the crab from its top shell, keeping the shell.

5 Push out the crab's mouth and its abdominal sac immediately below the mouth, and discard.

6 Pull away the feathery gills around the central chamber and discard them. Scrape out all the semi-liquid brown meat from the shell and set aside.

COOK'S TIP
It is vital to stir constantly to darken the roux without burning. Should black specks appear at any stage of cooking, discard the roux and start again.

7 Using a rolling pin, crack the claws in as many places as necessary to extract all the white meat. Pick out the white meat from the fragile cavities in the central body of the crab. Set aside all the crabmeat, brown and white.

8 Put the spidery legs, back shell and all the other pieces of shell into the pan with the corn cobs. Simmer for a further 15 minutes, then strain the stock into a clean pan and boil hard to reduce to 3½ pints/9 cups.

9 Meanwhile, melt the butter in a small pan and sprinkle in the flour. Stir constantly over a low heat until the roux is the color of rich cream.

10 Off the heat, slowly stir in 8 fluid ounces/1 cup of the stock. Return to the heat and stir until it thickens, then stir this thickened mixture into the pan of strained stock.

11 Add the corn kernels, return to the boil and simmer for 5 minutes.

12 Add the crabmeat, cream and scallions and season with cayenne, salt and pepper (preferably a mixture of black and white). Return to the boil and simmer for a further 2 minutes.

13 Ladle the soup into warmed bowls and serve with hot French bread or grissini breadsticks.

Energy 273kcal/1136kJ; Protein 7.7g; Carbohydrate 17.5g, of which sugars 6.1g; Fat 19.6g, of which saturates 11.3g; Cholesterol 60mg; Calcium 40mg; Fiber 0.9g; Sodium 255mg.

LEMON AND PUMPKIN MOULES MARINIÈRE

BASED ON THE CLASSIC FRENCH SHELLFISH DISH, THIS MUSSEL SOUP IS THICKENED WITH FRESH PUMPKIN AND FLAVORED WITH DILL AND LEMON. THIS IS A VERY ELEGANT AND IMPRESSIVE SOUP, IDEAL FOR SERVING AT A SPECIAL DINNER PARTY.

SERVES 4

INGREDIENTS

2¼ pounds fresh mussels
1¼ cups dry white wine
1 large lemon
1 bay leaf
1 tablespoon olive oil
1 onion, chopped
1 garlic clove, crushed
1½ pounds pumpkin or squash
3¾ cups vegetable stock
2 tablespoons chopped fresh dill
salt and ground black pepper
lemon wedges, to serve

1 Scrub the mussels in cold water and pull away the dark hairy beards protruding from the shells. Discard any open mussels that do not shut when tapped sharply, and put the rest into a large pan. Pour in the white wine.

2 Pare large pieces of rind from the lemon and squeeze the juice, then add both to the mussels with the bay leaf. Cover and bring to the boil, then cook for 4–5 minutes, shaking the pan, until all the mussels have opened.

3 Drain the mussels in a colander over a large bowl. Reserve the cooking liquid and the mussels.

4 Remove and discard the lemon rind and the bay leaf, and any mussels that have not opened.

5 When the mussels are cool enough to handle, set aside a few in their shells for the garnish. Remove the remaining mussels from their shells. Pour the reserved cooking liquid through a strainer lined with cheesecloth to remove any sand or grit.

6 Heat the oil in a large, clean pan. Add the onion and garlic and cook for 4–5 minutes, until softened.

7 Peel the pumpkin, remove the seeds and pith and roughly chop into chunks. Add the pumpkin flesh and the strained mussel cooking liquid to the pan. Bring to the boil and simmer, uncovered, for 5–6 minutes.

8 Pour in the vegetable stock and cook for a further 25–30 minutes, until the pumpkin has almost disintegrated.

9 Cool the soup slightly, then pour into a food processor or blender and process until smooth.

10 Return the soup to the rinsed pan and season well. Stir in the chopped dill and the shelled mussels, then bring just to the boil.

11 Ladle the soup into warmed soup plates and garnish with the reserved mussels in their shells. Serve lemon wedges with the soup.

Energy 161kcal/678kJ; Protein 14.3g; Carbohydrate 4.2g, of which sugars 3.3g; Fat 4.6g, of which saturates 0.8g; Cholesterol 30mg; Calcium 203mg; Fiber 1.7g; Sodium 161mg.

CLAM AND BASIL SOUP

SUBTLY SWEET AND SPICY, THIS SOUP IS AN IDEAL APPETIZER FOR SERVING AS PART OF A CELEBRATION DINNER. TO MAKE THE SOUP REALLY SPECIAL, BUY A JAR OF CLAMS IN THEIR SHELLS FROM AN ITALIAN DELICATESSEN, AND STIR SOME INTO THE SOUP BEFORE SERVING.

SERVES 4–6

INGREDIENTS

2 tablespoons olive oil
1 medium onion, finely chopped
leaves from 1 fresh or dried sprig of
    thyme, chopped or crumbled
2 garlic cloves, crushed
5 or 6 fresh basil leaves, plus extra
    to garnish
¼–½ teaspoon crushed red chiles,
    to taste
4 cups fish stock
12 fluid ounces/1½ cups bottled
    strained tomatoes
1 teaspoon granulated sugar
3½ ounces/scant 1 cup frozen peas
2½ ounces/⅔ cup small pasta shapes,
    such as chifferini, rigatoni or penne
8 ounces frozen shelled clams
salt and ground black pepper

1 Heat the oil in a large pan, add the onion and cook gently for about 5 minutes until softened but not colored.

2 Add the thyme, then stir in the garlic, basil leaves and chiles.

3 Add the stock, tomatoes and sugar to the pan, with salt and pepper to taste. Bring to the boil, then lower the heat and simmer for 15 minutes, stirring from time to time to prevent sticking.

4 Add the frozen peas and cook for a further 5 minutes.

5 Add the pasta to the stock mixture and bring to the boil, stirring. Lower the heat and simmer for about 5 minutes or according to the packet instructions, stirring frequently, until the pasta is *al dente*.

6 Turn the heat down to low, add the frozen clams and heat through for 2–3 minutes. Taste and adjust the seasoning. Serve hot in warmed bowls, garnished with basil leaves.

COOK'S TIPS
• Frozen shelled clams are available at delicatessens and good supermarkets. If you can't get them, use bottled or canned clams in natural juice (not vinegar).
• To make the fish stock, ask your fish counter for heads, bones and trimmings from white fish. Lobster or crab shell pieces may also be used. Boil the trimmings with chopped onion, celery, carrot, herbs and a little white wine.

Energy 123kcal/518kJ; Protein 8.9g; Carbohydrate 13g, of which sugars 3g; Fat 4.3g, of which saturates 0.7g; Cholesterol 25mg; Calcium 42mg; Fiber 1.5g; Sodium 585mg.

SPANISH SEAFOOD SOUP

THIS HEARTY SOUP CONTAINS ALL THE COLORS AND FLAVORS OF THE MEDITERRANEAN. IT IS SUBSTANTIAL ENOUGH TO SERVE AS A MAIN COURSE, BUT CAN ALSO BE DILUTED WITH A LITTLE WHITE WINE AND WATER TO MAKE AN ELEGANT APPETIZER FOR SIX.

SERVES 4

INGREDIENTS

1½ pounds raw shrimp, in the shell
3¾ cups cold water
1 onion, chopped
1 celery stick, chopped
1 bay leaf
3 tablespoons olive oil
2 slices stale bread, crusts removed
1 small onion, finely chopped
1 large garlic clove, chopped
2 large tomatoes, halved
½ large green bell pepper,
  finely chopped
1¼ pounds small clams or
  mussels, cleaned
juice of 1 lemon
3 tablespoons chopped fresh parsley
1 teaspoon paprika
salt and ground black pepper

COOK'S TIP
Good fish and shellfish dishes are normally based on proper fish stock (including the juices saved from opening mussels). This is equivalent to the French *court bouillon*, and takes 30 minutes' simmering. The method used here is one of the quickest, because the shrimp heads come off neatly, and the rest of the shells are simply added as they are removed.

1 Pull the heads off the shrimp and put them in a pan with the cold water. Add the onion, celery and bay leaf and simmer for 20–25 minutes.

2 Peel the shrimp, adding the shells to the stock as you go along.

3 Heat the oil in a wide, deep flameproof casserole and fry the bread slices quickly, then reserve them. Fry the onion until it is soft, adding the garlic towards the end.

4 Scoop the seeds out of the tomatoes and discard. Chop the flesh and add to the casserole with the green pepper. Fry briefly, stirring occasionally.

5 Strain the stock into the casserole and bring to the boil. Check over the small clams or mussels, discarding any that are open or damaged.

6 Add half the clams or mussels to the stock. When open, use a slotted spoon to transfer some of them out onto a plate. Remove the clams or mussels from the shells and discard the shells. (You should end up having discarded about half of the shells.) Meanwhile, repeat the process to cook the remaining clams or mussels.

7 Return the clams or mussels to the soup and add the shrimp. Add the bread, torn into little pieces, and the lemon juice and chopped parsley.

8 Season to taste with paprika, salt and pepper and stir gently to dissolve the bread. Serve immediately in soup bowls, providing a plate for the empty shells.

Energy 234kcal/978kJ; Protein 23.3g; Carbohydrate 11.3g, of which sugars 4.5g; Fat 10.9g, of which saturates 1.7g; Cholesterol 67mg; Calcium 216mg; Fiber 2g; Sodium 1193mg.

OYSTER SOUP

OYSTERS MAKE A DELICIOUS SOUP THAT IS REALLY LUXURIOUS. SERVE IT AS AN APPETIZER FOR A SPECIAL DINNER PARTY OR CELEBRATION MEAL.

2 Heat the mixture over medium heat until small bubbles appear around the edge of the pan, being careful not to allow it to boil. Reduce the heat to low and add the oysters.

3 Cook, stirring occasionally, until the oysters plump up and their edges begin to curl. Add the paprika and season the soup to taste.

4 Warm six soup plates or bowls. Place a pat of butter in each bowl, ladle in the soup and garnish with chopped parsley.

SERVES 6

INGREDIENTS
   16 fluid ounces/2 cups milk
   16 fluid ounces/2 cups light cream
   5 cups shucked oysters, with their
     liquor reserved
   a pinch of paprika
   1 ounce/2 tablespoons butter
   salt and freshly ground black pepper
   1 tablespoon chopped fresh parsley,
     to garnish

1 Combine the milk, light cream and oyster liquor in a heavy pan.

Energy 385kcal/1609kJ; Protein 26.5g; Carbohydrate 17.6g, of which sugars 12.2g; Fat 22.6g, of which saturates 13.8g; Cholesterol 174mg; Calcium 430mg; Fiber 0g; Sodium 1112mg.

ASPARAGUS SOUP WITH CRAB

A BEAUTIFUL GREEN SOUP WITH THE PURE TASTE OF FRESH ASPARAGUS. THE CRAB IS ADDED AT THE LAST MOMENT AS A LUXURIOUS GARNISH.

SERVES 6–8

INGREDIENTS

3–3½ pounds fresh asparagus
1 ounce/2 tablespoons butter
6¼ cups chicken stock
2 tablespoons cornstarch
2–3 tablespoons cold water
4 fluid ounces/½ cup whipping
  cream
salt and ground black pepper
6–7 ounces white crabmeat,
  to garnish

1 Trim the woody ends from the bottom of the asparagus spears and cut the spears into 1-inch pieces.

2 Melt the butter in a heavy pan or flameproof casserole over medium-high heat. Add the asparagus and cook for 5–6 minutes, stirring frequently, until it is bright green but not browned.

3 Add the stock and bring to the boil, skimming off any foam that rises to the surface. Simmer over medium heat for 3–5 minutes, until the asparagus is tender, yet crisp. Reserve 12–16 of the asparagus tips for the garnish.

4 Season the soup, cover and continue cooking for 15–20 minutes, until the asparagus is very tender.

5 Puree the soup in a blender or food processor and pass the mixture through the fine blade of a food mill back into the pan. Return the soup to the boil over a medium-high heat. Blend the cornstarch with the water and whisk into the boiling soup to thicken, then stir in the cream. Adjust the seasoning.

6 To serve, ladle the soup into warmed bowls and top each with a spoonful of the crabmeat and a few of the reserved asparagus tips.

Energy 157kcal/652kJ; Protein 9.7g; Carbohydrate 7.6g, of which sugars 4g; Fat 9.9g, of which saturates 5.6g; Cholesterol 38mg; Calcium 87mg; Fiber 3.2g; Sodium 147mg.

SEAFOOD WONTON SOUP

THIS IS A VARIATION OF THE POPULAR WONTON SOUP THAT IS TRADITIONALLY PREPARED USING PORK. IN CHINA IT WOULD BE SERVED AS A SNACK, OR DIM SUM, RATHER THAN AS AN APPETIZER TO A MEAL.

SERVES 4

INGREDIENTS

2 ounces raw jumbo shrimp
2 ounces queen scallops
3 ounces skinless cod fillet,
   roughly chopped
1 tablespoon finely chopped
   fresh chives
1 teaspoon dry sherry
1 small egg white
½ teaspoon sesame oil
¼ teaspoon salt
large pinch of ground white pepper
20 wonton wrappers
2 romaine lettuce leaves, shredded
3¾ cups fish stock
fresh cilantro leaves and garlic
   chives, to garnish

1 Peel and devein the shrimp. Rinse, dry on paper towels and cut into pieces.

2 Rinse and dry the scallops. Chop into pieces the same size as the shrimp.

COOK'S TIP
The filled wonton wrappers can be made ahead, then frozen for several weeks and cooked straight from the freezer.

3 Place the cod in a food processor and process until a paste is formed. Scrape into a bowl and stir in the shrimp, scallops, chives, sherry, sesame oil, salt and pepper.

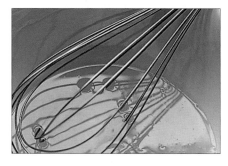

4 Lightly beat the egg white and add to the seafood filling. Mix well, cover and leave in a cool place to marinate for 20 minutes.

5 Make the wontons. Place 1 teaspoon of the seafood filling in the center of a wonton wrapper, then bring the corners together to meet at the top. Twist them together to enclose the filling. Fill the remaining wonton wrappers in the same way. Tie with a fresh chive if you like.

6 Bring a large pan of water to the boil. Drop in the wontons. When the water returns to the boil, lower the heat and simmer gently for 5 minutes or until the wontons float to the surface. Drain the wontons and divide them among four heated soup bowls.

7 Add a portion of lettuce to each bowl. Bring the fish stock to the boil. Ladle it on top of the lettuce and garnish each portion with cilantro leaves and garlic chives. Serve immediately.

Energy 92kcal/388kJ; Protein 10.7g; Carbohydrate 10.8g, of which sugars 0.9g; Fat 0.7g, of which saturates 0.2g; Cholesterol 39mg; Calcium 44mg; Fiber 0.7g; Sodium 74mg.

RED PEPPER SOUP WITH LIME

THE BEAUTIFUL, RICH RED COLOR OF THIS SOUP MAKES IT AN ATTRACTIVE APPETIZER OR LIGHT LUNCH. FOR A SPECIAL DINNER, TOAST SOME TINY CROUTONS AND SPRINKLE THEM INTO THE SOUP.

SERVES 4–6

INGREDIENTS

1 large onion, chopped
4 red bell peppers, seeded
  and chopped
1 teaspoon olive oil
1 garlic clove, crushed
1 small fresh red chilli, sliced
3 tablespoons tomato paste
3¾ cups chicken stock
finely grated rind and juice of
  1 lime
salt and ground black pepper
shreds of lime rind, to garnish

1 Cook the onion and peppers gently in the oil in a covered pan for about 5 minutes, shaking the pan occasionally, until just softened.

2 Stir in the garlic, chile and tomato paste. Add half the stock, then bring to the boil. Cover and simmer gently for about 10 minutes.

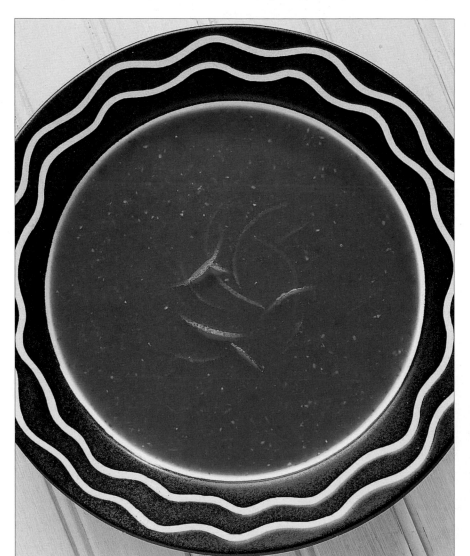

3 Cool slightly, then puree in a food processor or blender. Return to the pan and add the remaining stock, the lime rind and juice, and salt and pepper.

4 Bring the soup back to the boil, then serve immediately, with a few strips of lime rind sprinkled into each bowl.

Energy 66kcal/274kJ; Protein 2.2g; Carbohydrate 12.5g, of which sugars 11g; Fat 1.1g, of which saturates 0.2g; Cholesterol 0mg; Calcium 25mg; Fiber 2.8g; Sodium 24mg.

RED ONION AND BEET SOUP

THIS ATTRACTIVE, RUBY-RED SOUP, WITH ITS CONTRASTING SWIRL OF YOGURT, WILL LOOK STUNNING AT ANY DINNER PARTY.

SERVES 4–6

INGREDIENTS

1 tablespoon extra virgin
  olive oil
12 ounces red onions, sliced
2 garlic cloves, crushed
10 ounces cooked beets, cut
  into sticks
5 cups vegetable stock or water
2 ounces/1 cup cooked soup pasta
2 tablespoons raspberry vinegar
salt and ground black pepper
plain yogurt or mascarpone
  and chopped fresh chives,
  to garnish

1 Heat the olive oil in a large pan or flameproof casserole and add the onions and garlic.

COOK'S TIP
Substitute cooked barley for the pasta to give extra nuttiness to the flavor.

2 Cook gently for about 20 minutes or until the onion is soft and tender, stirring occasionally to prevent it sticking to the base of the pan.

3 Add the beets, stock or water, cooked pasta and vinegar, and heat through. Season and garnish with swirls of yogurt or mascarpone and chives.

Energy 87kcal/366kJ; Protein 2.8g; Carbohydrate 15.1g, of which sugars 7.6g; Fat 2.2g, of which saturates 0.3g; Cholesterol 0mg; Calcium 30mg; Fiber 1.9g; Sodium 53mg.

SPICED CREAMED PARSNIP SOUP <u>WITH</u> SHERRY

PARSNIPS ARE A NATURALLY SWEET VEGETABLE, AND THE MODERN ADDITION OF CURRY POWDER COMPLEMENTS THIS PERFECTLY, WHILE SHERRY LIFTS THE SOUP INTO THE DINNER-PARTY REALM.

2 Cut the parsnips into even-size pieces, add to the pan and coat with butter. Stir in the curry powder.

3 Pour in the sherry and cover with a *cartouche* (see Cook's Tip) and a lid. Cook over a low heat for 10 minutes or until the parsnips are softened, making sure they do not color.

4 Add the stock and season to taste. Bring to the boil then simmer for about 15 minutes or until the parsnips are soft. Remove from the heat.

5 Allow to cool for a while then purée in a blender or food processor.

6 When ready to serve, reheat the soup and check the seasoning. Ladle into warmed soup bowls and add a swirl of plain yogurt.

COOK'S TIPS
• A *cartouche* is a circle of waxed paper that helps to keep in the moisture, so the vegetables cook in their own juices along with the sherry.
• Avoid buying large parsnips, which can be rather woody and lacking in flavor.

SERVES 4

INGREDIENTS
  4 ounces/½ cup butter
  2 onions, sliced
  2¼ pounds parsnips, peeled
  2 teaspoons curry powder
  2 tablespoons medium sherry
  5 cups chicken or vegetable stock
  salt and ground black pepper
  plain yogurt, to serve

1 Melt the butter in a pan, add the onion and sweat gently without allowing it to color.

Energy 437kcal/1820kJ; Protein 5.9g; Carbohydrate 39.5g, of which sugars 20.2g; Fat 28.7g, of which saturates 16.8g; Cholesterol 67mg; Calcium 134mg; Fiber 12.9g; Sodium 218mg.

STAR-GAZER VEGETABLE SOUP

IF YOU HAVE THE TIME, IT IS WORTH MAKING YOUR OWN STOCK—EITHER VEGETABLE OR, IF YOU PREFER, CHICKEN OR FISH—FOR THIS RECIPE.

SERVES 4

INGREDIENTS
- 1 yellow bell pepper
- 2 large zucchini
- 2 large carrots
- 1 kohlrabi
- 1½ 3¾ cups well-flavored vegetable stock
- 2 ounces rice vermicelli
- salt and ground black pepper

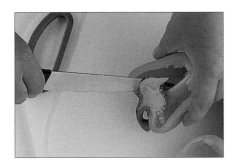

1 Cut the pepper into quarters, removing the seeds and core. Cut the zucchini and carrots lengthwise into ¼-inch slices and slice the kohlrabi into ¼-inch rounds.

2 Using tiny cookie cutters, stamp out shapes from the vegetables or use a very sharp knife to cut the sliced vegetables into stars and other decorative shapes.

COOK'S TIP
Sauté the leftover vegetable pieces in a little oil and mix with cooked brown rice to make a tasty risotto.

3 Place the vegetables and stock in a large pan and simmer for 10 minutes, until the vegetables are tender. Season to taste with salt and pepper.

4 Meanwhile, place the vermicelli in a bowl, cover with boiling water and set aside for 4 minutes. Drain, then divide among four warmed soup bowls. Ladle over the soup and serve.

Energy 96kcal/399kJ; Protein 3.4g; Carbohydrate 19.1g, of which sugars 8.9g; Fat 0.8g, of which saturates 0.2g; Cholesterol 0mg; Calcium 58mg; Fiber 3.1g; Sodium 20mg.

PUMPKIN SOUP <u>WITH</u> ANIS

LIQUORICE-FLAVORED ANIS ADDS A TOUCH OF EXCITEMENT TO THIS WINTER SOUP. HOT BREAD MAKES AN IDEAL ACCOMPANIMENT.

SERVES 4

INGREDIENTS

1½ pounds pumpkin
2 tablespoons olive oil
2 large onions, sliced
1 garlic clove, crushed
2 fresh red chiles, seeded
  and chopped
1 teaspoon curry paste
3 cups vegetable or chicken stock
1 tablespoon anis
salt and ground black pepper
⅔ cup light cream, to serve

COOK'S TIP
Use hollowed-out small squashes or pumpkins as individual soup bowls.

1 Peel the pumpkin, remove the seeds and chop the flesh roughly.

2 Heat the oil in a large pan and fry the onions until golden. Stir in the garlic, chiles and curry paste. Cook for 1 minute, then add the chopped pumpkin and cook for 5 minutes more. Pour over the stock and season.

3 Bring to the boil, lower the heat, cover and simmer for about 25 minutes.

4 Process until smooth in a blender or food processor, then return to the clean pan. Add the anis and reheat. Taste and season if necessary. Serve the soup in individual heated bowls, adding a spoonful of cream to each portion.

Energy 188kcal/780kJ; Protein 3.6g; Carbohydrate 12.5g, of which sugars 9.3g; Fat 13.2g, of which saturates 5.5g; Cholesterol 21mg; Calcium 107mg; Fiber 3.1g; Sodium 14mg.

FRENCH ONION SOUP WITH COGNAC

COGNAC ADDS A DELICIOUS KICK TO THIS TIME-HONORED, CLASSIC FRENCH SOUP AND MAKES IT SPECIAL ENOUGH TO SERVE AT A DINNER PARTY.

SERVES 4

INGREDIENTS

   2 tablespoons olive oil
   1 ounce/2 tablespoons butter
   3 onions (about 1 pound total
     weight), sliced
   1 teaspoon soft light brown sugar
   2 garlic cloves, crushed
   5 cups vegetable or chicken stock
   4 tablespoons cognac
   4 slices French bread
   1 tablespoon Dijon mustard
   4 ounces/1 cup Gruyère cheese,
     grated
   salt and ground black pepper

COOK'S TIP
Don't rush the browning of the onions. Their sweetness emerges through long, gentle cooking.

1 Heat the oil and butter in a heavy pan and cook the onions very gently for about 30 minutes until they are very soft. Sprinkle the brown sugar and garlic over and cook until the onions are golden brown.

2 Stir in the stock and cognac, with salt and pepper to taste. Bring to the boil, then lower the heat and simmer for about 30 minutes.

3 Just before serving, toast the bread under a hot broiler on one side only. Turn the slices over, spread them with the mustard and cover with the grated cheese. Broil until all the cheese has melted and is golden.

4 Ladle the soup into warmed bowls and float the toasted bread on top. Serve immediately.

Energy 395kcal/1646kJ; Protein 12.3g; Carbohydrate 31.4g, of which sugars 7.5g; Fat 21g, of which saturates 10.4g; Cholesterol 41mg; Calcium 290mg; Fiber 2.5g; Sodium 496mg.

CHILLED VEGETABLE SOUP <u>WITH</u> PASTIS

FENNEL, STAR ANISE AND PASTIS GIVE A DELICATE ANISEED FLAVOR TO THIS SOPHISTICATED SOUP, WHICH IS IDEAL AS AN APPETIZER FOR A DINNER PARTY.

2 With a slotted spoon, remove the star anise, then process the vegetables until smooth in a blender or food processor, and place in a clean pan.

3 Stir in the light cream, bring to the boil, taste and and adjust the seasoning if necessary.

4 Strain into a bowl, cover and leave until cold.

5 To serve, stir in the pastis, pour into bowls, add a swirl of heavy cream or crème fraîche and garnish with chives.

COOK'S TIP
To chill the soup quickly, stir in a spoonful of crushed ice.

SERVES 6

INGREDIENTS
   6 ounces leek, finely sliced
   8 ounces fennel, finely sliced
   1 potato, diced
   3 star anise, tied in a piece of
      cheesecloth
   1¼ cups light cream
   2 teaspoons pastis
   6 tablespoons heavy cream or
      crème fraîche
salt and ground black pepper
chives, finely chopped, to garnish

1 Pour 3¾ cups boiling water into a pan, add the sliced leek and fennel, the diced potato and the star anise, and season to taste with salt and pepper. Bring to the boil and simmer for 25 minutes.

Energy 219kcal/909kJ; Protein 3.3g; Carbohydrate 8.9g, of which sugars 3.1g; Fat 17.9g, of which saturates 11.2g; Cholesterol 48mg; Calcium 70mg; Fiber 1.9g; Sodium 27mg.

WINTER MELON SOUP WITH TIGER LILIES

THIS SIMPLE SOUP USES TWO TRADITIONAL SOUTHEAST ASIAN INGREDIENTS—WINTER MELON TO ABSORB THE FLAVORS AND TIGER LILIES TO LIFT THE BROTH WITH A FLORAL SCENT.

SERVES 4

INGREDIENTS

    12 ounces winter melon
    1 ounce tiger lilies, soaked in hot
      water for 20 minutes
    salt and ground black pepper
    1 small bunch each cilantro and
      mint, stalks removed, leaves
      chopped, to serve
For the stock
    1 ounce dried shrimp, soaked in
      water for 15 minutes
    1¼ pounds pork ribs
    1 onion, peeled and quartered
    6 ounces carrots, peeled and cut
      into chunks
    1 tablespoon *nuoc mam*
    1 tablespoon soy sauce
    4 black peppercorns

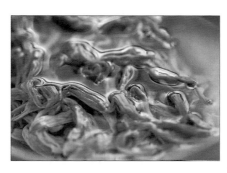

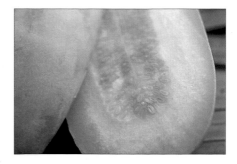

1 To make the stock, drain and rinse the dried shrimp. Put the pork ribs in a large pan and cover with 8 cups water. Bring to the boil, skim off any fat, and add the dried shrimp and the remaining stock ingredients. Cover and simmer for 1½ hours, then skim off any foam or fat. Continue simmering, uncovered, for a further 30 minutes. Strain and check the seasoning. You should have about 6¼ cups.

2 Halve the winter melon lengthwise and remove the seeds and inner membrane. Finely slice the flesh into half-moons. Squeeze the soaked tiger lilies dry and tie them in a knot.

3 Bring the stock to the boil in a deep pan or wok. Reduce the heat and add the winter melon and tiger lilies. Simmer for 15–20 minutes. Season to taste, sprinkle the cilantro and mint over the top, and serve immediately.

Energy 57kcal/241kJ; Protein 4.4g; Carbohydrate 9.6g, of which sugars 9g; Fat 0.4g, of which saturates 0.1g; Cholesterol 32mg; Calcium 101mg; Fiber 1.6g; Sodium 309mg.

INDEX

French onion soup with Gruyère croutes 418–19